7 Day

University of Plymouth Library

Subject to status this item may be renewed
via your Voyager account

http://voyager.plymouth.ac.uk

Exeter tel: (01392) 475049
Exmouth tel: (01395) 255331
Plymouth tel: (01752) 232323

The Politics of Regulation

THE CRC SERIES ON COMPETITION, REGULATION AND
DEVELOPMENT

Series editors: Paul Cook, *Professor of Economics and Development Policy and*
Martin Minogue, *Senior Research Fellow, Institute for Development Policy and*
Management, University of Manchester, UK

Titles in the series include:

Leading Issues in Competition, Regulation and Development
Edited by Paul Cook, Colin Kirkpatrick, Martin Minogue and David Parker

The Politics of Regulation
Institutions and Regulatory Reforms for the Age of Governance
Edited by Jacint Jordana and David Levi-Faur

The Politics of Regulation

Institutions and Regulatory Reforms for the Age of Governance

Edited by

Jacint Jordana and David Levi-Faur

THE CRC SERIES ON COMPETITION, REGULATION AND
DEVELOPMENT

Edward Elgar

Cheltenham, UK • Northampton, MA, USA

Published by
Edward Elgar Publishing Limited
Glensanda House
Montpellier Parade
Cheltenham
Glos GL50 1UA
UK

Edward Elgar Publishing, Inc.
136 West Street
Suite 202
Northampton
Massachusetts 01060
USA

A catalogue record for this book
is available from the British Library

Library of Congress Cataloguing in Publication Data

The politics of regulation : institutions and regulatory reforms for the age of
    governance / edited by Jacint Jordana, David Levi-Faur.
        p. cm. — (The CRC series on competition, regulation and development)
    Includes index.
    1. Trade regulation. 2. Economic policy. 3. Trade regulation—Europe. 4.
Europe—Economic policy. I. Jordana, Jacint, 1962– II. Levi-Faur, David. III. Series.

HD3612.P66 2004
382'.3—dc22
                                                                    2003068789

ISBN 1 84376 464 4 (cased)

Printed and bound in Great Britain by MPG Books Ltd, Bodmin, Corwall

Contents

Figures

Tables

Contributors

Damien Geradin is a professor of Law at the University of Liège and at the College of Europe, Bruges. He has also held visiting appointments at a number of universities, including King's College London, the University of Paris II (Panthéon-Assas), the University of Peking, Columbia Law School, Harvard Law School, UCLA School of Law, and Yale Law School. His works focuses on competition law and the regulation of network industries.

Fabrizio Gilardi is a researcher at the Institute of Political and International Studies of the University of Lausanne, Switzerland. He wrote his PhD dissertation on delegation to independent regulatory agencies in Western Europe, and has published in the *Journal of European Public Policy*, the *Swiss Political Science Review*, and *Politische Vierteljahresschrift*. He currently works on the diffusion of regulatory reforms in various fields.

Nicolas Jabko received a PhD from the University of California at Berkeley, and teaches political science at Sciences Po, Paris. He has published articles in the *Journal of European Public Policy*, *Comparative Political Studies*, *Revue Française de Science Politique* and *Security Studies*. His current research projects are on European political economy and transatlantic relations.

Jacint Jordana is Associate Professor in the Department of Political and Social Sciences at the Universitat Pompeu Fabra (Barcelona). His research interest focuses on the analysis of collective action, regulatory public policy and Latin American governance. He has recently edited the volume *Governing Telecommunications and the New Information Society in Europe* (Edward Elgar, 2002).

Christoph Knill is Professor of Political Science at the University of Konstanz, where he holds the chair on Comparative Public Policy and Administration. His particular research interests include comparative public policy, public administration and European governance. He is author of *The Europeanization of National Administrations. Patterns of Institutional Change and Persistence* (Cambridge University Press, 2001).

David Levi-Faur is a senior lecturer at the Department of Political Science, University of Haifa (leave and sabbatical, 2000–2004) and a senior fellow of the Regulation Network, RSSS, at the Australian National University. His major fields of interest are comparative political economy and comparative public policy. He currently specializes in multi-level analysis of the origin and diffusion of regulatory reforms. He was visiting scholar and research associate at the London School of Economics, the University of California, Berkeley, the University of Amsterdam, the University of Utrecht, the University of Manchester and the University of Oxford. His papers have been published in leading journals in the relevant fields (such as the *Journal of Public Policy*, the *Journal of European Public Policy*, *Review of International Relations*, *Studies in Comparative International Development*, the *Journal of Socio-Economics*, the *European Journal of Political Research and Comparative Political Studies*).

Andrea Lenschow received a PhD in Political Science from New York University (1996), and has been Assistant Professor of Political Science at Salzburg University from 1997 to 2003. As of October 2003 she will be Junior Professor at the University of Osnabrueck. In her research she has focused in particular on theories of institutionalism and implementation research in the field of environmental policy in Western Europe. She as edited the volume *Environmental Policy Integration. Greening Sectoral Policies in Europe* (Earthscan, 2002) and co-edited with Christoph Knill the book *Implementing EU Environmental Policy: New Directions and Old Problems* (Manchester University Press, 2000). Currently she is participating in an EU-funded project on Environmental Policy Convergence in Europe.

Martin Lodge is Lecturer in Political Science and Public Policy at the Department of Government and the ESRC Centre for Analysis of Risk and Regulation at the London School of Economics and Political Science. His research interests include the comparative study of regulation, especially network regulation, as well as comparative public administration and policy. His publications include *On Different Tracks: Designing Railway Regulation in Britain and Germany* (Praeger, 2003).

Joseph A. McCahery is Professor of International Business Law at Tilburg University Faculty of Law and a research fellow at the Tilburg Institute of Law and Economics and the European Corporate Governance Institute (Brussels). He holds a visiting appointment at Leiden University Faculty of Law. Previously, he held an appointment at Warwick University, where he also received his PhD degree. He was a law clerk for Judge Nathaniel R. Jones of the United States Court of Appeals for the Sixth Circuit. He has written widely on corporate law, corporate finance, the political economy of federalism, and securities regulation.

Iain McLean is Professor of Politics, Oxford University and a fellow of Nuffield College. He has worked on case studies of railway and mine regulation. Publications include 'Railway regulation as a testbed of rational choice'; *Aberfan: government and disasters*, with Martin Johnes (Ashley Drake, 2000), and *Rational Choice & British Politics: an analysis of rhetoric and manipulation from Peel to Blair* (Oxford University Press, 2001).

Anthony Ogus is Professor of Law, and Research Fellow at the Centre for Regulation and Competition, in the University of Manchester. His main research interest is in law-and-economics and its application to regulation. He has written *Regulation: Legal Form and Economic Theory* (Oxford University Press, 1994). He is currently studying regulation in developing countries.

David Sancho is a lecturer at the Political and Social Sciences Department of University Pompeu Fabra (UPF) and at present holds the position of Vice Dean of Management and Public Administration Studies at this university. His various research fields are centred on the study of public policies and governmental intervention: regulation, telecommunication policy, promotion of the information society and modernization strategies of public management through the use of the new information and communication technologies.

Patrick Schmidt is an assistant professor of Political Science at Southern Methodist University, Dallas, Texas. Before this he was the John Adams Research Fellow at the Centre for Socio-Legal Studies and a research fellow of Nuffield College, Oxford. Publications include: *Lawyers and Regulation: The Politics of the Administrative Process* (forthcoming, Cambridge University Press). His current fieldwork focuses on the involvement of lawyers in the regulation of global financial markets.

Volker Schneider is Professor of Political Science at Konstanz University, where he holds the Chair on Empirical Theory of the State. His research interests are state theory, organized interests, evolution of political institutions and policy networks. He has recently published: *Private Organizations in Global Politics* (with Karsten Ronit) (Routledge, 2000), and 'Institutional Reform in Telecommunications: The European Union in Transnational Policy Diffusion' (in Maria Green Cowles et al., *Transforming Europe*, Cornell University Press, 2001).

Colin Scott is Reader in Law in the Centre for the Analysis for Risk and Regulation at the London School of Economics. Key publications include the co-authored studies *Telecommunications Regulation: Culture, Chaos and Interdependence Inside the Regulatory Process* (Routledge, 2000) and *Regulation Inside Government* (Oxford University Press, 1999).

Marc Tenbücken has studied Politics and Management at the Universities of Constance and Geneva, and at MIT. Currently he is working as an academic assistant and preparing his PhD thesis. His research interest are policy processes in the European Union and regulatory reform in infrastructure sectors. He has recently published *Corporate Lobbying in the European Union* (Peter Lang, 2002).

Series editors' preface

We are glad to welcome, as the second book published in this series on *Regulation, Competition and Development*, a set of contributions by researchers working on both developed and developing economies, which examine the significant issues associated with making comparisons across these types of economy. Particular emphasis is placed on the way in which broader conceptions of the regulatory state address issues of effective governance, public accountability, more efficient processes of competition, and expansion into social policy sectors. The chapters focus on the political and institutional characteristics of the reform being commonly proposed and adapted in processes of regulatory reform. In doing so, they provide an important addition to the existing literature on the politics and governance of regulation.

Issues of regulation and competition have long been matters of both public policy discussion and academic research in developed economies, but until recently were relatively unexamined in relation to developing economies. The Centre on Regulation and Competition (CRC) was established in 2001, with funding from the UK Department for International Development, to conduct research into issues of competition, regulation and regulatory governance in developing countries. It works through a network of partnerships both in the UK and overseas, in Ghana, India, Malaysia, the Philippines, South Africa and Sri Lanka. This new series represents one of the many forms of dissemination of both conceptual studies and research findings, including conferences, workshops, journal publication, and policy briefs. We aim to make this series a focal point for future research on competition, regulation and regulatory governance in developing countries and hope that it will have a major impact on effective and socially beneficial transfer of knowledge across countries and regions of the world.

Paul Cook
Martin Minogue
Series editors
July 2003

Editors' preface

This book is the fruit of a collaborative research network that links scholars of the politics of regulation. The impetus for the establishment of the network is the belief that the politics of regulation is an under-researched area, especially outside the United States. The issue became especially important following the rise of the regulatory state and the diffusion of regulatory reforms around the world. The aims of the collection are twofold. The primary aim is to develop sound conceptual and analytical studies that shed light on the politics of regulation. In this, we hope the book will make a contribution in the tradition of Marver Bernstein, Theodore Lowi and James Wilson, who made influential contributions to the study of the politics of regulation. The second aim of the book is to shed light on the politics of regulation in the age of governance. We suggest that the economic, social and political context of regulation has been radically transformed in the last two decades. The spread of regulation as a mode of governance around the world obliges us to re-examine our theories and to develop new tools of analysis. The contributors to this collection have taken significant steps in these directions.

In order to stimulate scholarly and interdisciplinary dialogue, we organized a series of research workshops with the primary support of the European Science Foundation (ESF). The first workshop was held at Nuffield College, University of Oxford, on 25–26 May 2002, and the second at the Universitat Pompeu Fabra, Barcelona, on 29–30 November 2002; a third workshop was held in the Centre for Study of Law and Society, University of California at Berkeley, 25–26 April 2003. Most chapters in this book were originally presented and discussed in these workshops. The papers were reviewed by the editors and other scholars, and were subsequently reworked and revised in three editorial sessions. We wish to thank all the participants in the workshops and the reviewers, who contributed greatly to the quality of the present volume. We are also indebted to the authors for their willingness to answer all our numerous requests and comments.

A project like this would not be possible without financial support from a number of organizations. We would like to express our indebtedness to the European Science Foundation, the Spanish Ministry for Science and Technology, the Department of Political and Social Sciences (Universitat Pompeu Fabra), the Centre on Regulation and Competition (IDPM, University of Manchester), the Centre for Study of Law and Society (University of

California at Berkeley), the Department of Politics and International Relations (University of Oxford), Nuffield College Politics Group (University of Oxford), the Department of Political Science (University of Haifa) and the Generalitat de Catalunya. All these institutions were very encouraging to our collaborative work, and their generosity allowed us to organize the workshops. In these institutions it is a pleasure to acknowledge the help of John Darwin (chair of the Politics Group at Nuffield College), Mark Philp (Department of Politics and International Relations, Oxford), Philipe Row and Kerstin Sahlin-Andersson (European Science Foundation), and Paul Cook and Martin Minogue (Centre on Competition and Regulation, University of Manchester). David Levi-Faur would like to express his thanks to Professor Jeremy Richardson, former head of the Centre for European Politics, Economics and Society of the University of Oxford, where he was originally based, and also to his colleagues at the University of Haifa, and especially the Chair of the Department of Political Science, Professor Avraham Brichta, who allowed him generous leave and sabbatical during 2000–2004. The project was also facilitated by a seven-month research position at the Centre on the Study of Regulation and Competition, the University of Manchester.

It is our pleasure to name some of the scholars who encouraged and helped us with this project. We would like to thank to the following, who generously commented on particular aspects of the project: Ian Bartle (University of Bath), John Braithwaite (Australian National University), Fabio Franchino (University College London), Sharon Gilad (University of Oxford), Fabrizio Gilardi (University of Lausanne), Ken Hanf (Universitat Pompeu Fabra), Peter Humphreys (University of Manchester), Martin Lodge (London School of Economics), Michael Moran (University of Manchester), Bronwen Morgan (University of Oxford), Ulrika Morth (Stockholm University), Anthony Ogus (University of Manchester), Colin Scott (Australian National University and London School of Economics), and Raphael Schapiro (University of Oxford).

Jacint Jordana and David Levi-Faur
Barcelona and Oxford
August 2003

1. The politics of regulation in the age of governance

Jacint Jordana and David Levi-Faur[*]

Scholarly interest in regulation as a mode of governance – and of the regulatory state as its most characteristic feature – has increased substantially in the last decade. One of the most important driving forces of this interest is growing scholarly awareness of the global wave of regulatory reforms. Since the mid-1980s governance through regulation has ceased to be a peculiarity of the American administrative state but has become a central feature of reforms in the European Union (Majone, 1994, 1997), Latin America (Manzetti, 2000; Jordana and Levi-Faur, 2003), East Asia (Jayasuriya, 2001), and developing countries in general (Cook et al., 2004).[1] These recent developments have had a profound impact on our understanding of the regulatory state. While the studies of eminent scholars of regulation such as Marver Bernstein (1955), Theodore Lowi (1964, 1985) and James Wilson (1980) are still required reading, much has changed in the governance of the capitalist economy since the mid-1980s, hence in the degree of academic attention given to the politics of regulation. Regulation as an art and craft of governance, as an institutional reality, as a field of study, and as a public discourse is more salient and celebrated nowadays than ever before. However, the challenges are as great as the achievements. Not least, the degree of change in the ways governance through regulation is exercised can hardly be exaggerated.

Most intriguing is the expansion of regulatory modes of governance to more and more spheres of life and political arenas. Four issues are especially important here. First, the institutional advance of regulation in the context of privatization and the neo-liberal hegemony presents a paradox. In an era in which regulation has become synonymous with red tape, and deregulation has become a major electoral platform of the New Right, regulatory authorities have been created in unprecedented numbers and with unprecedented autonomy. Second, the development of proactive policies for the promotion of economic competition (regulation-for-competition) represents a departure from the past.[2] If the regulatory agencies that were established in the United States during the New Deal era legitimized monopolies, the new regulatory authorities that are now established all over the world are committed to active promotion of competition, using modern regulatory techniques (more rules, more competition: see Vogel, 1996). This might lead to institutional structures and policies that are basically more mercantilist than liberal (Levi-Faur, 1998).[3] Third, the incremental transfer of regulatory knowledge and institutions from economic to social spheres is encouraging to the extent that regulatory institutions have some clear advantages over ministries, and that the mere fact of reform opens new possibilities for effective governance. Yet it is also a cause for concern, since social regulation is advancing slower than economic regulation. Finally, while the American regulatory state that was created in four waves of institutional construction and deconstruction after the late nineteenth century availed of celebrated 'prophets' (McCraw, 1984) and had clear political affiliation (Vogel, 1989; Rose-Ackerman, 1992), the political forces that sustain, promote, and diffuse the regulatory state, and the benefits and costs that it imposes on business, are still unclear.

The sections of this chapter discuss four important implications of the recent advance of the regulatory state for the study of regulation. The first is the evolution and transformation of the notion of regulation, in particular the coexistence of multiple and sometimes fairly confusing meanings. The second is the changing relations between competition and regulation and their implications for the role of politics in general and the state in particular in the governance of the capitalist economy. The third is the political character (or colour) of the regulatory state, in particular the extent to which it is part of the neo-liberal order. The fourth issue is the political foundations of the regulatory state, considering the possibility that the changing social context of regulation has had a major impact on its rise. This aspect is captured through a discussion of the alleged decline in public trust in major political and social institutions in general and in the rise of the regulatory state in particular. One way to understand the relations between trust and the rise of the regulatory state is to suggest that 'we audit, and we regulate, when we cease to trust' (Moran, 2000, 10). Another way focuses on the changing patterns of trust allocation by the public rather than the alleged decline of trust (O'Neill, 2002, 9–10). Whatever the pattern of causality is, it might be valuable to discuss the relationship between the two. The major point that we advance, largely with the consent of the other contributors to this collection, is that the emergence of the regulatory state is much more than a by-product of neo-liberalism. To support this argument in this chapter we draw some *preliminary* outlines based on a trust-centred interpretation of the regulatory state.

THE VARIOUS MEANINGS OF REGULATION

Regulation is a popular subject of study in several disciplines across and beyond the social sciences. It is studied by scholars who advance different theoretical perspectives, who use various research methodologies, and who hold different assumptions about the relations between regulation and the political process. Not surprisingly, the various definitions of regulation reflect specific disciplinary concerns, are oriented towards different research methods, and reflect to a significant extent the unique personal, national and historical experience of the formulator of the definition. In these circumstances it would be futile and somewhat nonsensical to offer one authoritative definition of the notion of regulation that holds across the divides. Still, some benefit may accrue from the exchange of ideas between these various approaches through a discussion of the various meanings and a clarification of how they reflect different research agendas and disciplinary concerns. To tackle this task we draw mainly on Baldwin et al. (1998), who identify three main meanings for the notion of regulation: (a) targeted rules; (b) all modes of state intervention in the economy; and (c) all mechanisms of social control, by whomsoever exercised (cf. Ogus, 1994, 1–3; Doern and Wilks, 1998, 6).

The three meanings of regulation are described in Figure 1.1 in three circles that expand from the narrowest meaning of regulation (I) to its broadest (III). In its narrowest and simplest sense, 'regulation refers to the promulgation of an authoritative set of rules, accompanied by some mechanism, typically a

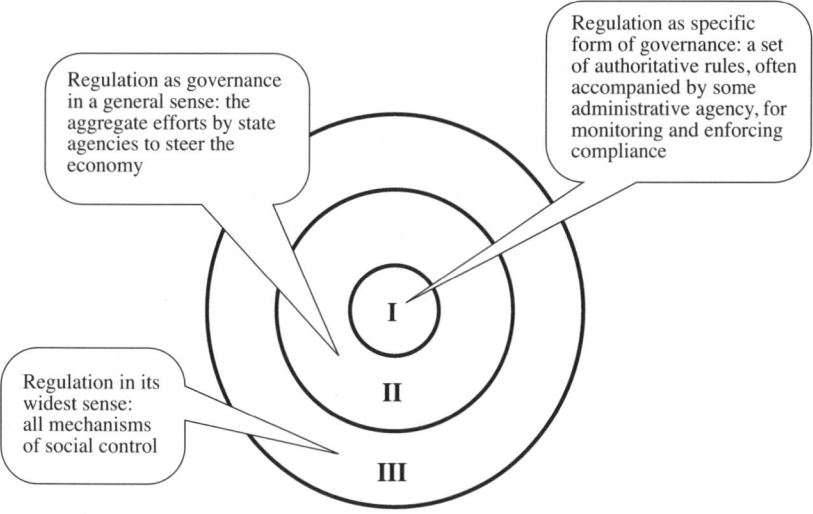

Source: Baldwin et al. (1998).

Figure 1.1 The three meanings of regulation

public agency, for monitoring and promoting compliance with these rules'
(Baldwin et al., 1998, 3). A second meaning of regulation refers to 'all the
efforts of state agencies to steer the economy' (ibid.). This meaning is broader
than the first since it includes, in addition to rule-making, measures such as
taxation, subsidies, redistribution and public ownership. The third meaning of
regulation is broader still, and encompasses all mechanisms of social control,
including unintentional and non-state processes. According to Baldwin et al.
(1998, 4), it extends

> to mechanisms which are not the products of state activity, nor part of any
> institutional arrangement, such as the development of social norms and the effects
> of markets in modifying behaviour. Thus a notion of intentionality about the
> development of norms is dropped, and anything producing effects on behaviour is
> capable of being considered as regulatory. Furthermore a wide range of activities
> which may involve legal or quasi-legal norms, but without mechanisms for
> monitoring and enforcement, might come within the definition.

We suggest that the three meanings to some extent reflect the changes that
we have identified in the economic and social context of regulation. In
addition, they reflect different research agendas and different disciplinary
concerns. Let us start with the pre-1990s transatlantic difference in the
meaning of regulation. Until the end of the 1980s scholars outside the United
States tended to employ the word 'regulation' to denote the general
instruments of government for the control of the economy and society
(meaning II). The notions of 'regulation' and 'intervention' were used almost
interchangeably (Majone, 1994, 77). The situation was different in the United
States, where the notion of regulation had acquired a narrower meaning in
response to the rise in the number of independent regulatory institutions and
the consequent crystallization of regulatory practices into a theory of
governance (meaning I). The global spread of the wave of regulatory reforms,
and especially the establishment of independent regulatory institutions in
various sectors of the economy (especially in the utilities), led to some
convergence in the meanings of regulation: towards the narrowest and away
from the second, which had more general use. This movement was
strengthened by a shift in the way some economists used the notion of
regulation. As noted by Ogus (2001, ix), economists, unlike lawyers (and, we
add, political scientists in the United States), used to employ the word
'regulation' in its broad sense. This meaning was acceptable and probably
successful in conveying a widespread distaste for over-regulation, yet it was
rather too broad, given the growth of institutional economics and law-and-
economics scholarship. We therefore suggest that even in the economics
profession the narrower meaning ('targeted rules') has grown increasingly
popular.

At the same time, it seems that the third meaning of regulation (all mechanisms of social control) is making headway in the socio-legal and the constructivist literature. This seems to be driven by the growth of (semi-)consensual international regimes for the governance of 'global problems' such as weapons of mass destruction and climate change. We have referred to this development as the increasing multiplicity of the levels of governance. New regulatory regimes are at least partly established through voluntary agreements, without recourse to strong monitoring and enforcement mechanisms and with apparent disregard for values of 'national sovereignty'. The normative questions that arise from this definition, the problems of monitoring and enforcement mechanism, and the interests in supranational and international regulatory regimes make this notion of regulation especially attractive for lawyers, sociologists of law, and scholars of international relations and international political economy.

Many variations in these notions of regulation might be found in the literature, and it is not impossible that the popularity of these notions will decline at some time in the future and that others will make headway. We should not look for an exhaustive and consensual definition across different disciplines and research agendas, but for a specific context and goal that shape the particular meaning of the notion of regulation. Let us move on to the changing relations between regulation and competition.

THE CHANGING RELATIONS BETWEEN REGULATION AND COMPETITION

Not only the meaning of regulation but also the relations between regulation and competition have changed in the last two decades. It was only in the early 1970s that George Stigler could write with much conviction and force that 'regulation and competition are rhetorical friends and deadly enemies: over the doorway of every regulatory agency ... should be carved: Competition Not Admitted' (Stigler, 1975, 183). While this notion of the relations between regulation and competition is still part of public and political discourse, it hardly reflects any longer the relations between competition and regulation. Regulation and competition became aligned in a way that was inconceivable to Stigler, and is still difficult for many to appreciate. The regulatory toolbox has expanded and, most importantly, contains new techniques of 'regulation-for-competition'. These techniques refine the work of the regulators and thus represent a professional advance in regulatory techniques. With the help of new digital technology, these techniques facilitate much of the spread of freer markets alongside the consolidation of regulatory regimes. At a different level, they allow the regulators to align themselves with the neo-liberal agenda and to regain legitimacy in an environment of 'regulatory flux'.[4]

It might be useful to start with a clarification of five notions that are used in the literature to capture the relations between competition and regulation. Deregulation, re-regulation, regulation-of-competition, regulation-*for*-competition and meta-regulation convey different and sometimes conflicting dimensions of the much wider phenomenon of regulatory reform and liberalization. Deregulation is the reduction of economic, political and social restrictions on the behaviour of social actors (in our context, mainly business). In the early 1970s, when Stigler wrote about the clash between regulation and competition, he implied that the elimination of regulation (that is, deregulation) was a necessary condition for competition. The notion of re-regulation is often used to imply that regulatory reforms and liberalization in general result in new settings of regulation rather than in deregulation. The notion of re-regulation is vague as to the nature and goals of the new regulation, and therefore has rather limited use in clarifying the relations between competition and regulation. The advantage of the notions of regulation-*of*-competition and regulation-*for*-competition over the notion of re-regulation is that they reflect 'positive' relations between regulation and competition and suggest that it may be possible to promote competition via administrative controls (see Table 1.1).[5]

Regulation-*of*-competition and regulation-*for*-competition differ in the degree of intervention by state authorities and in the capacities of the state to monitor and enforce competition. While both require the establishment and the strengthening of governance capacities, regulation-*for*-competition requires far more intrusive capacities. This is best indicated by the contrast between economy-wide responsibilities of national competition authorities in the case of regulation-*of*-competition, and sector-specific responsibilities of regulatory authorities in the case of regulation-*for*-competition. The broader responsibilities of national competition authorities allow them less influence on market actors who know their industry well. These broader responsibilities also imply that competition authorities adopt a reactive approach to anti-competitive measures. In regulation-*for*-competition, the responsibilities of regulatory authorities are narrowly confined to a sector or industry, but they usually give those authorities much more influence over market actors. Unlike the reactive approach of competition authorities, these sector-specific authorities are today proactive and involved in market design and market control to an unprecedented extent.

Finally, meta-regulation of competition implies that in addition to the direct regulation of the actions of individuals and corporations, the process of regulation itself becomes regulated. In our context of the promotion of competition via political power, it means that the government monitors

Table 1.1   Types of competition and types of regulation

Type of competition	Types of regulation	Regulatory authority	Examples
Deregulated	Self-regulating markets	No regulation (retreat of the state)	Moving from certification to liability laws in order to protect consumers
Regulated	Regulation-*of*-competition	National competition authorities	Prevention of concentration through the regulation of mergers, cross-ownership, etc.
Regulated	Regulation-*for*-competition	Sector-specific authorities and national competition authorities	Interconnection regimes in telecommunications, unbundling the network
Meta-regulated	Enforced self-regulation of competition rules	Sector-specific authorities and national competition authorities	Institutionalization of internal mechanisms of self-regulation that correspond with the legal requirements of competition law in general and the regulatory regime in particular.

Source: Partly based on Levi-Faur (1998).

the self-monitoring of corporations and other organizations as to the compliance of their employees with the rules of competition (see Morgan, 2003; Parker, 2002).[6] Direct intervention and enforcement are replaced here with allegedly lighter demands on economic actors to institutionalize processes of self-regulation. Yet if the intrusiveness of the state is to be judged by how far it can change social and corporate behaviour, this type of regulation should be considered as intrusive as regulation-*for*-competition.

While regulatory reforms certainly involve some aspects of deregulation, they also involve regulation-*for*-competition, regulation-*of*-competition, and meta-regulation. These last three forms of regulation, which are often ignored by neo-liberals, allow the relatively harmonious growth of the regulatory state in the context of pervasive regulation.

WHAT IS THE REGULATORY STATE?

It is often claimed that we live in the era of the 'Regulatory State' (Majone, 1994; 1997; Loughlin and Scott, 1997; McGowan and Wallace, 1996, Hood et al., 1999). Indeed, among a large number of candidates for a convincing label that captures the essence of recent changes in the governance of the capitalist economy, this one has proved especially popular (Moran, 2002, 391). Yet this notion raises several questions, of which some of the more significant are discussed here. What is the 'regulatory state'? Is it a scholarly fiction or a political reality? To what extent is it a global rather than a national phenomenon? Is it a product of the neo-liberal project of liberal world economy? And, consequently, what are the political affiliations (or colours) of the regulatory state?[7]

First, then, what is the regulatory state? We suggest three possible answers – the minimal, the prudent, and the over-ambitious – each of which has some advantages for the study of regulation. A minimal answer would be that it is a fiction that provides 'a sort of intellectual brazier around which [scholars of regulation] can all gather, to warm our hands and speak to each other, in a world of increasingly fragmented academic professionalism' (Moran, 2002, 411–2). Who cares, asks Moran, about the shape of the brazier or what is the fuel for the flames, as long as it helps moderate the crisis of communication in the social sciences? This minimalism seems to have some advantages as it reminds us not only that we employ the notion of regulation differently across and even within different disciplines, but that the importance of regulation and regulatory institutions in the governance of the economy is a contested issue. The downside of this minimalism is that it may be counter-productive to the consolidation of cross-disciplinary research and to attracting more scholars to the study of regulation. Fictitious entities are rather less attractive to scholarly research (and to funding institutions) than real entities.

From another perspective the term regulatory state 'suggests [that] modern states are placing more emphasis on the use of authority, rules and standard-setting, partially displacing an earlier emphasis on public ownership, public subsidies, and directly provided services. The expanding part of modern government, the argument goes, is *regulation* ...' (Hood et al., 1999, 3; see also Majone, 1997). Unlike the first, this second answer points to tangible dimensions of the regulatory state. By using the notion of modernity so often, it also suggests the existence of intimate relations between new and refined instruments of regulation that did not exist before, or at least were not widely used, and the development of regulatory institutions that operate them.[8] Paradoxically, the tangible effects of the regulatory state might be apparent in the growth in the discourse of regulation in scholarly, media and policy-making circles. Yet beyond the instruments and the discourse, numerous new institutions have gained autonomy from ministerial control, are staffed by experts, and command considerable resources. Their proliferation around the globe supplies some tangible support for the view that the regulatory state is more than a scholarly fiction.

Some caution, however, is in order here. First, the advance of the regulatory state is conditioned by sectoral characteristics as it clearly advances in some sectors more than others. Second, multiple forms of control, not just one, are employed in the governance of the capitalist economy; several modes of regulation coexist even in heavily regulated sectors (Pagoulatos, 1999). Third, the regulatory state does not develop in a vacuum and is not meant to operate as a sole source of regulatory control. At best, it can be embedded successfully in older layers of governance that were created for different purposes and in different eras (see Jordana and Sancho, Chapter 13, this volume). Fourth, dependent on national institutions and state traditions, it may well be that there are several types of regulatory state rather than one (Lodge, 2002, 177). Finally, caution is also advised with regard to the 'locus' of the regulatory state. For some it is a global phenomenon, driven by the emergence of a new convention on the best practice in economic governance (or more critically, the effects of imitation: Levi-Faur, 2002). For some it is basically an aspect of regional integration, which occurs in the context of liberalization and the rise of technocratic forms of legitimacy (for example, Majone, 1994, 1997). For others regulation is mainly a political and administrative process that occurs and matters at the national level: hence studies of the 'Regulatory State in Germany' and 'The Regulatory State in Britain' (Muller, 2002; Moran, 2003). For others still the regulatory state is a sectoral phenomenon: hence studies of *The Politics of Banking* (Moran, 1984) and even *The Politics of Central Banks* (Elgie and Thompson, 1998). While each of these interpretations might have some validity, it is necessary to develop research designs that will capture the increasing 'multi-levelness' of the regulations and regulatory politics (see Levi-Faur, Chapter 8, this volume).

The over-ambitious answer sees the regulatory state as *the* major aspect in the transformation of the governance of capitalist economies since the 1980s. Rule-making, according to this answer, will marginalize if not replace war-making, taxing and spending – the three most visible functions of the modern state. Variations across sectors, nations and international regimes are temporary or minor aspects of the shift towards convergence on the regulatory state. This approach sees the rise of the regulatory state as only one dimension of historically and institutionally entrenched modes of governance such as the welfare state, the developmental state and the stabilization state. Finally, the over-ambitious answer would analyse the regulatory state in an *a*historical manner. It ignores the effects of path-dependencies, sequencing of policy steps, and timing in general. While such an answer is hardly found in the scholarly literature in the full-fledged and somewhat caricatured form presented here, we hope that our discussion of the over-ambitious approach will serve as a warning rather than a viable answer to the question of what the regulatory state is.

We can now approach a second, no less important, issue that touches on the nature of the regulatory state. We have suggested that the term 'regulatory state' is one of the convincing labels that capture the essence of the transformation of the capitalist economy. This is all but paradoxical, since the rise of neo-liberalism was supposed to result in deregulation, the retreat of the state, and the triumph of markets and business interests (cf. Ayres and Braithwaite, 1992, 7–12). Could it be that the regulatory state is just a different expression of the same interests and policy goals? In other words, what is the political affiliation of the regulatory state? What are the political forces that support its expansion? Is it a product of the neo-liberal hegemony or is it a pink creature of the 'third way'?

There were times when the regulatory state had very unambiguous colours and a clear political identity. In the United States, where independent regulatory institutions occupied centre stage in the administrative machinery of government, the regulatory state was a product of popular political struggles against entrenched business interests. True, as some were only too happy to point out, business interests supported some forms of regulation (especially at the federal level); but this support hardly contradicts our argument. The creation of the regulatory state in the United States from the end of the nineteenth century through the New Deal and the postwar periods is the hallmark achievement of the American left, and indeed, at least from the point of view of the American extreme right, its colours were all too red. But to the European left, where nationalization rather than regulation was the widespread response to the rise of big business and public social concerns, the American regulatory state seemed rather pink.[9] What one sees, we learn again, depends (somewhat) on one's viewpoint.

This becomes all the more clear when one considers the different views on the current nature of the changes in the governance of the capitalist economy and the role of regulatory institutions in them. Jill Hills (1993), for example, portrayed the reforms in British telecommunications as a move 'back to the future', that is, towards the nineteenth century Night Watchman state. A similar view is reflected in Dunleavy's (1995) characterization of the change in the governance of the economy as the 'hollowing out' of the state. Indeed, even Majone's (1997) description of the change in the governance of

European economy as moving 'from the Positive State to the Regulatory State' has similar echoes. The insinuation that the regulatory state is less positive and 'less red' than its predecessors seems to underestimate the capacities of regulatory authorities to promote social goals and to overestimate the social benefits of public ownership.

A more balanced account of the regulatory state, we suggest, is offered by Ayres and Braithwaite (1992), and the regulatory state and the process of reform are more open-ended than is generally assumed. Such a view is best reflected in Braithwaite's (2000) recent conceptualization of the change in the political economy of the capitalist economy. A seafaring metaphor, borrowed from Osborne and Gaebler (1992), which distinguishes *steering* (leading, thinking, directing, guiding) from *rowing* (enterprise, service-provision), allowed Braithwaite to capture three different types of states across two centuries of capitalist economy, as presented in Table 1.2. While in the nineteenth century it was civil society that did the steering and rowing, the postwar State took over responsibility for both steering and rowing. The regulatory state that was born on a global scale in the 1980s represents a new division of labour. While the state is responsible for steering, civil society took over the functions of service provision and enterprise.[10]

Table 1.2 The transformation of governance and the nature of the regulatory state

	The Night Watchman State (nineteenth century)	The Postwar State (1945–1970s)	The Regulatory State (1980s–)
Steering	Civil society	State	State
Rowing	Civil society	State	Civil society

Source: Based on Braithwaite (2000).

The intriguing feature of Braithwaite's use of this metaphor is the relative freedom that it grants the regulatory state. Steering is not confined to certain goals and destination, so the 'policy boat' is not confined to shallow water. The regulatory state may opt for a variety of social and economic goals. It can be market enforcer, social planner, night watchman, or any combination of the three. National and sector-specific choices are thus not limited: the regulatory state can be captured by any organized interest or act in a fashion relatively autonomous of social forces. In other words, the jury is still out and the true colours of the regulatory state are still to be determined.

TRUST AND THE REGULATORY STATE

While the jury in our previous section is still deliberating, one might speculate about the criteria that it will adopt when making its judgement on the political affiliation of the regulatory state. It seems safe to suggest that a decision will be taken with reference to the performance of the regulatory state (not an easy task for our juries). Yet the jury might also want to consider the motives and the context that shaped the rise of the regulatory state. It will probably consider three options. The first suggests that the regulatory state is a technocratic solution to the problem of (lack of) expertise of policy-makers and more generally their time constraints. The second assumes the supremacy of the 'structural' power of business (Poulantzas, 1969; Lindblom, 1977) and suggests that delegation solves the problem of political credibility by imposing constraints on policy change. Unlike the first interpretation, which emphasizes the technocratic nature of the regulatory state, the second perceives it as a solution to the inherent tension between the demands of the capitalist order and democracy. Let us present each of the two before suggesting a trust-centred perspective.

The advantages of delegation from politicians to experts were already recognized in the American context. In the mid-1950s Marver Bernstein could write:

> In general, the commission form has been championed by those who believe that administrative regulation requires a high degree of expertness, a mastery of technical detail, and continuity and stability of policy. These requirements, it is alleged, can only be met by a board of commissioners functioning in a neutral environment, free from partisan political considerations. (Bernstein, 1955, 4)

Similarly, in the current European context, Majone emphasizes that 'regulation is not achieved simply by passing a law, but requires detailed knowledge of, and intimate involvement with, the regulated activity' (Majone, 1994, 81).[11] Intimate knowledge of the regulated activity is continuously raised as a reason for autonomous regulatory agencies and for granting wide discretion to regulators. At the same time it challenges the idea of democratic governance by elected officials by introducing an additional layer of decision-making, which is only indirectly accountable to the electorate.

The second interpretation of the rise of the regulatory state in general and delegation in particular is the credibility explanation. In their most basic form, these explanations suggest that governments delegate powers mainly in order to enhance the credibility of their policies to potential investors (Majone, 1999, 4; Franchino, 2002). Short-term electoral cycles, growing regulatory competition, and increasing international interdependence create the basic conditions for the delegation of authority to both domestic and international institutions (Majone, 1999). The issue of credible commitment is therefore intimately connected with the change in the context of regulation. Governments that are entangled with growing regulatory competition are pushed to transfer control through institutionalized forms of delegation as a way to enhance their credentials in the eyes of transnational business. At the same time, delegation of authority to supranational institutions is used as a tool by governments to project their commitment to international cooperation (Majone, 1999).

Yet a third interpretation of the extensive use of delegation and of the rise of regulation as a major mode of governance focuses on the role of trust and the dynamics of trust-building. For some, the decline of trust is a major characteristic of modern life. For Putnam (1993) and Fukuyama (1995), for example, the distinction between low-trust and high-trust societies promises to shed light on central issues such as the causes of economic development. For others, the major issue is not necessarily a decline of trust but its distribution in interpersonal, communal and political settings. Trust is given to some institutions and actors and is withheld from others (again, the general trends of this dynamic process are still much debated). Specifically in the context of regulation, it was suggested that the trends of the alleged decline in the public's trust in social, economic and political institutions might have important implications for the rise of regulation as a mode of governance (Power, 1997; Moran, 2000; 2002). The decline of public trust in economic and political institutions is celebrated in the outbreak of public scandals in the mass media (Moran, 2000, 2001, 2002) as well as in growing attention to blame-shifting strategies of politicians (Hood, 2002). At the same time the decline of trust might be behind the rise of the 'audit society' (Power, 1997, 142–7), the decline in some forms of self-regulation (Moran, 2000, 5–6), and the rise of the regulatory state *within* the state (Hood et al., 1999). Yet even in the context of regulation the suggestion that trust is declining in modern societies is not universally shared. How else can we explain the promotion of high-trust strategies of self-regulation that are popular not only among scholars of regulation but also among practitioners (Morgan, 2003; Parker, 2002)?[12] Since the issues of the alleged decline of trust and its effects on social and economic performances are contested, and since we aim to sketch only preliminary outlines of its effects on the regulatory state, we will limit ourselves here to the demonstration of four advantages of the trust-centred perspective on explanations that emphasize the role of expertise and 'policy credibility' in the context of government business relations. These four advantages may encourage other scholars to discuss the issues of trust and regulation, which are only partially developed here, more thoroughly.

First, trust-centred explanations make better sense than the other two explanations in regard to related concepts of the 'audit explosion' (Power,

1997) and the 'Regulatory State inside the state' (Hood et al., 1999). The notions of 'audit explosion' and 'audit society' capture the increasing degree to which modern societies are committing themselves to various kinds of auditing practices. According to Michael Power, the 'audit explosion' represents more than functional needs and is a reflection of sociological currents and our attempts at social control in the face of uncertainties and risks. Auditing is an effort to enhance trust via the supply of information, yet it comes at a price: 'one needs to trust the auditor and the audit process itself' (Power, 1997, 136). Similarly, Hood and his colleagues shed light on the fact that regulation is not only a game played between society and state actors but is also done inside the state (Hood et al., 1999). Here is another explosion of regulation, which is not a product of the dependency of the capitalist order on private investment:

> [T]the sum of regulation inside UK government amounted to a surprisingly large enterprise, approaching if not exceeding the scale of regulation of private business. It was an 'industry' which seemed to have grown topsy-like ... (Hood et al., 1999, 5)

The common denominator of observations on the 'audit explosion' and 'regulation inside the state' is that they place the process of regulation in its broader context. Regulation is increasing not only in sectors and arenas where expertise and capital are badly needed, but also far beyond. Observers suggest that the rise of the regulatory state is propelled by concerns of business investment and the role of expertise in the policy process, but also by the dynamic process of trust-building between social and political actors (for example, politicians and the electorate), which goes far beyond purely economic considerations.

A second good reason why one should consider the role of trust in the rise of the regulatory state is the 'retreat from self-regulation' and the growing vulnerability of experts to social and political criticism. According to Moran (2000, 8), the retreat from self-regulation is one of the paradoxes of the regulatory state since it clashes with the argument 'that we are witnessing the advance of reflexive modes of governance by self-steering systems'. If one also considers the decline of liberal forms of corporatism, the rising role of 'enforced self-regulation', that is, 'self-regulated, or else ...' (Ayres and Braithwaite, 1992, 15), and the decline of professional authority as reflected in the constraints on self-regulation by professional associations (Moran, 2000, 5–6), it seems even more plausible that trust is central to the rise of the regulatory state. We transform systems of self-regulation or make sure that they work properly in order to build or rebuild systems of trust.

Third, trust-centred explanations might be more persuasive than explanations centred on expertise and policy credibility when one considers their applicability to social regulation (for example, health and safety, environmental issues and consumer protection) and especially the creation of autonomous agencies in these spheres. The progress of regulatory reform in these areas, following scandals, catastrophes and public pressure, may suggest that trust between politicians and the public might be an important factor in their consolidation. Once caveat is required, however. If, indeed, independent regulatory authorities in social arenas continued to lag behind the economic arenas, one might want to turn again to the politics of expertise and issues of policy credibility in order to account for the rise of the regulatory state. Yet if this gap between the popularity of independent regulatory authorities in social and economic spheres is only temporary, and similar levels of regulatory reform will be observable in the sphere of social regulation, it will be possible to argue even more forcefully for the importance of trust in understanding the institutional design of the regulatory state.

Finally, the problems of 'non-majoritarian institutions' in general and the demands for more transparency and accountability specifically are often portrayed as outcomes of the rise of the regulatory state (Majone, 1994, 1997). Yet the relationship between the demand for more transparency and accountability on the one hand and the rise of the regulatory state on the other might *not* be one of cause and effect. It might well be that the regulatory state and the demand for more transparency and accountability are both outcomes of the shift in the balance of trust between different professions and social groups. The regulatory state may itself be the solution to problems of transparency and accountability that are associated with the postwar state. Either way, there can be significant interactions between the nature of trust in society and the logic of regulation as a mode of governance. If this assertion gains some general acceptance, it will place the rise of the regulatory state in a context which is wider than what is offered in the current literature and will diminish still more the strength and explanatory power of neo-liberalism as the dominant perspective for explaining current changes in the governance of capitalism. All in all, we think that trust-centred explanations are interesting enough. While not in any way a substitute for political analysis, they may help us frame our analysis in broader terms, namely sociological, and thus somewhat challenge the dominance of the political-economy analysis in the study of regulation and the regulatory state.

THE CONTRIBUTIONS TO THIS VOLUME

The contributions to this volume are organized in two parts. The first part assembles chapters that explicitly discuss theoretical perspectives and their application to the study of regulation, combining different views and approaches. The framing and the evolution of regulatory institutions, the relation between regulators and private interests, and the interrelation between multiple actors and levels of regulation are among the basic issues examined here, considering alternative theoretical approximations. The chapters in the second part present a more comparative focus, either addressing specific problem areas (for example, European governance) or proposing analytical and interpretative frameworks to manage the study of the politics of regulation and their institutional context. As a whole, they shed light on some of the most important developments in the diffusion of regulatory reforms and new institutional forms around the world from what might be best described as a European perspective on the changes in the governance of the capitalist economy.

Chapter 2, by Anthony Ogus, provides an assessment of the status of the economic theory of regulation. In the 1970s and 1980s the economic theory of regulation, with seminal contributions from Stigler and other members of the Chicago School, provided some major insights into the origins and nature of regulation. The principal hypothesis that regulation benefited, and was therefore sought by, the regulated industries rather than other interested groups was an important antidote to the familiar public interest models. This work was complemented by that of the Virginia School, with its focus on rent-seeking behaviour. Anthony Ogus examines how well the economic theory of regulation has survived in an era of deregulation and regulatory reform. His conclusions are that the revitalized public interest approach to economic analysis, sometimes associated with the Yale School of law-and-economics, provides necessary tools for the study of contemporary regulatory policy-making.

Chapter 3, by Iain McLean, examines three events in the history of British regulation that exemplify some key theoretical debates (some of which are also raised in Chapter 2 by Anthony Ogus). McLean compares three distinct theories: the so-called public interest models, the economic theories of regulatory capture, and the adaptation of the median-voter hypothesis as an explanation for regulatory decision-making. The first case is railway regulation from 1825 to 1872, with four notable railway regulation acts. Of these, the Railway Clauses Consolidation Act 1845 and the Regulation of Railways Act 1844 remained a huge influence on regulation in both the UK and the USA throughout the nineteenth century. In this case, regulation of safety arose from electoral pressure; regulation of price and quantity was a political initiative from an exceptionally determined minister (W.E. Gladstone). The second case is about the consequences of a colliery waste tip that slid down a mountain of waste into Aberfan, a mining village in South Wales. To explain this regulatory failure McLean analyses why risk was not assessed properly, invoking cultural factors and the existence of regulatory capture. The third case refers to the wave of privatizations under Thatcher governments during the 1980s, without the prior establishment of new regulations; McLean analyses this as an example of policy guided by median-voter seeking. On the basis of these three cases, McLean argues that all three theories of regulation are viable, but not for all the cases: they are supported by different bodies of evidence, depending on each case. Information management, but also historical contingencies, seem to have an important role in explaining which theories best match which cases.

In Chapter 4 Fabrizio Gilardi focuses on explanations for the diffusion of independent regulatory agencies (IRAs) in Europe. The creation of such agencies can be observed in all West European countries and in a wide range of sectors, such as utilities, financial services, food safety, consumer protection and general competition. Why do governments delegate to agencies they can only partially control? Gilardi suggests that the most promising avenue for research is the new institutionalism in its three forms: rational choice, historical and sociological. Rational choice institutionalism has a long tradition in the US, where, in its principal–agent and transaction costs variants, it has been extensively used to analyse delegation to the executive and to bureaucracy. This constitutes an excellent starting-point for the study of delegation to IRAs, but more for the questions it raises than for the answers it offers. In effect, in the case of delegation to IRAs, what can be observed is that principals make agents purposely independent rather than, as predicted by principal–agent theory, designing control mechanisms that are as accurate as possible. This means that some powerful incentives must be present that lead governments to engage in this extreme form of delegation. Rational choice institutionalism identifies two such incentives. The first is the need to make credible commitments, and the second is the desire to mitigate the effects of the uncertainty of political property rights. In many regulatory settings, credible commitment capacity is a very valuable asset, as it is the only means for governments to achieve their goals. Delegation to IRAs is a way for governments to remove their future freedom of action, and thus to improve the credibility of their commitments. On the other hand, the problem of political uncertainty refers to the fact that elected politicians, by reason of the democratic process, are not able to exercise power for ever. This suggests that politicians should be expected to find a method to make their policy choices last well beyond the moment, which can be postponed but not avoided, when they lose their political property rights over a given policy area. This means that current politicians may wish to bind future politicians. Again, delegation to IRAs is a possible solution.

Historical institutionalism and sociological institutionalism, argues Gilardi, share many similarities, but it is useful to treat them separately. Beginning with historical institutionalism, the main argument is that 'functional pressures' such as those highlighted by rational choice institutionalism are strongly mediated by national institutions, and in particular by state traditions and structures. For example, Britain has a long tradition of regulation through commissions, whereas France has been much more suspicious of independent agencies, seeing them as threatening the unity of the state. In the end, the argument refers to path dependency: change is possible only on a given path. Thus, national and sectoral paths are likely to have an impact on the design of IRAs.

Sociological institutionalism, on the other hand, strongly emphasizes institutional isomorphism. Social processes legitimize certain types of institutional choices rather than others. From this perspective the creation of IRAs is explained by the fact that governments seek legitimacy for their regulatory policies, which can be achieved by using socially valued institutional models such as IRAs. The three forms of institutional isomorphism – coercive, mimetic and normative – are thus likely to be at the origin of the diffusion of IRAs across Europe. The last part of the chapter is devoted to a discussion of the observable implications of the three theories, as well as of the available empirical evidence. The concluding section summarizes the main arguments and sketches a research agenda on IRAs in Western Europe.

Chapter 5, by Damien Geradin and Joe McCahery, critically examines the theory of regulatory competition. The departure point of this theory is that governments compete for factors of production – and also to attract habitants – when they regulate. Thus, regulation should satisfy citizen preferences if competition is effective. In general, it is argued that decentralized regulation produces more efficient results, because at the level of local government competition is greater (there are more governmental units competing). Damien Geradin and Joe McCahery summarize the main lines of this theoretical perspective and point to their normative implications. They then criticize the oversimplification of the theory and suggest an alternative approach, labelled 'regulatory co-opetition'. This approach considers three main dimensions of competition and cooperation, including 'extra-governmental', in which non-governmental actors also play a role. They argue that this multi-dimensional approach clarifies the complexity of actual regulatory strategies, in which different combinations of competition and cooperation are present in relationships between different actors involved in the regulatory arena. Each dimension influences the regulatory behaviour of actors, creating pressures and opportunities. If public interest theories and rent-seeking theories are based on hypotheses about the fundamental interest lying behind the actors' behaviour, regulatory competition theory, but also the alternative co-opetition model, are based primarily on some hypothesis about the aggregate effects of multiple actors with regulatory powers. Although this interpretative framework is mostly inspired by economic reasoning on the functioning of markets, is appears clear that the politics of regulation has to be analysed somewhat to make sense of regulatory developments, in so far as too many options remain open.

The move towards the regulatory state has attracted much attention to issues of accountability and transparency. In Chapter 6 Martin Lodge highlights various perspectives on these problems. The 'traditional' legal literature centres on political-constitutional concerns, 'transaction cost' accounts point to the importance of 'slack' for 'other-regarding' actions, and a 'traditional public service'-oriented literature suggests changes in the public service ethos and accountability owing to perceived marketization via regulatory reform. This chapter advances beyond traditional subjects by underlining the doctrinal basis of the different criticisms and accounts of regulation. Martin Lodge's argument is advanced in three steps. First, he explains the diversity in accounts of accountability and transparency in the literature by locating them in distinct administrative doctrines. Second, he advances a 'transparency toolbox' to distinguish various 'value-free' instruments through which regulation can be made accountable and transparent. These instruments are then linked to the contrasting administrative doctrines of fiduciary trusteeship and consumer sovereignty to show the variety of potential instruments through which accountability and transparency may be incorporated into regulation. In the third part of the chapter Lodge discusses the factors that impact on the selection of instruments, drawing both on analytical concerns (based on the transaction-cost literature) and on empirical evidence, from the developed world as well as the developing world. Accountability and transparency are not just 'good things' that should be enhanced as much as possible, he concludes, but essentially are contested instruments. Any solution to these problems affects the distribution of power in any regulatory regime, involves trade-offs, and provokes responses that can be self-defeating. For this reason they are important instruments in the battlefields of the politics of regulation.

In Chapter 7 Colin Scott examines governance 'beyond' the regulatory state. Three core assumptions of the regulatory reforms are scrutinized: regulation is instrumental in character; the state is necessarily central to regulatory governance; and state law is a central instrument of regulatory governance. The chapter focuses on one aspect of the critique concerning the centrality of state law to regulation. It argues for shifting the focus of analysis from law to the wider range of norms and mechanisms through which control is asserted or achieved, however indirectly.

The issue at the heart of Scott's approach is the extent to which we can or should think of regulatory governance functioning in a manner not dependent on state law or within which state law is not central. Scott explores different theories in search of support for the notion of the post-regulatory state – in which state law is not the key to regulation – such as the limits of control by the law, or the dimensions present in guaranteeing a basic social order. The theories reviewed focus on the relation between social order and state regulation and on the existence of multiple sources of social order (such as iterated cooperation and cohesive communities). This line of theoretical reasoning based on socially emergent properties represents the opposite extreme to the intentional perspectives based upon individual interests, but also addresses regulatory behaviour and regulatory institutions of all kinds, not only formal ones.

Together, these first six contributions shed light on some basic theoretical perspectives on the politics of regulation. They either explain regulatory results by reference to the conscious purposes of politicians and bureaucrats (Ogus, McLean), or explain regulatory landscapes by analysing the development of formal rules and institutions – by aggregate effects of competition and cooperation (Geradin and McCahery), or by strategic considerations, mimetic reactions, or cultural traditions of decision-makers (Gilardi). The two last chapters explain the discourse and notions of transparency and accountability as derivatives of different conceptions of democratic order (Lodge) and the interplay between formal and informal regulatory rules in the functioning of a regulatory order – the post-regulatory state (Scott).

The second part of the book addresses the analysis of the politics of regulation from a different methodological perspective. Instead of formulating an interpretative adaptation or model based on general theories, its analytical purpose takes as a departure point comparative perspectives aiming to derive non-obvious conclusions from the comparison of different cases. Chapter 8, by David Levi-Faur, deals with problems of comparative analysis in a global world where variations occur simultaneously in different arenas of political action. Levi-Faur identifies four popular comparative approaches to the study of politics and policy in general and regulation in particular. These are titled: the national patterns approach (NPA), the policy sector approach (PSA), the international regime approach (IRA), and the temporal patterns approach (TPA). While these approaches are not necessarily contradictory, they represent different assumptions about the determinants of political and regulatory change. Each of these approaches omits some important sources of variations and commonalties in the regulation of the economy and society. Levi-Faur presents a technique that could maximize their explanatory power in the context of medium-N comparative designs, especially those designs that combine two or more comparative approaches to the study of regulatory change. This technique complements the stepwise approach of Steven Vogel and further strengthens the ability of the researcher to increase the number of cases without compromising the strengths of the case-oriented approach.

Chapter 9, by Nicolas Jabko, discusses the political foundations of the regulatory state. Jabko takes issue with the approach that attributes the worldwide multiplication of independent regulatory authorities to the evolving functional requirements of a modern economy, namely the shift away from *dirigiste* policies and towards a more market-based model of public supervision of the economy. Based on a comparative analysis of new regulatory mechanisms recently set up in the European Union, Jabko argues that the emergence of the regulatory state at the European Union level is the result of political manoeuvring rather than evolving functional requirements. In sectors where market forces and technological modernization prevail, old-style regulators constantly have to adapt in order to defend their turf; therefore, would-be regulatory entrepreneurs are generally out-manoeuvred, and new regulatory agencies are rarely created. By contrast, regulatory innovation occurs often in policy sectors where technological evolution is so slow that significant increases in economic efficiency cannot come from incremental regulatory intervention; under certain conditions, the very inertia of this situation creates manoeuvring room for new regulatory–political initiatives. In sum, the chapter concludes that regulatory innovation is more a function of politics than of economic modernization.

Chapter 10, by Christoph Knill and Andrea Lenschow, focuses on two central issues: changes in the nature of the regulatory state and the emergence of multiple regulatory forms. However, the authors use the comparative method in a different way. Taking as a case study the European Union – which has witnessed not only the shift of regulatory activities to a new institutional centre, but with this shift also the evolution of new regulatory patterns – they identify and compare four different modes of regulation in the governance of the European Union. These are new instruments, regulatory standards, self-regulation and the open method of coordination. Then a discussion is developed about the different political dimensions to which they are linked. Thus, each mode of regulation is considered to be linked to a specific mechanism of steering. The authors present an evaluation of the problems of governance that each mode of regulation implies.

Chapter 11, by Marc Tenbücken and Volker Schneider, deals with regulatory reforms and institutional innovations in the field of telecommunications. Comparing the OECD countries, the authors observe that all Western industrial nations have opened their telecommunications markets, dismantled state monopolies, and established national regulatory authorities (NRAs). Liberalization measures starting in the United States in the early 1980s triggered a global chain-reaction that eventually reached every Western industrial nation. However, a closer look at the national level reveals that significant national differences prevail in the institutional transposition of the reform process. The authors demonstrate that despite convergence, considerable differences exist between the NRAs in terms of their organizational structure and regulatory competencies. The international diffusion process did not lead to the adoption of a unitary NRA model. Whereas the impact of the organizational structure on the level of independence is quite similar across countries, significant national differences exist in the delegation of regulatory functions to NRAs. The results obtained from the cross-national comparison enable the authors to create an index, ranking NRAs according to their degree of independence with respect to the government.

Chapter 12, by Patrick Schmidt, is devoted to the role of lawyers in regulatory processes. As a highly influential professional collective, lawyers play a central role in many aspects related to regulation, and often research in this area fails to take account of the overwhelmingly 'legal' character of regulatory politics. Patrick Schmidt analyses this issue by examining the significance of legal interactions in the networks of actors concerned with regulation in the US, taking as a case study the effective running of the Occupational Safety and Health Agency (OSHA) dealing with interest groups, courts and other governmental units. Drawing on extensive interviews and documentary evidence, the chapter explores the way agenda-setting and issues for decision are presented in legal language in the context of credible threats from potential litigants and courts. The author defends the hypothesis that the legal foundation of regulatory politics does more than provide certain incentive structures and tools for individual actors, although it certainly does that. In the aggregate, as the OSHA case suggests, a focus on legal interactions explains the organic development of policy-making and policy output, as the development of precedents and legal norms in particular cases shapes the playing-field for continuing interaction. In sum, this chapter shows us the importance of professional and cultural values and procedures as imbued in micro-level regulatory interactions.

The final chapter, by Jacint Jordana and David Sancho, concentrates on regulatory designs and institutional constellations, and basically consists of an examination of how political institutions work within the regulatory state. Considering that innovations such as National Regulatory Authorities (NRAs) do not exist in a political vacuum, the authors observe that new regulatory institutions are embedded in institutional settings that were created in previous historical periods and for different forms of public action. Therefore, the accumulation of different institutions with intervening capabilities apparently tends to make the role of institutions for decision-making in regulatory policy much more complicated than in most traditional interventionist policies. This institutional accumulation resulted in more complex institutional settings that combined comprehensive and specialized public bodies aiming to shape public policy according to different public mandates and with different and often contradictory goals. Thus, delegation to autonomous regulatory agencies represents in fact only one segment of the whole institutional arena in which regulatory policy is made and implemented.

To make sense of this type of situation, the authors discuss several dimensions for analysing it, in particular by addressing two basic issues: the distribution of responsibilities in the regulatory arena, and the nature of power structures in the institutional constellation. The number of veto players, the character of delegation to NRAs, and also the possible existence of time-stabilizers are the basic decision-making procedures considered in the chapter as devices that intervene in the configuration of the institutional constellation for the making of regulatory policy. Overall, this final chapter is intended as a framework for comparative analyses of institutions involved in regulatory policy, considering that, after the diffusion of regulatory reforms and institutions in recent decades, it is necessary to adopt a more general view of institutional interdependencies in regulation than the traditional Anglo-Saxon configurations offer.

CONCLUDING REMARKS

Probably, the most challenging issue facing analysts of the politics of regulation is the transformation of politics from the 'craft of governing' to the 'art of governance' (Rosenau and Czempiel, 1992: Rhodes, 1997). 'Governance' has become a standard way of characterizing politics in a world where interdependencies between political actors, policy outcomes and policy process are increasingly common, across countries, regions, sectors and issues (Gourevitch, 1978; Tsebelis, 1990), and where governments are no longer the exclusive actors at the international arena. While these aspects are particularly salient in the European Union policy process (Grande, 1996; Kohler-Koch, 1996; Hooghe and Marks, 2001), they are evident globally. The politics of regulation nowadays often occurs in complex multi-level arenas, where some actors can play simultaneously at several levels. The goals of these multi-level actors are often obscured from observers who focus their attention on only one arena of policy-making (Tsebelis, 1990). At the same time, new institutions are being created to deal with these new settings, so the institutional arena of policy-making is becoming increasingly complex and the regulatory state is alleged to increase the fragmentation of the state (Jayasuriya, 2001, 101–2). All the contributors to this book have set their studies in the context of these changes. We are confident that some significant progress has been made here, and also that the road ahead in the study of the politics of regulation, while still full of challenges, is one of the most intriguing and interesting that a new generation of scholars might want to take.

NOTES

* We are happy to acknowledge the helpful comments on a draft version from John Braithwaite, Margit Cohn, Sharon Gilad, Fabrizio Gilardi, Nicolas Jabko, Martin Lodge, Bronwen Morgan, Anthony Ogus, Colin Scott, Patrick Schmidt and Volker Schneider. All errors are ours.

1. The rise of the regulatory state is by no means equal across regions. For the slow advance of the regulatory state in the Arab world, see Levi-Faur (2003).
2. Indeed, they not only depart from the past but also create new unanticipated consequences; see Wilks and Bartle (2002).
3. Mercantilist approaches to economic management in general and economic development in particular emphasize the role of the state in the promotion of markets and capitalism. Neo-liberal approaches tend to marginalize the role of the state and to perceive the relations between state and markets in zero-sum terms.
4. We owe this term to Ayres and Braithwaite (1992, 14), who emphasize that the process of change was not as uni-dimensional as the neo-liberals hoped and the leftists lamented.
5. We prefer them to notions of re-regulation as they depict the rationale of the reforms, something that the notion of re-regulation leaves open.
6. The notion of meta-regulation is simple. At heart, writes Morgan, 'it captures a desire to think reflexively about regulation, such that rather than regulating social and individual action directly, the process of regulation itself becomes regulated' (2003, 2). She further distinguishes between thin and thick notions of meta-regulation, where the thicker version imposes some substantive constraints on policy choice and is more intrusive in its approach towards the market (ibid., 37).
7. Each of these questions deserves further attention, which is beyond the scope of this chapter. Again, we aim to provide here a platform for future research rather than set forth a definitive answer.
8. One example is auctioning the right to use the airwaves or an airport slot (Milgrom, 2000). Another is the use of price-control mechanisms such as PRI-X (Baldwin and Cave, 1999, 226–38).
9. This (pink) view of American capitalism fails to recognize the similarities since the 1930s of American and European approaches to social regulation (health and safety, consumer protection and environment). We owe this point to Anthony Ogus.
10. One problem that our table leaves unsolved regards the implications of globalization. What is civil society in the light of transnational operators? We thank Martin Lodge for this comment.
11. Indeed, Epstein and O'Halloran (1999, 5) suggest that 'What divides the modern administrative state from its predecessors is the delegation of broad decision-making authority to a professional civil service'.
12. For a critical perspective on the effectiveness of self-regulation (and probably of high-trust strategies of regulation in general), see Hutter (2001).

BIBLIOGRAPHY

Ayres, Ian and John Braithwaite (1992), *Responsive Regulation: Transcending the Deregulation Debate*, Oxford: Oxford University Press.

Baldwin, Robert and Martin Cave (1999), *Understanding Regulation*, Oxford: Oxford University Press.

Baldwin, R., C. Scott and C. Hood (1998), 'Introduction', in R. Bardwin, C. Scott and C. Hood (eds), *A Reader on Regulation*, Oxford: Oxford University Press, pp. 1–55.

Bernstein, M.H. (1955), *Regulating Business by Independent Commission*, Princeton: Princeton University Press.

Braithwaite, John (2000), 'The New Regulatory State and the Transformation of Criminology', *British Journal of Criminology*, **40**, 222–38.

Braithwaite, John and Peter Drahos (2000), *Global Business Regulation*, Cambridge: Cambridge University Press.

Cook, Paul, Colin Kirkpatrick, Martin Minogue and David Parker (2004) (eds), *Leading Issues in Competition, Regulation and Development*, Cheltenham, UK and Northampton, USA: Edward Elgar.

Doern, G. Bruce and Stephen Wilks (eds) (1998), *Changing Regulatory Institutions in Britain and North America*, Toronto: University of Toronto Press.

Dolowitz, David and David Marsh (2000), 'Learning from Abroad: The Role of Policy Transfer in Contemporary Policy Making', *Governance*, **13** (1), 5–24.

Drori, S. Gili, Meyer W. John, Ramirez O. Francisco and Schofer Evan (2003), *Science in the Modern World Polity*, Stanford: Stanford University Press.

Dunleavy, Patrick (1995), 'The Globalization of Public Services Production: Can Government be "Best in World"?', *Public Policy and Administration*, **9** (2), 36–64.

Eisner, Marc Allen (2000), *Regulatory Politics in Transition*, Baltimore: Johns Hopkins University Press.

Elgie, Robert and Helen Thompson (1998), *The Politics of Central Banks*, London: Routledge.

Epstein, David and Sharyn O'Halloran (1999), *Delegating Powers: A Transaction Cost Politics Approach to Policy Making under Separate Powers*, Cambridge: Cambridge University Press.

Franchino, Fabio (2002), 'Efficiency or Credibility? Testing the Two Logics of Delegation to the European Commission', *Journal of European Public Policy*, **9** (5) 677–94.

Fukuyama, Francis (1995), *Trust: the Social Virtues and the Creation of Prosperity*, London: Hamish Hamilton.

Gilardi, Fabrizio (2002), 'Policy Credibility and Delegation to Independent Regulatory Agencies: A Comparative Empirical Analysis', *Journal of European Public Policy*, **9** (6), 873–93.

Gourevitch, Peter (1978), 'The Second Image Reversed: The International Sources of Domestic Politics', *International Organization*, **32**, 881–911.

Grande, Edgar (1996), 'The State and Interest Groups in a Framework of Multi-Level Decision Making: The Case of the European Union', *Journal of European Public Policy*, **3**, 318–38.

Haas, M. Peter (1992), 'Introduction: Epistemic Communities and International Policy Coordination', *International Organization*, **46** (1), 1–36.

Hills, Jill (1993), 'Back to the Future: Britain's 19th Century Telecommunications Policy', *Telecommunications Policy*, **17**, 186–99.

Hood, Christopher (2002), 'The Risk Game and the Blame Game', *Government and Opposition*, **37** (1), 15–37.

Hood, Christopher, Henry Rothstein and Robert Baldwin (2001), *The Government of Risk*, Oxford: Oxford University Press.

Hood, Christopher, Colin Scott, Oliver James, George Jones and Tony Travers (1999), *Regulation Inside Government: Waste-Watchers, Quality Police, and Sleaze-Busters*, Oxford: Oxford University Press.

Hooghe, Liesbet and Gary Marks (2001), *Multi-Level Governance and European Integration*, Lanham, MD: Rowman and Littlefield.

Hutter, Bridget (2001), 'Is Enforced Self-regulation a Form of Risk Taking? The Case of Railway Health and Safety', *International Journal of the Sociology of Law*, **29**, 379–400.

Jayasuriya, Kanishka (2001), 'Globalization and the Changing Architecture of the State: The Politics of the Regulatory State and the Politics of Negative Co-ordination', *Journal of European Public Policy*, **8** (1), 101–23.

Jordana, Jacint and David Levi-Faur (2003), 'The Rise of the Regulatory State in Latin America: A Study of the Diffusion of Regulatory Reforms across Countries and Sectors', paper presented at the Annual Meeting of the American Political Science Association, Philadelphia, 27–29 August.

Kohler-Koch, Beates (1996), 'Catching up with Change: The Transformation of Governance in the European Union', *Journal of European Public Policy*, **3**, 359–80.

Levi-Faur, David (1998), 'The Competition State as a Neomercantilist State: Restructuring Global Telecommunications', *Journal of Socio-Economics*, **27** (6), 665–85.

Levi-Faur, David (2002), 'Herding towards a New Convention: On Herds, Shepherds, and Lost Sheep in the Liberalization of Telecommunications and Electricity Industry', Nuffield College Working Paper in Politics, W6-2002, Oxford.

Levi-Faur, David (2003), 'When Diffusion Does Not Work: Regulatory Reforms in the Arab World and Latin America Compared', unpublished manuscript.

Lindblom, E.C. (1977), *Politics and Markets*, New York: Basic Books.

Lodge, Martin (2002), *On Different Tracks; Designing Railways Regulation In Britain and Germany*, Westport: Praeger.

Loughlin, Martin and Colin Scott (1997), 'The Regulatory State', in Patrick Dunleavy, Ian Holliday, Andrew Gamble and Gillian Peele (eds), *Developments in British Politics* 5, Basingstoke: Macmillan, pp. 205–19.

Lowi, Theodore (1964), 'American Business, Public Policy, Case Studies, and Political Theory', *World Politics*, **16**, 677–715.

Lowi, Theodore (1972), 'Four Systems of Politics, Policy and Choice', *Public Administration Review*, **32**, 298–310.

Lowi, T. (1985), 'The State in Politics. The Relation between Policy and Administration', in R.G. Noll (ed.), *Regulatory Policy and the Social Sciences*, Berkeley: University of California Press, pp. 67–105.

Majone, Giandomenico (1994), 'The Rise of the Regulatory State in Europe', *West European Politics*, **17**, 77–101.

Majone, Giandomenico (1996), *Regulating Europe*, London: Routledge.

Majone, Giandomenico (1997), 'From the Positive to the Regulatory State. Causes and Consequences of Changes in the Mode of Governance', *Journal of Public Policy*, **17** (2), 139–67.

Majone, Giandomenico (1999), 'The Regulatory State and its Legitimacy Problems', *West European Politics*, **22** (1), 1–24.

Majone, Giandomenico (2001), 'Two Logics of Delegation. Agency and Fiduciary Relations in EU Governance', *European Union Politics*, **2** (1), 103–22.

Manzetti, Luigi (2000) (ed.), *Regulatory Policy in Latin America: Post-Privatization Realities*, Miami: North–South Center Press.

McCraw, Thomas (1984), *Prophets of Regulation*, Cambridge, MA: Belknap Press.

McGowan, F. and H. Wallace (1996), 'Towards a European Regulatory State', *Journal of European Public Policy*, **3** (4), 560–76.

Milgrom, Paul (2000), *Auction Theory for Privatisation*, Cambridge: Cambridge University Press.

Moran, Michael (1984), *The Politics of Banking: The Strange Case of Competition and Credit Control*, London: Macmillan.

Moran, Michael (2000), 'From Command State to Regulatory State?', *Public Policy and Administration*, **15** (4), 1–13.

Moran, Michael (2001), 'The Rise of the Regulatory State in Britain', *Parliamentary Affairs*, **54**, 19–34.

Moran, Michael (2002), 'Review Article: Understanding the Regulatory State', *British Journal of Political Science*, **32**, 391–413.

Moran, Michael (2003), *The British Regulatory State: High Modernism and Hyper Innovation*, Oxford: Oxford University Press.

Morgan, Bronwen (2003), *Social Citizenship in the Shadow of Competition: The Bureaucratic Politics of Regulatory Justification*, Aldershot: Ashgate.

Muller, M. Markus (2002), *The New Regulatory State in Germany*, Birmingham: Birmingham University Press.

Ogus, Anthony (1994), *Regulation: Legal Form and Economic Theory*, Oxford: Clarendon Press.

Ogus, Anthony (2001), *Regulation, Economics and the Law*, Cheltenham, UK and Northampton, USA: Edward Elgar.

O'Neill, Onora (2002), *A Question of Trust*, The BBC Reith Lectures 2002, Cambridge: Cambridge University Press.

Osborne, David and Ted Gaebler (1992), *Reinventing Government*, Reading, MA: Addison-Wesley.

Pagoulatos, George (1999), 'European Banking: Five Modes of Governance', *West European Politics*, **22** (1), 68–94.

Parker, Christine (2002), *The Open Corporation: Effective Self-Regulation and Democracy*, Cambridge: Cambridge University Press.

Poulantzas, Nikos (1969), 'The Problem of the Capitalist State', *New Left Review*, **58**, 67–78.

Power, Michael (1997), *The Audit Society: Rituals of Verification*, Oxford: Oxford University Press.

Putnam, Robert (1993), *Making Democracy Work: Civic Traditions in Modern Italy*, Princeton: Princeton University Press (with Robert Leonardi and Raffaella Y. Nanetti).

Radaelli, Claudio (2000), Policy Transfer in the European Union: Institutional Isomorphism as a Source of Legitimacy', *Governance*, **13** (1), 25–43.

Rhodes, R.A.W. (1997), *Understanding Governance*, Buckingham: Open University Press.

Rose-Ackerman, Susan (1992), *Rethinking the Progressive Agenda: The Reform of the American Regulatory State*, New York: The Free Press.

Rosenau, N. James and Ernst-Otto Czempiel (eds) (1992), *Governance without Government: Order and Change in World Politics*, Cambridge, Cambridge University Press.

Sabatier, Paul and Hank Jenkins-Smith (eds) (1988), 'Special Issue: Policy Change and Policy-Oriented Learning: Exploring an Advocacy Coalition Framework', *Policy Science*, **21** (2–3), 123–277.

Stigler, George (1975), *Citizens and the State: Essays on Regulation*, Chicago: University of Chicago Press.

Sunstein, Cass R. (1990a), *After the Rights Revolution*, Cambridge, MA: Harvard University Press.

Sunstein, Cass R. (1990b), 'Paradoxes of the Regulatory State', *University of Chicago Law Review*, **57**, 407–41.

Tsebelis, G. (1990), *Nested Games: Rational Choice in Comparative Politics*, California: University of California Press.

Vogel, David (1989), *Fluctuating Fortunes: The Political Power of Business*, New York: Basic Books.

Vogel, Steven (1996), *Freer Markets, More Rules; Regulatory Reform in Advanced Industrial Countries*, Ithaca and London: Cornell University Press.

Wilks, Stephen and Ian Bartle (2002), 'The Unanticipated Consequences of Creating Independent Competition Agencies', *West European Politics*, **25** (1), 148–72.

Wilson, James Q. (1980), *The Politics of Regulation*, New York: Basic Books.

PART I

Theories of regulation for the age of governance

2. W(h)ither the economic theory of regulation? What economic theory of regulation?

Anthony Ogus[*]

INTRODUCTION

The first part of the title to this chapter should provoke an obvious sceptical question: what is a jurist doing, writing a chapter on economic theory for an audience or readership made up primarily of political scientists? My answer is twofold: the way in which economists have approached regulation has had a profound impact on regulatory scholarship and policy; but an outsider is well placed to comment on that impact, particularly if that person comes – like myself – with a lawyer's understanding of what has been happening to regulation within recent years.

One interpretation of my title suggests a simple, but plausible, hypothesis. The economic theory of regulation, as conventionally understood, was developed during the 1960s and 1970s and did much to explain how the regulation of that period came into being and why it failed. The theory is much less adept at explaining the phenomenon of deregulation which occurred in the 1980s and 1990s and, as a consequence, its influence is much in decline.

This simple story has an intuitive appeal, but, as the second part of my title suggests, it is too simple. In the first place, there is some ambiguity about what is to be regarded as 'theory'. It should not be confused with economic analysis, which uncontroversially has a major role to play in regulatory policy-making. In any event, there has been no single economic theory; rather, several with different tools and with different implications. Further, while some of the theories are purely predictive, others combine prediction with normative evaluation. Then there is some confusion regarding the subject-matter of their models. Many economists have (to a lawyer) a narrow vision of 'regulation', focusing almost exclusively on what can be referred to as 'economic regulation' and which is applied to markets in respect of which there is inadequate competition. These economists tend to ignore 'social regulation', the justification for which arises from other forms of market failure.

From all this it should be clear that I see one of my principal tasks as that of unravelling the different approaches and concepts which intertwine in this area. But I will also go further; I will argue that the obsession to find an all-embracing economic theory which 'explains' regulation diverts attention away from the important fact that economic analysis is playing an increasingly significant role in relation to regulatory policy, whether that be to enhance intervention or else to deregulate. In my concluding remarks, I attempt to provide some tentative reasons why economic analysis appears to have increasingly influenced policy-making in recent years.

ECONOMIC REGULATORY ANALYSIS

It seems to me that much of the confusion surrounding the economic theory of regulation has its source in a failure to distinguish between 'theory' and 'analysis'. I assume that the application of economic analysis by policy-makers and others to regulation is uncontroversial. Nevertheless, it may be helpful if I summarize what is involved (Ogus, 1994). Using the conventional tools of microeconomics, in relation to any given area of government intervention, economic analysis can attempt to:

- identify the failure of the market which justifies intervention;
- select the method of intervention which predictably will correct that failure at least cost.

For the first of these tasks, the incidence of market failure will normally arise from externalities (market transactions generate significant external effects which are not reflected in the pricing of the transaction), information deficits (the information available to some of those engaging in the market transactions is seriously imperfect), or inadequate competition (on the supply or demand side there are insufficient alternatives); or some combination of these. Regulation which is predominantly justified by the first two forms of market failure is often and conveniently referred to as 'social' regulation, for example health and safety regulation, environmental and consumer protection; that arising from the third as 'economic' regulation, for example price controls imposed on natural monopolies.

However, the mere existence of an identified failure is not sufficient, by itself, to justify regulation, as that term is normally understood. It may be possible to correct the failure by appropriate market transactions (Coase, 1960) or by the application of private law remedies, not involving state action (Ogus, 1994, 25–7). It then becomes a question for analysis whether these private forms of market failure correction are less or more costly than regulatory interventions. If the latter, we can add to the three identified forms of market failure, as justifying regulation: significant transaction or coordination costs; and failure of private law.

The second task, that of selecting the method of intervention which will correct the failures at least cost, is of course more complex as it comprises a number of dimensions (Rose-Ackerman, 1988; Ogus, 1998a). To facilitate exposition, I shall focus on choice of instruments, levels of intervention and institutional arrangements.

In selecting the appropriate regulatory instrument, policy-makers will obviously need access to technical economic expertise on such matters as the degree of competition within a market of privatized utilities, rendering price controls unnecessary, or the method of determining efficient prices for monopolized industries (Foster, 1992). But the economic input can obviously address a far wider range of policy issues. Thus in determining whether, in relation to hazardous activities, *ex ante* controls (for example licensing) are to be preferred to *ex post* ongoing standards, it is necessary to balance the social costs arising from imperfect enforcement of the latter against the heavier administrative costs of the former (Shavell, 1993). So also, in choosing between specification (input) standards and performance (output) standards, account should be taken of the impact of information costs as to the cheapest technologies of control (lower for the regulatory agencies or for the regulated firms) and of monitoring and other enforcement costs (Ogus, 1994, 166-8). And the same variables are relevant to the choice, much debated, between command-and-control instruments of this kind and financial incentives, for example pollution taxes (Ogus, 1998b).

As regards the desirable level of regulatory protection, one would expect that the economic notion of what is optimal, the point at which the marginal costs of the controls are equal to their marginal benefits, should be a relevant goal for regulatory policy-makers and, in many cases, that will require sophisticated assessment techniques for risk contingencies (Viscusi, 1998), the evaluation of such problematic 'goods' as human life and health and a clean environment, and the level of discounting to be used for future costs and benefits (Zerbe and Dively, 1994).

I turn finally to the institutional arrangements. It is important to appreciate here that what have traditionally been regarded as matters for lawyers and political scientists have been the subject of profound economic analysis. Thus the questions of allocating the power of regulatory decision-making between legislature, executive, independent (or quasi-independent) regulatory agencies and the judiciary, and the breadth of discretion to be conferred on the relevant institutions, have been addressed by economists using notably principal–agent theory (Bishop, 1990). The main thrust of this analysis is to identify what institutional and procedural arrangements will create the appropriate incentives for efficient outcomes. And the same approach is crucial for the related, but independent, question of regulatory enforcement: given the goal of optimal enforcement (increases to regulatory compliance justifying the administrative costs), what level of monitoring and what incidence of sanctions are most likely to achieve it (Polinsky and Shavell, 1979)?

FROM ECONOMIC ANALYSIS TO PUBLIC INTEREST THEORY

To what extent can an 'economic theory of regulation' be derived from these inputs into the policy process? The answer much depends on how the inputs are presented. To begin with, we can assume that some of them will be in the form of predictions. So, for example, if the response of a given firm or individual to regulatory sanctions is inelastic (the tendency to comply will not alter much as a penalty increases), to achieve a given level of enforcement, it will predictably be cheaper to invest more in monitoring conduct (Cooter, 1984, 1528). Propositions of this kind involve positive analysis and can be regarded as part of an 'economic theory of regulation', but the concept is artificial because the proposition relates to behaviour which, though it occurs in a regulatory context, could well occur elsewhere.

In contrast, much of the analysis can be presented as normative propositions. If the analysis is aimed at inducing allocatively efficient outcomes, then indeed we have an 'economic theory of regulation'. Take the two following statements:

1. In devising occupational health and safety standards, regulators should aim to secure the optimal level of care.
2. In reviewing the prices set by energy suppliers, regulators should discourage cross-subsidization from industrial consumers to domestic consumers.

Both statements assume that the goal is allocative efficiency – presumably based on the Kaldor–Hicks criterion[1] – with the implication that it is the exclusive goal. Now there may be some economists who postulate allocative efficiency as the exclusive policy goal, but there cannot be many. A normative economic theory of regulation, in this sense, is untenable. It is widely accepted that good policy-making involves a tradeoff between efficiency and other goals (Okun, 1975).

The two statements could be amended to reflect such a perspective, as follows:

1. To maximize aggregate social welfare in devising occupational health and safety standards, regulators should aim at securing the optimal level of care.
2. To maximize aggregate social welfare, in reviewing the prices set by energy suppliers, regulators should discourage cross-subsidization from industrial consumers to domestic consumers.

Implicit now is the recognition that the regulation[2] may be formulated also to pursue non-economic goals, for example distributional justice. Thus, for the purposes of (1), the efficient level of safety may nevertheless be rejected as imposing an unacceptably high level of costs on particular groups within the community. And, as regards (2), the view may be taken that the economically justified price of (say) water may be too high for some consumers in some parts of the country and that an appropriate[3] way of dealing with this is through cross-subsidization. This is not to say that the economic analysis becomes irrelevant to the policy-making process, because it can then be used to indicate what sacrifice would have to be incurred, in terms of aggregate social welfare, in order to achieve the given distributional objective.

Analysis of the kind described in this section has, nevertheless, been interpreted as giving rise to another 'economic theory of regulation'. This is positive rather than normative, and attempts to explain the existence and form of regulation by reference to its economic justifications; as such it is generally referred to as the 'public interest theory of regulation' (Den Hertog, 2000, 225–34). So if, for example, those practising architecture must first obtain an occupational licence, this regulatory requirement is explained by the forms of market failure to which such practice gives rise (information asymmetries and externalities) and by the perception that occupational licensing is the perceived cheapest mode of correcting such failure.[4]

Taken literally, this 'theory' has become less and less convincing. The 'rational' use of the administrative process in furtherance of the public interest was the hallmark of public law scholarship of the 1930s and 1940s (see, especially, Landis, 1938) and that clearly had a major influence on juristic ideas of the postwar period. When I was a lawyer learning my craft in the 1960s, I may have held the naive view that politicians and others involved in the promulgation of legislation by and large pursued what they thought was in the 'public interest'. However I – and I assume others like me – would not have elevated that expectation into a prediction that legislation was always and exclusively made in the public interest, and therefore certainly not into an explanation of the content of the statute book. Nor do I see that because welfare economists contribute to the policy process by specifying the conditions which would justify regulation and by identifying the least costly regulatory form, they should necessarily be regarded as articulating an explanatory 'theory' of regulation.

Undoubtedly the economic contribution of this period can be criticized on the ground that much of it failed to give sufficient attention to variables which had a major impact on the effectiveness of regulation (Posner, 1974). It was, for example, too often assumed that regulators had, or could acquire at low cost, the necessary information, and the problems, and therefore also costs, of monitoring and enforcement were often ignored. Given these inadequacies, we can easily understand how the first wave of economic involvement in regulatory policy-making may be partly responsible for what is often described as 'regulatory failure'. As we shall see, the criticisms led, in due course, to a broader, and arguably more satisfactory, conventional economic input into the policy process.

In other respects, the 'public interest economic theory of regulation' was too much of an Aunt Sally in the great debate of regulation which occurred in the 1970s. The criticism of it, that politicians and other actors have motivations other than altruism, is platitudinous. It nevertheless did provoke an inquiry into whether it was possible to provide a comprehensive explanation of how legislative decisions are made; and this led to the development of a private interest explanatory economic theory of regulation.

EXPLANATORY PRIVATE INTEREST THEORY

Explaining regulation by reference to individual utility-maximizing behaviour has had such a major impact on regulatory theory generally, that it is often identified as being *the* economic theory of regulation (for example Peltzman, 1989). The basic idea is that regulation is a commodity made available in the political 'market-place' and 'supplied' by politicians and bureaucrats by reference to the demand of those who will benefit from its promulgation; but there are several important variants.[5] For Stigler (1971), the trade was principally between politicians and industries which would benefit from regulatory subsidies and barriers to entry. While different groups could furnish political support, the 'price' necessary to secure the 'purchase', the transaction was most likely to be entered into by those groups which could coordinate their influence at lowest cost, thus tending to favour producers over, for example, consumers.[6] The problem with this is that it does not explain why in many instances regulation benefited consumers, for example by the cross-subsidization of utility prices. To meet this problem Peltzman (1976) proposed a more generalized notion of maximizing political support: politicians devise transfers such that, at the margin, the gain in votes from beneficiaries just exceeds the loss in votes from those who pay.

These versions of private interest theory were used most prominently and plausibly in relation to economic regulation, particularly price controls. Here the impact of regulation on consumer prices was direct and easily noticeable, thus facilitating the political response. What then of social regulation where the impact of regulation might be less marked? The key here was to recognize how interventionist measures which were ostensibly designed to protect consumers (or other largely dispersed groups, such as environmentalists) in fact served to protect specific producer interests. This was generally achieved by restricting the entry of newcomers. The obvious example is a licensing system which purports to restrict supply to 'safe' or 'reliable' producers, but which, because of the barrier to entry, often serves simply to enhance the profits of incumbents (Maurizi, 1974). So also where a regulatory regime decrees by means of a so-called 'grandfather clause' that certain standards should apply only to new producers (Breyer, 1982, 115). A third example occurs where the regime adopts measures the compliance cost of which does not vary with output, thereby discriminating against small firms and removing competitive pressure from larger firms (Ogus, 1994, 172).

The extent to which empirical evidence substantiates the private interest theory, or a particular variant of it, is disputed. Most commentators seem to accept that it was reasonably successful at explaining the incidence of economic regulation (at least in the USA) before the 1980s (Keeler and Foreman, 1998). It appears to have been less successful in relation to the deregulation which subsequently occurred[7] and more generally to social regulation, where, in some areas – for example environmental protection – there has been a significant expansion of interventionist controls favouring diffuse groups rather than producer groups.

Of course, there have been attempts either to explain the latter phenomena in a way which is compatible with the theory or to refine the theory in some way. Thus, as regards deregulation, it has been argued that the rents generated by the initial intervention over time become dissipated and the beneficiaries then were motivated to inducing alternative arrangements, such as self-regulation, which in its turn generates rents (Jarrell, 1984). On the Peltzman version of the theory, which emphasizes the more general political appeal of regulatory policies, it becomes important for politicians to preserve a balance between different pressures within a given supporting coalition and deregulation may benefit part of that coalition (Peltzman, 1989, 38). A similar point may be made in relation to social regulation: in developing the broad package of measures necessary to achieve the coalition, placating the interests of single-issue voters may play a decisive role (Weingast, 1981). And that may override the fact that such voters, for example, environmentalists or consumers, constitute a diffuse group, in contrast to the producer groups who oppose them.

Nevertheless, the theory can also be criticized on a more abstract level. Many of us are uneasy with the basic assumption that politicians and bureaucrats are driven exclusively or even predominantly by self-seeking motives; intuition suggests that ideology and altruism are equally important (Farber and Frickey, 1991). Finally, it should be noted that if a Peltzman-like model of broad political appeal is adopted, the theory converges with a public interest approach which includes distributional justice as one of its justifications for intervention (Keeler and Foreman, 1998, 215). Of course public interest theory may attempt to articulate objective notions of what are 'fair' distributions, but it is not unlikely that those who perceive the *status quo ante* to be 'unfair' and who would benefit from transfer payments will exert an influence on policy-making in exactly the way predicted by the private interest theory.

NORMATIVE PRIVATE INTEREST THEORY

Adherents of the Virginia School of public choice have been critical of the fact that much, perhaps most, of what has been written within the private interest theory tradition has been predictive, rather than normative, and indifferent to the efficiency implications of the analysis. Now, contrary to what is often assumed, such implications are not always easy to state. Let us first acknowledge that if – as is customary for public policy purposes – the Kaldor–Hicks test of efficiency is adopted, then regulatory measures which are subject to typical democratic processes are likely to pass the test, because majority economic interests are likely to prevail (Hovenkamp, 1990, 86). If, conversely, as predicted by some versions of private interest theory, interest group activity enables minorities to benefit at the expense of the majority, then the result is likely to be inefficient.

Quite independent of this, the main thrust of the Virginian analysis is to focus on the inefficiencies arising from the activities involved in seeking regulatory benefits; hence their branch of private interest theory is often referred to as 'rent-seeking theory' (Tollison, 1982). Their main point is that the resources devoted to the campaigns to acquire regulatory wealth transfers are, from society's point of view, entirely wasted: they do not contribute to a wealth-enhancing activity (Tullock, 1967).

Whatever normative conclusions are drawn directly from private interest theory, it is clear that the insights revealed by the theories have had a major impact on public lawyers' thinking about constitutional arrangements (Ogus, 1998a, 490). 'We need to know who wins and who loses and by how much, when thinking about public policy. Not only is this a necessary part of strategic public management, it is crucial to a normative consideration of whether the legislation is in the public interest' (Mashaw, 1989, 145). The apparent vulnerability of public institutions to capture by private interests as well as to the self-interest of the decision-makers themselves suggested an enhancement of principles requiring officials and agents to apply standards of transparency and administrative rationality to their decision-making. On the other hand, and more specifically, the notion that legislatures function primarily to confer benefits on private interest groups has suggested to some the futility of the conventional principle of statutory interpretation, requiring courts to ascertain the public interest goal of legislators (Easterbrook, 1984).

RENEWAL OF PUBLIC INTEREST ANALYSIS

Our last 'theory', effectively a reinvigorated version of the earlier public interest economic analysis, may be seen as a reaction to what some saw as the excessively negative implications of private interest theory. Economists have made a major input into regulatory policy-making, albeit one which has been subject, like any other, to political manipulation. And it is no mere coincidence that this renewal of the public interest approach has taken place during the era of deregulation. As many commentators have shown (see, for example, Howse et al., 1990), 'deregulation' has been in most instances not a total removal of government controls, but rather an attempt to develop better targeted and less costly forms of regulation. In the context of economic regulation, this has meant a greater use of devices to stimulate competition, as well as a more refined approach to imitating market-based pricing decisions. As regards social regulation, it has involved a re-examination of rigid command-and-control methods, replacing some by financial incentives and setting more general objectives, leaving it to the industry or individual firms to devise particular rules to meet them (Ogus, 2000). To identify more clearly the developments of public interest economic analysis in relation to each area of deregulation, it is appropriate to deal with them separately.

The majority of contemporary economists who would describe themselves as 'regulatory economists' are obsessed by economic regulation[8] and their analytical tools have been significantly developed in the last two decades (Crew and Kleindorfer, 2002). There has been a sophisticated exploration of principal–agent theory as it affects regulatory decision-making (Laffont and Tirole, 1993), arising from the perception that the principal (the regulator) is heavily reliant on how the agent (the regulated firm) responds to incentive structures. Such incentives must be developed against a background in which the firm has informational advantages over the regulator. Predictions have also emerged as to how allowing the firm to retain some of the profits derived from such advantages may lead to better incentives for cost constraints (Baron,

1991). Another branch of the literature has applied the increasingly popular game theory to bargaining strategy between the regulator and the firm (for an early example, see Sharkey, 1982).

Insights from analysis of this kind have made significant and practical contributions to a variety of policy problems that contemporary regulators have had to confront, for example in relation to access pricing and network structuring (Crew and Kleindorfer, 2002, 16–20). But their impact on matters such as universal service obligations and cross-subsidization has been less marked, for the obvious reason that these matters extend into areas of political, and therefore non-economic, judgement.[9]

In relation to deregulatory policy in the social regulation sectors, there have been increasing demands from government for economic expertise. An influential paper published by OECD in 1994 called for economic analysis to become a central feature of legislative and regulatory processes (OECD, 1994, ch. 5). This has fostered what has variously been described as the 'New Haven' or 'Progressive School' of law-and-economics, the protagonists of which 'are similar to Chicagoans in recognising the value of markets in promoting efficiency and the importance of economic incentives in both the private and public sectors. They are trying to get the economic incentives right, not eliminate them' (Rose-Ackerman, 1988, 344). Their main input into policy-making has been through the medium of regulatory impact analysis (or regulatory appraisal), which relies heavily on cost–benefit analysis. Under OECD encouragement (see especially OECD, 1997), this has become such a widespread feature of the administrative arrangements governing the preparation and reform of regulation, that one commentator has suggested that we are living in a 'Cost–Benefit State' (Sunstein, 1996).

Although, as a tool of government policy-making, cost–benefit analysis has been around for some time, its systematic use in a regulatory context effectively dates from President Reagan's famous Executive Order 12,291 of 1981 (McGarity, 1991). This required federal regulatory agencies, before promulgating new regulations, to submit a regulatory impact analysis, quantifying the potential benefits and costs. Refined under succeeding administrations (for a short history, see Hahn and Sunstein, 2002), it provided a model for developments in other jurisdictions (for a survey, see OECD, 1997).

Arguably in no other previous way has economic analysis had such a direct impact on social regulatory policy-making. But that impact should not be exaggerated or misunderstood, because its limits are important. Cost–benefit analysis can never provide a determinative indicator of what is socially desirable because, at most, it provides information only as to the impact of a given reform on aggregate social welfare (Adler and Posner, 1999). Although the disaggregation of costs and benefits, indicating how they fall on different sections of the community may – and in some jurisdictions has – become part of the exercise, what weighting to be attributed to outcomes is a matter of political, not economic, judgement. Moreover, the quantification of certain benefits is highly speculative, particularly when they are based on subjective perceptions and/or involve a degree of uncertainty.

It follows from all this that regulatory impact analysis, and cost–benefit analysis in particular, is a valuable complement to, rather than a substitute for, political decision-making. Its significance lies more in its procedures, imposing a discipline on the officials responsible for regulatory policy-making, than on providing a decisive indicator of 'good' regulation (Froud et al., 1998). No one has yet, to the best of my knowledge, posited a 'cost–benefit theory of regulation'.

CONCLUSIONS

It should be clear from this last section that, in recent years, economic analysis has come to play a key role in regulatory policy development. The reasons why this has occurred are not so easy to identify but some suggestions may be offered. In the first place, at a time when the notion of the 'regulatory state' is under challenge, it is understandable that efforts are being made to distance regulatory processes from government. And, if there is a perceived need for 'experts' who can proffer 'objective' solutions to regulatory problems, what group can appear to fit this bill so well as economists, particularly in the area of economic regulation, where issues of competition, pricing and network management are the main preoccupations? It should be noted, too, that there is an increased demand for the services of economists, both as consultants to regulated firms and as expert witnesses in litigation (Kovocic, 2002). Clearly the two phenomena are related: the more that regulators rely on economic expertise, the more that regulated firms will need the same to challenge decisions which are unfavourable to them, particularly as regulatory systems are becoming increasingly affected by adversarial legalism (Kagan, 2001).

The role of economists in relation to social regulation is less obvious, but here we can observe a tension between the apparent popular demands for increasing protection against a multitude of risks and the recognition by governments that meeting all such demands is not feasible. For political reasons, the latter point cannot easily be conceded and in the circumstances the best way of resolving the tension might be to engage economists to undertake risk assessment and management, and regulatory impact analysis.

The recognition of these trends should not, however, disguise what we have seen to be the limits of the contributions of economic analysis. Subjective evaluations are required in many policy areas, including importantly risk assessment and management, and economists can have little to say on distributional justice objectives or how they are to be traded-off against efficiency considerations.

What then of economic theory? I have attempted to show how economists have been too obsessed with finding an overall theoretical framework which will provide a complete explanation of the existence and incidence of regulation. The public interest approach, which assumes that law is made exclusively to generate aggregate social welfare is too naive; and the private interest theory which relates it entirely to the furtherance of personal and group welfare is excessively cynical. Both sets of theories have nevertheless been helpful in focusing attention on how the different institutions of regulatory decision-making can be used either to advance the ostensible goals of regulation or else to subvert those goals to private ends.

NOTES

* In this revised version of the paper, I wish to acknowledge the assistance I have derived from comments made by the two editors, three referees and participants at the workshop.
1. A policy is Kaldor–Hicks efficient if the aggregate gains to whomsoever exceed the aggregate losses to whomsoever.
2. The switch in the subject of the sentence from 'regulator' to 'regulation' is deliberate: where the regulator is independent of government, a desirable allocation of decision-making powers might entrust efficiency to the regulator, leaving the government (as democratically elected, responsive to political pressures) to deal with distributional issues: McCrudden (1999).
3. It is generally considered that devising a system of transfer payments to assist poorer people to pay the cost-justified price is economically preferable to cross-subsidizaton: Foster (1992).
4. A public interest theory does not necessarily have to be confined to economic, that is efficiency, goals. It can embrace, for example, distributional aims. But then its definition and its capacity to become operational are problematic because there is no way scientifically to measure efficiency against distributional equity.
5. For an extended survey, see Peltzman (1989).
6. Drawing on the pioneering analysis of Olson (1965).
7. 'Not one economist in a hundred practising in the early 1970s predicted the sweeping changes that were soon to happen' (Peltzman, 1989, 3).
8. A survey of 'regulatory economics' in the last 20 years in Crew and Kleindorfer (2002) does not even mention social regulation!
9. The problem of regulators being expected to make decisions which have both economic and political dimensions is recognized in a report of the UK's Better Regulation Task Force (2001, 28–9).

REFERENCES

Adler, M.D. and E.A. Posner (1999), 'Rethinking Cost–Benefit Analysis', *Yale Law Journal,* **109**, 165–247.
Baron, D.P. (1991), 'Information, Incentives, and Commitment in Regulatory Mechanisms: Regulatory Innovation in Telecommunications', in M.A. Einhorn (ed.), *Price-caps and Incentive Regulation in Telecommunications*, Norwell, MA: Kluwer Academic, pp. 47–75.

Better Regulation Task Force (2001), *Economic Regulators*, London: Cabinet Office.

Bishop, W. (1990), 'A Theory of Administrative Law', *Journal of Legal Studies*, **19**, 489–530.

Breyer, S. (1982), *Regulation and its Reform*, Cambridge, MA: Harvard University Press.

Coase, R.H. (1960), 'The Problem of Social Cost', *Journal of Law and Economics*, **3**, 1–44.

Cooter, R. (1984), 'Prices and Sanctions', *Columbia Law Review*, **84**, 1523–60.

Crew, M.A. and P.R. Kleindorfer (2002), 'Regulatory Economics: Twenty Years of Progress?', *Journal of Regulatory Economics*, **21**, 5–22.

Den Hertog, J. (2000), 'General Theories of Regulation', in B. Bouckaert and G. De Geest (eds), *Encyclopedia of Law and Economics*, vol. III, *The Regulation of Contracts*, Cheltenham, UK and Northampton, USA: Edward Elgar, pp. 223–70.

Easterbrook, F.H. (1984), 'Foreword: The Court and the Economic System', *Harvard Law Review*, **98**, 4–60.

Farber, D.A. and P.P. Frickey (1991), *Law and Public Choice: A Critical Introduction*, Chicago: University of Chicago Press.

Foster, C.D. (1992), *Privatization, Public Ownership and the Regulation of Natural Monopoly*, Oxford: Blackwell.

Froud, J., R. Boden, A. Ogus and P. Stubbs (1998), *Controlling the Regulators*, London: Macmillan.

Hahn, R.W. and C. Sunstein (2002), 'A New Executive Order For Improving Federal Regulation? Deeper And Wider Cost–Benefit Analysis', *University of Pennsylvania Law Review*, **150**, 1489–552.

Hovenkamp, H. (1990), 'Legislation, Well-Being and Public Choice', *University of Chicago Law Review*, **57**, 63–116.

Howse, R., J.R.S. Prichard and M.J. Trebilcock (1990), 'Smaller or Smarter Government?', *University of Toronto Law Journal*, **40**, 498–541.

Jarrell, G.A. (1984), 'Change at the Exchange: Causes and Effects of Deregulation', *Journal of Law and Economics*, **27**, 273–312.

Kagan, R.A. (2001), *Adversarial legalism: The American way of law*, Cambridge, MA: Harvard University Press.

Keeler, T.E. and S.E. Foreman (1998), 'Regulation and Deregulation' in P. Newman (ed.), *The New Palgrave Dictionary of Economics and the Law*, London: Macmillan, vol. 3, pp. 213–21.

Kovocic, W. (2002), 'Economic Regulation and the Courts: Ten Cases That Made A Difference', *Journal of Regulatory Economics*, **21**, 23–34.

Laffont, J.-J. and J. Tirole (1993), *A Theory of Incentives in Procurement and Regulation*, Cambridge, MA: MIT Press.

Landis, J.M. (1938), *The Administrative Process*, New Haven: Yale University Press.

Mashaw, J.L. (1989). 'The Economics of Politics and the Understanding of Public Law', *Chicago-Kent Law Review*, **65**, 123–60.

Maurizi, A. (1974), 'Occupational Licensing and the Public Interest', *Journal of Political Economy,* **82**, 399–413.

McCrudden, C. (1999), 'Social Policy and Economic Regulators: Some Issues from the Reform of Utility Regulation' in C. McCrudden (ed.), *Regulation and Deregulation: Policy and Practice in the Utilities and Financial Services Industries*, Oxord: Clarendon Press, ch. 10.

McGarity, T. (1991), *Reinventing Rationality: The Role of Regulatory Analysis in the Federal Bureaucracy*, Cambridge: Cambridge University Press.

OECD (1994), *Improving The Quality Of Laws And Regulations: Economic, Legal And Managerial Technique*, Paris: OECD.

OECD (1997), *Regulatory Impact Analysis: Best Practices in OECD Countries*, Paris: OECD.

Ogus, A. (1994), *Regulation: Legal Form and Economic Theory*, Oxford: Clarendon Press.

Ogus, A. (1998a), 'Law-and-Economics from the Perspective of Law' in P. Newman (ed.), *The New Palgrave Dictionary of Economics and the Law*, London: Macmillan, vol. 2, pp. 486–92.

Ogus, A. (1998b), 'Corrective Taxes and Financial Impositions as Regulatory Instruments', *Modern Law Review*, **61**, 767–88.

Ogus, A. (2000), 'New Techniques for Social Regulation: Decentralisation and Diversity', in H. Collins, P. Davies and R. Rideout (eds), *Legal Regulation of the Employment Relation*, London: Kluwer Law International, 83–98.

Okun, A. (1975), *Equality and Efficiency: The Big Tradeoff*, Washington, DC: Brookings Institution.

Olson, M. (1965), *The Logic of Collective Action*, Cambridge, MA: Harvard University Press.

Peltzman, S. (1976), 'Towards a More General Theory of Regulation', *Journal of Law and Economics*, **19**, 211.

Peltzman, S. (1989), 'The Economic Theory of Regulation After a Decade of Deregulation', *Brookings Papers on Economic Activity: Microeconomics*, 1–41.

Polinsky, A.M. and S. Shavell (1979), 'The Optimal Tradeoff between the Probability and Magnitude of Fines', *American Economic Review*, **69**, 880–91.

Posner, R.A. (1974), 'Theories of Economic Regulation', *Bell Journal of Economics and Management Science*, **5**, 335–58.

Rose-Ackerman, S. (1988), 'Progressive Law and Economics – And the New Administrative Law', *Yale Law Journal*, **98**, 341–68.

Sharkey, W.W. (1982), 'Suggestions for a Game Theoretic Approach to Public Utility Pricing and Cost Allocation', *Bell Journal of Economics*, **13**, 57–68.

Shavell, S. (1993), 'The Optimal Structure of Law Enforcement', *Journal of Law and Economics*, **36**, 255–87.

Stigler, G.J. (1971), 'The Theory of Economic Regulation', *Bell Journal of Economics and Management Science*, **2**, 3–21.

Sunstein, C.R. (1996), 'Congress, Constitutional Moments, and the Cost–Benefit State', *Stanford Law Review*, **48**, 247–309.

Tollison, R.D. (1982), 'Rent Seeking: A Survey', *Kyklos*, **35**, 575–602.

Tullock, G. (1967), 'The Welfare Costs of Tariffs, Monopolies and Theft', *Western Economic Journal*, **5**, 224–32.

Viscusi, W.K. (1998), *Rational Risk Policy*, Oxford: Clarendon Press.

Weingast, B.R. (1981), 'Regulation, Reregulation, and Deregulation: The Political Foundations of Agency Clientele Relationships', *Law and Contemporary Problems*, **44**, 147–77.

Zerbe, R.O. and D.D. Dively (1994), *Benefit–Cost Analysis in Theory and Practice*, New York: HarperCollins.

3. The history of regulation in the United Kingdom: three case studies in search of a theory[1]

Iain McLean

INTRODUCTION

Regulation has existed for as long as governments have interfered in private actions: that is, for ever. The economic theory of regulation was revitalized by the neoclassical revolution (Stigler, 1971). In the last 25 years, political scientists have also identified a distinct 'politics of regulation' (see especially Wilson, 1980). Majone (1994) has gone so far as to claim that European democracies have become 'regulatory states' in which government has retreated as direct controller of the means of production, but advanced as an indirect regulator of them. Others label this the replacement of 'government' by 'governance'.

Theories of regulation may be grouped into public interest, regulatory capture, and median-voter classes. The public interest theory states that regulation is the solution to certain sorts of market failure, especially market failure due to natural monopoly (see especially Foster, 1992). A normative version states that given such failure, regulation *ought* to occur. A positive version (that no scholar known to me is brave or foolhardy enough to espouse) would state that given such market failure, regulation *does* occur. However, what Wilson (1980, 370) calls 'policy entrepreneurs' may create a public interest if they persuade enough people to believe that it is in the public interest to do what they advocate.

Regulatory capture, endorsed by a wide ideological range of scholars, from Marxists to the public choice movement (Virginia branch), is both positive and normative. In a strong positive version, it predicts that regulation comes into existence to serve the interest of the regulated (Kolko, 1965; Ayres and Braithwaite, 1991; Feaver, 1997; Laffont and Martimort, 1999). A weaker positive version would hold that, once regulation has come into existence (for whatever, perhaps exogenous, reason), it is captured by the interest being regulated. A normative implication, much favoured by UK governments since

1979, is that self-regulation is A Bad Thing (except, curiously, for lawyers – but then Lady Thatcher is a lawyer).

The median voter theory in this context emanates principally from the public choice movement (Chicago branch). Chicago economists pioneered the theory of regulatory capture (especially Stigler, 1971) but now take a mellower view. The median-voter theorem (Black, 1958) states that, assuming that politics in the relevant arena has only one issue dimension, the outcome under any defensible voting system will be the favourite issue position of the median voter in that dimension. In its Chicago application to any economic policy arena such as trade policy or optimal regulation, it implies that policy in each dimension sits stably at the (possibly weighted) median point of the interests concerned. In relation to regulation, the Chicago position might be characterized as Virginia without attitude. Yes, regulators may be captured, in any given policy area, by the regulated industry. That simply shows, *ex post*, that the regulated industry was more intense, or better informed, than those who would have gained from a different pattern of regulation. All is for the best in the best of all possible worlds. A young economist and an old economist were once walking past the Palmer House Hilton. The young economist said 'Look! there's a $100 bill on the sidewalk!' Without looking down, the old economist said, 'There can't be. If there had been, somebody would have picked it up' (compare Wittman, 1995 with Olson, 2000).

Regulation has existed for ever, but regulation for defensible reasons of economic or social policy is more recent. Expropriation of citizens and distribution of the spoils to the king's (general's, president's) favourites is not treated as regulation in this chapter. Even this restriction is not enough to make the subject tractable. Many examples of regulation in pre-nineteenth century politics (and indeed since) may have originated in what seemed to be good ideas at the time rather than (or in addition to) naked expropriation of one group in favour of another. Therefore I further restrict the field of study to regulation for (what would now be seen as) defensible reasons of economic or social policy. In so doing I consciously break the historian's first rule, 'The past is another country; they do things differently there.' However, it enables me to start in the early nineteenth century, when both economic regulation (beginning with the Regulation of Railways Act 1844) and social regulation (of industrial conditions and transport safety) took recognizably modern forms in the UK.

The cases studied are:

- the origin of railway regulation from 1825 to 1872;
- regulatory failure in the Aberfan disaster (1966); and
- the tardy development of a new pattern of regulation after 1979.

The first two cases draw on my previously published work; the third deals with the obvious puzzle of why political agents after 1979 were so slow to realize that extensive privatization would entail extensive re-regulation. I use the cases to show that the regulatory state is older than Majone claims; that all three theories of regulation have something to contribute; and that while the history of social (risk) regulation in the UK (cf. Hood et al., 2001) is continuous since the early nineteenth century, that of economic regulation is discontinuous – the principles behind it were lost in the 1870s and not rediscovered until the 1980s.

CASE 1. RAILWAY REGULATION FROM 1825 TO 1872

Risk regulation of the railways in the United Kingdom dates back to the 1840s. Inspectors of Railways were first appointed under an Act of 1840. Because the Act stipulated that the inspectors must not have a connection with any railway company, they were drawn from the Royal Engineers and their reports always stated their military rank. They still do. Their first report in 1841 demanded that their powers of regulation be strengthened, a demand partly met in 1842.

The Regulation of Railways Act 1844 (7 & 8 Vict. c85) was pushed through Parliament by the 34-year-old W.E. Gladstone, President of the Board of Trade, despite fierce opposition from the railway companies. It mostly covers economic regulation. The Act gave Parliament the powers, from 21 years after its passage, to cap the rates of, or to nationalize, any new line which was earning more than 10 per cent a year. The 'parliamentary train' clause required every company to run at least one third-class all-stations train, comprising covered vehicles with seats, each way every weekday at an average speed (including stops) of not less than 12 mph and a fare of not more than a penny a mile. Other sections obliged companies to carry the mail, troops and police; to allow public telegraph lines to be erected along their rights of way; and to open their own telegraph systems to public use. Companies complied with the 'parliamentary train' clause as minimally as possible, with the mandatory train leaving town at about 6 am. ('The idiot who, in railway carriages, / Scribbles on window-panes, / We only suffer / to ride on a buffer / of *Parliamentary trains!*' – W.S. Gilbert, *The Mikado*). This pattern of service persisted until the Beeching reforms of British Railways in 1963.

Gladstone's Act shaped the US 1887 Interstate Commerce Act, which itself shaped subsequent regulation in the USA (Breyer, 1982, 6, 199; McCraw, 1984, 13). It was a pioneering effort at economic regulation, but the economics behind it were lost in the late nineteenth century and not rediscovered until the late twentieth. The ideology of classical economics, in which the bureaucrats of the Board of Trade were soaked and to which Peel and Gladstone were both converted (Brown, 1958, 20–33, 214–31; Feuchtwanger, 1989, 43; Shannon, 1982, 117–20) strongly favoured free trade, but not regulation. Thus, the case poses stiff challenges to orthodox political economy.

Gladstone's risk regime survives to this day. Between 1844 and 1923 there were further highly charged, and highly publicized, attempts to tighten the regulation of railway safety and/or rates. Victorians knew very well that there was a 'railway interest' comprising MPs and peers who were directors of railway companies, who led the opposition to further regulation. *Bradshaw's Railway Almanack* published a list of them every year from 1847 until 1923. Victorian regulation remains under-researched (but see Alderman, 1973; Foreman-Peck, 1987; Foster, 1992; Gourvish, 1972; Kostal, 1994; Lubenow, 1971; Parris, 1965; Williams, 1952; Schapiro, 2003).

Every railway that wished to open to the public had first to obtain a private Act of Parliament. Parliament gave the company eminent domain rights; in return it laid down maximum toll rates. Railway Acts were modelled on earlier turnpike road and canal acts. Parliamentarians assumed that the railways would, like turnpike roads, provide the track, on which others would run goods and passenger vehicles. The railways' tolls for track use were regulated, but the charges for carriage were not. The Stockton & Darlington Railway (1825) did work somewhat like a turnpike. But by 1830, it was clear that the turnpike model was impracticable. Increasing speeds and long braking distances meant that only one body could decide when a train could enter a track section. Any entrepreneur who put a private locomotive on the track would be at the mercy of the railway company as soon as he ran out of water. Gladstone's officials argued in 1841

> [t]hat Railway Companies using locomotive power possess a practical monopoly for the conveyance of passengers ..., and that under existing circumstances this monopoly is inseparable from the nature of these establishments, and ... [t]hat this monopoly is the result of circumstances contemplated neither by the Legislature nor by the Companies themselves, the extensive powers contained in their Acts of incorporation having been obtained under the impression that the interests of the public were sufficiently secured by fixing a maximum rate of tolls, and providing for free competition in the supply of locomotive power and other means of conveyance.

Accordingly, they proposed that 'the public interests shall not suffer from the mistaken view taken in the infancy of the science of locomotion, and that for this purpose the powerful monopolies ... should be subjected to the supervision and control of the Board of Trade' (*Parliamentary Papers*, House of Commons, 1841 First Session, vol. XXV. Hereafter cited as *P.P.*, year, volume).

The Railway Department found their man in Gladstone. He had entered politics as a Tory determined to protect the Church of England as a state church. However, Sir Robert Peel picked him out as an able administrator and gave him a junior government job in the short administration of 1834–5. In 1841, the Tories won a clear General Election victory. Peel offered Gladstone the Vice-Presidency of the Board of Trade. This disappointed Gladstone, who had hoped to rule Ireland: 'the science of politics deals with the government of men, but I am set to govern packages' (Feuchtwanger, 1989, 41). His education in free trade, regulation and lobbying continued intensively through his four years in office, moving up to President in 1843. Sir James Graham, Peel's Home Secretary, said 'Gladstone could do in four hours what it took any other man sixteen to do, and he worked sixteen hours a day' (Shannon, 1982, 115–16).

The tariff reductions of 1842 confronted him with aggrieved producer-groups who stood to lose their monopoly rents:

> B of Trade and House $12^3/_4 - 6^3/_4$ and $9^1/_4 - 1^1/_2$ [i.e. 12.45 to 18.45 and 21.15 to 01.30]. Dined at Abp of Yorks. Copper, Tin, Zinc, Salmon, Timber, Oil, Saltmeat, all are to be ruined, and all in arms. (Diary for 15.3.1842 in Foot and Matthew, 1974, 187. Hereafter cited as Gladstone, diary, date.)

He scorned lobbyists. In 1844, when the railway companies lobbied Peel against Gladstone's bill, he forced them to admit that their delegation had not been authorized by their Boards *(Copies of any Memorial to Sir Robert Peel, by certain Directors and others connected with Railway Companies, against the Railways Bill now before this House; and of any Correspondence thereupon between the Board of Trade and the aforesaid Memorialists P.P., 1844, XLI).*

Gladstone's Bill of 1844 was a personal crusade, without Cabinet support (Parris, 1965, 55–6). By 1844 railways had proved themselves and were earning large dividends. Therefore there was a sudden rush to promote new schemes, and the Private Bill Office had more railway bills in hand than ever before. But Gladstone did not think that the entry of new railway companies would bring the railway business into competitive equilibrium. Rather, if Parliament were to allow competing routes between the same towns, 'it would afford facilities to exaction ... an increase of the evil, ... a mere multiplication of monopoly' *(Hansard*, 3rd series, vol. 72, cols 232–6. Hereafter cited as *H.*, vol., cols). Hence Gladstone proposed:

- a power to cap the rates of new railways after a period of years, to a level such that their dividends would be held at 10 per cent of the value of their issued capital;
- a power to nationalize any such lines after the same period of time;
- a change in Private Bill procedure to enable the Board of Trade to scrutinise all railway bills affecting the same part of the country

together, and to decide which route it was most in the public interest to permit;

● to improve the standard of third-class travel. He stated that there was 'very strong feeling on this subject, both within the House, and out of doors', and added that third-class passengers could see all too plainly the difference between their carriages and those for first- and second-class passengers. (Compare the third-class open trucks of the Bodmin & Wadebridge Railway with contemporary first- and second-class carriages at the National Railway Museum, York.)

Gladstone's economic reasoning replicated that of the then unknown French economist A.-A. Cournot (Foster, 1992). Most companies were discriminating monopolists. They charged fares which guaranteed a substantial operating profit, but which just undercut stagecoach fares. They segregated third-class from upper-class trains for fear that passengers would leak on to the cheaper coaches. They negotiated exclusive deals with some road carriers to take passengers and goods to places not on the railway, and excluded others from station yards or refused to carry their goods *(Fifth Report of the Select Committee on Railways, Minutes of Evidence, P.P.,* 1844, XI; Hawke, 1970, 360; Gourvish, 1972, 34–44, 71; Kostal, 1994, ch. 5). Gladstone perceived that it was difficult or impossible to enforce competitive behaviour by direct regulation. It was also unrealistic to expect competition between companies to do the job. New companies' Acts might merely be 'improperly used as efficient instruments of extortion against the subsisting Companies, to whom might be offered only the alternative of losing their traffic or of buying off opposition'. Even if a new company built its line rather than let itself be bought off, Gladstone 'cannot conceive that two bodies, or even three, acting by compact executive Boards, and secure against the entrance of any other party into the field, will fail to combine together'.

George Hudson, the 'Railway King' and leader of the lobby against Gladstone's Bill, cheerfully admitted to Gladstone's Select Committee that he had offered the rival Leeds & Selby Railway a sum of money to 'shut up their line', which they had accepted *(Fifth Report* ..., p. xii, Minutes of Evidence, 333, q. 4395. *P.P.,* 1844, XI).

Thus Gladstone concluded that the railway market was bound to fail. There were two games to consider: the game between an existing (natural monopolist) company and the government, and the game between an existing company and a new entrant. In the first game, the company was likely to be able to fend off attempts to regulate its rates directly because of information asymmetry. The company knew its full schedule of rates and the government did not; therefore attempts to regulate rates simply led to the company reformulating them in a slightly different form, so that would-be regulators or plaintiffs would have to start all over again. As to the second game, Gladstone saw further than Cournot. Companies would not simply adjust their production in response to each other's activities. Rather, they would collude and share monopoly rent: as they were 'acting by compact executive Boards' they would reach the cooperative (collusive) equilibrium in their prisoners' dilemma game. Gladstone therefore asserted

> the undoubted right and power of the State to promote the construction of new and competing Lines of Railway, as a means of protection to the Public against the consequences of the virtual monopoly which former Acts have called into existence. (*Fifth Report* ... p. xii)

Between March and June 1844, Gladstone's Select Committee produced six reports and took minutes of evidence which occupy 682 pages of the large-format *Parliamentary Papers*. Gladstone dominated the enquiry from start to finish. He first offered the railway interest a corporatist 'Hypothetical Outline', which asked the railways to guarantee 'a means of communication for the poorer classes, in carriages protected from the weather, at a moderate charge'. These rules need only apply to one train a day, and railways could carry other third-class traffic (if any) by whatever arrangements they liked. His main offer in return to the companies was 'The principle that competing lines, as such, and without a legitimate traffic of their own, ought not to be encouraged when better arrangements can be made' (Appendix to *Fifth Report* ..., *P.P.*, 1844, XI). Hudson failed to understand the deal (*Fifth Report* ..., Minutes of Evidence, pp. 320–33, qq. 4203–395. *P.P.*, 1844, XI).

Gladstone therefore forced the Third Report of the Select Committee over the objections of its two railway-director members. This stated that the railways' monopoly 'is ... regarded, even at the present day, with considerable jealousy by the Public at large', jealousy which could be expected to grow 'if the profits of Railways generally should be augmented in any very great degree'. Gladstone held two bargaining counters. One was that the railways needed an Act to reverse a recent rating (property-tax) decision hostile to them. The other was the discovery that many railways had been issuing illegal and unsecured 'loan notes' over and above the debt they were allowed by their Acts to issue. Gladstone offered clauses in the regulatory bill to legalize the notes that had been already issued. He used these chips to get the Parliamentary Train clause applied to all companies, old and new,

> as it rests upon the principle that the Companies affected by it are voluntary Suitors for the aid of the Legislature, to enable them, in some instances, to legalise transactions which they have conducted without the sanction of the law; in others to extend and enlarge, for their own benefit, the concerns in which they are engaged; and that it is open to those Companies to accept the aid, with the conditions attached to it, or to decline both the one and the other (*Fifth Report* ... *P.P.*, 1844, XI).

Gladstone introduced his Bill aggressively. He complained that in discriminating against some road carriers 'the Railroad had gone among individual traders very much like a triton among the minnows'. He evoked the spectacle of a sinister interest combining railway directors and the 'deeper power in the opposition, and he might as well use plain language, ... Parliamentary agents and solicitors'. He ridiculed the claims of the railway interest that the Bill was 'a shock' to property and pointed out that railway shares had continued to rise since the Third Report announced his intention to legislate. He concluded:

> I shrunk from a contest with Railway Companies ... but being persuaded that justice is not with them, but against them ... I do not shrink from the contest. I say that although Railway Companies are powerful, I do not think they have mounted so high, or that Parliament has yet sunk so low, that at their bidding you shall refuse your sanction to this bill. ... (Loud cheering). *(H.,* 76, 489, 502, 508–9)

Almost no participant in the debate except Gladstone discussed economic regulation; most discussed safety or the Parliamentary Train clause. The Second Reading was carried by 186 to 98 – 'a satisfactory division' (diary, 11.7.1844). However, Gladstone was forced to enter a further round of discussions with Hudson, in order not to lose the Bill in the 1844 session (Lambert, 1964, 106–7; Hyde, 1934, 159–77). In Committee, Gladstone substantially diluted the powers of the Board of Trade, and the Bill was enacted without a division. The rate regulation and state purchase powers remained in a weaker form. By comparison with his Bill, Gladstone had suffered a defeat. The sophisticated proposals of the Bill might have enabled the government to enforce regulation despite the companies' information advantages; the version enacted did not. Even so, the knowledge that the state control plans remained must have influenced rational railway investors and managers. One sure way of avoiding nationalization would be to ensure that your rate of return remained below 10 per cent; a way to ensure that in turn was to build unprofitable branch-lines, as conspicuously happened in late Victorian times, and avoid regulation by over-capitalization. British railways from 1844 to 1923 may therefore be evidence for the hypothesis that regulated industries evade the effects of regulation by over-capitalization (Averch and Johnson, 1962). Furthermore, by comparison with his starting position, the Hypothetical Outline, Gladstone had gained more regulation. The rate revision power was in the Hypothetical Outline, but the state purchase power was not. The powers relating to the telegraph, also not in the Hypothetical Outline, passed unchallenged, perhaps because there was no distributional coalition of telegraph manufacturers and operators.

In 1864, when the opportunity to purchase or rate-cap railways under the 1844 Act was becoming imminent, Gladstone was Chancellor of the

Exchequer in a Liberal government. He was no more hostile to state purchase in principle than in 1844, and he drew up a scheme for implementing his own legislation. But the government did not pursue it after a Royal Commission on Railways recommended against doing so (*Report of the Royal Commission on Railways, P.P.*, 1867, XXXVIII; Matthew, 1986, 119).

Rowland Hill, who had turned the state-run Post Office into a profitable corporation in 1840, was a member of the 1867 Royal Commission. His Minority Report recommended nationalizing the rail infrastructure, using the 1844 powers, and adopting a highly ingenious scheme for franchising local operations suggested by Edwin Chadwick. Chadwick (1859) ranks with Gladstone as an economist but not as a politician. His paper opens with a table showing that the British railway industry performed worse than those of France, Belgium, Prussia, or Austria, all of which had wholly or partly state-run railways. British construction costs, working expenses and fares were the highest, dividends were the lowest, and the accident record was the worst, of the five nations studied. Chadwick puts these failures down to the failure of 'competition in the field' and advocates instead 'competition for the field' – a principle which, he says, should also be applied to public health utilities such as sewerage and burials. Companies should be required to tender for the monopoly right to operate services on a given sector of the network for a limited time. Not until the 2003 tendering round did the UK rail regulator catch up with Edwin Chadwick's idea.

It got nowhere. The majority of the Royal Commission rejected nationalization and economic regulation, for a mixture of good and bad reasons. Chadwick alleged that the Commission was hobbled by its members from the railway interest. But, since most of the 1844 Act was not retrospective, they could not have used it to take control of the whole network. They pointed out that most of Britain's trunk lines had been authorized by pre-1844 Acts and could not be compulsorily purchased.

There was one more attempt to grapple with economic regulation of the railways, in a joint Commons and Lords Select Committee of 1872 (*P.P.*, 1872, XIII). This committee noted that Parliament had always opposed railway amalgamations, on the assumption that a larger railway was a more monopolistic one, more prone to the monopolistic behaviour that Gladstone denounced in 1844. However, the railway which most nearly had a local monopoly, the North Eastern Railway, had the highest dividend, the lowest fares, and the most consumer satisfaction of any British railway. Faced with this challenge to their economic understanding, the 1872 Select Committee retired hurt. Subsequent attempts to control railway rates by tribunal also failed (Foster, 1992, ch. 2 *passim*). Risk regulation on the railways was much more successful, although not well costed. Various Acts strengthened the Inspectors, especially one of 1889 requiring continuous brakes after a tragic runaway accident at Armagh. Increased union and public pressure also brought regulation of railwaymen's maximum hours, after accidents caused by signalmen falling asleep during 24-hour shifts.

Which theory of regulation throws most light on this history? The median-voter hypothesis is supported as to risk regulation. Railway accidents are salient enough for the public to notice. It is not supported as to price and quantity regulation, where only Gladstone, Chadwick and Hill understood the economic issues. The regulatory capture hypothesis is not supported. In 1844 Gladstone actually offered the companies a 'capture', that is, a corporatist bargain, in the Hypothetical Outline. The companies rejected the deal. So Gladstone drew up a fiercely interventionist Bill which became a moderately interventionist Act. The companies admittedly saw off the clauses they most disliked; but if regulatory capture were true, they would have been able to see off the rest as well. The public interest hypothesis stands as the most correct of those examined. Gladstone was in Wilson's (1980) terminology a successful policy entrepreneur. Chadwick and Hill had both succeeded as policy entrepreneurs elsewhere (sanitation and the Post Office respectively), but failed on railway regulation.

CASE 2: ABERFAN

On 21 October 1966, a colliery waste tip slid down Merthyr Mountain into the mining village of Aberfan, in south Wales. It engulfed the village school and several houses, killing 144 people, of whom 109 were children. The ensuing Tribunal established that the National Coal Board, the public corporation which owned the tip, had for many years been tipping on a slope on top of springs which lubricated the tip and made it inherently unstable; that it had slipped twice before, in 1944 and 1963; that the Coal Board had given (at best) misleading answers to residents and the local authority who had complained about the danger the tip posed; and that the Board's liability for the disaster was 'incontestable and uncontested' (Davies, 1967, 131. For details, see McLean and Johnes, 2000, chs 1–2).

All of this was known by 1967. Much more remained unknown until all the Aberfan papers in the Public Record Office were opened in 1997. We now know that the Chairman of the National Coal Board, the Rt Hon. Lord Robens of Woldingham, fought long, hard and successfully to save his Board and himself after the publication of the 'devastating'[2] Tribunal report. Nobody was prosecuted, sacked, or demoted. The Rt Hon. Lord Robens and his Board remained in place. At the end of his term at the Coal Board the Rt Hon. Lord Robens was appointed to chair the official committee on health and safety at work which wrote the current UK law on that subject. The Rt Hon. Lord

Robens forced the charitable Disaster Fund to pay £150000 towards the cost of removing the remaining unsafe tips from above Aberfan. This was unlawful under charity law, yet the Charity Commission offered the Fund no protection. Ron Davies, the incoming Secretary of State for Wales, repaid the £150000 at par at the change of government in 1997. Two regulatory bodies – the Charity Commission and HM Inspectorate of Mines and Quarries – failed grievously to protect the citizens of Aberfan, or of the UK more generally. Parts of the explanation (McLean and Johnes, 2000, chs 3, 6–8) throw light on regulatory failure.

The trouble goes back to nationalization. 'Unfortunately, the minister mainly responsible for the nationalization statutes, Herbert Morrison, was not a Gladstone' (Foster, 1992, 4). The Morrison template was first used for the nationalization of London Transport in 1930 and then for the widespread nationalizations, mostly of utilities, by the Attlee Labour government between 1945 and 1951. Electricity, gas, some transport modes and telecoms (always publicly owned since the early days of telephones) all have some characteristics of natural monopolies, although none was ever completely so. The grounds for nationalizing coal and steel were different, and grounded in the history of British socialism. Morrison knew what he did not want; less clearly what he wanted. The clear negative idea derived from the threat of syndicalism. Its most powerful advocate, Noah Ablett, argued in *The Miners' Next Step* ([Ablett] 1912) for 'the taking over of all industries, by the workmen themselves ...'

> [A]ll miners, &c., have this in common; they delve in the earth to produce the minerals, ores, gems, salt, stone, &c., which form the basis of raw material for all other industries. Similarly the Railwaymen, Dockers, Seamen, Carters, etc., form the transport industry. Therefore, before an organised and self-disciplined working class can achieve its emancipation, it must coalesce on these lines.

Dangerfield (1936) saw the rise of syndicalism as part of the Strange Death of Liberal England. But he failed to notice that the syndicalists lost. Ablett's doctrine was so dangerous that it was squashed without trace. Whoever was to control the mining industry, in Morrison's view, it must not be the miners. Morrison understood the danger that public ownership controlled by the producers could degenerate into a producers' cartel. Therefore the Morrison template, although it put union representatives on the board, never permitted union representation from a given industry to be put on its own board. The Rt Hon. Lord Robens was a trade unionist – but from the shop workers' union, not any of the mining unions.

But Morrison – and the entire Labour Party – had fuzzy and unclear ideas about what the purposes of nationalization were. Most prominent was a perception that private ownership of the industries in question had 'failed the nation'. Winston Churchill supposedly remarked in 1926, during the General Strike, that he thought the miners' representatives were the stupidest people in the country until he met the coalowners. A second justification was that the industries nationalized under Attlee constituted the 'commanding heights' of the British economy. The questions 'Are they really?' and 'So what if they are?', so obvious today, were not raised then. The third justification was that public ownership enabled the British economy to be centrally planned. But the Morrison framework, in which each board was responsible for its own industry, and for making a surplus 'taking one year with another' (whatever that meant), precluded this.

The Victorian tradition of regulation had simply been forgotten. Risk regulation continued to work well in some industries – notably rail, where the independence of the Royal Engineers enthroned in Gladstone's time constituted an external check on industry managers. Aberfan proved that it did not exist in the coal industry. Economic regulation was swept away by the assumptions, first that nationalization made it irrelevant, and second that the duty of the nationalized industries was to maximize domestic output. Such mercantilism made sense in a world war, but not in 1966. Finally, lawyers worked in a hermetic world of their own.

Aberfan illustrates these three failures of regulation. The worst was the failure of HM Inspectorate of Mines and Quarries to notice that the Aberfan tips were lethal. The reason was cultural. In the coal industry, power, prestige and danger went together – underground. Underground mining was dirty and dangerous, and hundreds of lives were at stake when anything went wrong. Inspectors of Mines were drawn from the ranks. As the elite of the mining industry were underground workers, so the elite of the Inspectorate were underground workers. In the graphic words of the Aberfan Tribunal, 'We found that many witnesses ... had been oblivious of what lay before their eyes. It did not enter their consciousness. They were like moles being asked about the habits of birds' (Davies, 1967, 11).

Aberfan was not a reportable accident under the governing legislation, the Mines and Quarries Act 1954, because no mineworkers were injured. (When they saw the tip heave up before collapsing, the tipping gang went for a cup of tea before deciding what to do next. That action saved their lives.) After the disaster, the Inspectorate realized that it was vulnerable. The Minister, Richard Marsh, records being extensively briefed by the inspectorate that safety regulation was entirely a matter for them, not for him (Marsh, 1978, 113). In the event, the Tribunal let the Inspectorate off unaccountably lightly. Counsel for the Aberfan Parents' and Residents' Association, Desmond Ackner QC, was the most feared cross-examiner of his generation. He tore a sequence of Coal Board witnesses to shreds. But on the day that the Chief Inspector for South Wales was on the witness stand, Ackner was absent. His junior cross-examined the Inspector, and none of Ackner's killer questions were posed (Tribunal of Inquiry, Transcripts of Evidence, Merthyr Tydfil Public Library. Day 52: cross-examination of Cyril Leigh by Aubrey Myerson. See index at http://www.nuff.ox.ac.uk/politics/aberfan/witalph.htm.)

Mercantilism emerged during the debate about removing the remaining spoil heaps at Aberfan. The Coal Board's legal liability to do so (leaving aside any questions about its moral responsibilities) was, as the Tribunal had recorded, incontestable and uncontested. So why was it not forced to clear up the deadly mess it had created? Partly because of the failure of the Charity Commission, discussed in the next two paragraphs. But partly because mercantilism blinded all actors to elementary economics. A weary civil servant recorded 'The cost of all the consequences ... to an NCB in deficit, must fall in the end on the Exchequer' (J. Siberry, 06.11.67, PRO BD52/113). The most eye-opening document in the Aberfan papers is part of a briefing note for the Minister to use in the Commons debate on the disaster. A contractor called Ryan had claimed that he could remove the tips for one-fifth of the Coal Board's publicly stated price, if allowed to recover and sell the coal they contained. (The Coal Board knew that it could do the job for a third of its publicly stated price.) If challenged on this point (in the event, he was not), the Minister was advised to explain that letting contractors sell recovered coal

> displaces deep mined coal when the mines cannot be closed fast enough and their stockpiles are swollen ... If non-NCB tips are concerned the contractor can sell the coal cheaply to the detriment of the NCB ... [T]he coal recovery operation merely removes the coal to the enrichment of Mr Ryan but leaves the tip area in a shambles ... (In confidence NCB confirm that this has been Ryan's position.)

The fact that someone other than the NCB could produce coal more cheaply than the Board was given as a reason for *not* doing it. Beyond that, the reader may wish to check the dictionary meaning of 'shambles' ('5. transf. and fig. a. A place of carnage or wholesale slaughter; a scene of blood.' *OED Online*, s.v. 'shamble'); and wonder at the world in which senior civil servants could accept the word of the National Coal Board that other people left tips in shambles.

The Charity Commission objected to the Disaster Fund's sponsoring the memorial that stands in Aberfan cemetery, and to its making flat-rate payments. According to the Commission, the trustees ought to have reviewed each case individually to check 'whether the parents had been close to their children and were thus likely to be suffering mentally' (W.E.A. Lewis, Charity Commissioner, 08.09.67, quoted by McLean and Johnes, 2000, 140). Though threatened with personal liability, the trustees stood firm, at the risk of making payments to parents who may not have been suffering mentally.

Having spoken when it should have remained silent, the Commission then remained silent when it should have spoken. The raid on the Disaster Fund to pay £150000 towards the removal of the tips was unquestionably unlawful under charity law. No blame attaches to the charity trustees, whom the Rt Hon. Lord Robens was putting under intolerable pressure by refusing to pay the full cost of removal. Substantial blame attaches to the Charity Commission for failing to protect either donors to, or beneficiaries from, the fund from this raid (McLean and Johnes, 2000, ch. 6).

All of the above failings can be blamed on the loss of the Victorian regulatory culture. Although Morrison had tried to ensure that the miners did not run the mines for the benefit of the miners, in the arena of safety regulation Noah Ablett unfortunately got his way. There could be no clearer case of regulatory capture. Regulation had become a private game for the regulators and the regulated (in the case of the Charity Commission for the regulators alone).

CASE 3: THE UNACCOUNTABLY SLOW RETURN OF REGULATION TO THE UK.

Levi-Faur (2002) has studied the 'herding' effects of utility liberalization. 'Herding' corresponds to what others have called 'information cascades'. One nation (or one individual) does something unprecedented, such as (Lohmann, 1994) demonstrate openly against the East German regime or (Levi-Faur, 2002) liberalize telecoms. The effects that everyone predicted fail to occur. So the next least risk-averse person (nation) joins the first. Which in turn induces the next least risk-averse ... and before long, the whole herd has followed its leader, ending with (respectively) the collapse of the regime and the liberalization of telecoms in the Maldives.

These stylized stories have interesting quirks. The model cannot itself say why the first demonstrator (liberalizer) acts. That has to be explained exogenously. In the stylized story (not Levi-Faur's) of utility liberalization, the UK under the mould-breaking leadership of Margaret Thatcher was the first to liberalize. Others followed in a herd upon observing the beneficial consequences. The Iron Lady is the exogenous force.

But Chile, unlike the UK, did it economically the right way round, setting a framework for regulating telecoms and liberalizing afterwards. Why is the leader of the herd always taken to be the UK, not Chile? And why was the UK so slow to (re-)regulate? As to the first question, it is harder for a herd of democracies to follow a military dictatorship than another democracy. The second is more challenging. The following summary is drawn from McLean (2001).

Margaret Thatcher was Prime Minister from 1979 until toppled by her own party on Thanksgiving Day 1990. What we now think of as Thatcherite economics was less coherent at the time than many of both Mrs Thatcher's admirers and her detractors have made it sound. It had already been spelt out, first by Enoch Powell, and then by Keith Joseph, when Mrs Thatcher became Prime Minister. Her Conservative predecessor Edward Heath had come to power in 1970 on a manifesto which promised to 'check any abuse of dominant market power or monopoly ... identify and remove obstacles that prevent effective competition and restrict initiative' (Craig, 1975, 332). It contained no explicit promises of privatization. As in Chile, that takes things in the order that economists prefer. But Heath failed to press ahead with it, because he (like everybody else at the time except Powell) thought that selling free-market capitalism to the electorate was impossible if unemployment soared to one million. Powell and Joseph failed because they never captured power. Thatcher succeeded. Nevertheless, that Thatcherism was not a unified ideology – or, if it was, only in retrospect – emerges most clearly from the hesitant start to her economic liberalism in office.

It is convenient to divide economic Thatcherism into three eras, defined by her three General Election victories. Thatcherism I lasted from 1979 to 1983, Thatcherism II from 1983 to 1987, and Thatcherism III from 1987 to her fall in 1990. The Conservatives had ample room to manoeuvre in 1979. They had not won the election; Labour had lost it. Their most successful poster ('Labour isn't working') was an attack on Labour rather than a promise to do better. This was just as well, as during Thatcherism I, unemployment rose to levels last seen in the 1930s. By the second quarter of 1983 it had reached 2.9 million on seasonally adjusted figures (12.1 per cent). Until 1979, all modern UK prime ministers had assumed that unemployment at that level was incompatible with a stable and civilized society. By experiment, Mrs Thatcher showed that it was compatible with stability. There were riots in inner-city Liverpool and London in 1981, but no general threat to public order. The unemployed were politically excluded and never became an electoral force either. Although the 1981 levels of unemployment and economic decline would certainly have led the Conservatives to defeat had the Falklands War not come along, it did. Under Thatcherism I, a government that had presided over three million unemployed was re-elected. Unemployment continued to rise until the third quarter of 1986.

Many commentators see the huge surge in unemployment as an inevitable consequence of the macroeconomic policy of Thatcherism I. Mrs Thatcher and her Chancellor, Geoffrey Howe, resolutely turned their backs on Keynesian economics. They met the rise in unemployment not with an increase in public spending but with a tightening of the money supply. Some commentators accuse them of deliberately letting unemployment rip in order to kill the power of the trade unions. This is to go too quickly for conspiracy theory. It is more likely that Thatcher and Howe did not anticipate that their monetarism would take such a huge toll on employment. If they had anticipated it, they would have known that they would have to modify it to have any hope of winning the next election.

Unlike monetary policy, union policy was prominent in the 1979 election manifesto. It was not nearly as radical as Mrs Thatcher wished, because the policy area was still controlled by James Prior, her Heathite first Secretary of State for Employment. But in monetarism, and the associated policy of controlling public spending by setting cash limits (Pliatzky, 1989, 53), the Conservatives found by experiment the means to destroy trade union power that had eluded the head-on assault of the Heath government. Controlling inflation by a consensual agreement on incomes policy had patently failed in 1979. The Conservatives could quite truthfully say to trade unions and their members that they would abandon it, and restore free collective bargaining. They did not reveal to unions and their members – because nobody asked them to – what they would do instead. In the event, allowing unemployment to let rip cowed unions in all sectors. Cash limits cowed those in the public sector, as they imposed a very direct tradeoff between pay rates and employment levels throughout the public service. And the 'winter of discontent' of 1978–79 gave the overt restrictions on union activity introduced by Thatcher the legitimacy that earlier attempts had lacked. Even so, she proceeded very cautiously, restrained by Prior until she felt strong enough to move him in 1981. Radical change to the legal position of unions came later. And in a crucial strategic retreat, the government backed away from a confrontation with the National Union of Mineworkers (NUM) in 1981, increasing subsidies to the coal industry rather than insisting on closures or reductions of the industry's losses.

Privatization was barely mentioned in the 1979 manifesto. The first few privatizations were mostly of profitable state holdings. They were done in order to raise money, not for any of the wider and more diverse motives that appeared under Thatcherism II and III. They realized under £500 million a year (Vickers and Yarrow, 1988, ch. 6 and Table 6.1). More significant was the sale of council houses to their tenants at deep discounts, labelled the Right to Buy. It was a last-minute addition to the 1979 manifesto as the Conservatives discovered from their focus group research how popular the idea was (Butler and Kavanagh, 1980, 190; Garrett, 1994, 109). It gave some voters a powerful vested interest in Conservative victory, and it broke up a powerful, concentrated electoral force with a vested interest in Labour victory. Careful analysis (Heath and Garrett, 1991; Garrett, 1994) shows that council tenants who bought their homes under the Right to Buy were already more pro-Conservative than the remainder. But council house buyers remained more loyal to the Conservatives as other groups slipped back in 1987 and 1992.

Privatization took centre stage after the 1983 General Election. Its two main objectives were political. One was the extension of popular capitalism; the other was the break-up of a united public sector interest group. The extension of popular capitalism was typified by the 'Tell Sid' advertising campaign used to sell shares in British Gas. Sid was a working man, slow on the uptake, who had failed to realize what a bonanza he would join if he bought shares in British Gas. For the shares to be a bonanza they had to be underpriced. Table 3.1 shows the immediate gains made by share purchasers in the main privatizations of Thatcherism II.

Having sold these shares at a huge discount, the Conservatives then put a double argument to their purchasers. 'You have made a huge gain with us – reward us. And you might make a huge loss if Labour wins the next election – protect yourself. For both reasons, vote Conservative'. In November 1986 Norman Tebbit, then Chairman of the Conservative Party, wrote to those who had brought British Telecom shares as follows:

> On Monday 8 September, Labour's industry spokesman announced his plans for your British Telecom shares.
> This is what Labour has agreed to do.
> If they win the next General Election, they will immediately confiscate your shareholders' rights. Then they will make you sell your shares for 130p each (which is dramatically less than the current market value ...
> We, on the other hand, believe in putting these companies into real 'public ownership', by which we mean ownership, through shares, by members of the public like yourself ...
> The most effective way to stop Labour's attack on your savings, and your pension, is to make sure they don't get back into power. Think how much a Labour government could cost you. Then send me a donation for our Fighting Fund.
> (Facsimile reproduced in McLean, 1989, Fig. 3.4)

Table 3.1   Principal UK privatizations 1983–87: immediate profits

Company	Gross proceeds of sale, £m	Date of share offer	First day premium, %
British Telecom	3916	03.12.84	33.0
British Aerospace	550	14.05.85	12.0
Cable & Wireless	602	13.12.85	0.5
TSB	1360	10.10.86	35.5
British Gas	5603	08.12.86	9.0
British Airways	900	11.02.87	35.0
Rolls-Royce	1360	20.05.87	36.0

Source: Vickers and Yarrow (1988), Table 7.1; cases which occurred between the 1983 and 1987 General Elections and where the gross sale proceeds were £500 million or more.

Second, all pre-1979 attempts to control wage inflation had foundered on the rock of public sector pay. Once one group of workers had settled for a given percentage wage increase, no other organized group would settle for less. This effect was not confined to the public sector. But in the public sector, the government was the paymaster. It would be blamed for any of the resulting strikes and disruption that followed from any attempt to impose wage restraint, as had happened most recently in the Winter of Discontent that made Prime Minister Thatcher possible. After privatization, it was no longer up to the government to set the wages of telephone, gas, or airline staff. And cash limits enabled the government to tell workers in the core public sector: 'you can have more pay and fewer jobs, or the same number of jobs and no more pay. The choice is yours.'

The influential critique by Vickers and Yarrow (1988) showed that privatization had not promoted economic efficiency. Economic efficiency required tough regulation. Otherwise, a public monopoly might simply give way to a private monopoly. If a government aims to increase economic efficiency, privatization as such is irrelevant; what matters is the opening of industry to competition. But the popular capitalism of Thatcherism II depended on giving Sid both a quick buck and an assurance of long-term profits. The quick buck was easy – underprice the sale. But the long-term advantage depended on the company being allowed to continue to make monopoly profits. Accordingly, Thatcher II did not break up the privatized companies, nor ensure that new entrants could get fair access to customers of the former state monopolist. The privatisation of British Airports Authority (BAA), completed just after the 1987 election, had an added twist. The value of airport terminals is hugely boosted by the duty-free concessions they can auction. But the tax anomaly that allows international travellers to avoid paying excise duty on spirits and cigarettes 'is arbitrary, and inefficient, and there is no distributional reason' for it (Vickers and Yarrow, 1988, 360). It is a tax transfer from the poor to the rich, and from those with good health habits to those with bad health habits. By selling BAA, the government privatized an arbitrary source of tax privilege.

The privatizations of Thatcherism III made better economic, but worse political, sense than their predecessors. In this era, each utility acquired a tough regulator who imposed the so-called RPI–X formula on prices. Each utility was allowed to increase its prices each year by no more than the average increase in the Retail Price Index, minus an amount X determined by the regulator, to ensure that the real consumer price of utilities declined. RPI–X was proposed in 1983, but the first company it was applied to, British Telecommunications (BT), was making such huge efficiency gains through technical change that it was not a binding constraint. Telecoms were privatized with a duopoly of suppliers (BT and Mercury) and a regulator (Oftel), neither of which ate into BT's profitability. Only in the third Thatcher term did some privatized utilities find RPI–X seriously irksome.

Between 1987 and 1990 electricity, rail and coal were privatized. The electricity companies were privatized in a more pro-competitive way than British Gas or British Telecom; accordingly, prices have come down sharply, but electric Sid has made fewer windfall gains. If he held on his shares until 2002, he would by now be looking very foolish. British Rail was compulsorily broken up into small components – too small, as events since the fall of Mrs Thatcher seem to have shown. And the government finally saw off the National Union of Mineworkers (the job that Harold Macmillan had hired the Rt Hon. Lord Robens to do) by selling most of the remaining deep-mining coal capacity to a single firm, RJB Mining, which had almost vanished by 2000.

This case epitomises median-voter politics. A wise commentator (Samuel Brittan) has said that people always overestimated Mrs Thatcher's grasp of economics while underestimating her grasp of politics. The sequence 'Privatize first, regulate later' makes no economic sense. It makes very good political sense in a democracy. Chile, which was not a democracy, could follow an economic logic that the UK could not. Even the UK could not have followed the logic it did but for the accident of the Falklands War, without which Mrs Thatcher would have led the Conservatives to crashing defeat in the 1983 General Election. Privatization, first suggested to Mrs Thatcher by her marketing advisers and brilliantly exploited by Mr (now Lord) Tebbit, was an excellent median-seeking device. It may have been a lousy economic device, but that should not surprise a Chicago political economist.

Why, though, did the same median-voter logic not inhibit efficient regulation under Thatcherism III? From 1987 to 1989 the Conservatives had so much political space at their command that they no longer needed to worry about the median voter. Before the 1987 election, the Tebbit letter seemed essential because the 1983 Falklands windfall had evaporated and the Labour Party was rapidly moving to the centre away from its extremist positions of 1983. If the interests of the median voter clashed with economic efficiency, the latter must give way. Winning a third term in 1987 without the Falklands factor gave Mrs Thatcher breathing space. Labour had imploded earlier; now the Liberal–Social Democrat alliance reached its nadir in 1989. In 1990 Mrs Thatcher's breathing space contracted, resulting ultimately in her Thanksgiving Day massacre. Her successor John Major won a quite unexpected victory in 1992, so that the pro-competitive reforms of Thatcherism III had space to continue through a further term. They became bipartisan when Labour became New Labour under Tony Blair (beginning in 1994). Efficient regulation under Thatcher III seems more a case of public interest than of median-voter effects, although if there were policy entrepreneurs they were not so much Mrs Thatcher and her ministers as some of the regulators (such as Don Cruickshanks) and academic commentators (such as John Vickers, later to become a regulator-in-chief).

CONCLUSION

All three theories of regulation are viable, but none of the three contains the whole truth. Historical contingency matters. Cases 1 and 3 feature unusually strong politicians at work: Gladstone imposing what he saw as a public interest regime, and Mrs Thatcher successfully seeking a median voter in multidimensional space. Case 2 features an unusually strong industry leader, the Rt Hon. Lord Robens, riding roughshod over weak politicians. No surprise, then, that different theories of regulation are supported in each of the three cases.

In regulatory politics, the party with information is the party with power. Asymmetric information implies asymmetric power. Gladstone, Chadwick, and the later Railway and Canal Rates Commission (Foster, 1992, ch. 2) were defeated by asymmetric information. The railway companies knew their rates, costs and profits; nineteenth-century governments did not. Governments looked for low-information tools to regulate utilities. The Victorian device of capping their rate of return failed. Not until RPI–X did government discover a cheap means of monitoring utilities' performance.

In risk regulation, the information asymmetries worked in the opposite direction. A regulator such as HM Inspectorate of Railways could impose technical standards on new railways whether or not they were reasonable. Before Armagh, they had nearly mandated a technically useless continuous braking system (Parris, 1965, 210–17). These information asymmetries persist to the present day, with the risk regulator of the railway sometimes mandating inappropriate regimes. Aberfan proved that the coal industry regulator and the regulated were equally moles unaware of the habits of birds. Government was a closed shop which did not open until 1997.

NOTES

1. Special thanks are due to my previous co-authors Christopher Foster and Martin Johnes; to participants in the regulation conference at Barcelona and other members of the Regulation Network who sent me their comments on earlier drafts; and to Stewart Wood for his acute criticisms of case study 3. I acknowledge the assistance of the British Academy under research grant no. APN6714, and of the Economic & Social Research Council under research grant no. R000222677.
2. So called by Prime Minister Harold Wilson: PRO, PREM 13/1280.

REFERENCES

[Ablett, Noah and others] (1912), *The Miners' Next Step*, Tonypandy: Robert Davies & Co., http://www.llgc.org.uk/ymgyrchu/Llafur/1926/MNS.htm.

Alderman, G. (1973), *The Railway Interest*, Leicester: Leicester University Press.

Averch, H. and D.L. Johnson (1962), 'Behavior of the firm under regulatory constraints', *American Economic Review*, **52**, 1052–69.

Ayres, Ian and John Braithwaite (1991), 'Tripartism: Regulatory capture and empowerment', *Law and Social Inquiry*, **16**, 435–96.

Black, Duncan (1958), *The Theory of Committees and Elections*, Cambridge: Cambridge University Press.

Breyer, S. (1982), *Regulation*, Cambridge, MA: Harvard University Press.

Brown, L. (1958), *The Board of Trade and the Free Trade Movement 1830–1842*, Oxford: Clarendon Press.

Butler, D.E. and D. Kavanagh (1980), *The British General Election of 1979*, London: Macmillan.

Chadwick, Sir E. (1859), 'Results of different principles of legislation and administration in Europe; of competition for the field, as compared with competition within the field, of service', *Journal of the Statistical Society of London*, **22**, 381–420.

Craig, F.W.S. (1975), *British parliamentary election manifestos 1900–1974*, London: Macmillan.

Dangerfield, George (1936), *The Strange Death of Liberal England*, London: Constable.

Davies, Edmund (chairman) (1967), 'Report of the Tribunal appointed to inquire into the Disaster at Aberfan on October 21st, 1966', HL 316, HC 533, London: HMSO.

Feaver, D. (1997), 'A regulatory analysis of Australia's anti-dumping law and policy: Statutory failure or regulatory capture?', *Australian Journal of Public Administration*, **56** (4), 67–77.

Feuchtwanger, E.J. (1989), *Gladstone*, 2nd edn, London: Macmillan.

Foot, M.R.D. and H.G.C. Matthew (eds) (1974), *The Gladstone Diaries vol. iii 1840–1847*, Oxford: Clarendon Press.

Foreman-Peck, J. (1987), 'Natural monopoly and railway policy in the nineteenth century', *Oxford Economic Papers*, **39**, 699–718.

Foster, C.D. (1992), *Privatization, Public Ownership and the Regulation of Natural Monopoly*, Oxford: Blackwell.

Garrett, Geoffrey (1994), 'Popular Capitalism: The Electoral Legacy of Thatcherism', in A. Heath et al., *Labour's Last Chance: the 1992 election and beyond*, Aldershot: Dartmouth, pp. 107–23.

Gourvish, T.R. (1972), *Mark Huish and the London & North Western Railway*, Leicester: Leicester University Press.

Great Britain, *Parliamentary Papers*, various volumes.

Hansard (*Parliamentary Debates, Third Series*), various dates.

Hawke, G.R. (1970), *Railways and Economic Growth in England and Wales 1840–1870*, Oxford: Clarendon Press.

Heath, A. and G. Garrett (1991), 'The Extension of Popular Capitalism', in A. Heath et al., *Understanding Political Change: The British Voter 1964–1987*, Oxford: Pergamon, pp. 120–35.

Hood, C., H. Rothstein and R. Baldwin (2001), *The Government of Risk: Understanding Risk Regulation Regimes*, Oxford: Oxford University Press.

Hyde, F. (1934), *Mr Gladstone at the Board of Trade*, London: Cobden-Sanderson.

Kolko, Gabriel (1965), *Railroads and Regulation, 1877–1916*, Princeton, NJ: Princeton University Press.

Kostal, R. (1994), *Law and English Railway Capitalism 1825–1875*, Oxford: Clarendon Press.

Laffont, J. and D. Martimort (1999), 'Separation of regulators against collusive behavior', *Rand Journal of Economics*, **30** (2), 232–62.

Lambert, R.S. (1964), *The Railway King*, 2nd edn, London: Allen & Unwin.

Levi-Faur, D. (2002), 'Herding towards a New Convention: On herds, shepherds, and lost sheep in the liberalization of the telecommunications and electricity industries', Nuffield College Working Papers in Politics, 2002-W6, Oxford.

Lohmann, S. (1994), 'The dynamics of information cascades: the Monday demonstrations in Leipzig, East Germany, 1989–1991', *World Politics*, **47**, 42–101.

Lubenow, W.C. (1971), *The Politics of Government Growth: Early Victorian Attitudes towards State Intervention 1833–1848*, Newton Abbot: David & Charles.

McCraw, T.K. (1984), *Prophets of Regulation*, London: Belknap Press.

McLean, I. (1989), *Democracy and New Technology*, Cambridge: Polity Press.

McLean, I. (2001), *Rational Choice & British Politics: An Analysis of Rhetoric and Manipulation from Peel to Blair*, Oxford: Oxford University Press.

McLean, I. and M. Johnes (2000), *Aberfan: Government and Disasters*, Cardiff: Welsh Academic Press.

Majone, G. (1994), 'The rise of the regulatory state in Europe', *West European Politics*, **17**, 77–101.

Marsh, Richard (1978), *Off the Rails: an autobiography*, London: Weidenfeld & Nicolson.

Matthew, H.C.G. (1986), *Gladstone 1809–1874*, Oxford: Clarendon Press.

Olson, Mancur (2000), 'Big Bills left on the Sidewalk: Why some Nations are Rich, and others Poor', in Olson and Kähkönen (eds) (2000), pp. 37–60.

Olson, Mancur and Satu Kähkönen (eds) (2000), *A Not-so-dismal Science: A Broader View of Economies and Societies*, Oxford: Oxford University Press.

Parris, H. (1965), *Government and the Railways in the 19th Century*, London: Routledge.

Pliatzky, Leo (1989), *The Treasury under Mrs Thatcher*, Oxford: Basil Blackwell.

Schapiro, R. (2003), 'Public or private ownership? Urban utilities in Britain, 1870–1914', D. Phil. thesis Oxford University.

Shannon, R. (1982), *Gladstone, vol. 1, 1809–1865*, London: Hamish Hamilton.

Stigler, G. (1971), 'The theory of economic regulation', *Bell Journal of Economics and Management Science*, **2**, 3–21.

Vickers, J. and G. Yarrow (1988), *Privatization: An Economic Analysis*, Cambridge, MA: MIT Press.

Williams, P.M. (1952), 'Public opinion and the railway rates question in 1886', *English Historical Review*, **67**, 37–73.

Wilson, J.Q. (1980), 'The Politics of Regulation', in J.Q. Wilson (ed.), *The Politics of Regulation*, New York: Basic Books, pp. 357–94.

Wittman, Donald (1995), *The Myth of Democratic Failure: Why Political Institutions are Efficient*, Chicago: University of Chicago Press.

4. Institutional change in regulatory policies: regulation through independent agencies and the three new institutionalisms

Fabrizio Gilardi*

One of the most widespread institutions of modern regulatory governance is the so-called independent regulator (OECD, 2002, 91)

The question remains: can new institutionalists develop institutionalist propositions about institutional change, or a new institutionalist theory/theories of institutions?
(Gorges, 2001, 142)

1. INTRODUCTION

This book studies regulatory change, and fosters a broad comparative view on regulatory processes and outcomes. The age of governance has seen the expansion of regulation as a distinctive mode of social coordination, both at national and supranational level (Knill and Lenschow, Chapter 10, this book; Jakbo, Chapter 9, this book). The present chapter deals with the institutional side of regulatory change, and more specifically with the establishment, in all countries and many sectors, of independent regulatory agencies (IRAs). Indeed, IRAs are one of the main distinctive features of the regulatory state that has been rising in Europe since the 1990s (Majone, 1997a). They can be defined as public organizations with regulatory powers that are neither directly elected by the people, nor directly managed by elected officials. In other words, they are non-majoritarian institutions (Thatcher and Stone Sweet, 2002) carrying out regulation. Examples include the British Office of Telecommunications (Oftel), the German Bundeskartellamt, the French

Commission des opérations de bourse (COB), and the Italian Autorità per l'energia elettrica e il gas, just to name a few.

In spite of growing academic interest, many aspects of regulation through IRAs remain unclear, including the basic question of where IRAs come from in the first place. IRAs are never the only institutional option for the regulation of markets, yet governments have increasingly decided to rely on them to carry out regulation. How can delegation of regulatory competencies to IRAs be explained? The major goal of this chapter is to compare different explanatory strategies about this important institutional innovation. The first aim is to develop hypotheses capable of accounting for cross-national, cross-sectoral and historical variations of the institutional characteristics of regulatory policies. The theoretical perspective adopted here is that of the new institutionalism. Institutional change is both a central theme and a problematic issue for institutional theory (Rothstein, 1996, 153–6), which has already been used with some success to explain many different forms of such change, including institutional change in regulation. The new institutionalism, rather than being a monolithic theory, is composed of three main branches, namely rational choice, sociological and historical (see below). In the perspective of hypothesis development, this has the advantage of forcing the researcher to cover a much broader spectrum of possible explanations.

The focus on the new institutionalism also gives the opportunity to carry out an applied study of its capacity to deal with institutional change, which contrasts sharply with the usual highly theoretical or even meta-theoretical discussions. Tackling this important issue from an empirical starting point is likely to provide new insights for institutional theories of institutional change, and will also highlight the relative weaknesses and strengths of the new institutionalism variants. The second goal of the chapter, then, is to compare the three new institutionalist variants on their ability to theorize institutional change. The main problem with this comparison is that the three new institutionalisms embody not only different theoretical arguments, but also distinctive methodologies. For example, historical institutionalists tend to be more qualitative-oriented than rational choice ones. However, not only do the three branches communicate and exchange insights,[1] but they also share a 'common core' (Immergut, 1998).

The rest of the chapter is structured as follows. The next section introduces the new institutionalism in its three variants. Rational choice institutionalism looks at how utility-maximizing actors design rules that constrain behaviour. Sociological institutionalism has a broader view of institutions that includes norms, and stresses their cognitive dimension. Historical institutionalism tries to combine insights from both and emphasizes the importance of looking at time processes. The main criticism of the three theories is that they are biased towards stability and unfit to explain institutional change.

Their capacity to do so in the case of IRAs will serve as a basis for their comparison.

I will then move from the general to the particular by presenting in turn rational choice, sociological and historical institutionalist explanations of the creation of IRAs. Rational choice institutionalism suggests that the establishment of IRAs can be a solution for the problems of choice over time, and in particular credible commitments and political uncertainty. Sociological institutionalism argues that IRAs can be established due to their symbolic properties rather than for the functions they fulfil, and that they may have become taken for granted as the appropriate way to carry out regulation. Historical institutionalism, finally, emphasizes that functional pressures for the creation of IRAs are mediated by existing institutional arrangements through path-dependent processes.

In the conclusion, I compare the three theories. Each leads to distinct predictions, which, however, are not always competing. This raises the common problem of observational equivalence, where different causes lead to the same outcome, and which makes empirical analysis more difficult. Second, since each theory magnifies some aspects of the establishment of IRAs and neglects others, theory choice should depend essentially on the question asked.

2. THE THREE NEW INSTITUTIONALISMS AND THEIR CRITICS

New institutionalist theory emerged against the background of, and in reaction to, the behaviouralist revolution within political science (Immergut, 1998, 6). In opposition to behaviouralism, the new institutionalism holds that expressed preferences are not necessarily identical to true preferences, that the aggregation of individual preferences can be inefficient and imperfectly translated into outcomes or decisions, and that, on the normative side, the utilitarian standard for the identification of the public interest as the sum of individual interests is inappropriate. These three points, and in particular a concern with the problems of how individual preferences are formed and aggregated, constitute the common core of the new institutionalism (Immergut, 1998).

The new institutionalism, however, is not a coherent theory, but is rather composed of three distinct branches, usually termed rational choice, sociological and historical (Hall and Taylor, 1996). Rational choice institutionalism has two main features. First, actors are conceptualized as rational utility-maximizers whose behaviour is shaped and constrained by institutions, defined as rules of the game. Second, institutions are seen as the result of deliberate design. Their shape is determined by the benefits they can provide to the relevant actors, and can thus be conceptualized as 'congealed preferences' (Riker, 1980). Sociological institutionalism, on the other hand, is rooted in organization theory and relies on a broader definition of institutions, including not only formal rules and procedures, but also norms. It emphasizes the cognitive impact of institutions, which supply guidelines and shortcuts for behaviour. Institutional origins and change are not seen as the results of purposive design, but as phenomena that have strong symbolic dimensions. Historical institutionalism, finally, draws on insights of both theories, on which it tries, with only moderate success, to build a distinctive coherent view of the interactions between actors and institutions (Hay and Wincott, 1998; Hall and Taylor, 1998). Several distinctive features can be identified (Thelen, 1999; Pierson and Skocpol, 2002). First, hypotheses tend to flow from empirical puzzles rather than from the divergence between theoretical predictions and observed patterns, and are often focused on questions of substantive interest for a broad audience. The theoretical ambitions are limited to the building of middle-range rather than general theory. Second, there is a marked historical view of institutions, whose study is seen to imply an analysis of time processes. Third, the preferences of actors can be endogenous, that is, influenced by institutions. Finally, there is a tendency to focus on macro-contexts and the combined effects of institutions and processes in the analysis of the outcomes of interest.

As a foretaste of the next sections, Table 4.1 summarizes the main arguments and hypotheses on the creation of IRAs. Rational choice insists on the role of IRAs in solving the problems of choice over time in regulation, and in particular credible commitments and political uncertainty. Sociological institutionalism stresses the importance of normative structures in leading symbolic diffusion of organizational arrangements, and posits that delegation to IRAs increases in scope as these become a taken-for-granted institutional form. Historical institutionalism, finally, emphasizes that path-dependent processes limit the possibilities for change, which however becomes possible when the mechanisms sustaining the dominant institutional arrangements weaken.

The problem of institutional change is, in spite of its centrality, one of the major weak spots of institutional theory. According to Gorges (2001), the main problem is that the new institutionalism, being naturally biased towards stability, supplies explanations of change that tend to rely on elements that are exogenous to the theory and, in particular, are extra-institutional. Gorges (2001) seems to use the two formulations as synonymous, but there is an important difference. Saying that explanations of institutional change should be fully within the domain of institutional theory does not imply that institutions themselves must be at the origin of change. In effect, the

Table 4.1   Institutional change in regulation: summary of new institutionalist arguments and hypotheses on the establishment of IRAs

Theory	General argument about the establishment of IRAs	Specific hypotheses on the establishment of IRAs
Rational choice institutionalism	IRAs help in solving the problems of choice over time in regulation	Regulation through IRAs occurs because politicians try to improve the credibility of their policies and try to solve the political uncertainty problem
Sociological institutionalism	Normative structures lead to symbolic diffusion of IRAs	Regulation through IRAs occurs because they are taken for granted as the appropriate organizational form for regulators
Historical institutionalism	Regulation through IRAs is affected by path dependence	Contingent institutional arrangements mediate functional pressures for the establishment of IRAs. More radical change occurs when the effects of the mechanisms sustaining institutions vanish

characteristic of the new institutionalism is that its focus is not so much on institutions as on the relationship between actors and institutions (see also Hay and Wincott, 1998). This means that an explanation of institutional change that relies on actors and/or on the relationship between actors and institutions is perfectly acceptable. It is, however, important, as Gorges (2001) stresses, that the role of non-institutional factors in institutional change be clearly conceptualized, so that the conditions under which institutional and non-institutional variables matter, as well as the relationship between the two, are unambiguous. Further, Gorges (2001) also emphasizes that explanations of institutional change should have comparative power. A final criterion for comparison and evaluation is the capacity to deal with time. In effect, as Pierson (2003) convincingly argues, many institutional phenomena are characterized by causal processes with long time horizons, and it is thus important that theories of institutional change can account for this.

To sum up, successful explanations of institutional change should not rely on arguments that are exogenous to the theory, should unambiguously specify the theoretical conditions of institutional change, should be able to provide hypotheses with comparative scope, and should take the time dimension seriously. The performance of the three new institutionalisms along these dimensions will be assessed in the conclusion.

3.   RATIONAL CHOICE INSTITUTIONALISM: CREDIBILITY, POLITICAL UNCERTAINTY AND DELEGATION TO IRAS

The nature of delegation to IRAs is peculiar and cannot be explained by conventional arguments. In particular, standard principal–agent theory (Moe, 1984; Bendor, Glazer and Hammond, 2001) is ill equipped to deal with this type of delegation. The central claim of principal–agent models is that delegation is beneficial but also dangerous, because the agent can use its informational advantages for its own benefit, rather than for that of the principal. In the case of IRAs, however, governments make agencies purposely independent rather than, as predicted by principal–agent theory, designing as accurate control mechanisms as possible, although controls do exist. The same point is made by Moe, who stresses that insulating an agency from politics is a structural design that politicians 'would never favor on technical grounds alone' (Moe, 1995, 137). Hence, there must be some other reasons.

Within rational choice, the most promising avenue for research when studying delegation to IRAs seems to be the one stressing the consequences of the fact that choices must often be made over time (Loewenstein and Elster, 1992). Two problems derive from this fact, namely credible commitments and political uncertainty.

3.1   Credible Commitments

Credible commitment capacity has been shown to be necessary for economic growth and investment, because it provides a guarantee against public expropriation for economic actors (Stasavage, 2002; Henisz, 2000). In addition, credibility is a valuable asset for politicians when they carry out regulatory policy (Majone, 1997b, 2001). The outcome of regulatory policies depends crucially on the response of a myriad of actors, notably investors. Coercion is often not a viable option. Rather, policy-makers have to credibly signal their commitment to the announced course of action. Kydland and Prescott (1977), in the paper that is at the origin of this stream of literature, give the following example. Consider a government not wishing to have houses built on a flood plain, and thus announcing that the costly flood-control measures will not be created. In the absence of a law prohibiting the construction of houses there, rational actors know that, if houses begin to be built there, then the government will have incentives to build protections. The outcome is that both houses and flood-control mechanisms are built.

For several reasons, people, and especially elected politicians, may be prone to time-inconsistent preferences such as the one just described. Time inconsistency 'occurs when the best policy currently planned for some future period is no longer the best when that period arrives' (Cukierman, 1992, 15). As Elster (2000) stresses, this need not be caused by unforeseen changes in the environment, nor by a subjective change in the preferences of the agent. It may be caused by the mere passage of time. This phenomenon is known as 'hyperbolic discounting' of the future, which means that 'individuals have a strong preference for the present compared to all future dates, but are much less concerned with the relative importance of future dates' (Elster, 2000, 25).

The important consequence is that, in the face of this time-inconsistency problem, solutions are likely to be sought. In the context of regulatory policy, one possible solution is delegation of powers to an independent agency. It is a way for governments to bind themselves, or, in other words, to remove their future freedom of action, not unlike Ulysses facing the Sirens. Delegation may be an effective mechanism for precommitment because the agent may not suffer from the same temptation of opportunism, in reason of its preferences, legal mandate, or time horizon.

The nearly ideal-typical situation where governments face credible commitment problems is monetary policy, where policy-makers have to credibly signal their willingness to keep inflation low (for an overview of the literature see Berger, de Haan and Eijffinger, 2000). Short of this credibility, economic actors are likely to anticipate governments' unwillingness to support the (electoral) costs of a conservative course of action, which leads to inflationary tendencies. Expected inflation leads to actual inflation. Economists suggest two main solutions, namely fixed rules and delegation to independent and conservative central banks, both removing governments' discretion.

In the more general case of regulatory policies, it has been argued that credibility problems are most likely to arise when governments engage in privatization and liberalization reforms (Spiller, 1993; Levy and Spiller, 1994). In these situations, governments have to attract private investors, which requires a credible commitment to investor-friendly courses of action. This is particularly true in sectors such as utilities, which are characterized by important sunk costs and thus higher risk. However, as Gilardi (2002) has shown, such problems are equally present in all economic regulatory policies, and are not limited to cases where competitive markets are created. For social regulation, on the other hand, where consumers rather than investors are the main target of policies, credibility is less necessary.

3.2   Political Uncertainty

A second hypothesis is that delegation is linked to the problem of political uncertainty (Moe, 1990, 1995; Horn, 1995, 16–19; Horn and Shepsle, 1989). According to Moe (1995, 124), 'the right to exercise public authority can be thought of as a property right of sorts. These rights are used ... to make choices about policy and the structure of government.' The problem is that, unlike in the economy, in a democratic political system these political property rights are uncertain because they are bound to be periodically reallocated. Moreover, this reallocation will be operated without any compensation for the losers (Moe, 1990, 227). This means that, before caring about the transaction costs that characterize economic organization and institutions, political actors have to secure their property rights, which are political in nature and consist of authority over policy. To this extent, political actors, in opposition to economic ones, are concerned with more than simply making efficient choices about how to use their property. While the property rights of economic actors are guaranteed by democratic states, those of political actors are not, precisely because of the democratic nature of the state. As a consequence, the first concern of political actors will be securing their property rights when they have the opportunity to do so. The uncertainty of political property rights is then very likely to play a key role in the design of political institutions. In particular, this may lead legislators to design bureaucracies that they cannot control (Moe, 1995, 131).

There has recently been a renewed theoretical interest in the role of political uncertainty in political processes. Swank and Dur (2001) argue that politicians set up permanent advisory units not only to obtain expertise, but also to affect the actions of their successors. De Figueiredo (2002), on the other hand, develops a formal model showing that electorally weak groups attempt to protect their policies by insulating them while they are in power. These studies show that political uncertainty can be usefully distinguished from credible commitment, although the two problems are intimately related and, for our purposes, lead to the same outcome. The main conceptual difference between the two is that, while political uncertainty cannot be dissociated from the characteristics of the electoral process, the time-inconsistency problem, which is at the basis of the credibility issue, can and does affect actors that do not have to care about elections. An illustrative example is that of a benevolent dictator: despite being outside the democratic process, he may still have time inconsistent preferences and thus suffer from low credible commitment capacity.

3.3 Empirical Evidence

Is the creation of IRAs motivated by credibility and/or political uncertainty concerns? Available evidence does not abound, but does suggest that these two factors matter. Gilardi (2002) examines the empirical consistency of the credibility hypothesis. He finds that the extent of independence accorded to regulators is positively affected by the economic nature of regulation, and negatively by the number of veto players. This result supports the hypothesis, as credibility problems are more severe when governments have to deal with investors rather than consumers, and veto players, since they lead to policy stability, can be conceived as a functional equivalent of delegation as a means of precommitment.

De Figueiredo (2003), on the other hand, studies the delegation of veto power for budget to governors ('line-item veto') in the US, and supplies evidence that it may be used as an insulation mechanism. The line-item veto has a restrictive effect on budget, and the author finds that it tends to be used by conservatives when they perceive their future electoral prospects to be weak. A similar result is found by Volden (2002), who analyses delegation to bureaucracies for the Aid to Families with Dependent Children, and finds that declining coalitions are more likely to engage in extensive delegation. Also, casual evidence supporting the political uncertainty hypothesis is supplied by Vogel (1996, 131), who claims that the Thatcher administration favoured independent regulators in order to prevent capture by the Labour Party.

Overall, it can be said that rational choice institutionalist hypotheses have not been tested extensively, but available evidence seems to be supportive of their basic claims. When designing regulatory institutions, politicians seem to care about both credibility and political uncertainty.

4. SOCIOLOGICAL INSTITUTIONALISM: SYMBOLIC DIMENSIONS OF THE DIFFUSION OF IRAS

Rational choice institutionalism implicitly assumes that governments act independently from each other. IRAs are created because governments want to solve the credibility and/or political uncertainty problem, and what other governments do is irrelevant. Sociological institutionalism, on the other hand, posits that one of the main explanatory factors of delegation to IRAs is the fact that governments behave interdependently, or, in other words, look at the behaviour of other governments before deciding whether to establish an independent regulator. This means that sociological institutionalist explanations are situated in a diffusion perspective. In effect, the specificity of diffusion processes is that they are characterized by interdependent behaviour (Brune and Garrett, 2000; Simmons and Elkins, 2003).

Although there is no consensus in the literature on the appropriate theoretical specification of diffusion mechanisms, it seems useful to differentiate between goal-oriented and symbolic drivers of diffusion. Goal-oriented diffusion mechanisms include Bayesian and bounded learning. In Bayesian learning (Meseguer, 2002), governments are assumed to act after updating their beliefs about the benefits of a given policy by looking at the experience of others. Bounded learning, on the other hand, can be conceptualized as a bounded rationality version of rational or Bayesian learning (Weyland, 2002). In this case, actors try to get relevant information from the observation of the behaviour of others, but, rather than on Bayesian updating, they rely on 'cognitive shortcuts' such as representativeness, availability and anchoring (McDermott, 2001; Weyland, 2002). In both cases, however, the functions policies can perform matter. The interdependence of actors stems from the fact that, by looking at each other, they try to get relevant information that can help them in their decision.

Borrowing models from others, however, need not be 'a utilitarian activity designed to solve extant problems' (Weyland, 2002, 9). In this case, the interdependence of actors is not based on a goal-oriented effort, but, rather, on the importance of shared values and norms. The identification and conceptualization of symbolic (in opposition to goal-oriented) drivers of diffusion of organizational forms is at the centre of sociological institutionalism.

4.1   Legitimacy and Taken-for-grantedness as Drivers of Diffusion

Sociological institutionalism is concerned with the constitutive role of culturally legitimate models of organization and action (Clemens and Cook, 1999, 442). There are basically two related reasons why organizations can be created independently from the functions they can accomplish. First, the set-up of an organization can be a ceremony intended to provide legitimacy to certain decisions by diverting the attention from more substantial concerns (Meyer and Rowan, 1977, 349). In the case of IRAs, governments may create independent regulators so as to legitimate other decisions, such as liberalization of utilities. As IRAs become valued by the broader institutional environment (which includes norms and values), establishing them may enhance the legitimacy of certain policy choices. Second, over time some organizational forms can become 'taken for granted' (Hannan and Carroll, 1992), while others disappear from the 'domain of the possible', and this independently from the functions they can perform. In this perspective, IRAs are not established as a legitimation device, but simply because other options are not even considered, while IRAs have become the normal or obvious thing to do in given contexts.

An important methodological problem is how the effects of ceremonial adoption and taken-for-grantedness (TFG) can be measured. In the 'population ecology' literature (Hannan and Carroll, 1992, Ruef, 2000) it is conventionally argued that TFG is crucially affected by organizational density, defined as the number of organizations in a given population. Widespread identification and recognition is the precondition to a status in which an organizational form is taken for granted. Identification and recognition, in turn, depend primarily on the number of organizations that have taken up a given form. Organizational density is also likely to affect the extent to which an organizational form is seen as an 'appropriate' solution to a given problem, and the extent to which it is ceremonially adopted to improve legitimacy.

In particular, organizational density is expected to have an impact on organizational foundings, that is, the number of similar organizations that are created in a given period. The relationship between the total number of organizations in the population and the number of new organizations is assumed to have the form of an inverted U, with the number of foundings rising initially with increasing density to some point and then declining with further increases in density (Carroll and Hannan, 1989a, Ranger-Moore et al., 1991; Baum and Oliver, 1992). The argument is that at low levels of density, that is, when there are few organizations in the population, each new organization enhances the legitimacy of that organizational form. When that form has become prevalent, however, that is, when many organizations have adopted it, its legitimacy is already high and thus further proliferation will not have much effect on the extent to which it is taken for granted. On the other hand, as the number of organizations increases to high levels, each new organization increases competition for resources and discourages foundings. Thus, high levels of density should be negatively associated with new foundings, and the whole relationship between the total number of organizations and the number of newly created organizations assumes an inverted-U shape.

How relevant is this hypothesis for IRAs? The first part is straightforward: when there are few IRAs, each new IRA increases the legitimacy of this type of organization and should thus have a positive effect on subsequent IRA creations. This argument is very similar to that advanced by McNamara (2002) for independent central banks and by Radaelli (2000) for institutional isomorphism in general. That legitimacy increases at declining rates seems also a reasonable assumption. On the other hand, the hypothesis that, once IRAs become largely widespread, the effect of density on foundings becomes negative is more problematic. In effect, while the assumption that competition for scarce resources increases with high levels of density is reasonable for organizations such as newspapers (Carroll and Hannan, 1989a) or banks and insurance companies (Ranger-Moore et al., 1991), such competition simply does not exist for public bodies such as IRAs. There is nevertheless another mechanism that is likely to have the same effect, namely the fact that the population of IRAs, unlike that of other private organizations, cannot go beyond a given size. This means that as the size of the IRA population increases, the number of potential newcomers decreases. Even though there is not competition for scarce resources, then, the fact that the population of IRAs has a limited size leads to the same conclusion: with a high number of IRAs, the effect of density on foundings becomes negative. It is very important to understand, however, that this hypothesis holds only if the unit of analysis is the population of IRAs (or a sub-population), and one is interested in how many new IRAs are created each year (or during another lapse of time) in that group. If the unit of analysis is the single regulator (for example, the regulator for financial markets in Portugal) and one is interested in when it becomes independent, however, the impact of density should be always positive, because there is no competition mechanism. For other organizations, such as those typically studied in the population ecology literature, on the other hand, the inverted-U hypothesis should hold both if the unit of analysis is a group and if it is a single organization.

Given its parsimony, it will come as no surprise that this conceptualization of TFG in terms of organizational density has been subject to extensive debate. The conceptualization has been criticized in reason of its (excessive) simplicity and its indirect measurement of the concept (Zucker, 1989; Baum and Powell, 1995). Hannan and Carroll (1995; Carroll and Hannan, 1989b) have defended it on pragmatic grounds: density allows researchers to carry out extensive comparisons, both longitudinal and cross-sectional. It is important to note, however, that the relationship between density and adoptions is one of the main and most robust results of diffusion research (Weyland, 2002), which applies to all sorts of phenomena, including some, such as the diffusion of diseases, where TFG has no meaning whatsoever. Finally, the operationalization has been extended to achieve a more direct measurement, notably through the concept of relational density, defined as 'the number of formal relations between the members of a population and key institutions in the environment' (Baum and Oliver, 1992, 540).

4.2 Empirical Evidence

The abundant evidence of the impact of norms on the diffusion of private organizations is not matched by similar evidence for IRAs. There have none the less been recent attempts to examine the empirical relevance of sociological institutionalist arguments for the creation of IRAs. Gilardi (2003) has studied the impact of the number of existing IRAs (density) on the probability that new IRAs are created at both the aggregate and the individual level. When looking at IRAs as a population, the inverted-U relationship between density and new foundings highlighted by the population ecology literature is confirmed. The analysis at the individual level, where the unit of analysis is the single IRA rather than the population, partially confirms the relevance of density in explaining the decision to set up an IRA, even after controlling for other variables related to functional pressures for delegation, such as privatization and liberalization. Also, as predicted by the theory, at the individual level the inverted-U pattern disappears, and the relationship between density and the probability that a new IRA is created becomes monotonic. The empirical evidence for sociological institutionalist hypotheses is thus strong enough to justify further efforts in this direction.

5. HISTORICAL INSTITUTIONALISM: PATH-DEPENDENCE, MEDIATING FACTORS AND DELEGATION TO IRAS

Path-dependence is one of the key components of historical institutionalism because it embodies two of its core elements, namely the importance of institutions and that of the time dimension in the study of politics (Pierson, 2000, 264). Some will disagree with the choice to bind historical institutionalism to path-dependence. This narrow focus can however be justified by the need to discipline a quite eclectic approach. Path-dependence seems a good way to give a common ground to rather diverse historical institutionalist analyses of IRAs.

5.1 Path Dependence as a Common Ground for Historical Institutionalist Studies of IRAs

Despite its increasing popularity among scholars, only seldom has path dependence been used with sufficient discipline (Pierson, 2000; Mahoney, 2000). Before discussing the implications of path-dependence for the study of IRAs, then, it is important to define rigorously this basic concept.

According to Mahoney (2000), path-dependent processes are characterized by three main features. Note that these features concern *all* path-dependent processes and are *minimal* conditions (Mahoney, 2000, 510). First, path-dependent sequences are highly sensitive to events that take place in the early stages. While initial conditions do not determine the final outcome (Goldstone, 1998, 834), early events have a decisive impact on the path the process will follow. Second, these early events are contingent, meaning that they cannot be explained on the basis of available theory. This does not mean they cannot be explained at all, but only that the explanation lies outside the reach of the theory that is used. An example is the introduction of the QWERTY keyboard. This event is to be considered contingent because this type of keyboard was less efficient than the Dvorak type, thus the latter, according to neo-classical economic theory, should have been selected (Mahoney, 2000, 515; David, 1985, 336). Third, contingent events lead to relatively deterministic processes. This can also be thought of as inertia: 'once processes are set into motion and begin tracking a particular outcome, these processes tend to stay in motion and continue to track this outcome' (Mahoney, 2000, 511).

Path-dependent processes can be decomposed in two moments. There is first a 'critical juncture' during which an institutional arrangement is adopted. A crucial feature of this institutional creation is that it is contingent, that is, unexplainable by available theory or knowledge. If the critical juncture can be explained, then it does not lead to a path-dependent process (Mahoney, 2000, 513; Goldstone, 1998, 834). Once the institution is in place, the path is followed, in a relatively deterministic manner, because several mechanisms may be at work, all providing 'positive feedback' or 'increasing returns' to the original institutional choice. In politics, these mechanisms include the use of political authority to enhance power asymmetries, the coordination benefits deriving from institutions, and the assets political actors develop on the basis of existing institutions (Thelen, 1999; Pierson, 2000; Pierson and O'Neil Trowbridge, 2002). Historical institutionalist analyses, then, are focused on the critical junctures that give rise to institutions, and on the mechanisms that sustain a given institutional path (Thelen, 1999). If the research is on institutional change, particular emphasis will be put on instititutional reproduction mechanisms, and on how their effects vanished at a given moment, leading to a break in the path.

Recent theoretical advances have sought to provide a better account of change in path-dependent processes (Crouch and Farrell, 2002). This work addresses the important question of how institutionalist theory, which is naturally biased towards institutional persistence, can explain institutional change without relying exclusively on exogenous factors. The argument of Crouch and Farrell (2002) exploits the fact that secondary paths coexist along the dominant one. Although changing path is costly, it is not impossible, and the authors specify the conditions under which such change is likely. In particular, they emphasize that perturbations in the environment, dealing with different environments, or playing simultaneous games, give agents incentives not to neglect alternative paths, which is extremely useful when the agent wants to leave the dominant path. Although the theory is presented at a high level of generality, it is extremely promising for the enhancement of path-dependent arguments of institutional change, even for empirical research.

These arguments on path dependence can be linked to historical institutionalist studies of delegation to IRAs. In particular, Thatcher (2002; see also Thatcher and Stone Sweet, 2002) argues that, while functional pressures such as those highlighted by rationalist analyses do play an important role in explaining delegation, they are strongly mediated by several 'contextual factors'. This is a common historical institutionalist argument. Vogel (1996), for example, finds in his study of regulatory reforms under globalization that governments have undertaken reforms that reinforce distinctive national trajectories based on different underlying ideas about the appropriate role of the state in the market and on structural features of the political economic context. Common pressures for reforms are mediated by national institutions. In other words, change is carried out along distinct and well-established (national) institutional paths. This reasoning embodies a clear path-dependent argument.

The mediating factors stressed by Thatcher (2002) are learning and isomorphism, political leadership, state traditions and structures, and the broader context of state reforms. In a path-dependent perspective, state traditions and structures seem the most relevant aspect. According to Thatcher (2002), the set-up of IRAs was easiest in the UK by reason of the long tradition of regulatory commissions, dating back to the nineteenth century in the case of railways. In France, on the other hand, the concern with the unity of the state has long been an obstacle for the creation of IRAs.

Although in these analyses path-dependence is not invoked explicitly, it appears quite clearly in the background, and indeed it could provide a common and sound theoretical basis to otherwise rather diverse approaches. In effect, if the establishment of IRAs is part of a path-dependent process, then the observable implications should be, among others, institutional inertia (Mahoney, 2000, 511; Pierson, 2000, 263), which is something close to the claim that state traditions and structures mediate pressures for institutional change (Thatcher, 2002). The presence of path-dependence, however, should be demonstrated rather than assumed or suggested. As discussed above, this would involve (1) the identification of the critical juncture (which must be contingent) where the relevant institutional arrangements emerged (for example the tradition of regulatory commissions in the UK, or of self-regulation in Germany), (2) the identification of the mechanisms that sustained them, and (3) the demonstration that these played a key role in the adaptation to functional pressures for the creation of IRAs.

5.2 Empirical Evidence

Although there is no study that has explicitly framed the analysis of the creation of IRAs in the path-dependence terms sketched above, several recent studies do suggest that path-dependent mechanisms may have been at work.

Döhler (2002) examines the emergence of IRAs in Germany and suggests that the constitutional doctrine of ministerial responsibility has played a key role in shaping the organizational form of regulators. The ministerial responsibility doctrine stems from the 'departmental principle' (*Ressortprinzip*) embodied in Article 65 of the constitution, which stipulates that agencies and administration have a subordinate status and cannot escape ministerial control. It seems that the emergence of this doctrine can, to a certain extent, be considered 'contingent', since Döhler (2002) stresses that it did not emerge as a series of conscious decisions. What is lacking, however, is a discussion of the mechanisms that have sustained that institutional arrangement. This is particularly important as some recent IRAs, such as the telecoms regulator (RegTP) created in 1998, were granted more autonomy, drawing on the example of the Cartel Office. Following path-dependence theory, this departure from the path could be explained by the weakening of the mechanisms that had sustained the relevant institutional arrangements so far. Alternatively, following Crouch and Farrell (2002), it could be argued that the creation of the RegTP is an example of how alternative paths can re-emerge.

Other similar studies could be presented (for example Böllhoff, 2002; Bartle et al., 2002), but this example suffices to illustrate the main point. There is definitely evidence that history matters in the set-up of IRAs, which supports historical institutionalism, but on the other hand this does not stand up to the expectations of the more sophisticated arguments and hypotheses developed in recent theoretical advances (Pierson, 2000; Mahoney, 2000; Crouch and Farrell, 2002).

6. CONCLUSION

This chapter attempted to discipline the study of institutional change in regulation by comparing the strategies to which the three new institutionalist branches lead when they are used to explain delegation to IRAs. First, the chapter aimed at developing hypotheses on regulation through IRAs across countries and sectors. As summarized in Table 4.1 in the second section, each new institutionalist branch offers a distinctive view. Rational choice stresses the role of institutions in solving the problems of choice over time. In particular, IRAs are seen as a means to improve the credibility of regulatory policies by (partially) removing control from elected officials who, in reason of the democratic process, have a short time horizon and may face incentives to renege on commitments. A lack of credibility is problematic because it discourages private investment. On the other hand, the democratic process implies that policies can be changed or even undone when a new party or coalition gains power. When they face this type of uncertainty, political actors have incentives to lock in policies as long as they can, and insulating policy from politics through an independent agency is a means to do so.

Sociological institutionalism rejects this functional view of institutions, and emphasizes the importance of normative structures and symbolic diffusion. In this perspective, organizations are created not because of the function they perform, but because of their symbolic properties. The set-up of IRAs, then, is seen as an attempt to gain legitimacy for policy choices without having to justify them, and also as the result of their being progressively taken for granted as the natural or obvious institutional design for regulatory policies. Historical institutionalism, finally, puts a strong emphasis on path-dependent process that severely limit, though do not rule out, the possibilities for change once a given institutional path has been embraced. Pressures for the creation of IRAs, then, are mediated by the prevailing institutional arrangements as long as the mechanisms that sustain them hold. Although these three explanations clearly differ in most respects, they do not lead exclusively to competing predictions. This raises the common problem of observational equivalence, where the same outcome can be explained by different causes, and which complicates empirical analysis.

The second goal was to examine the capacity of the three new institutionalisms to deal with this important form of institutional change. We have just seen that they draw attention to different aspects of delegation to IRAs. This demonstrates that each has a distinctive view of institutional change, but what remains to be discussed is how they perform against the standards set by critics of the new institutionalism.

Table 4.2 compares how the three theories conceptualize institutional change in regulation along the four problematic dimensions discussed in the second section, namely the status of the institutional change in the theory (whether it is exogenous or endogenous), the treatment of non-institutional factors (whether it is systematic or *ad hoc*), the potential for comparisons, and the importance of the time dimension. Rational choice institutionalism does not have to look outside its boundaries to account for institutional change. Delegation to IRAs is explained by two general problems of choice over time, namely credible commitments and political uncertainty. Non-institutional factors, in this case functional pressures for delegation, are clearly identified and their role in explaining the outcome is presented in detail. This implies that the theory easily leads to comparative hypotheses, both cross-national and cross-sectoral. On the other hand, the role of time and history is sharply under-conceptualized, and is in fact reduced to the longitudinal variation of functional pressures.

Table 4.2   New institutionalist accounts of institutional change in regulation: an assessment

	Rational choice institutionalism	Sociological institutionalism	Historical institutionalism
Status of institutional change (endogenous/ exogenous)	Endogenous: credibility and political uncertainty problems drive delegation to IRAs	Exogenous for the first IRAs, endogenous for the others: the theory explains why IRAs spread, but not why the first IRAs are established	The theory can integrate endogenous change, but scholars rely heavily on exogenous arguments
Treatment of non-institutional factors (systematic/ *ad hoc*)	Systematic: functional pressures are clearly identified	*Ad hoc*: non-institutional factors are borrowed from other theories	*Ad hoc*: non-institutional factors are borrowed from other theories
Comparative strength	Cross-national and cross-sectoral variations of pressures for delegation can be systematically predicted	Cross-sectoral variations more easily explained than cross-national variations	Comparisons are possible, but the theory is biased towards case studies
Time dimension	Longitudinal variations are reduced to variations in functional pressures	The theory accounts for longitudinal dynamics, but the role of time and history is underdeveloped	Time and history are fully taken into account

The sociological institutionalist account of change is ambivalent. On the one hand, it is silent on the creation of the first IRAs, which are supposed to be established for some functional reasons that are not discussed. On the other, it develops sophisticated arguments to explain the spread of IRAs, which is driven by the fact that this organizational form progressively becomes taken for granted at the expense of alternative solutions. This means that the theory embodies a dynamic argument that can account for longitudinal processes, although the precise role of time and history remains unclear. Also, the theory is more apt to investigate cross-sectoral rather than cross-national variations, as TFG is often better conceptualized at the sectoral than at the national level.

Finally, historical institutionalism can in principle account for institutional change without relying on external advice, but is stronger in explaining why change occurs (notably because the mechanisms sustaining previous institutional arrangements disappear or weaken) than the precise direction of change. The latter is explained through exogenous factors borrowed from other theories. In the case of IRAs, the trigger of change is often identified in the functional pressures for delegation highlighted by rational choice. Although the theory can lead to comparative hypotheses, it seems biased towards case studies aiming at the detailed examination of how certain path-dependent processes are sustained or break. On the other hand, this ensures that time and history are fully taken into account.

It appears clear from this comparison that there is no best theory. Rather than being a relativistic conclusion, this observation highlights the weaknesses that each theory has to overcome if it wants to supply a good explanation of institutional change in regulation, and, second, stresses that, at their current stage of development, some theories are better for some questions. If one is interested in broad comparisons, historical institutionalism is not an ideal starting point. If the focus is on long-term dynamics, rational choice is not enough. And if one wants to study the functional rationales for the set-up of IRAs, then sociological institutionalism has little to say.

Despite these differences, the two main elements of the new institutionalist 'common core' (Immergut, 1998), namely the fact that both individual preferences and their aggregation are problematic, are present in the argument the three branches provide on delegation to IRAs. Rational choice stresses the prevalence of strategic choices over the long term (versus the expression of short-term preferences), as well as the role of institutions in facilitating preference aggregation when regulatory choices are carried out over time; sociological institutionalism emphasizes the importance of symbolic dimensions in shaping preferences over IRAs, and gives a more prominent place to institutional structures than to actors; and historical institutionalism highlights the impact of contingent events and mediating factors in shaping preferences over delegation to IRAs.

In conclusion, this analysis will have attained its objective if it has succeeded in clarifying the key claims of three major theories in relation to recent forms of institutional change in regulation, and in supplying a starting point for the development of testable hypotheses. It is hoped that it will also encourage scholars to address more explicitly the theoretical foundations of their analyses of regulatory institutions.

NOTES

* I wish to thank Ian Bartle, Dietmar Braun, Alex Fischer, Fabio Franchino, Olivier Giraud, Silja Häusermann, Jacint Jordana, David Levi-Faur, Sarah Nicolet, Yannis Papadopoulos and participants in the Oxford workshop for their very useful comments on previous versions of this chapter. I alone am responsible for its content.
1. It is particularly historical institutionalism that exhibits a strong tendency to integrate insights from the two other branches.

REFERENCES

Bartle, Ian, Markus M. Müller, Roland Sturm and Stephen Wilks (2002), 'The Regulatory State: Britain and Germany Compared', London: Anglo-German Foundation for the Study of Industrial Society.

Baum, Joel A.C. and Christine Oliver (1992), 'Institutional Embeddedness and the Dynamics of Organizational Populations', *American Sociological Review*, **7**, 540–59.

Baum, Joel A.C. and Walter W. Powell (1995), 'Cultivating an Institutional Ecology of Organizations: Comment on Hannan, Carroll, Dundon, and Torres', *American Sociological Review*, **60**, 529–38.

Bendor, Jonathan, Amihai Glazer and Thomas Hammond (2001), 'Theories of Delegation', *Annual Review of Political Science*, **4**, 235–69.

Berger, Helge, Jacob de Haan and Sylvester C.W. Eijffinger (2000), 'Central Bank Independence: An Update of Theory and Evidence', Discussion Paper No. 2353, London: Centre for Economic Policy Research.

Böllhoff, Dominik (2002), 'The New Regulatory Regime – The Institutional Design of Telecommunications Regulation at the National Level', in Adrienne Héritier (ed.), *Common Goods: Reinventing European and International Governance*, Lanham: Rowman & Littlefield.

Brune, Nancy and Geoffrey Garrett (2000), 'The Diffusion of Privatization in the Developing World', paper for presentation at the APSA Annual Meeting, Washington, DC, 30 August–3 September.

Carroll, Glenn R. and Michael T. Hannan (1989a), 'Density Dependence in the Evolution of Populations of Newspaper Organizations', *American Sociological Review*, **54**, 524–41.

Carroll, Glenn R. and Michael T. Hannan (1989b), 'On Using Institutional Theory in studying Organizational Populations (Reply to Zucker)', *American Sociological Review*, **54** (4), 545–8.

Clemens, Elisabeth S. and James M. Cook (1999), 'Politics and Institutionalism: Explaining Durability and Change', *Annual Review of Sociology*, **25**, 441–66.

Crouch, Colin and Henry Farrell (2002), 'Breaking the Path of Institutional Development? Alternatives to the New Determinism', MPIfG Discussion Paper 02/5, Köln: Max-Planck-Institut für Gesellschaftsforschung.

Cukierman, Alex (1992), *Central Bank Strategy, Credibility, and Independence: Theory and Evidence*, Cambridge, MA: The MIT Press.

David, Paul A. (1985), 'Clio and the Economics of QWERTY', *American Economic Review*, **75** (2), 332–7.

De Figueiredo, Rui J.P. (2002), 'Electoral Competition, Political Uncertainty, and Policy Insulation', *American Political Science Review*, **96** (2), 321–33.

De Figueiredo, Rui J.P. (2003), 'Budget Institutions and Political Insulation', *Journal of Public Economics*, forthcoming.

Döhler, Marian (2002), 'Institutional Choice and Bureaucratic Autonomy in Germany', *West European Politics*, **25** (1), 101–24.

Elster, Jon (2000), *Ulysses Unbound. Studies in Rationality, Precommitment, and Constraints*, Cambridge: Cambridge University Press.

Gilardi, Fabrizio (2002), 'Policy Credibility and Delegation to Independent Regulatory Agencies: A Comparative Empirical Analysis', *Journal of European Public Policy*, **9** (6), 873–93.

Gilardi, Fabrizio (2003), 'Spurious and Symbolic Diffusion of Independent Regulatory Agencies in Western Europe', paper presented at the workshop 'The Internationalization of Regulatory Reforms', University of California, Berkeley, 25–26 April.

Goldstone, Jack A. (1998), 'Initial Conditions, General Laws, Path Dependence, and Explanation in Historical Sociology', *American Journal of Sociology*, **104** (3), 829–45.

Gorges, Michael J. (2001), 'New Institutionalists Explanations for Institutional Change: A Note of Caution', *Politics*, **21** (2), 137–45.

Hall, Peter A. and Rosemary C.R. Taylor (1996), 'Political Science and the Three New Institutionalisms', *Political Studies*, **44**, 936–57.

Hall, Peter A. and Rosemary C.R. Taylor (1998), 'The Potential of Historical Institutionalism: A Response to Hay and Wincott', *Political Studies*, **46**, 958–62.

Hannan, Michael T. and Glenn R. Carroll (1992), *Dynamics of Organizational Populations. Density, Legitimation, and Competition*, Oxford: Oxford University Press.

Hannan, Michael T. and Glenn R. Carroll (1995), 'Theory Building and Cheap Talk about Legitimation: Reply to Baum and Powell', *American Sociological Review*, **60**, 539–44.

Hay, Colin and Daniel Wincott (1998), 'Structure, Agency and Historical Institutionalism', *Political Studies*, **46**, 951–7.

Henisz, Witold J. (2000), 'The Institutional Environment for Economic Growth', *Economics and Politics*, **12** (1), 1–31.

Horn, Murray J. (1995), *The Political Economy of Public Administration. Institutional Choice in the Public Sector*, Cambridge: Cambridge University Press.

Horn, Murray J. and Kenneth A. Shepsle (1989), 'Commentary on "Administrative Arrangements and the Political Control of Agencies": Administrative Process and Organizational Form as Legislative Responses to Agency Costs', *Virginia Law Review*, **75**, 499–508.

Immergut, Ellen M. (1998), 'The Theoretical Core of the New Institutionalism', *Politics and Society*, **26** (1), 5–34.

Kydland, Finn E. and Edward C. Prescott (1977), 'Rules Rather than Discretion: The Inconsistency of Optimal Plans', *Journal of Political Economy*, **85** (1), 73–491.

Levy, Brian and Pablo T. Spiller (1994), 'The Institutional Foundations of Regulatory Commitment: A Comparatiive Analysis of Telecommunications Regulation', *Journal of Law, Economics, and Organization*, **10** (2), 201–46.

Loewenstein, George and Jon Elster (eds) (1992), *Choice Over Time*, New York: Russell Sage Foundation.

Mahoney, James (2000), 'Path Dependence in Historical Sociology', *Theory and Society*, **29**, 507–48.

Majone, Giandomenico (1997a), 'From the Positive to the Regulatory State', *Journal of Public Policy*, **17** (2), 139–67.

Majone, Giandomenico (1997b), 'Independent Agencies and the Delegation Problem: Theoretical and Normative Dimensions', in Bernard Steuenberg and Frans van Vught (eds), *Political Institutions and Public Policy*, Dordrecht: Kluwer Academic Publishers, pp. 139–56.

Majone, Giandomenico (2001), 'Nonmajoritarian Institutions and the Limits of Democratic Governance: A Political Transaction-Cost Approach', *Journal of Institutional and Theoretical Economics*, **157**, 57–78.

McDermott, Rose (2001), 'The Psychological Ideas of Amos Tversky and Their Relevance for Political Science', *Journal of Theoretical Politics*, **13** (1), 5–33.

McNamara, Kathleen (2002), 'Rational Fictions: Central Bank Independence and the Social Logic of Delegation', *West European Politics*, **25** (1), 47–76.

Meseguer, Covadonga (2002), *Bayesian Learning about Policies*, Madrid, Centro de Estudios Avanzados en Ciencias Sociales, Instituto Juan March de Estudios e Investigaciones.

Meyer, John W. and Brian Rowan (1977), 'Institutionalized Organizations: Formal Structure as Myth and Ceremony', *American Journal of Sociology*, **83** (2), 340–63.

Moe, Terry M. (1984), 'The New Economics of Organization', *American Journal of Political Science*, **28**, 739–77.

Moe, Terry M. (1990), 'Political Institutions: The Neglected Side of the Story', *Journal of Law, Economics, and Organisation*, **6** (Special Issue), 213–53.

Moe, Terry M. (1995), 'The Politics of Structural Choice: Toward a Theory of Public Bureaucracy', in Oliver E. Williamson (ed.), *Organization Theory. From Chester Barnard to the Present and Beyond*, expanded edn, Oxford: Oxford University Press, pp. 116–53.

OECD (2002), *Regulatory Policies in OECD Countries. From Interventionism to Regulatory Governance*, Paris: OECD.

Pierson, Paul (2000), 'Increasing Returns, Path Dependence, and the Study of Politics', *American Political Science Review*, **94** (2), 251–67.

Pierson, Paul (2003), 'Big, Slow-Moving, and ... Invisible: Macro-Social Processes in the Study of Comparative Politics', in James Mahoney and Dietrich Rueschmeyer (eds), *Comparative Historical Analysis in the Social Sciences*, Cambridge: Cambridge University Press, pp. 177–207.

Pierson, Paul and Shannon O'Neil Trowbridge (2002), 'Asset Specificity and Institutional Development', paper presented at the APSA Annual Meeting, Boston, 29 August–1 September.

Pierson, Paul and Theda Skocpol (2002), 'Historical Institutionalism in Contemporary Political Science', in Ira Katznelson and Helen Milner (eds), *The State of the Discipline*, New York: W.W. Norton, pp. 693–721.

Radaelli, Claudio M. (2000), 'Policy Transfer in the European Union: Institutional Isomorphism as a Source of Legitimacy', *Governance*, **13** (1), 25–43.

Ranger-Moore, James, Jane Banaszak-Holl and Michael T. Hannan (1991), 'Density-Dependent Dynamics in Regulated Industries: Founding Rates of Banks and Life Insurance Companies', *Administrative Science Quarterly*, **36**, 36–65.

Riker, William H. (1980), 'Implications from the Disequilibrium of Majority Rule for the Study of Institutions', *American Political Science Review*, **74** (2), 432–46.

Rothstein, Bo (1996), 'Political Institutions: An Overview', in Robert E. Goodin and Hans-Dieter Klingemann (eds), *A New Handbook of Political Science*, Oxford: Oxford University Press, pp. 133–66.

Ruef, Martin (2000), 'The Emergence of Organizational Forms: A Community Ecology Approach', *American Journal of Sociology*, **106** (3), 658–714.

Simmons, Beth and Zachary Elkins (2003), 'The Globalization of Liberalization: Policy Diffusion in the International Political Economy', paper presented at the workshop 'The Internationalization of Regulatory Reforms', University of California, Berkeley, 25–26 April.

Spiller, Pablo T. (1993), 'Institutions and Regulatory Commitment in Utilities' Privatization', *Industrial and Corporate Change*, **2** (3), 387–450.

Stasavage, David (2002), 'Private Investment and Political Institutions', *Economics and Politics*, **14** (1), 41–63.

Swank, Otto H. and Robert A.J. Dur (2001), 'Why Do Policy Makers Give (Permanent) Power to Policy Advisers?', *Economics and Politics*, **13** (1), 73–94.

Thatcher, Mark (2002), 'Delegation to Independent Regulatory Agencies: Pressures, Functions and Contextual Mediation', *West European Politics*, **25** (1), 125–47.

Thatcher, Mark and Alec Stone Sweet (2002), 'Theory and Practice of Delegation to Non-Majoritarian Institutions', *West European Politics*, **25** (1), 1–22.

Thelen, Kathleen (1999), 'Historical Institutionalism in Comparative Politics', *Annual Review of Political Science*, **2**, 369–404.

Vogel, Steven K. (1996), *Freer Markets, More Rules. Regulatory Reform in Advanced Industrial Countries*, Ithaca: Cornell University Press.

Volden, Craig (2002), 'Delegating Powers to Bureaucracies: Evidence from the States', *Journal of Law, Economics and Organization*, **18** (1), 187–220.

Weyland, Kurt (2002), 'The Diffusion of Innovations: A Theoretical Analysis', paper presented at the 2002 APSA meeting, Boston, 29 August–1 September.

Zucker, Lynne G. (1989), 'Combining Institutional Theory and Population Ecology: No Legitimacy, No History (Comment on Carroll and Hannan)', *American Sociological Review*, **54** (4), 542–5.

5. Regulatory co-opetition: transcending the regulatory competition debate

Damien Geradin and Joseph A. McCahery

INTRODUCTION

The reduction in barriers to trade and the liberalization of financial markets, transportation and telecommunications have created the basis for the increase in flows of factors of production between jurisdictions (Bratton and McCahery, 1997). As countries move to a more liberalized domestic economy, questions of competition between jurisdictions abound. With the prospect of increased capital mobility, it is becoming conventional wisdom that national governments are forced to perform their economic policy functions more efficiently since governments that yield optimal levels of public goods may be more successful in the competition between jurisdictions for attracting mobile resources. The concern to attract mobile resources has shaped entire areas of governmental policy and plays a determinative role for firms locating new plants. Arguments in favour of decentralization follow from the economics of competition between jurisdictions. The theory of regulatory competition tells us that allowing for more decentralization helps to remove much of the asymmetrical information problems, reduces the prospects of regulatory capture, and enhances the introduction of a range of alternative solutions for similar problems. The economic advantages of decentralization undoubtedly provided a strong argument for politicians within federal systems to introduce the dynamic of diversity as a counterbalance to the discretion of central government (Inman and Rubinfeld, 1997a; McKinnon and Nechyba, 1997; Choi and Guzman, 2001).[1]

Regulatory competition is an economic theory of government organization that equates decentralization with efficient results.[2] The theory makes an analogy between law and commodities,[3] and then asserts that lower level governments – local, state, or national, as opposed to federal or supranational – should compete for citizens and factors of production when they regulate. It predicts that such competitively determined regulation will satisfy citizen preferences. The prediction has a normative implication for legal and political theory: just as price competition disciplines producers of private goods for the benefit of consumers, so regulatory competition promises to discipline government for the benefit of taxpaying citizens. Regulatory competition has been brought to bear on the entire range of federalism discussions, usually to support a devolutionary initiative or to oppose a proposal for federal intervention.[4] The theory originated in public economics with the publication of the Tiebout model in 1956, which, in turn, influenced its own field profoundly (Dowding et al., 1994). Theoretical arbitrage to legal contexts occurred early in the history of law and economics. But, in contrast to regulatory competition's development in its home field, where it remained closely tied to the study of the production of public goods by state and local governments, lawyers, economists and political scientists in the United States have applied it across an expanse of subject matter, from corporate law and banking to environmental law and trade law (Esty and Geradin, 2001b; Inman and Rubinfeld, 2000; Weingast, 1995).

After becoming a fixture on the landscape of American federalism, regulatory competition expanded to venues worldwide (Bratton et al., 1996). It has been brought to bear within other federal and quasi-federal systems. Most notably it has figured in discussions on strategies for integration with the European Union, especially in the context of the centralization versus subsidiarity debate crucial to many countries in the EU (Van den Bergh, 1996, 1998). The European Union Treaty agreed by the European Council at Maastricht in 1991 provides for the principle of subsidiarity according to which the Community should only intervene when it is better placed than the Member States to act.[5] Yet a prominent feature of the Maastricht Treaty is the transfer of a range of regulatory functions to the Community level. One justification for this policy is that market integration requires national monetary and fiscal policy be coordinated by a centralized institution (Kletzer and von Hagen, 2000; Alesina and Wacriarg, 1999; Bednar et al., 1996).

The post-Maastricht debate has given rise to two divergent positions concerning the optimal allocation of political and economic power in the EU. The debate over the appropriate location of power is conducted in the domain of efficiency, equity and accountability. On the one hand, the decision to centralize policy at the federal level is primarily defended on the basis that it permits the Community to internalize significant spillovers by redistributing risk across regions.[6] Centralization, taking the form of harmonization of rules, is also often perceived as necessary to eliminate barriers to trade, as well as distortions of competition (Inman and Rubinfeld, 1997a). On the other hand, decentralized policies provide incentives for states to commit to efficiency-enhancing regulation. Subsidiarity favours the view that economic policy-making should be restricted to lower levels of government unless there exist credible circumstances for regulatory power to be centralized (Inman and

Rubinfeld, 1998). What subsidiarity captures is the sense that competition between jurisdictions provides a counterbalance to the drive for enhanced integration based on centralized coordination of national laws and policies (Woolcock, 1996).

In the debate over whether to undertake regulation by central or a lower-level authority, proponents of legal federalism look to the economic theory of jurisdictional competition to provide support for devolutionary initiatives. Proponents of deregulation insist that there is a strong connection between decentralization, competitive behaviour and efficient results (Romano, 1993, 2001). Regulatory competition is thought to follow from a robust economic theory that supports two general assertions. First, competitive forces shape a wide range of regulatory outcomes at state and local levels because menus of regulation figure significantly in the location decisions of citizens and factors of production. Second, the competition results in a market that equilibrates regulatory outcomes and citizen preferences. Two conditions must obtain, however – the lower-level regulation must not generate significant externalities and borders must remain open for the free movement of capital and labour (Easterbrook, 1994). Given satisfaction of these conditions, the lower-level market for regulation (if left free to operate by the central government) will provide an 'empirical answer' to important policy questions, since only the public goods and regulatory restrictions for which citizens are willing to pay will survive (Weingast, 1995). Central government intervention inhibits the operation of the market, and therefore is at best unnecessary and at worst results in deadweight anti-competitive costs. There emerges a presumption in favour of locating regulatory authority at lower-level units (CEPR, 1993; Seabright, 1996).

We argue that economic theory, in fact, supports neither the sequence of assertions nor the bottom-line presumption in the theory outlined above. In doing so, we do not deny the existence of regulatory competition, however. There are entire areas of law that manifestly have been shaped by competition (Romano, 2001; Bar-Gil et al., 2002; Levinson, 1996; Macey, 2000; Stewart, 2002). State and local governments also make taxing and spending decisions where competition clearly plays a determinative role – stadium deals for professional teams and tax breaks for local firms locating new plants being the most obvious examples. Nor do we deny that competition can have beneficial effects. Nor does our argument imply wholesale rejection of the body of legal scholarship on regulatory competition. To the contrary, we find that situation-specific legal applications provide a source of material for demonstrating the theory's shortcomings. We even agree that regulatory competition may be termed a federalism value – at least at a broad structural level.

In this chapter, we argue that both race-to-the-bottom[7] and regulatory competition theories – and the resulting centralization and decentralization strategies that they imply – are overstated from a descriptive point of view and unsatisfactory from a normative one. The world is diverse and complex and regulatory competition should reflect and parallel this complexity. A theoretical work by Daniel Esty and one of us provides a study of the patterns of regulatory theory, which we build on in section 3 (Esty and Geradin, 2001a). We argue therefore that optimal governance requires a flexible mix of competition and cooperation between governmental actors, as well as between governmental and non-governmental actors. This approach is called 'regulatory co-opetition'.[8]

This rest of this chapter is divided into three sections. Section 2 provides a critical overview of regulatory competition theory, which today represents the dominant academic thinking about regulatory structure (Bratton and McCahery, 1997). We recognize the merits of regulatory competition but see the prevailing theory as incomplete and unnuanced. Our fundamental critique is two-fold. First, we argue that in many instances the 'locational rights' market created by competition among regulators fails and that some form of cooperation between and among jurisdictions is required to prevent inefficient outcomes. Thus, contrary to the position defended by most regulatory competition theorists, we conclude that, in the real world as opposed to the world of theory (and building on observations from the United States and the European Union), the welfare-enhancing effects of decentralization cannot be presumed. Second, we argue that standard regulatory competition theory posits too limited a mechanism for exerting real competitive pressure on governmental actors (Esty, 1998). Competition between horizontally arrayed jurisdictions represents only one of the forms of pressure that disciplines state actors and drives governmental efficiency. Competition between governmental actors at different levels of power (for example state versus federal officials), between stakeholders within a single governmental unit (for example DG MARKT versus DG Environment), or between government decision-makers and non-governmental organizations (NGOs) may also prove valuable (Esty, 1999). In fact, these multiple dimensions of competition, combined with mechanisms of cooperation, seem likely to enhance regulatory efficacy and efficiency more than simple interjurisdictional horizontal competition.

Section 3 develops regulatory co-opetition as an alternative model. This theory builds on the view that the best regulatory systems require a mix of competition and cooperation across various levels of government, within the branches or departments of a government, and between regulators and non-governmental actors. The analysis of regulatory co-opetition, as developed by Esty and Geradin (2001a), has three main dimensions: (1) *inter*-governmental (reflecting the dynamics of competition and cooperation *among* governments, both horizontally and vertically arrayed); (2) *intra*-governmental (arising from the give-and-take between departments and officials *within* governments); and (3) *extra*-governmental (driven by the simultaneously *cooperative* and *competitive* relations between governmental and non-governmental actors).

Section 4 offers a brief summary and our conclusions. We argue, in particular, that the diversity of the regulatory challenges that governments face and the complexity of the world in which we live demand regulatory strategies that are pluralistic, not simplistic. Sometimes regulatory competition will prove to be advantageous; in other cases, some form of collaboration will produce superior results. More often, a combination of competition and cooperation will be optimal.

2.   REGULATORY COMPETITION: A CRITICAL OVERVIEW

The concept of regulatory competition can be traced to Charles Tiebout's (1956) original article arguing that a decentralized governmental system, with horizontally arrayed jurisdictions competing to attract residents on the basis of differing tax and benefit structures, produces efficient outcomes. The Tiebout model focuses on citizen-voter tastes for local public goods in the hypothetical context of a city resident contemplating a move to the suburbs and choosing among a number of towns. The model makes three assumptions. First, locational decisions will reveal individual preferences for public goods and levels of taxation: rational, forward-looking individuals, after surveying the range of available choices, will act in accordance with their preferences for location-specific bundles of goods. Second, a local public goods equilibrium can be established, if like producers of private goods and services, local government units compete with their public goods offerings to attract in-migration. Third, the promotion of competition between local governments should lead to an optimal balance between level of taxation and the provision of public goods. Given all this, there arises a general presumption favouring the provision of public goods at the local level. Notice that the essence of regulatory competition is that it provides a medium which ensures that the competition among jurisdictions takes place.

Taken literally, Tiebout's model has policy implications for only a limited class of government activities (Bratton and McCahery, 1997). It addresses the production of 'public goods', that is, goods and services produced by public authorities for which people are willing to pay taxes, such as police and fire protection, primary education, roads and sewers. Scholars since Tiebout have developed the analysis for firms (Oates and Schwab, 1988). In recent years, the original model of public goods production has been extended to government output of regulation. Under the expanded view, the public consumes and pays for regulatory outcomes such as contract enforcement, environmental regulation, health and safety standards, and stable labour relations (Myles, 1995). The extended Tiebout model assumes that governments are suppliers of legal structures and products. Like producers of any other good, these actors could and should be disciplined by market forces. Competitive pressures, so the theory goes, force governments to produce their regulatory products at competitive 'prices' (so that the benefits of governmental intervention exceed the costs) on pain of losing their customers, in this case citizens or businesses (Easterbrook, 1983). The normative strength of the theory lies in the hope that competition will stimulate experimentation, innovation, and product differentiation in regulation, as in markets for products (Calabresi, 1995). The process of refining the product (regulatory requirements and approaches) to meet consumer (societal) desires thus leads to the adoption of more efficient laws and enhances social welfare.

For regulatory competition theorists, centralized systems of standard-setting should be seen as regulatory cartels which, as any other form of collusion between competitors, inhibit the operation of the market, raise prices and reduce economic efficiency. Such intervention should therefore be eliminated or narrowed to the greatest extent possible.[9] Fundamentally, regulatory competition theory generates a strong presumption in favour of governmental action on a decentralized basis (Revesz, 1992). It is assumed that by increasing the lower units' subject-matter jurisdiction, decentralization expands opportunities for competitive lawmaking. Significantly, many of the benefits thus claimed for decentralization obtain whether or not it precipitates an outbreak of competition. Reducing the size of the regulatory unit narrows the variance in the distribution of preferences, reduces the likelihood that preferences will be bundled and, presumably, ameliorates some problem of asymmetrical information (Woolcock, 1996). Regulation, thus adapted to local conditions, is more likely to approach the ideal of consonance with citizen preferences.[10] At the same time, decentralization increases the probability that a diverse range of preferences will come to be manifested in regulation promulgated by one or another jurisdictions (Seabright, 1996). The localized experimentation, thus fostered, makes it possible for a range of regulatory strategies to appear, while simultaneously limiting the negative impact of unsuccessful experiments (Romano, 1993).

Finally, decentralization reduces the scope of the central government monopoly and ameliorates the negative effect of regulatory capture. Capture leads to bigger dead-weight costs when authority is exercised at higher levels of government. Local authorities have a lesser capacity to damage the economy. They cannot impose tariffs and quotas on imports; their licensing arrangements have a limited reach; and their limited resources reduce the capacity to offer significant subsidies. Incentives to interest groups, accordingly, decrease as authority vests in lower levels. These units of course remain subject to small-scale influence activities (Dixit et al., 1997). But, at this point, horizontal competition can have a disciplinary effect that minimizes the losses stemming from capture arrangements. Given mobility of people and factors, the imposition of costly and restrictive interest group legislation in one jurisdiction benefits a neighbouring jurisdiction with a less costly regime. As the factors vote with their feet, they affect the incentives of lawmakers – inefficient wealth transfers to favoured groups become less attractive than regulations that enhance the wealth of the larger population.

The list of relative advantages of decentralization and competition coalesces into a race to the top when projected into the standard evolutionary framework. Thus extended, the Tiebout model promises an efficient allocation of industrial activity among horizontally situated jurisdictions (Revesz, 1992). In a dynamic environment, the competitive forces that achieve this result should assure that only efficient regulation continues in effect. Over time, then, competition raises the quality of all regulation. In contrast, centralization and its secondary counterpart of coordination across junior units emerge as the regulatory equivalent of price-fixing, presumptively retarding the competitive evolution of efficient law. Accordingly, the proponents of central government intervention must bear the burden of showing why market forces will not eliminate the problem in due course.

Two universally recognized exceptions to this presumption of favouring decentralization should be noted. First, borders must be kept open so factor and citizen mobility can bring competitive discipline to regulation (Easterbrook, 1983). Authority to suppress anti-competitive lawmaking must be vested at higher levels of government, through either judicial or legislative intervention. The Commerce Clause of the United States Constitution is a case in point as it can be used by federal courts to strike down protectionist state measures, as well as by the federal government to pre-empt state legislation. Second, this higher authority must police the externalities pursuant to economic theory's command that the scope of regulation match the domain of its costs and benefits. Competing governments have an incentive to regulate so as to facilitate cross-border externalization by their citizens.[11] The classic example occurs when a jurisdiction excepts from its environmental laws a given type of pollution knowing that prevailing winds will blow the permitted particles across borders. Here, not only does the producer externalize a cost, but those affected by the externality have no voice regarding its regulation and have not traded their sufferance for higher incomes. With externalities, multiple jurisdictions can even race to the bottom, justifying either intervention by a higher-level unit or intergovernmental cooperation to remedy the situation (Stewart, 1993).

A third exception, for welfare and redistribution policies is widely (if not universally) acknowledged (Oates, 1972). Competing local governments have incentives to encourage new investment and immigration by rich citizens and to discourage immigration by poor citizens. It follows that a decentralized system probably leads to a lower level of government-mandated wealth redistribution than its citizens might prefer. This third exception would also justify centralized welfare provision (or central intervention to impose minimum welfare standards) (Gillette, 1994).[12]

3. THE DEBATE IN LEGAL FEDERALISM: THE RACE TO THE TOP VERSUS THE RACE TO THE BOTTOM

3.1 The Model and its Implications

The jurisdictional competition paradigm crosses the barrier that separates the public and private spheres to recast the public sector in private terms. Policy inquiry is diverted from the government's role as a benevolent maximizer of social welfare both in the provision of traditional public goods and as an economic regulatory to an exclusive preoccupation with the processes that bring the rules into existence. The legal federalism debate focuses on the legitimacy of this barrier-crossing. Proponents argue that the ensuing race to the top will ensure high standards of government service. Opponents respond that competitive government actors will forsake their mission and thereby race to the bottom.

To see this race-to-the-bottom perspective, consider how a proponent of a public interest approach would respond to the race-to-the-top theory. From a public interest perspective, dismantling federal regulations to encourage junior-level competition amounts to a betrayal of the public interest. With competition, the content of regulation and the level of public goods and taxation are dictated by the private preferences of a narrow, arbitrarily identified class of itinerant at-the-margin consumers, rather than by a dispassionate and responsible calculation of public welfare. The individual jurisdiction, forced to cater to the preferences of this narrow class, loses its ability to pursue its notion of the best interests of the citizens committed to remain within the jurisdiction for the long term. At the same time, dismantling federal regulations deprives disaggregated groups of states and localities of the technical ability to regulate multistate businesses, with the mere threat of disinvestments sufficing to move legislatures to satisfy firms' preferences (Stewart, 1993).

The race-to-the-bottom view shares an important point with its race-to-the-top opposite: both assume that government actors intensely compete for factors of production. Under the race-to-the-bottom theory, however, the race proceeds downward because competition forces the pursuit of policies further and further removed from the public interest. The characterization invites the remedy of pre-emptive centralization. If, for a particular subject matter, the race necessarily proceeds to the bottom, then a higher-level government should regulate the subject matter whether or not the competition presently determines the content of regulation at junior levels. This is best known as the justification for the federalism of environmental law.

The environmental law literature also contributes a restatement of race-to-the-bottom positions in economic terms. This provides that, without centralization, competition for production factors would leave states in a prisoner's dilemma respecting environmental standards (Sarnoff, 1997; Swire, 1996). The threat of production factors defecting to a competing state would deter any individual state from promulgating environmental standards consistent with its preferences. The greater the competition, the greater the disparity between the level of environmental protection in the public interest and that evolving in practice.

Proponents of jurisdictional competition have rebutted this description (Revesz, 2000). They argue that the prisoner's dilemma rests on a set of heroic assumptions, specifically the presence of fixed preferences for strict regulation across many jurisdictions, each of which believe that cost–benefit tradeoffs should not be applied to the subject matter. Competition for factors of production and collective action problems then undermine the jurisdiction's ability to adhere to the stated policy, producing a suboptimal result (Revesz, 1992). The critics contend that a more realistic set-up would depict a world of scarce resources in which the inevitable cost–benefit tradeoffs between levels of regulation and income would prevent the assumption of any *a priori* fixed preferences for a given level of regulation. Without fixed preferences across jurisdictions, a jurisdiction cannot assume that cooperation will yield higher payoffs, such that a prisoner's dilemma is no longer inevitable.[13] It remains possible in theory; but, say the critics, in practice it is unlikely that absolute, normatively based preferences, whether for stricter environmental rules or some other form of regulation, would exist across jurisdictions (Majone, 1991).[14]

The race-to-the-top view has the better of this discussion. Where once the race-to-the-top and the race-to-the-bottom views competed for attention as pragmatic opposites of equal strength, we now see a general presumption in competition's favour (Daines, 2001; Romano, 2001). The result is said to follow from economic theory; regulatory competition pursuant to the Tiebout framework has survived critical theoretical inspection, while the race-to-the-bottom view has not (Revesz, 1992). In the next section, we survey the limitations of the jurisdictional competition approach.

3.2 Limitations of the Model

Market failure

The virtues of regulatory competition derive from the forces generated by a functioning and competitive market for legal products. There are, however, a host of reasons to believe that this market rarely operates in the manner envisioned by regulatory competition optimists and is, in fact, often marked by market failures, notably a lack of adequate (never mind *perfect*) information (Esty, 1999). Because the market for locational rights is relatively *imperfect*, untrammelled regulatory competition cannot be counted on to produce optimal outcomes.[15] While these market shortcomings are not universally or uniformly present, their real-world frequency makes a strong presumption in favour of decentralized governance or high expectations from simple strategies of regulatory competition unwise.[16]

Externalities   Externalities represent a primary cause of failure in locational rights markets (Seabright, 1996). The inefficiency of markets where private and social costs diverge has long been understood (Pigou, 1918), and the extension of this principle in the public goods context to circumstances where a harm (or benefit) to be regulated falls outside the jurisdiction of the regulating authorities has nearly as long a history (Baumol and Oates, 1988). If regulators ignore impacts beyond their own jurisdictions, the standards they set will be systematically suboptimal (too low if they overlook transboundary regulatory benefits and too high if they disregard transboundary regulatory costs). A variety of such uninternalized externalities threatens market failure and allocative inefficiency with regard to decentralized regulation.

Externalities can be found in many realms but particularly plague certain regulatory domains such as environmental protection (Stewart, 2002). The classic externality is a *physical* pollution spillover such as air emissions blowing across political boundaries. For many years, for example, Britain did not control sulphur emissions from its power plants because most of the adverse effects were felt in Scandinavia or elsewhere. Given the prevailing winds, Britain did not suffer especially from acid rain, but its air pollution standards were suboptimal from an overarching perspective because it failed to internalize the costs of the pollution that fell beyond British borders. A similar acid rain dynamic exists between the United States and Canada as well as between China and Japan.

Externalities may also be *economic*.[17] Weak enforcement of antitrust rules or intellectual property rights in one nation may have a negative impact on the profits of foreign-based producers whose products are thereby squeezed out of the market. To the extent that these spillover effects are not based on market-clearing effects, but rather driven by strategic behaviour, suboptimal results must be anticipated.

To avoid welfare losses and market distortions, such externalities must be corrected through some form of interjurisdictional collective action. The theoretical logic behind the need for regulatory collaboration at an overarching level in the face of transboundary externalities is not much disputed even by regulatory competition advocates (Revesz, 1992). What remains contested is the pervasiveness and scale of such market-disrupting externalities. We believe that the degree of uninternalized externalities may, in fact, vary widely from one field of regulation to the next – with important implications for how much relative emphasis can be placed on regulatory competition.

Imperfect information   A second cause of market failure undermining the potential gains from regulatory competition derives from information deficiencies. For markets to work efficiently, the buyers must have 'perfect' information, which, in the context of regulatory competition, means sufficient data to determine whether the government is delivering an appropriate level of regulation and doing so in a cost-effective manner. The buyers (businesses and citizens) must also be fully informed about the alternative regulatory packages offered by competing jurisdictions, and they must be aware of the options that they have to exit or move.

This information may not be readily accessible. Some aspects of the requisite data will be relatively easy to obtain and to compare so long as the competing jurisdictions share the same language and legal traditions. For instance, an American company may well be able to identify state laws and regulatory burdens that might apply to its operations as it contemplates building a new factory somewhere in the United States. The same information-gathering will prove more difficult, however, in the European Union – or among other groups of independent nations – because of the greater cultural and regulatory heterogeneity of their component entities. In addition, information costs will often be prohibitive when the buyer is not a firm but an individual trying to determine where to live, when the scope of the inquiry covers a large number of regulatory variables (environment, health, safety, tax burden, support services, and so on) or when the options encompass many jurisdictions.

The likelihood of information-deficiency-induced market failures also mounts in some regulatory realms because of the high level of underlying uncertainty about regulatory costs and benefits (Esty, 1999). Thus, while average citizens may be able to judge whether the roads that a town provides are adequate, they will not be well positioned to determine whether the degree of air pollution protection provided by a particular jurisdiction matches their needs.

One other information problem should be mentioned, this one lying on the supply side. Law production results from deliberative, political processes. If asymmetrical information exists amongst competitive lawmakers, or one set of regulators fails properly to account for the choices of others, no equilibrium matching of regulation and preferences will result (Majone, 1996). Alternatively, one jurisdiction may inaccurately predict the tradeoff calculus prevailing in another, setting its regulatory standard lower (or higher) than necessary (Stewart, 1993). In either case, later development of a potentially full set of information will at least create an opportunity for a cure. Given competitive forces, neither interest group deals nor political stasis should get in the way of adjustment. Relative stakes should be pertinent once again: the greater the capital investment riding on a particular regulation, the less of a problem information asymmetries should present.

In sum, where the regulatory cost–benefit calculus is relatively clear, certain and visible, regulatory competition will be more likely to yield welfare benefits. But, in realms where the costs or benefits of governmental intervention are more obscure, operation of the market in locational rights may not enhance social welfare.

Lack of mobility   The lack of mobility of market participants may also lead to regulatory market failure. For regulatory competition to work, 'buyers' of standards and the legal regimes that support them must be able to move to the jurisdiction that offers the package of costs and benefits that most closely matches their own needs and values.[18] But the assumption of perfect mobility may not reflect reality.

The Tieboutian vision of 'people voting with their feet' bears little resemblance to the real world. Significant transaction costs will attend the individuals' changes of domicile. These costs will vary depending on both the distance of the move and the relevant conditions of the housing market and employment market. These costs relate directly to the geographic size of the home and target jurisdiction. The larger the community, the greater the cost barrier to the move, and thus citizens become less mobile (Mueller, 1989). Furthermore, cultural barriers and tradition affect mobility. In Europe, for example, the vast majority of people live all of their lives in their countries, and even towns, of origin (Bratton and McCahery, 2001). The elasticity of population migration as a function of policy variability appears, in fact, to be rather low.

In the case of businesses, market requirements and regulatory barriers dramatically constrain mobility. Many companies serve local markets or have large amounts of capital tied up in immovable assets. Thus, threats to migrate are often empty. Moreover, legal regimes can hinder mobility. The ability of European firms to move (by 'rechartering') in other Member States has been impeded, moreover, by the 'real seat' doctrine – the rule that the law governing the corporation is that of its actual seat of business, not simply that of a state in which it has filed appropriate papers or keeps a mailing address (Rammeloo, 2001; Charny, 1991). Experts agree that application of this doctrine in most Member States has been a key factor preventing the famous Delaware incorporation phenomenon from occurring in Europe (Cheffins, 1997; Edwards, 1999; McCahery and Vermeulen, 2001). The upshot of this discussion for regulatory competition theory is a notion of differential mobility: in advanced economies, capital mobility will exceed that of labour, particularly across national borders. The incidence of regulatory competition will reflect the differentials. We are unlikely to see competition for residents across national borders along the lines predicted by Tiebout's model of American local government. Instead, as we have seen in the context of securities regulation, national regulators will be competing to offer low-cost regulatory products to highly mobile factors. In effect, immobile factors of production – individuals in different countries or locations – will be competing for the only really mobile factor: capital (Bratton and McCahery, 2001).

Economies of scale and transaction cost savings   Economic theory teaches that if economies of scale are important, a single supplier may be more efficient than several competing suppliers. When regulatory economies of scale are present, centralized standard-setting procedures may thus be more efficient than regulatory competition.[19]

Some aspects of regulation are more technically complicated or analysis-intensive, making them susceptible to economies of scale that might overwhelm any benefits from multiple jurisdictions competing with diverse regulatory approaches. Some elements of regulation, moreover, are driven heavily by 'facts' that do not vary geographically – for example the safe level of human exposure to carcinogens – rather than by divergent circumstance and values. It may make sense, therefore, for bank regulation to be decentralized across the 50 US federal states or 15 EU member states. But having each US state or EU member state undertake the exhaustive and expensive analysis necessary to set its own pesticide residue tolerances makes less sense.

Absent centralized functions, independent regulators will either duplicate each other's analytic work or engage in time-consuming and complex negotiations over the division of technical labour. The poorer the jurisdiction, moreover, the more likely it is that its regulators will lack basic technical capacity and the resources necessary to do a competent and analytically rigorous job. Likewise, the smaller the regulating entity, the more likely it is to suffer from a lack of scientific, technical and analytic economies of scale. This reasoning does not mean that all food safety or air and water pollution standards should be set (or implemented) by central authorities. It simply suggests that at least *some* regulatory functions will be more efficiently carried out on a centralized basis while other activities will probably be more appropriately handled by decentralized governmental bodies (Esty, 1996).

Collective action – or high degrees of regulatory cooperation – will likewise be more efficient than regulatory competition when interjurisdictional trade is significant and cross-border regulatory transaction costs are high. For instance, inconsistent safety standards for internationally traded goods will generate substantial costs for producers and may even discourage them from exporting their products. Producers may need to spend vast sums on lawyers to spell out the particularized rules of each jurisdiction and then further amounts to tailor their products to local market requirements (Sykes, 1995). Even the most minor regulatory differences can have large economic implications. In such circumstances, it is generally recognized that convergence of standards or some form of mutual recognition policy will be desirable.[20]

Public choice and political problems The regulatory competition theory presumes that regulators know the interests of their constituents and act upon them (Revesz, 1992). If, however, special interests manipulate the standard-setting process or other public choice failures distort the regulatory options available to businesses and citizens, the market for locational rights will not function efficiently (Esty, 1996). Much of the recent debate over the value of regulatory competition turns on how pervasive public choice failures are presumed to be (Dua and Esty, 1997).

Incentive pictures on both the supply and demand side become more complex when we shift our attention to the competition for individuals and factors of production. Here, unlike cost–benefit calculations in conventional product markets, which on both the supply and demand side focus on the price and quality of a single product and result in the consummation or rejection of a two-party transaction, political cost–benefit calculations tie bundles of issues together. With regulation, the legal product's effect on local firms can present complex conflicts of interest. If, for example, the regulation is a new environmental control, government actors must consider the welfare effects on all constituents of polluting firms resident in the jurisdiction, in addition to effects on the residents who do (or do not) bear the cost of pollution. Differential effects present problems of preference aggregation, difficult political calculations, and problematic definition of the political interest.

The environmental law example brings us to the problem of winners and losers – all affected actors may not be satisfied with the regulatory result, whether or not competitively determined. The theory remits the losers to self-protection through relocation to a more satisfactory jurisdiction. But that suggestion may not solve the resulting problem of preference aggregation, given bundled regulatory products, information asymmetries, associational ties, cultural preferences and the out-of-pocket costs of a move. Furthermore, if interest groups favouring pollution effectively organize themselves so as to capture regulators throughout the class of horizontally situated jurisdictional alternatives, the list of clean air alternatives will dwindle. Losers may retain access to the regulatory policy process, after all. Given differential mobility, nothing in the competition model prevents this result.

This situation of horizontal capture characterizes the system of corporate law in the United States. Here mobility is relatively cheap and the legal product can be purchased separately; accordingly, factor preferences do determine the content of lawmaking. But the horizontally constituted legal structure remits the relocation decision to one interested group, corporate management, and excludes another whose interests often conflict, corporate shareholders. This ties the supply-side rent incentive to management's interest. Juridical path dependencies and collective action problems prevent the shareholders from exploiting any opportunities to register their influence on the law of any of the 50 available jurisdictions so as to make the competitive system work for their benefit. The result is regulatory capture constituted by a competitively driven lawmaking system. Since management's preferences vastly outweigh those of the shareholders in the resulting legal regime, it is suboptimal in the evaluation of most observers.

Competitive incentives   The black-box conception of the extended Tiebout model severely limits the model's explanatory capacity. With regulation, self-interested production does not necessarily imply the production of value-maximizing rules. Entrepreneurs produce for pecuniary gain, just as do government actors in the public choice model. Governments, unlike firms, do not labour under an immediate threat of bankruptcy that comes from excess production costs and high prices. As a result, agency problems in the production of public goods tend to be more substantial than those within firms.

Certainly, government actors sometimes can be relied on to produce value-enhancing rules. Presumably, this occurs when tax revenues, export earnings, jobs, technology, or other positive externalities yielded by the attraction of factors of production also happen to yield appropriate political benefits, either in the form of electoral advantage, satisfaction of the demands of favoured interest groups, or the satisfaction incident to enhancing public welfare.[21] It is less certain that this incentive relationship can be assumed as a systematic proposition. Indeed, where it does exist it can be ephemeral. Unlike firms, which must hew to the profit incentive, the objectives of government suppliers change over time with voter preferences.

The exercise of opening up regulatory competition's black box and inquiring as to competitive incentives shows that special conditions tend to obtain in those cases in which government entrepreneurship becomes wrought into the lawmaking structure. Consider corporate charter competition in this regard. There we do see recognizable buyer–seller relationships, but it also turns out that corporate charter competition is not a game that every state can play. Significant competitive incentives do not show up across the class of potential suppliers. Small jurisdictions tend to take the leading competitive roles. Similar conditions obtain in parallel cases of sale of juridical status – small island states tend to offer themselves as tax havens; Liberia, Panama, and Greece lead in the registration of ships. The explanation prevailing for Delaware probably applies across the board. Corporate franchise fees amount to 15 per cent of Delaware's tax base; the same cash flow would be a trivial percentage of the tax base of a much larger state.[22] Given a limited market, competitive success has a larger impact on the smaller government budget of a small jurisdiction. Political and financial incentives to create (or enter) a legal product market arise when such a significant payoff is held out. The incentive relationship lends plausibility to the product market in turn. The small jurisdiction's propensity to fiscal dependence on its legal business provides a structural assurance that customer interests will take precedence over all competing interests in local political deliberations (Bratton and McCahery, 1995; Bebchuk and Ferrell, 2001; Kahan and Kamar, 2002).

Network externalities Even when incentives to compete clearly are present, additional incentive problems may inhibit the evolution of the efficiency of law produced by state competition. Network externality models (Klausner, 1993), for example, show that a demand-side problem can cause suboptimal equilibria to evolve and product innovation to be chocked off in situations of intense competition. Supply-side problems may also arise. Product innovation presupposes an incentive to invest. The patent deters entry by competitors, assuring a potential return on investment in research and development. Conversely, if an innovation can be copied by a rival, then new technologies will not efficiently replace old technologies. Legal innovation leads to the production of public goods and carries no patent protection. As a consequence, competing states will have insufficient incentives to invest resources in producing efficient rules. State legislatures will see no point in entering a race to innovate if any resulting lead will be exhausted in a very short period of time (Ayres, 1996). The result of network and learning effects is that the continuous use of the dominant legal rule or code, even if not optimal, will further reduce the incentives for lawmakers to innovate. The reluctance to diverge from the existing framework means that even if new legal rules are created, parties will be unwilling to substitute the standard for non-standard terms. In short, the benefits that accrue to a standardized regime may be sufficient to outweigh the benefits that firms could gain by shifting to a new or modernized statute. Also, since potential first-users of new legislation do not have the advantage of future network benefits, such new forms may only emerge if the inherent benefits are of paramount importance. The switching costs constitute yet another reason that conservative lawmakers accept the *status quo*. The uncertainty about the future benefits of the introduction or modernization of new rules leads to the persistence of inefficient rules and delays genuine legal innovation.

In the contest of US corporate law, for example, the ingredients of increasing returns may involve the externalities that lock in firms to an inferior legal regime. However, even though the mere existence of increasing returns could certainly lead to inefficiency in theory, some commentators argue that the necessary conditions for its occurrence are easily avoidable. For instance, Romano (2001) argues that states, like Delaware, internalize the network externalities that would otherwise produce inefficient rules. On this view, lawmakers will have an incentive to internalize the costs of inefficient law by promulgating new legislation designed to limit the costs of the dominant legal network. But, if the lawmaking system is constrained due to significant switching costs and high barriers to entry, lawmakers may be satisfied with maintaining the inefficient rules (Bebchuk et al., 2002).

Bundling and pricing   A problem lies concealed beneath the Tiebout model's assumption that mobile citizens choose jurisdictions based on levels of taxation and public goods. Private goods are produced and sold separately. Public goods typically are jointly produced and made available on a bundled basis. They are not individually priced.[23] Similarly, regulation tends to apply across the board. Public goods and regulations, moreover, often come in complex packages (Bratton and McCahery, 1997). Furthermore, those complex packages influence the choices of consumers who display greater heterogeneity than those in standard product markets (Rose-Ackerman, 1983). The resulting supply- and demand-side complexity does make it less likely that consumer preferences will have a disciplining effect on producers.[24] It thus comes as no surprise that public economists have noted that there are several assumptions about private goods that cannot be extended to local public goods or regulation (Laffont, 1998, 2001).

Too narrow set of competitors
The second aspect of our critique of the Tieboutian or neo-Tieboutian models of regulatory competition centres on the fact that they represent far too limited a mechanism for exerting real competitive pressure. Competition between horizontally arrayed jurisdictions represents only one of the ways that government officials might be disciplined. Other sources of competition, involving a larger set of competitors, should be envisaged.

First, traditional regulatory competition theory tends to overlook the fact that the structure of federalism is inherently competitive. Dividing power among local, state and federal (and, increasingly, international) authorities generates competing policy perspectives. If decision processes at one level of government are suboptimal or distorted by bureaucratic sloth, special interest lobbying, corruption, elite domination, self-serving politicians, or simply inadequate information and analytic limitations, these shortcomings can be highlighted and perhaps even redressed by having parallel decision-making processes operating at higher or lower levels of government (Esty, 1999).

The same logic applies to the presence of governance structures above the nation-state. The Organisation for Economic Co-operation and Development (OECD) provides a measure of competitive pressure in this regard. The OECD's widely publicized periodic 'national reviews' of its member countries in a variety of regulatory areas often reveal policy weaknesses. OECD 'guidelines' and information-sharing activities serve, moreover, as benchmarks for policy-makers. Similarly, the World Trade Organization (WTO) and other regional trade organizations provide a useful source of discipline against protectionist governmental trade policies (Abbott, 1996).

Another form of policy-making discipline that gets short shrift from many regulatory competition theorists is the competition that exists between the various branches or departments of a government. As Breton argues, government actors are inherently competitive (Breton, 1996). In many policy areas, government departments will struggle to push their own agendas. In the United States, for example, the EPA (Environmental Protection Agency) and the DOE (Department of Energy) compete vigorously over the design of climate change strategies. These two governmental entities come at the greenhouse gas emissions problem from very different starting points; they bring to the issue quite different bureaucratic strengths; and they draw support and information from highly divergent constituencies. Still another manifestation of competition between government departments with shared regulatory responsibility is the recent conflict between the Securities and Exchange Commission and the Commodities Futures Trading Commission over share futures trading contracts (Scott and Wellons, 2002; Macey, 1994). A similar form of rivalry can be observed in the European Union structure, where Directorate Generals often advance competing strategies to address a common policy issue. While DG Environment will be essentially concerned by the environmental effects of a proposed legislation, the DG Enterprise will be mainly preoccupied by its potential impact on competitiveness.

Finally, competitive pressures will also be generated by NGOs (Esty, 1998). In the intellectual marketplace, it is often NGOs that most aggressively offer alternative data or information, competing analysis and new policy options. In the United States, the work of the Environmental Defense Fund (EDF) to develop the tradable SO_2 permit system that is now embodied in the 1990 US Clean Air Act provides an example of NGO-based policy ideas driving the regulatory process. At the international level, the work being carried out by a number of NGOs to persuade the WTO and its members to integrate environmental and labour concerns into the multilateral trading system offers another illustration of the vitality of NGO policy-making activity as a mechanism for improving governance.

We thus believe that, in contrast with Tieboutian models of regulatory competition which focus on horizontal competition between jurisdictions, governmental performance can be and should be sharpened by multiple sources of policy development and pressure – playing out at both horizontal and vertical levels and involving both state and non-state actors. This model of co-opetition further diverges from traditional regulatory competition in so far as it argues that optimal regulatory outcomes cannot be achieved through *competitive* pressures alone. The regulatory process will almost always benefit from a degree of *cooperation* among governmental actors and between government officials and non-governmental actors. This collaboration may occur in the form of shared mechanisms for issue-spotting, joint information gathering or data exchange, divided or collaborative research and analytic work, technology or policy transfers, and a division of labour in policy implementation and evaluation (Freeman, 1997). Such cooperation often generates economies of scale, permits an efficient degree of division of labour, and allows for the governance structure to extract the benefits of both centralized and decentralized processes.

3.3   The Alternative Model: Regulatory Co-opetition

Regulatory co-opetition plays out, as we noted above, at different levels and involves several types of actors. Three forms of regulatory co-opetition can be distinguished: (1) *inter*-governmental; (2) *intra*-governmental; and (3) *extra*-governmental.

Inter-governmental regulatory co-opetition
This term refers to the dynamics of competition and cooperation taking place among governments. This model of co-opetition has both horizontal and vertical dimensions. A dynamic of co-opetition can take place among or between governmental actors at the same jurisdictional level (for example across the US federal states or EU member states) or between governmental actors at different jurisdictional levels (for example between US federal and state authorities or the EU and Member States).

The main difference between the horizontal dimension of inter-governmental co-opetition and Tieboutian models of regulatory competition is that, while both models recognize the virtues of competition among state actors, the former model also recognizes that the regulatory process may in certain circumstances benefit from collaboration among horizontally arrayed governments. As illustrated by the US and EU systems, such cooperation can take the form of harmonized standards, mutual recognition procedures, or – at a lower level on the 'integration' scale – exchanges of data, information and policy experience. In the EC, for example, the Council adopted a directive on mutual assistance in 1977, which was designed to facilitate the exchange of information relating to the assessment of taxes (Terra and Wattel, 1997).

A dynamic of horizontal co-opetition can also be beneficial at the global level. The twentieth century has been marked by rigorous economic competition between the US and Europe, and this interplay has had an impact on domestic regulatory policies. Major regulatory reforms within these blocks have often been stimulated by competitive pressures, especially the fear of deteriorating competitiveness. For instance, the opening to competition of the telecommunications and energy markets in Europe was in large measure based on the view that such markets were much less efficient than the deregulated US markets and that this inefficiency threatened the competitiveness of European industry generally (European Commission, 1987). Absent such competitive pressures, the grip of telecommunications and energy state monopolies on the European economy would probably have remained largely intact. Americans and Europeans increasingly collaborate on a range of regulatory issues in an effort to remove non-tariff barriers and thus to facilitate trade. For instance, bilateral regulatory harmonization and mutual recognition efforts have been undertaken by the United States and the European Union in the context of the New Transatlantic Agenda (Krenzler and Shonmaker, 1996). The two blocks have agreed to consult each other in the early stages of drafting regulations and to rely to a greater extent on each other's technical resources and expertise (European Commission, 1997). In recent years, the United States and the European Union have also increasingly cooperated in the antitrust field (Fox, 2001). Some degree of regulatory cooperation is also taking place on a multilateral basis. Although differences in levels of development, geographic circumstances, technical competence and risk preferences make collaborative standard-setting and enforcement difficult, a measure of regulatory harmonization has, nevertheless, been achieved under the auspices of the WTO. This process is most advanced in the intellectual property (Abbott, 1997) and telecommunications (Bronckers and Larouche, 1997) arenas. Pressure is now mounting for the adoption of multilateral rules on competition policy as well (Petersmann, 1996; Subramanian, 1997). To some extent, regulatory harmonization and cooperation efforts have also been undertaken by a variety of organizations (including the International Labour Organisation – ILO, OECD, International Standards Organization – ISO, and

Codex Alimentarius) in the areas of labour (Bercusson, 2001), chemical testing (Esty, 1994), food safety (Bredahl and Forsythe, 1989), and banking standards (Dewatripont and Tirole, 1994; Tirole, 2002). In the environmental field, little regulatory convergence has been achieved due to the weakness of the United Nations Environment Program (UNEP), the opposition of developing countries, and hesitancy (fear of downwards harmonization) among some environmental groups (Esty and Geradin, 1997).

The dynamics of co-opetition among governmental actors also has a vertical dimension. As noted above, federalism, with its division of power among federal, state and local authorities, is inherently competitive. Inefficiencies or incapacity at one level of government will often be corrected by intervention at the other levels. For instance, the almost complete absence of governmental environmental activity in Europe's southern Member States was corrected by regulatory intervention at the EU level. Similarly, the expansion of US federal intervention in the environmental field in the 1970s was, in part, due to the failure of existing state regimes to adequately protect the environment (Kraft and Vig, 1990).

On the other hand, failures on the part of the federal authorities to carry out their duties or the risk that centralized governance structures may be subject to 'capture' contributes to the case for some degree of decentralization. For instance, during the Reagan administrations in the 1980s, state enforcement of federal antitrust laws compensated for the limited federal enforcement of such laws (Hawk and Laudati, 1996). The competitive pressures created by a federal structure with several levels of government – each level searching to extend or maintain its scope of power and influence – thus creates a system of 'checks and balances' that forces each level to strengthen its regulatory performance.

As useful as the tension of regulatory competition can be, we believe that good governance often requires a simultaneous degree of cooperation across different levels of government. In the United States, a good bit of federal regulation, notably environmental programmes, depends in whole or in part on state implementation. Other examples of the value of cooperation abound. In fact, the shared regulatory responsibility between the federal and state levels of government is so central to the US governance structure that the system is often referred to as 'cooperative federalism' (Mott, 1990). In many ways, the EU relies on the same model with a significant element (perhaps even more so than in the American system) of cooperation between federal/central and member state authorities (Geradin, 1997).

We see a growing role for vertical competition. Not only has the capacity of state and local authorities improved dramatically in recent years (Esty, 1999), but the sophistication of international institutions is rising steadily. Today, many regulatory issues are examined at local, state/provincial, federal/national, regional, and/or global levels. As in the case of a federal structure, the existence of several levels of regulatory activity puts pressure on governmental actors to carry out their tasks effectively and efficiently.

The strength of the competitive pressure varies from one regulatory domain to the next. Some tiers in this hierarchy remain generally too weak to add much value. Local decision-making continues to be plagued by technical and analytic incapacity in many places. And many international institutions are too weak to impose real pressure on their member nations. Clearly, building sufficiently strong international governance structures that enhance the system of 'checks and balances' and contribute to the competitive regulatory dynamic represents one of the greatest challenges facing the world community in the context of growing economic interdependence.

Intra-governmental regulatory co-opetition

We use this term to refer to the dynamics of competition and cooperation taking place *within* governments.

The competition may be *intra*-branch, especially within a multi-ministry executive (Breton, 1996). Ministries will often hold competing views over the need for and the content of a proposed legislation. This dynamic strengthens the regulatory process by forcing those initiating the regulatory process to come up with innovative and analytically serious proposals and to justify their approaches against the alternatives proposed by others. This give-and-take depends as well on the presence of cooperative mechanisms – information-sharing, assignment of primary drafting responsibilities, and coordinated implementation – to prevent the rivalry between such bodies from degenerating and resulting in duplication of work, regulatory diseconomies of scale, or even decision-making stalemates.

A dynamic of co-opetition can also be observed among the branches of governments. Courts generally have the power to strike down unconstitutional laws. They thus represent a barrier against the most blatant legislative abuses. Conversely, in some instances, legislative intervention may also be used to correct the distortions created by inconsistent court decisions. A form of competition can therefore be observed between the judiciary and the legislature.[25] In some cases, the executive or judicial branches take the heat for stalemated legislatures. In the 1970s and 1980s, for instance, the European Court of Justice facilitated the free movement of goods with a series of decisions (the so-called *Cassis de Dijon* jurisprudence) declaring that a product that is lawfully produced and marketed in one Member State must be admitted in another Member State except where the latter can refer to 'essential requirements' (Weatherill and Beaumont, 1999). This principle of mutual recognition was designed to compensate for the legislative inaction of the Council of Ministers which, due to the rule of unanimity voting, was unable to achieve its programme of product standards harmonization.

In representative democracies, furthermore, there are regular contests for power (including competition for control of the regulatory apparatus) in the form of voting.[26] Governments adopting inefficient or ineffective regulatory regimes thus risk being driven out of power. Given the relative lack of mobility of citizens, we see the lively tensions of intra-governmental rivalry as a more serious kind of competitive pressure than the hypothetical risk of exit that lies at the heart of Tieboutian models of regulatory competition. And, of course, while political parties compete for power, they must also cooperate between elections in the governing process. Bipartisan support will often be needed for constitutional or other major regulatory reforms.

Extra-governmental regulatory co-opetition

We use this term to refer to the dynamics of competition and cooperation taking place between governmental and non-governmental actors. Co-opetition between governmental and non-governmental actors promises to sharpen governmental performance by unleashing NGOs to act as intellectual competitors in the policy-making domain (Esty, 1998). In many cases, NGOs are better positioned to compete with regulators than are other governmental officials. NGOs are entrepreneurial and move to new issues quickly. NGOs operate in a fiercely competitive marketplace for media and public attention as well as fundraising resources. These pressures create a strong incentive to come up with creative solutions to environmental problems and to 'sell' their solutions to the public and in the appropriate governmental arena.

NGOs, operating in a 'cooperative mode' *vis-à-vis* governments, can also contribute significantly to optimizing the functioning of policy-making processes. They often supply observations, data and information that help build the analytic foundation for decision-making. They also serve as conduits for information flows to and from citizens. In the United States infant formula marketing case, the activities of NGOs prompted Abbott-Ross and Bristol-Myers to alter their infant formula regulatory strategy. Beyond bringing critical information 'up' to decision-makers, such NGO participation in the regulatory process also permits the involved groups to disseminate information 'down' to the disaggregated public, helping citizens to understand decisions made by distant officials. Finally, NGOs, which are able to mobilize social disapproval against a company or product, often help foster the internalization of regulatory norms. For example, it is unlikely that the certification of diamond as 'war-free' or tropical hardwoods as 'sustainable' would have occurred but for the NGOs trying to create a new social norm (Murphy, 2003).

Industry associations also impose competitive pressures on governments.

Like citizens' groups, they will often aggressively come up with relevant data and information, competing analyses and new policy options. In the area of swap transactions, the International Swap and Derivatives Association (ISDA) was formed to create standard documentation to eliminate the battle of the forms. Since the creation of the two master agreements in 1987, the ISDA has created documentation for a range of other derivatives, which has had a strong effect on the growth of the market (Scott and Wellons, 2002).

Proponents of regulatory competition may contend that co-opetition may lead to increased regulatory 'capture' by interest groups and, thus, reduced governmental transparency and accountability. Putting environmental NGOs, industry associations and other interests against each other, however, works to flesh out viable policies, induce investment in the creation of policy analysis and other valuable information, and generate countervailing forces that provide a 'watchdog' mechanism and therefore a check on 'capture' (Bratton and McCahery, 1995). It could also be argued that competing NGOs and industry associations simply create a cacophony of voices that ultimately cancel each other out. But this vision would be too simplistic. Good governance is not a zero-sum game. Competition between groups for governmental attention forces these entities to generate useful and credible material and to develop 'winning' proposals. This dynamic ensures that government officials will be able to choose among a large set of policy options and hear well-honed arguments where difficult choices must be made.

The benefits of cooperation between governmental and industry actors should also not be overlooked. In the context of prudential supervision, the Committee on Banking Regulations and Supervisory Practices of the Bank for International Settlements (BIS) has sought, in response to identified weaknesses in the original Accord, to amend, since June 1999, the Basle Accord (Scott and Wellons, 2002). At first glance, the objective of the new Accord is to modernize the regulatory regime in light of the development of new financial instruments, which have influenced the behaviour of banks. The proposed new shift of the regulatory system, reflected in the second consultative proposal issued in January 2001, is based on a market-oriented approach that would allow banks to use an internal ratings-based systems (IRB) approach for rating credit risk of individual banks and external credit assessments by rating agencies to weigh the risk of loans to borrowers in certain classes. After joint efforts with the banking industry to identify expand and modify the IRB approach, the Commission and the major banks have reached an agreement about the parameters for IRB.

Cooperation between industry associations and governmental actors can also be observed at the global level. The International Organization of Securities Commissions (IOSCO), an international, non-governmental body which consists of autonomous government agencies, self-regulatory organizations and market actors, has been one of the central institutions responsible for promoting the harmonization of multinational offerings of securities, capital adequacy standards for securities firms, and accounting standards (Underhill, 1995). The aim of IOSCO's working party on securities, for example, is to provide technical support in identifying the disclosure practices and legal requirements that enhance the process of raising capital, the objective of which is the adoption of harmonized disclosure requirements (for example, a common prospectus for the major securities exchanges where multinational offers are typically underwritten) (Biancheri, 1998).

4. SUMMARY AND CONCLUSIONS

We have argued that regulatory competition theory makes a critical point: market forces and the tensions they generate provide an important set of incentives for creativity, innovation, efficiency and forbearance among regulators. But simplistic Tieboutian models of horizontally arrayed governments competing for citizens and factories neither describe the full potential for competition-driven regulatory discipline nor paint a convincing picture of how to squeeze optimal results out of governmental processes.

More importantly, the results to be achieved by traditional regulatory competition will vary depending on the context. Where the market for regulatory results (or locational rights) closely resembles perfect competition, stronger and more constructive (welfare-maximizing) pressures can be anticipated from Tieboutian competition. While we may favour a presumption of competition, exceptions must be made where this market fails, due to uninternalized externalities, information limitations, public choice failures, or strategic behaviour in standard-setting.

Given real-world experience, which suggests that some degree of market failure will almost always be present, regulatory co-opetition represents a better model for achieving optimal governance. Harnessing inter-governmental, intra-governmental, and extra-governmental competitive pressures and simultaneously facilitating a degree of cooperation among the various participants in the regulatory process promises systematically improved outcomes. In this diverse and complex world of regulatory challenges, there remains a good bit of research to be done to identify the variables that determine the optimal mix of competitive and cooperative forces. But we see considerable promise in promoting a degree of 'regulatory ecology' through which different species of regulators and other actors coexist in relationships that are sometimes competitive and at other times symbiotic.

Many issues remain unresolved, and further investigation is necessary in order to assess the robustness of these arguments. In this regard, it is important to focus attention on a few issues. First, the large literature on regulatory competition mostly examines normative claims about the effect of competition on institutions and rules. More should be known about the effect of competition on the development of law. Most of the empirical work has been conducted in the United States. There is a need for more studies in Europe to provide comparison cross-culturally and across a wider variety of regulatory fields. This would be valuable in providing insights into the projected benefits of regulatory competition, as well as highlighting the regulatory fields and systems that may not actually benefit from the presence of lower-level competition. Second, we should know the circumstances in which federal intervention provides a more efficient alternative to lower level regulation (Bratton and McCahery, 1995; Bebchuk and Ferrell, 2001). Third, we need better evidence about the circumstances in which effective regulatory cooperation takes place. The work we have described above has shown the factors that may support effective horizontal co-opetition.

We have no doubt that regulatory competition will continue to receive the same attention in the future as it has done in the past. The general trend should move away from the perspective that applies Tiebout's regulatory competition model and shifts to an approach that acknowledges the diversity in geographic circumstances and preferences, while arguing for variations in regulatory approaches.

NOTES

1. This analysis, of course, is important for political scientists and legal scholars who are concerned with the protection of individual rights, see Weingast (1995); Easterbrook (1983). Law and economics has illuminated the tradeoffs involved when selecting a principle of federalism (that is, between economic efficiency, political participation, and individual liberties, see Inman and Rubinfeld (1997b).
2. The basic idea underlying the theory is that reducing the size of the regulating unit narrows the variance in the distribution of preferences and reduces the likelihood that the preferences will be bundled. Regulation, thus adapted to local conditions, is more likely to approach the ideal of consonance with citizen preferences. At the same time, decentralization increases the probability that a diverse range of preferences will come to be manifested in regulation promulgated by one or another jurisdiction. The localized experimentation thus fostered makes it possible for a range of regulatory strategies to appear, while simultaneously limiting the negative impact of unsuccessful regulatory experiments. Decentralization reduces the scope of the central government monopoly and ameliorates the negative effects of regulatory capture, see Woolcock (1996); Breton (1996); Scharpf (1999).
3. Romano (1993) has suggested that statutory law should be viewed as a product that is supplied by governments and purchased by firms. Ayres (1996) and Kahan and Kamar (2002) argue that the leading state has a high-powered incentive to continuously update its statutes and to create additional litigation, which preserves its first-mover advantage and generates a flow of cases.
4. The discipline of law-and-economics has made important contributions to the study of institutions and legal rules; see Newman (1998). Law-and-economics research has advanced our understanding of a broad range of legal subjects and legal systems; see Mattei (1997).

Law-and-economics provides a powerful analytical framework for analysing the legal and regulatory issues involved in the assignment of authority to lower-level jurisdictions; see Bratton et al. (1996); Esty and Geradin (2001b).

5. The subsidiarity principle, set forth in paragraph 2 of Art. 5 (ex 3b) EC concerns subject matter as to which the EC and the Member States share competences. It imposes a burden of proof to justify action by the higher level of government, seeking to assure, first, that EC action taken in lieu of Member State action is justified, and, second, that any authority thereby accorded the EC is limited to the minimum necessary to achieve the articulated objective; see Dashwood (1996). As such, subsidiarity is not a principle of decentralization even if it incorporates a presumption in decentralization's favour. It is instead a principle that guides the upward and downward allocation of regulatory authority within the federation.

6. For an analysis of the tradeoffs between risk-sharing by centralized and decentralized governments, see Persson and Tabellini (1996).

7. The race-to-the-bottom approach assumes that, given full mobility, investors will migrate to the jurisdiction where they can earn the highest rate of return. The content of regulation and the level of public goods and taxation are dictated by governments competing for scarce investment capital; see Wilson (1996).

8. We borrow the concept of 'co-opetition' from Adam Brandenburg and Barry Nalebuff's book of the same name Brandenburg and Nalebuff (1996). The book explains that the optimal strategy for business is often a mix of competitive and cooperative actions.

9. If faithfully applied, the regulatory competition model would suggest that global free trade agreements are also unnecessary, since localities should adopt optimal trade policies on their own. Yet in the WTO arena, regulatory competition advocates recognize market failures of the kind discussed below. For a discussion of this apparent contradiction, see Farber (1997).

10. An incidental cost benefit can also be suggested. Reconciliation of preferences through political channels of dialogue and voting costs more than reconciliation through market transactions; see Gilson and Schwartz (2001).

11. If a law is not cost beneficial but involves no externalities, there is at least some local incentive to change it; if the costs are externalized, there is no local incentive to make a change. Product liability laws that favour locals exemplify this; see Schill (1991).

12. Daniel Shaviro (1992), makes an additional point: because here regulation and attendant politics come down to the determination of cash amount, localized preference diversity presents a less important value.

13. LeBoeuf (1994), offers a different formulation of this point. He notes that a state that imposes anti-pollution legislation transfers wealth away from industry to those who have a clean environment. If the redistributive move embodied in the legislation is Kaldor–Hicks superior (actors in the aggregate are better off although some are left worse off), then the state can make a second redistributive move (a tax break, for example) that compensates industry for the cost of compliance, and still be ahead on a net basis in the end. If the state does not make the second redistributive move, it presumably prefers the redistributive result of the anti-pollution legislation. If the state enacts no anti-pollution legislation, its residents presumably prefer to devote resources to capital investment. Federal intervention is, accordingly, redistributive.

14. Gastios and Seabright (1989) assert that a prisoner's dilemma at the international level alone does not provide a sufficient justification for a delegation of regulatory authority to the supranational level.

15. The market for corporate law, for example, suffers from a surfeit of agency problems on the demand side; see Bratton and McCahery (1995).

16. It is worth pointing out, moreover, that there is very little evidence about the performance of state competition. The most extensive body of empirical research focuses on the effect of state competition on shareholder wealth in Delaware; see Bhagat and Romano (2001) (surveying empirical studies). Unsurprisingly, the evidence is mixed. A number of studies show that firms reincorporating in Delaware have higher abnormal returns, which supports the arguments of the race-to-the-top proponents in US corporate law; see Daines (2001)

(finding evidence that companies in Delaware have higher Tobin's Q). But recent work challenged the main elements of Daines' study, suggesting that wide fluctuation of the Delaware co-efficient over the period of the study does not easily support the view that Delaware law improves firms' market value; see Bebchuk, Cohen and Ferrell (2002).

17. There is an ongoing debate, which we will not rehearse here, about whether economic externalities are 'real' or merely pecuniary; compare Revesz (1992) with Esty (1996).

18. The Tiebout model assumes full mobility of factors of production. Scholars note that this assumption is implausible. Formal showings confirm that the slightest relaxation of this assumption leads to inefficient public goods production; see Wilson (1996).

19. Industry sectors where large economies of scale can be achieved (for example electricity production and transmission) are generally considered to be 'natural monopolies'. Similarly, areas where important regulatory economies of scale can be achieved may be considered to be 'natural legal monopolies'; see Viscusi et al. (2001).

20. Esty and Geradin (1998) explain that 'harmonization' need not imply absolutely uniform standards. Alternative forms of harmonization or regulatory 'convergence' may permit some degree of standardization without the concomitant efficiency losses that single standards that do not match local needs generate. Harmonization debates themselves often entail competition over whose standards should be adopted. And agreement on a common standard need not bring an end to regulatory competition. Many forms of harmonization are flexible and open enough to allow continued debate over and refinement of the standards selected; see Leebron (1996).

21. Or, alternatively, the particular factor cuts an advantageous deal directly with the responsible government actor.

22. Romano (1993), maintains that there is a positive relationship between franchise revenue and corporate law responsiveness as evidence of state competition. Some, however, counter that the more appropriate measure of states' incentives to compete is marginal incorporation revenue; see Kahan and Kamar (2001). While Romano (2001) concedes the force of Kahan and Kamar's objection, she nevertheless speculates that since states enjoy the freedom to incorporate in the state of their choice, it may be that there may be a positive relation between marginal and total revenue.

23. We note, however, that this problem of joint supply can be ameliorated in theory through technological segregation or other forms of unbundling.

24. Many public economists find Tiebout's location model to be an unsatisfactory attempt to solve the problem of ascertaining individual's preferences respecting public goods; see Bratton and McCahery (1997) (summarizing literature).

25. As pointed out by Ogus (1999), competition may also take place between different court systems with overlapping jurisdictions. For instance, the struggle between the Chancery Courts and the Common Law rivals had a significant impact on the development of legal principles in the United Kingdom.

26. To some extent, political parties competing for power can be compared to firms engaged in a competitive bidding for a monopolistic franchise power to provide a service, the competition serving to ensure that the firm offering the most efficient prices and services will be selected; see Ogus (1999).

REFERENCES

Abbott, Frederick M. (1997), 'The Future of the Multilateral Trading System in the Context of TRIPS', *Hastings International and Comparative Law Review*, **20**, 661–82.

Abbott, Kenneth W. (1996), 'Defensive Unfairness: The Normative Structure of Section 301', in Jagdish N. Bhagwati and Robert E. Hudec (eds), *Fair Trade and Harmonization, Prerequisites for Free Trade*, vol. 2: Legal Analysis, Cambridge, MA: MIT Press, pp. 415–71.

Alesina, Alberto and Romain Wacriarg (1999), 'Is Europe Going Too Far?', *NBER Working Paper*, no. 6883.

Ayres, Ian (1996), 'Supply-side Inefficiencies in State Competition for Corporate Charters', in William W. Bratton, Joseph A. McCahery, Sol Picciotto and Colin Scott (eds), *International Regulatory Competition and Coordination: Perspectives on Economic Regulation in Europe and the United States*, Oxford: Oxford University Press, pp. 239–56.

Bar-Gil, Oren, Michal Barzuza and Lucian Bebchuk (2002), 'A Model of State Competition in Corporate Law', *Harvard Law School and John M. Olin Center for Law, Economics and Business, Working paper*.

Baumol, William J. and Wallace E. Oates (1988), *The Theory of Environmental Policy*, Cambridge: Cambridge University Press.

Bebchuk, Lucian and Allen Ferrell (2001), 'A New Approach to Takeover Law and Regulatory Competition', *Virginia Law Review*, 111–64.

Bebchuk, Lucian, Alma Cohen and Allen Ferrell (2002), 'Does the Evidence Favor State Competition in Corporate Law?', *California Law Review*, **90**, 1775–822.

Bednar, Jenna, John Ferejohn and Geoffrey Grant (1996), 'The Politics of European Federalism', *International Review of Law and Economics*, **16**, 279–94.

Bercusson, Brian (2001), 'Regulatory Competition in the EU System: Labour', in Daniel C. Esty and Damien Geradin (eds), *Regulatory Competition and Economic Integration, Comparative Perspectives*, Oxford: Oxford University Press, pp. 241–62.

Bhagat, Snajai and Roberta Romano (2001), 'Event Studies and the Law: Part II – Empirical Studies of Corporate Law', *Yale University, Working Paper*.

Biancheri, Carlo (1998), 'Cooperation Among Supervisory Authorities under the ISD', in Guido Ferranrini (ed.), *European Securities Markets – The Investment Services Directive and Beyond*, The Hague: Kluwer Law International, pp. 363–71.

Brandenburg, Adam and Barry Nalebuff (1996), *Co-opetition*, New York: Doubleday.

Bratton, William W. and Joseph A. McCahery (1995), 'Regulatory Competition, Regulatory Capture, and Corporate Self-Regulation', *North Carolina Law Review*, **73**, 1861–948.

Bratton, William W. and Joseph A. McCahery (1997), 'The New Economics of Jurisdictional Competition: Devolutionary Federalism in a Second-Best World', *Georgetown Law Journal*, **86**, 201–78.

Bratton, William W. and Joseph A. McCahery (2001), 'Tax Coordination and Tax Competition in the European Union: Evaluating the Code of Conduct on Business Taxation', *Common Market Law Review*, **38**, 677–718.

Bratton, William W., Joseph A. McCahery, Sol Picciotto and Colin Scott (eds) (1996), *International Regulatory Competition and Coordination, Perspectives on Economic Regulation in Europe and the United States*, Oxford: Oxford University Press.

Bredahl, Maury E. and Kenneth W. Forsythe (1989), 'Harmonizing Phytosanitary and Sanitary Regulations', *World Economy*, **12** (2), 189–206.

Breton, Albert (1996), *Competitive Governments: An Economic Theory of Politics and Public Finance*, Cambridge: Cambridge University Press.

Bronckers, Marco and Pierre Larouche (1997), 'Telecommunications Services and the World Trade Organization', *Journal of World Trade*, **31**, 5–48.

Calabresi, Stephen (1995), 'A Government of Limited and Enumerated Powers: In Defense of *United States v. Lopez*', *Michigan Law Review*, **94**, 752–831.

Centre for European Economic Policy Research (CEPR) (1993), *Making Sense of*

Subsidiarity: How Much Centralization for Europe?, London: Centre for Economic Policy Research.

Charny, David (1991), 'Competition Among Jurisdictions in Formulating Corporate Rules: An American Perspective on the "Race to the Bottom" in the European Communities', *Harvard International Law Journal*, **32**, 423–56.

Cheffins, Brian R. (1997), *Company Law: Theory, Structure and Organization*, Oxford: Oxford University Press.

Choi, Stephen J. and Andrew T. Guzman (2001), 'Choice and Interpretation in Corporate Law', *Virginia Law Review*, **87**, 961–90.

Daines, Robert (2001), 'Does Delaware Improve Firm Value?', *Journal of Financial Economics*, **62**, 525–58.

Dashwood, Alan (1996), 'The Limits of European Community Powers', *European Law Review*, **21**, 113–28.

Dewatripont, Mathias and Jean Tirole (1994), *The Prudential Regulation of Banks*, Cambridge, MA: MIT Press.

Dixit, Avinash, Gene M. Grossman and Elhanan Helpman (1997), 'Common Agency and Coordination: General Theory and Application to Government Policy Making', *Journal of Political Economy*, **105**, 752–69.

Dowding, Keith, P. John and S. Biggs (1994), 'Tiebout: A Summary of the Empirical Literature', *Urban Studies*, **31**, 767–97.

Dua, André and Daniel C. Esty (1997), *Sustaining the Asian Pacific Miracle: Environmental Protection and Economic Integration*, Washington, DC: Institute for International Economics.

Easterbrook, Frank (1983), 'Antitrust and the Economics of Federalism', *Journal of Law and Economics*, **26**, 23–50.

Easterbrook, Frank (1994), 'Federalism and European Business Law', *International Review of Law and Economics*, **14**, 125–32.

Edwards, Vanessa (1999), *EC Company Law*, Oxford: Oxford University Press.

Esty, Daniel C. (1994), *Greening the GATT: Trade, Environment and the Future*, Washington, DC: Institute for International Economics.

Esty, Daniel C. (1996), 'Revitalizing Environmental Federalism', *Michigan Law Review*, **95** (3), 570–653.

Esty, Daniel C. (1998), 'Non-Governmental Organizations at the World Trade Organization: Cooperation, Competition, or Exclusion', *Journal of International Economic Law*, **1** (1), 123–47.

Esty, Daniel C. (1999), 'Toward Optimal Environmental Governance', *New York University Law Review*, **74**, 1495–574.

Esty, Daniel C. and Damien Geradin (1997), 'Market Access, Competitiveness and Harmonization', *Harvard Environmental Law Review*, **21**, 265–336.

Esty, Daniel C. and Damien Geradin (1998), 'Environmental Protection and International Competitiveness: A Conceptual Framework', *Journal of World Trade*, **32**, 5–46.

Esty, Daniel C. and Damien Geradin (2001a), 'Regulatory Co-Opetition', in Daniel C. Esty and Damien Geradin (eds), *Regulatory Competition and Economic Integration, Comparative Perspectives*, Oxford: Oxford University Press, pp. 30–46.

Esty, Daniel C. and Damien Geradin (eds) (2001b), *Regulatory Competition and Economic Integration, Comparative Perspectives*, Oxford: Oxford University Press.

European Commission (1987), *Toward a Dynamic Economy – Green Paper on the Development of the Common Market for Telecommunications Services and Equipment*, COM (87) final (1987) 290.

European Commission (1997), *Regulatory Competition: Promoting Trade While Facilitating Consumer Protection*, joint statement of US–EU Summit, 5 December 1997.

Farber, Daniel (1997), 'Symposium: The Allocation of Government Authority: Environmental Federalism in a Global Economy', *Virginia Law Review*, **83**, 1283–319.

Fox, Eleanor M. (2001), 'Antitrust Law on a Global Scale: Races Up, Down and Sideways', in Daniel C. Esty and Damien Geradin (eds), *Regulatory Competition and Economic Integration*, Oxford: Oxford University Press, pp. 348–63.

Freeman, Jody (1997), 'Collaborative Government in the Administrative State', *University of California at Los Angeles Law Review*, **45**, 1–87.

Gastios, Konstantine and Paul Seabright (1989), 'Regulation in the European Community', *Oxford Review of Economic Policy*, **5**, 37–60.

Geradin, Damien (1997), *Trade and the Environment: A Comparative Study of EC and US Law*, Cambridge: Cambridge University Press.

Gillette, Clayton P. (1994), 'Expropriation and Institutional Design in State and Local Government', *Virginia Law Review*, **80**, 625–87.

Gilson, Ronald J. and Alan Schwartz (2001), 'Sales and Elections as Methods for Transferring Corporate Control', *Theoretical Inquiries in Law*, **2**, 783–814.

Hawk, Barry E. and Laraine L. Laudati (1996), 'Antitrust Federalism in the United States and Decentralization of Competition Enforcement in the European Union', *Fordham International Law Journal*, **20**, 20–49.

Inman, Robert P. and Daniel L. Rubinfeld (1997a), 'Rethinking Federalism', *Journal of Economic Perspectives*, **11**, 43–64.

Inman, Robert P. and Daniel L. Rubinfeld (1997b), 'The Political Economy of Federalism', in Dennis C. Mueller (ed.), *Perspectives on Public Choice*, Cambridge: Cambridge University Press, pp. 73–105.

Inman, Robert P. and Daniel L. Rubinfeld (1998), 'Subsidiarity and the European Union', in Peter Newman (ed.), *The New Palgrave Dictionary of Economics and Law*, London: Macmillian Reference Ltd, pp. 545–51.

Inman, Robert P. and Daniel L. Rubinfeld (2000), 'Federalism', in *The Encyclopedia of Law and Economics*, vol. 5, pp. 661–91.

Kahan, Marcel and Ehud Kamar (2001), 'Price Discrimination in the Market for Corporate Law', *Cornell Law Review*, **86**, 1205–56.

Kahan, Marcel and Ehud Kamar (2002), 'The Myth of State Competition in Corporate Law', *Stanford Law Review*, **55**, 679–749.

Klausner, Michael (1993), Corporations, Corporate Law and Networks of Contracts', *Virginia Law Review*, **81**, 757–852.

Kletzer, Kenneth and Jürgen von Hagen (2000), 'Monetary Union and Fiscal Federalism', *Centre for Economic Policy Research, Working Paper*, no. 2625.

Kraft, Michael E. and Norman J. Vig (1990), 'Environmental Policy from the Seventies to the Nineties: Continuity and Change', in Norman J. Vig and Michael E. Kraft (eds), *Environmental Policy in the 1990s*, Washington, DC: CO Press, pp. 3–26.

Krenzler, Horst G. and Astrid Shonmaker (1996), 'A New Transatlantic Agenda', *European Foreign Affairs Review*, **1**, 9–28.

Laffont, Jean-Jacques (1988), *Fundamentals of Public Economics*, Cambridge, MA: MIT Press.

Laffont, Jean-Jacques (2001), *Incentives and Political Economy*, Oxford: Oxford University Press.

LeBoeuf, Jacques (1994), 'The Economics of Federalism and the Proper Scope of the Federal Commerce Power', *San Diego Law Review*, **31**, 555–616.

Leebron, David W. (1996), 'Lying Down with Procrustes: An Analysis of Harmonization Claims', in Jagdish N. Bhagwati and Robert E. Hudec (eds), *Fair Trade and Harmonization, vol I: Economic Analysis*, Cambridge, MA: MIT Press, pp. 41–118.

Levinson, Arik (1996), 'Environmental Regulations and Industry Location: International and Domestic Evidence', in Jagdish H. Bhagwati and Robert E. Hudec (eds), *Fair Trade and Harmonization, Prerequisites for Free Trade, vol I: Economic Analysis*, Cambridge, MA: MIT Press, pp. 429–58.

Macey, Jonathan R. (1994), 'Administrative Agency Obsolescence and Interest Group Foundation: A Case Study of the SEC at Sixty', *Cardozo Law Review*, 909–49.

Macey, Jonathan R. (2000), 'The "Demand" for International Regulatory Cooperation: Public-Choice Perspective', in George A. Bermann, Matthias Herdegen and Peter L. Lindseth (eds), *Transatlantic Regulatory Cooperation, Legal Problems and Political Prospects*, Oxford: Oxford University Press, pp. 147–66.

Majone, Giandomenico (1991), 'Market Integration and Regulation: Europe After 1992', *European University Institute, Working paper*.

Majone, Giandomenico (1996), *Regulating Europe*, London: Routledge.

Mattaei, Ugo (1997), *Comparative Law and Economics*, Ann Arbor: University of Michigan Press.

McCahery, Joseph A. and Erik Vermeulen (2001), 'The Evolution of Closely Held Business Forms in Europe', *Journal of Corporation Law*, **26**, 855–78.

McKinnon, Ronald and Thomas Nechyba (1997), 'Competition in Federal Systems: The Role of Political and Financial Constraints', in John Ferejohn and Barry R. Weingast (eds), *The New Federalism: Can the States Be Trusted?*, Stanford, CA: Hoover Press, pp. 3–61.

Mueller, Dennis C. (1989), *Public Choice II*, Cambridge: Cambridge University Press.

Mott, Richard (1990), 'Federal–State Relations in US Environmental Law: Lessons from the American Experience', *European University Institute Working Paper, EPU*, no. 90/2.

Murphy, Dale D. (2004), *The Structure of Regulatory Competition: Corporations and Public Policies in a Global Economy*, Oxford: Oxford University Press.

Myles, Gareth D. (1995), *Public Economics*, Cambridge: Cambridge University Press.

Newman, Peter (1998), *The New Palgrave Dictionary of Economics and the Law*, London: Macmillan Reference Ltd.

Oates, Wallace E. (1972), *Fiscal Federalism*, New York: Harcourt Brace Jovanovich.

Oates, Wallace E. and Richard M. Schwab (1988), 'Economic Competition Among Jurisdictions: Efficiency Enhancing or Distortion Inducing?' *Journal of Public Economics*, **35**, 333–54.

Ogus, Anthony (1999), 'Competition Between National Legal Systems: A Contribution of Economic Analysis to Comparative Law', *International and Comparative Law Quarterly*, **48**, 405–18.

Persson, Torsten and Guido Tabellini (1996), 'Federal Fiscal Constitutions: Risk Sharing and Moral Hazard', *Econometrica*, **64**, 623–46.

Petersmann, Ernst-Ulrich (1996), 'International Competition Rules for Governments and Private Business', *Journal of World Trade*, **30**, 5–35.

Pigou, Arthur (1918), *The Economics of Welfare*, London: Macmillan.

Rammeloo, Stephan (2001), *Corporations in Private International Law*, Oxford: Oxford University Press.

Revesz, Richard L. (1992), 'Rehabilitating Interstate Competition: Rethinking the "Race-to-the-Bottom" Rationale for Federal Environmental Regulation', *New York University Law Review*, **67**, 1210–54.

Revesz, Richard L. (2000), 'Environmental Regulation in Federal Systems', *Yearbook of European Environmental Law*, **1**, 1–35.

Romano, Roberta (1993), *The Genius of American Corporate Law*, Washington, DC: American Enterprise Institute Press.

Romano, Roberta (2001), 'The Need for Competition in International Securities Regulation', *Theoretical Inquiries in Law*, **2**, 387–562.

Rose-Ackerman, Susan (1983), 'Tiebout Models and the Competitive Ideal: An Essay on the Political Economy of Government', in John M. Quigley (ed.), *Perspectives on Local Public Finance and Public Policy*, London: JAI Press, pp. 23–46.

Sarnoff, Joshua D. (1997), 'The Continuing Imperative (But Only from a National Perspective) for Federal Environmental Protection', *Duke Environmental Law Policy Forum*, 225–318.

Scharpf, Fritz (1999), *Governing in Europe, Effective and Democratic?*, Oxford: Oxford University Press.

Schill, Michael H. (1991), 'Uniformity or Diversity: Residential Real Estate Finance Law in the 1990s and the Implications of Changing Financial Markets', *California Law Review*, **64**, 1261–320.

Scott, Hal S. and Philip A. Wellons (2002), *International Finance – Transactions, Policy, and Regulation*, New York: Foundation Press.

Seabright, Paul (1996), 'Accountability and Decentralization in Government: An Incomplete Contracts Model', *European Economic Review*, **40**, 61–89.

Shaviro, Daniel (1992), 'An Economic and Political Look at Federalism in Taxation', *Michigan Law Review*, **90**, 895–968.

Stewart, Richard B. (1993), 'Environmental Regulation and International Competitiveness', *Yale Law Journal*, **102**, 2039–106.

Stewart, Richard B. (2002), 'The Importance of Law and Economics for European Environmental Law', *Yearbook of European Environmental Law*, **2**, pp. 1–45.

Subramanian, Arvind (1997), 'Multilateral Rules on Competition Policy – A Possible Way Forward', *Journal of World Trade*, **31**, 95–115.

Swire, Peter P. (1996), 'The Race to Laxity and the Race to Undesirability: Explaining Failures in Competition Among Jurisdictions in Environmental Law', *Yale Journal of Regulation*, **14**, 67–109.

Sykes, Alan O. (1995), *Product Standards for Internationally Integrated Goods and Markets*, Washington, DC: Institute of International Economics.

Terra, Ben J.M. and Peter J. Wattel (1997), *European Tax Law*, Deventer: Kluwer Fiscal Publishers.

Tiebout, Charles M. (1956), 'A Pure Theory of Local Public Expenditures', *Journal of Political Economy*, **64**, 416–24.

Tirole, Jean (2002), *Financial Crises, Liquidity, and the International Monetary System*, Princeton: Princeton University Press.

Underhill, Geoffrey R.D. (1995), 'Keeping Governments Out of Politics: Transnational Securities Markets, Regulatory Cooperation, and Political Legitimacy', *Review of International Studies*, **21**, 251–78.

Van den Bergh, Roger (1996), 'Economic Criteria for Applying the Subsidiarity Principle in the European Community: The Case of Competition Policy,' *International Review of Law and Economics*, **16**, 363–83.

Van den Bergh Roger (1998), 'Subsidiarity as an Economic Demarcation Principle and the Emergence of European Private Law', *Maastricht Journal of European and Comparative Law*, **5**, 129–52.

Viscusi, W. Kip, John M. Vernon and Joseph E. Harrington, Jr (2001), *Economics of Regulation and Antitrust*, Cambridge, MA: MIT Press.

Weatherill, Stephen and Paul Beaumont (1999), *EU Law, The Essential Guide to the Legal Workings of the European Union*, London: Penguin Books.

Weingast, Barry (1995), 'The Economic Role of Political Institutions: Market Preserving Federalism and Economic Development', *Journal of Law, Economics and Organization*, **11**, 1–31.

Wilson, John Douglas (1996), 'Capital Mobility and Environmental Standards: Is There a Theoretical Basis for a Race to the Bottom?' in Jagdish N. Bhagwati and Robert E. Hudec (eds), *Fair Trade and Harmonization, Prerequisites for Free Trade, vol I: Economic Analysis*, Cambridge, MA: MIT Press, pp. 393–427.

Woolcock, Stephen (1996), 'Competition Among Rules in the Single European Market', in William W. Bratton, Joseph A. McCahery, Sol Picciotto and Colin Scott (eds), *International Regulatory Competition and Coordination, Perspectives on Economic Regulation in Europe and the United States*, Oxford: Oxford University Press, pp. 289–322.

6. Accountability and transparency in regulation: critiques, doctrines and instruments

Martin Lodge[1]

The widely proclaimed rise of the regulatory state (Majone, 1997; Loughlin and Scott, 1997; Moran, 2002) has led to a renewed emphasis on debates concerning accountability and transparency. The perception of limited accountability and transparency of regulatory regimes has been at the forefront of criticisms by the media, the wider public, business and so-called public interest groups. For example, debates emerged to the extent to which regulators should be obliged to report to parliamentary committees and how transparent their decision-making should be vis-à-vis government departments, the industry and, more widely, citizens. Similarly, accountability and transparency have also become prominent features in the talk about 'governance', as promoted by diverse groups and organizations such as the World Bank, the International Monetary Fund and the OECD, and by non-governmental organizations, for example 'Transparency International'. Universal endorsement by such a diversity of actors suggests that the appeal of these terms is primarily based on them meaning different things to different people. Questions of who is accountable and transparent, to whom and on what terms therefore represent crucial dimensions in any regulatory regime and therefore deserve critical analysis. In addition, three partly overlapping discussions make the study of 'who is accountable to whom and for what' in the regulatory state particularly pertinent: first, questions as to the changing nature of policy-making and the impact of such institutional change on the quality of citizenship; second, questions of designing control mechanisms as discussed in the principal–agent literature; and third, debates as to the extent to which regulation is different to traditional public administration concerns (see also Scott, 2000, 40–43).

One of the features of the 'rise' of the regulatory state at the end of the twentieth century has been the rearranging of governmental architectures, control mechanisms and relationships between actors. The analysis of broad policy change has gone hand in hand with debates concerning the impact of such policy change on the quality and extent of citizenship rights. Apart from changing ownership structures in various service delivery domains, the rise of the 'regulatory state' has been associated with the creation of quasi-independent agencies, the supposed formalization of relationships between actors as well as the increasing and complex number of actors involved in the regulatory space (Loughlin and Scott, 1997; Scott, 2001, 2000; Hancher and Moran, 1989). This has resulted in over- and under-lapping relationships across regulatory regimes at the local, regional, national and international level, involving to a varying extent government departments, politicians, regulatory bodies, 'target populations', firms, shareholders and the wider public.[2] Sources of demands to be accountable and transparent range from coercion to more voluntary forms of acceptance.

Furthermore, the shift to the regulatory state is said to have created concerns about the democratic legitimacy of particular regulatory decision-making, given that such decisions are often not merely highly technocratic but highly value-based choices. Regulatory decision-making often involves politically sensitive tradeoffs, for example between values of economic efficiency, social and environmental objectives as well as security of supply concerns, which are seen to have been moved from majoritarian to non-majoritarian institutions (Baldwin and Cave, 1999, 286; see also Berry, 1979).

The move towards the regulatory state has also widely been held to imply a change in the quality of citizenship, namely a move from a political conception of citizenship to that of an economic agency. Whereas in the 'age' of the welfare state citizenship was seen to include rights to particular services, it is suggested that the age of the regulatory state has brought about a reduced conception of citizenship, limited to that of the individual provided with the contractual rights of a consumer (Stewart, 1992). This criticism has led to claims of increased economic inequality and hardship that are said to signify a deterioration in the quality of standards of citizenship (Haque, 2001, 71) and a decline in accountability (Falconer and Ross, 1999). As a result, the literature has been filled with contributions and suggestions on mechanisms enhancing the accountability of regulatory agencies via parliamentary oversight (see Graham, 1997), the choice of appropriate (rather than non-appropriate) accountability modes (Romsek, 2000), the use of both vertical and horizontal measures (via courts, professional standard-setters and auditors) (Scott, 2000, 43) and the significance attached to output- rather than input-based understandings of legitimacy (Majone, 1999). More generally, there has been an overall concern and demand, in the light of the perceived decline in trust in experts and political-administrative decision-making, for enhanced 'openness' of regulatory regimes, for example in risk regulation (see Hood et al., 2001, 151–63). Demands for 'openness' include advocacy for greater 'transparency' of existing rules, more inclusive participation and more substantial obligations to justify and report on decisions taken. Thus the concern here has been mainly with accounting for the changing ways of policy-making and its impact on the quality of democratic life and citizenship rights.

Another feature of the rise of the regulatory state is apparent in the principal–agent literature, which points to a wider discussion of accountability and transparency instruments given its concern with information asymmetries and incomplete contracting (for an overview, see Huber and Shipan, 2000). Thus a number of measures have been put forward to prevent 'shirking' or 'drifting' by the agent. At the same time, the principal–agent analysis, limited as it is in the light of the extensive number of relationships and interdependencies, points to at least three dimensions where an absence of accountability and transparency facilitates the possibilities for 'drift' as a consequence of limited control due to incomplete information. These involve *agency drift* by the regulated actor(s) through the evasion of control in the pursuit of self-interested action (potentially leading to 'capture' of the regulatory regime; Stigler, 1971), *bureaucratic drift* by regulatory and bureaucratic authorities enforcing regulation through selective or biased attention, budget- and turf-maximization strategies, and, finally, *coalitional drift*, where the governing coalition seeks to move beyond the policy preferences established by the enacting coalition. In the face of an inherent control problem, a variety of devices have been explored to prevent such 'drifting', ranging from 'police patrols' (through monitoring committees and the like), 'fire alarms' (of constituencies affected by adverse regulatory decisions), self-revelatory mechanisms such as cross-sanctions, and through structural–procedural devices which direct the regulatory decision-making process towards particular outputs (such instruments include decision-making and appointment rules, legislative direction and the like). These instruments operating at the *ex ante* and *ex post* stages of regulation apply across all three levels of 'drift' (see McCubbins et al., 1987; Horn, 1995; Epstein and O'Halloran, 1999; Macey, 1992; Levine and Forrence, 1990).[3]

Finally, regulatory activities are said to differ from other government activities in terms of their 'visibility' (Horn, 1995, 40). On the one hand, regulation allows governments to hide the true costs of their activities by imposing the costs of regulation on those parties affected by regulation. Thereby governments avoid the visibility of public budgets and the potential electoral backlash by anti-tax coalitions (in particular when the costs of regulation are targeted at diffuse or non-pivotal interests). On the other hand, regulation as a tool of government reduces information asymmetries as it imposes the cost of adjustment and implementation on regulated actors. This distribution of regulatory cost is said to facilitate informed participation by affected constituencies (although it assumes the ability to organize collective action by the affected parties). Furthermore, systems which allow for 'revolving doors' (the occurrence of transfer between public and private sector work) encourage decision-making 'in front of an audience': regulators seek to advance their future private sector careers through competent (if arguably short-termist) rather than biased or captured regulation (Makkai and Braithwaite, 1995).

These traditional discussions of accountability and transparency have been too limited in their focus, emphasizing the importance of input and parliamentary channels of holding regulators to account, while ignoring wider dimensions in which regulation should be held to account and be transparent. Similarly, what constitutes appropriate 'police patrols', 'fire alarms' or 'deck-stacking' via procedural controls is likely to attract considerable controversy. For example, there is likely to be disagreement about the internal account-ability of 'fire alarms', the extent of responsiveness by the standard-setting system to particular 'fire alarms' rather than others or the speed and representativeness of 'police patrols' exercising oversight.

This chapter seeks to highlight the potential diversity of instruments through which regulation and regulatory regimes can be held accountable and transparent. Accountability is defined as the obligation to account for regulatory (or any other type of) activities to another person or body; transparency is associated with prescribed standards of making regulatory activities accessable and assessable. As systems of control, regulatory regimes require three central elements: standard-setting, behaviour modification and information-gathering. Holding these three elements accountable and transparent is crucial for the functioning of any control system: without accountability and transparency, any non-arbitrary standard-setting or enforcement would be impossible. Nevertheless, *how* accountability and transparency are incorporated into regulatory regimes differs greatly in terms of who holds whom accountable for what type of activities and type of consequences. Moreover, there are particular tradeoffs from advocating one set of instruments over others.

The rest of this chapter explores these issues in three stages. The next section sets out five dimensions, built on three basic essential regulatory regime components noted above, across which accountability and transparency apply to regulatory regimes. It illustrates variety in accountability and transparency instruments by applying a simple 'transparency toolbox' across three administrative doctrines. This is followed by a brief empirical comparison of different regulatory regimes to highlight the empirical diversity of the ways in which regulatory regimes are being held to account. Examples are drawn from four EU member states' approaches towards network regulation. The final section points to tradeoffs when choosing particular regulatory instruments over others. This chapter is therefore less concerned with advocating a 'best-in-world' solution, but seeks to point to the diversity of potential instruments and their basis in particular administrative doctrines. This chapter seeks to highlight the potential diversity of instruments through which regulation can be held accountable and transparent while at the same time suggesting that accountability and transparency are not 'good things' in their own right of which we should simply have 'more', but that particular choices are based on administrative doctrines and invite particular tradeoffs.

ACCOUNTABILITY AND TRANSPARENCY AND REGULATORY REGIMES

Conventional understandings of accountability are concerned with the demands on an agent to report on certain activities and the ability to impose sanctions. Thus accountability is inherent to any system of control. As already noted, a regulatory regime as a system of control requires *at minimum* three central elements: detectors (for information-gathering), effectors (for behaviour modification) and a standard-setting machinery (Hood, 1983, 3–4). These three elements are essential in order to keep the control system within a preferred subset of all its possible states (Hood, 1986, 112). The following is concerned not with these three elements as such, but with the way in which they point to five crucial dimensions which require separate analysis and considerations in any discussion of accountability and transparency:

- the accountability and transparency of the decision-making process involved in the setting of rules and standards;
- the transparency of the rules to be followed;
- the accountability and transparency of the activities of regulated actors;
- the accountability and transparency of regulating actors;
- the accountability and transparency of so-called feedback processes.

Taking such a perspective broadens the discussion of accountability and transparency in regulation beyond the traditional emphasis given to the importance of decision-making to be made in a visible and a justifiable way (Stirton and Lodge, 2001, 474–7). Such traditional discussions thereby neglect the importance of 'responsiveness' and 'detection': the knowledge of what has been decided is not a particularly extensive form of transparency. Additional dimensions highlighted in this kind of analysis are, for example, the ways in which standard-setting machineries respond to the information gathered through detecting tools, the ways in which detection is held accountable and the way in which standard-setting is being held accountable. Holding 'detectors' to account seems particularly crucial as 'failure' has been widely associated with breakdown on the information-gathering dimensions of control systems. Thus the analysis needs to expand to account for the variety and multi-dimensionality of relationships within (even a stylized) regulatory regime. Furthermore, it needs to illustrate 'how to' establish appropriate mechanisms for the holding to account and transparency of particular actors.

How then can a regulatory regime be held accountable and be made transparent across its five accountability and transparency dimensions? The rest of this section attempts to provide a response in three steps; first, it introduces a basic toolbox of four tools through which accountability and transparency can be discussed; second, it surveys three distinct administrative doctrines that prescribe different ways in which the broad tools can be translated into policy instruments; third, these doctrines are applied to the five accountability and transparency dimensions of a regulatory regime, as discussed above.

Table 6.1   Transparency toolbox

Orientation of tools	Tool activation	
	Individual	*Collective*
Input-oriented	Voice	Representation
Output-oriented	Choice	Information

Table 6.1 introduces a 'transparency toolbox' of four basic mechanisms that potentially enhance transparency and accountability (see Stirton and Lodge, 2001, 478). The 'transparency toolbox' is based on two key dimensions. First, it distinguishes between tools that are either individually exercised or collectively provided. Thus information and representation are supposed to make regulation (and regulated service provision) transparent to users and citizens *en masse*, while voice and choice tools are provided to the individual for their discretionary use. Second, it distinguishes between input-oriented tools, those aimed at enhancing the quality of the process of regulatory decision-making and regulated service provision, and output-oriented tools, which facilitate the evaluation of provided regulation and regulated services. Voice seeks to enable user participation and redress, representation seeks to counter imbalances in collective action (for example through the enfranchisement of public interest groups in regulatory decision-making processes; Ayres and Braithwaite, 1992), choice aims to enhance selection, while information seeks to redress potential information asymmetries, thereby enhancing the quality of choice. Nevertheless, as such, the toolbox provides

only little content as to 'how to fix' or enhance the accountability and transparency of regulatory regimes. Such content is provided by administrative doctrines that put forward particular principles or ideas of what should be done in administration in the light of particular policy problems (see Hood and Jackson, 1991, 9–19).

Building on the analysis of doctrines in public management, three different ways of 'how to' design and discuss regulatory transparency can be distinguished, 'fiduciary trusteeship', 'consumer sovereignty' and 'empowered citizenship' (Hood, 1997, 1998). All three provide distinct understandings as to how accountability should be designed (in particular by who to whom) into a regulatory regime and with what type of instruments.[4]

The *fiduciary trusteeship* doctrine has been particularly prominent in 'traditional' public administration (Hood, 1986, 181–4). It resonates with those criticisms of the 'regulatory state' that are troubled by the blurring of the 'public–private' divide (for example, Haque, 2001). Concerning the regulation of public service provision, it is assumed that 'producers' know best, given high information costs, with customers being a divided group and incapable of collective action, potentially willing to accept undesirable risks given lack of expertise. Such expertise is provided by public-interested technocrats able to counter concentrated interests, to balance against public pressure for 'knee-jerk responses' (the immediate, non-considered response to sudden demands) or to deal with issues of long-term, but low-level salience, such as nuclear energy refuse, medical treatments, the consumption of particular foodstuffs or even holiday locations. Accordingly, regulation should be exercised in an orderly, legally structured way that minimizes the discretion of all parties to safeguard certainty in the regulatory process by reducing the potential for arbitrary (and discretionary) decision-making. Accountability is conducted via oversight and review by authoritative and responsible experts. In terms of transparency tools, this doctrine emphasizes the importance of representation (through elected officials and specialist bodies) and of limited voice for individuals, through elected representatives. Put differently, regulatory activity is said to be accountable once it is suitably justified, at best in front of a knowing audience of experts or competent political representatives.

Arguments based on the *fiduciary trusteeship* doctrine warn against the risk of a downward drive of regulatory standards ('Delaware effect') once competition (or choice) between different standards is allowed, while direct citizen involvement is regarded as setting a dangerous precedent that downgrades the importance of expert decision-making and judgement, opening regulation up to ill-informed decisions and potentially leading to more widespread challenges to hierarchical authority, undermining authoritative activity due to hyper-accountability. However, it is questionable whether individuals require this kind of paternalism across all areas of regulation, and how far such a concept should be stretched in its application. While we may agree on the necessity of oversight by expertise in highly complex domains, we may be less willing to accept such paternalism when it comes to the monitoring and sanctioning of individual leisure pursuits or the mere choice of phone-set designs. Furthermore, it is debatable whether the assumption of trust in experts and their judgement is not rather naive, given experts' self-interest and biased understandings (such as 'groupthink' syndromes), pointing to further questions about the accountability of these bodies and the accountability and transparency of their selection mechanisms.[5] Finally, it is doubtful whether a belief in 'authority' will provide straightforward solutions when it comes to 'wicked issues' involving multidimensional problems in highly uncertain environments lacking any form of political and societal consensus. Instead such problem constellations seem to require strong participatory and inclusive processes across all five dimensions of the regulatory regime.

The *consumer sovereignty* doctrine, in contrast, regards citizens as the best judges of their own needs, who should be allowed to take their own decisions when it comes to choosing public services or in accepting risks. Therefore, individuals are regarded as capable of informed choice and their choices are sufficient to hold producers to account for their behaviour. Public authority over economic rents is to be minimized, as it is most likely to be abused by self-interested activities of those in authority. Thus, the significance of competition is emphasized, allowing the individual a maximum possible degree of voluntary choice on the extent and nature of consumption of any particular good (Hood, 1986, 171–2), relying also on the self-interest of the providers of the regulated product to be accountable by providing information and being concerned about their reputation. Therefore, providers find it in their interest to be accountable and transparent in their activities to increase their chances of survival.

The principles of competition and rivalry are not merely limited to the accountability and transparency of the ways through which public services are provided but applies to regulation more generally. Thus rivalry may exist between competing regulatory standards and certificates (such as shipping classification and registration schemes). Furthermore, rivalry and diversity, which need not necessarily occur within one single policy domain, induce cross-organizational policy learning and 'discovery' processes. Furthermore, distrust in hierarchical decisions could potentially be minimized through competitive means of selection of regulators with distinctive policy packages. Accordingly, this doctrine emphasizes the transparency tools of information and choice, the former in particular contributing to the quality of the latter.

However, as with fiduciary trusteeship, the applicability of the consumer sovereignty doctrine faces some challenges. It is questionable to what extent an individual should be able to choose risk-taking activities, as long as the question of 'acceptable' externalities (that is, the imposition of costs on others due to individual behaviour) has remained unresolved. Furthermore, there are potentially certain domains where the demand for choice or the possibility of transparent 'controlled experiments' between different standards may be unacceptable to the wider public. A choice between a safe and an unsafe plane or ship may lead to discounts on price to the individual consumer of the plane's or the ship's services, but the consequences of a plane crash or major maritime spillage may impose higher costs on the wider public than the individual benefits arising from the existence of choice.[6]

The third doctrine builds on *empowering citizens*. It suggests that the two earlier doctrines either run the risk of concentrating power, thereby facilitating elitist regulatory decision-making processes or of disadvantaging certain individuals over others, given different capabilities to understand perceived complexities of market processes. Thus this doctrine does not only advocate maximizing input-oriented participation and placing a maximum of scrutiny on the regulatory process (for example, rotating mandates of regulators), but regards such activity as also having transformative effects on the participating citizen, thereby supposedly contributing to the existence of an involved and informed citizenry (Bozeman, 2002, 148).[7] Therefore accountability and transparency mechanisms emphasize the importance of reducing social distance between those who regulate (and produce) and those affected by regulatory activity. This reduced social distance is directed at the involvement in the processes in particular; it pays less attention to issues of enhancing the quality of choice for the individual.

In terms of the transparency toolbox, this doctrine emphasizes the importance of voice, representation and information. Information is seen as important given inherent distrust of authority and elitist decision-making, which therefore requires a maximum of public scrutiny; this is linked to mechanisms of representation, where the contribution from a cross-section of constituencies may be linked to principles of rotation and the mandating of regulators. Similarly, voice is regarded as crucial in that it allows for the contribution of 'laypeople' to the regulatory decision-making which otherwise is reserved to experts and their particular biases. There are, as with the other doctrines, certain limitations as to the extent to which regulation can be made truly egalitarian. It seems to ignore the costs involved in participation (while also the predicted transformative impact may be questioned) and the potential occurrence (so often bemoaned by so-called experts) of 'irrational' decision-making by including too much publicness. Similarly, there are limitations as to the extent to which authority can be distrusted (or rather the potential costs of such distrust), given the need to acquire some expertise to regulate particular activities, while mandating devices may cause considerable tensions given the incomplete nature of such mandating 'contracts' and the difficulty of establishing universally acceptable decision-making procedures which may be regarded as leading to universally accepted outcomes.

Table 6.2, besides summarizing the above argument across the four basic tools of the 'transparency toolbox', suggests how the different doctrines locate authority in different ways. It thereby clarifies how the different administrative doctrines seek to enhance the quality of decision-making for the particular set

Table 6.2   Transparency toolbox across three doctrines

	Fiduciary trusteeship	Consumer sovereignty	Citizen empowerment
Locus of authority	Technocratic authority	Individual consumer	Participation in collective decision-making
Choice	Election of political representatives	Election of regulators/ politicians/choice of regulatory standards and in public services	Public discourse and choice on value conflicts
Voice	Public hearings, letters to authorities and political representatives	Complaint handling	Localized input and encouragement of value statements
Representation	Consumer councils	Competition among public interest groups	Direct citizen involvement, rotating mandates, peer group pressure
Information	White Papers, Annual Reports, government/ regulator statements	Benchmarking, financial transparency requirements	Mandating of representatives, maximum scrutiny and exposure of rival views

of (legitimate) actors making authoritative choices. Thus, while the fiduciary trusteeship doctrine regards experts and technocrats as legitimate authorities, consumer sovereignty and citizen empowerment doctrines point to individual consumers and participatory decision-making processes as legitimate loci for authoritative decision-making. Furthermore, certain instruments share universal endorsement across the three doctrines, but with different justifications; thus, for example, participation in elections is universally endorsed; however, while one doctrine regards it as an important measure of competition, the other regards it as legitimating the use of authority, while the third points to the importance of participation in its own right.

Having looked across the application of a very basic 'transparency toolbox' across three doctrines, indicating of what type of instruments would be advocated by particular worldviews in contrast to others, a similar exercise can be undertaken across all the five dimensions of a regulatory regime, as set out earlier. Table 6.3 provides an overview of instruments particularly emphasized by the various administrative doctrines. It does not aim to provide an exhaustive survey, but seeks to illustrates the argument.

Table 6.3 illustrates the key difference of advocated instruments across the five accountability and transparency dimensions of any regulatory regime. The first dimension, the accountability and transparency of the standard-setting process, points to the differences in conception as to the appropriate locus of authority, and to differences in terms of process. Similarly, across the three doctrines there are substantial variations in advocated instruments when it comes to the transparency of rules that are to be implemented, ranging from a reliance on professional standards, the existence of legal codes (including competition law) and those that involve access and participatory rights.

The third dimension, of choice of instruments to advance the accountability and transparency of regulated actors and activities, seeks to avoid 'capture' or 'creative compliance'. Potential answers to such incentives range from the creation of oversight bodies, to a concern with the incentive structures and information revelation requirements to a mixture of lay participation in oversight and in the running of the regulated activities. The fourth dimension concerns the accountability and transparency of the regulator, with the primary emphasis being on avoiding goal displacement through bureaucratic self-interest. While according to the 'fiduciary trusteeship' doctrine, such behaviour is to be controlled through reporting, legal duties and technocratic oversight, the 'consumer sovereignty' doctrine suggests instruments of choice, such as election to regulatory offices and regulatory standards as ways to control regulatory activities. 'Citizen empowerment'-based instruments in contrast stress the importance of heterogeneous participation, encouraging public discourse on competing values of regulation for holding the 'effecting' capacity of regulatory regimes to account.

Table 6.3   Accountability and transparency across regulatory regimes

	Fiduciary trusteeship	Consumer sovereignty	Citizen empowerment
Decision-making process involved in the setting of rules	Legislative and technocratic decision-making	Competition between sets of rules, individual choice	Inclusion, 'discourse' between contrasting worldviews
Transparency of the rules to be followed	Professional standards and legality	Contractual obligations, competition law	Publicness of access and procedural rules
Accountability and transparency of regulated activities	Oversight through supervision by experts, political competition for office, consumer representation duties	Competition and benchmarks, information revelation requirements, individual focus	Oversight through lay participation, local production
Accountability and transparency of controls on regulated activities	Reporting duties and legalism	Competition between standards and agencies, choice mechanism, information revelation, legal redress	Involvement, mandated supervision, public interest group involvement
Accountability and transparency of feedback processes	Reviews by experts (royal commissions and task forces)	Evolution of competitive orders, mutual adjustment through discovery processes	Immediate participation, including affected constituencies

Finally, the 'feedback' side of the regulatory regime requires to be held to account and transparent in order to allow for the unbiased updating of regulatory standards and activities. While the first doctrine advocates the importance of expert-driven reviews, the alternative doctrines point to the importance of maintaining variety and diversity in order to encourage learning and mutual adjustment processes, while more egalitarian doctrines stress the importance of participatory discourse and value-based reviews.

Such a 'toolbox' device offers one way to approach accountability and transparency in regulation from a different perspective to the traditional concerns of empirical accountability of particular institutional arrangements. It also provides a basis for empirical analysis in at least two ways. One way is to assess whether the empirical world of regulation conforms to the ways in which costs and benefits from exercising choice in various policy domains are distributed. Therefore, the costs to the individual to exercise choice have to be weighted against the costs of being restrained by collectively binding decisions. Thus domains characterized by low information costs could be predicted to rely on instruments based on the consumer sovereignty doctrine. A second way is to use the toolbox to assess, in a comprehensive way, the existing instruments that are supposed to advance the accountability and transparency of particular regulatory regimes or to compare national regulatory regimes, enquiring whether there is cross-national or cross-sectoral diversity or trends towards increasing commonality or even convergence. The following section provides a brief overview of accountability and transparency approaches in network regulation across a set of Western European countries.

COMPARING ACCOUNTABILITY AND TRANSPARENCY INSTRUMENTS IN NATIONAL NETWORK REGULATION IN EUROPE

The toolbox of regulatory transparency points to the potential variety in which regulation can be held to account. It also allows for the empirical investigation of regulatory regimes, moving beyond stale debates concerning parliamentary accountability and towards a more complex understanding of regime characteristics and dynamics. Comparative assessments have pointed to the diversity of ways in which national regulatory regimes have attempted to hold the provision of public services accountable. This section briefly compares the experiences in Britain, Germany, Sweden and Ireland in the area of network regulation, an area where change has arguably been most noticeable in terms of change in industry–state relations. The first three states represent three countries with different 'welfare state traditions'; Ireland represents an example of a regulatory reform 'latecomer'. Without seeking to develop an account of either the regulatory reforms (for example, their differences in timing, extent and degree of regulatory reforms across policy domains) as such or of the various instruments that have been employed (see Lodge, 2001, 2002), this section illustrates the prevalence of nationally diverse approaches towards accountability and transparency, while at the same time pointing to some broad similarities in terms of policy trends.

In terms of choice, all states witnessed a substantial increase in the ways in which users are able to select services, albeit at different speeds across sectors (as considered elsewhere in this volume) and states, reflecting to some extent the different sectoral dynamics and levels of pressures provided by EU-driven initiatives. However, even where formal liberalization took place, this did not necessarily affect the extent of choice being exercised. For example, in the case of electricity in Germany, despite a complete formal liberalization of its market, there was only limited active choice by consumers. The extent of *choice* also differed considerably across policy sectors. In telecommunications, there was substantial choice given EU-driven liberalization as of 1 January 1998 (although Ireland was granted a temporary derogation), but in practice there were significant differences. For example, Germany witnessed the immediate exercise of *choice* based on provisions that allowed for call-by-call selection and unified billing, whereas such mechanisms were absent in the UK despite the latter's longer record of a (partly) liberalized market. In Sweden, choice was extended to the postal sectors (and emerged in certain cities). Across European countries, *choice* in the railway domain was mainly constricted to 'competition for the market' in tendering for particular services rather than choice for the individual user.

Apart from the increasing prevalence of *choice* in network industry services, there was also, however, a growth of supplementary instruments that were supposed to advance the quality of choice, by enhancing that quality and by strengthening alternative accountability and transparency mechanisms. Thus there was, across time, a substantial strengthening of *voice*-based instruments in British network regulation, in particular following the 1992 Competition and Services (Utilities) Act that placed a very strong emphasis on consumer satisfaction and harmonized provisions across regulatory regimes for the (by then) privatized utilities. Similarly the Swedish competition authority and the postal and telecommunications regulator, the PTS, moved increasingly into monitoring consumer complaints. In contrast, Germany saw only very little interest in providing for venues to raise complaints. Ireland set out complaint regimes in its licences in electricity, while in telecommunications the regulator became increasingly interested in monitoring complaints. In terms of *information*, there was similarly a mixed response. Both Germany and Sweden saw a rapid expansion of privately provided price comparisons for electricity and telecommunications, but little information regarding service quality. Ireland offered hardly any information on price or services, while the UK witnessed a very belated response by the regulatory agencies in terms of information provision. By 2003, Oftel had initiated industry-led price and service quality information services, while the energy consumer watchdog, 'energywatch', was responsible for providing comparative pricing and service quality information. There were far less prominent tendencies in terms of *representation*. Germany, Sweden and Ireland relied mainly on general consumer interest watchdogs. It was only the UK that relied, based on inherited structure from the days of nationalized enterprises, on sector-specific consumer councils. Developments in the late 1990s and early 2000s saw the development of both stronger consumer representation in the case of energy, where 'energywatch' was provided with substantially more resources in the wake of the 2000 Utilities Act and lesser representation in telecommunications, where the communications regulator, Ofcom, was to include a consumer and practitioner panel in its decision-making instead of a sectoral consumer watchdog.

In sum, across regulatory regimes for network industries in Western Europe, there has been an increasing shift not only towards choice through market liberalization, but also an, albeit varied, growth of accompanying transparency mechanisms, in particular voice (complaints) and information, although with substantial variations across states and domains. Table 6.4 provides a limited overview for four European states as an example of such a comparative approach. Similarly, in Commonwealth Caribbean countries (Lodge and Stirton, 2001), despite a more limited move towards choice, there has been an increasing awareness that political representatives do not necessarily provide a complete transparency and accountability regime; this has led to more individualized measures, such as complaint procedures, more in-depth detection measures and increased consumer representation functions by regulatory bodies.

Such an empirical picture, although limited, does not point to an overall decline of accountability and transparency as a consequence of the shift towards the 'regulatory state' *per se*. Instead of debating the deteriorating impact of a perceived 'marketization' of particular activities on the quality of 'citizenship', the analysis of the extent to which accountability and transparency are provided through instruments informed by distinct doctrinal choices offers a more useful way to explore analytical and empirical difference. It also allows for an investigation of how and whether these instruments were effective, especially in contrast to those instruments employed in the age of the 'positive' state.

TRADING OFF TRANSPARENCY AND ACCOUNTABILITY

Having illustrated the variety of instruments available across administrative doctrines, this section illustrates crucial tradeoffs across a number of central issues in holding regulatory regimes accountable and transparent. It therefore

Table 6.4   *Overview of national transparency mechanisms in network regulation*

Mechanism	Britain	Ireland	Germany	Sweden
Voice	Increasing emphasis on complaint handling	Formalization of complaint handling	Limited regulatory information service	Not part of licence requirement – uneven compliance to regulator
Representation	Consumer councils, towards diverse representation within regulatory bodies	Consideration of industry ombudsman	No representation beyond regulatory authority	Involvement of regulator and consumer associations
Choice	Increasing emphasis on choice. Shift of agencies towards competition	Latecomer – choice in telecoms most prominent	Enhanced choice in telecoms; hurdles in electricity	Widespread liberalization
Information	Price, service comparison provided/ delegated by regulators	Limited – under consideration	Numerous private price comparisons	Private price comparison

points to the limitations of claims (by any of the three doctrines under discussion) advocating 'more' transparency. Without claiming to be exhaustive, this section discusses three central themes, pointing to particular tradeoffs in the consequences of effecting accountability, in the setting of standards, and in the degree of responsiveness to public pressure.

The first theme concerns the potential consequences of who is being held accountable to whom. As accountability and transparency are crucial for holding the regulatory regime in a desired subset of possible outcomes and outputs, it can be questioned whether certain measures of holding to account and transparency may not invite undesired side-effects. For example, when things are seen to go wrong, one of the central claims is that someone has to be seen to have been responsible for the misconduct or the particular undesired outcome (to prevent the so-called 'many-hands' problem; see Bovens, 1998).[8] One further crucial question concerns how 'transparent' such holding to account is supposed to be and what type of sanctions are associated with the possible finding of misconduct. Open systems arguably encourage behaviour to reduce all forms of risk exposure or even more unaccountable task evasion, which then is even more difficult to detect, let alone to correct. Such avoidance behaviour may be further facilitated in cases of strong sanctions. Progress is said to require trial-and-error processes within an 'open' environment to allow for improvement, debate and learning. A fear of sanctions will encourage the narrow-minded 'going by the book', the potential export of regulated activities to other territories with less 'tough' regulatory regimes and the potential crowding out of desirable activities given high regulatory compliance costs. The related issue concerns 'who' should be held to account when things 'go wrong'. An emphasis on finding the person 'in charge' may very well identify a particular culprit of a particular wrongdoing, but it is most unlikely to address the question whether such behaviour was induced by dysfunctional wider systems. Most studies of 'failure' have pointed to the importance of dysfunctional organizations rather than individual wilful wrongdoing.

The second theme points to problems of setting standards and how these are being held to account. The fiduciary trusteeship doctrine implies a relatively certain state of affairs – experts are assumed to be able to come to some form of quantitative analysis as to what standards are likely to offer greater benefits than costs or what type of risks are deemed irrelevant or insignificant. Such an account can be challenged on two related counts. First, the need to quantify scenarios is often seen as already restricting empirical complexity, thereby potentially fitting a solution to the 'wrong problem'. Second, in so-called 'wicked issues' (as noted above), standard-setting by experts may generate even more distrust and contestation, given inherent value and technocratic conflicts and lack of any form of direction, central control or consensus. An alternative version, advocated in particular by the 'citizen empowerment' worldview, is to generate open contests between the different views via encouraging discourse. However, such processes may deepen existing conflict cleavages, may require longer time periods than is feasible for regulatory responses and may generate conditions such as increasing elite cartelization or opinion fragmentation.

The third theme points to the level of responsiveness of regimes to external pressure. While many claim that regulatory regimes should be open to the preferences of the 'public', it is not always clear what constitutes the 'public' and what type of assessment of 'public opinion' should be used. In fact, increasing the importance of 'participation' may advance rather than reduce the advantages of organized over diffuse groups. Furthermore, the degree to which regulatory regimes should be resilient to outbreaks of public demands for regulatory activities (following, for example, fatal bites by dogs considered as 'dangerous') is contested in the literature (Breyer, 1993). A further concern is the biased ways in which institutions respond to demands for regulatory activity; in the dangerous dogs case, for example, it is notable that, in cross-national perspective, the regulatory activities are usually not directed at 'middle-class' dog breeds and types, despite their prominence in incident statistics (Lodge and Hood, 2002). Moreover, claims to accountability and transparency are likely to encourage a trend towards increasing juridification and potential gridlock: if all activities are to be held accountable and transparent and are linked to a high-complaint culture, then regulatory activities are bound to become increasingly rigid.

Such questions suggest that asking for 'more' accountability and transparency, or, more generally, openness does not only involve questions of selecting administrative doctrine and instruments; it also points to certain limitations and consequences of particular instruments and techniques. Accountability and transparency are therefore not goals in themselves, their purpose is to maintain a system in a certain range of desired states. Furthermore, whatever doctrine is advocated in the promotion of accountability and transparency is likely to invite particular tradeoffs and tensions, leading to continuous challenges to the existing regimes.

CONCLUSION

One aspect of the regulatory reforms of recent decades has been a further diversification of public services; such diversification requires a diversified understanding of accountability and transparency. Where responsibility for the provision of certain goods in a 'public interested' way is shared between state and non-state actors, the challenge is to provide for appropriate coordination and oversight. Focusing on a regulatory regime perspective and highlighting the various dimensions across which accountability and transparency matter accepts an empirical reality of complex relationships within a regulatory state and allows for a diversity of actors to perform accountability and transparency obligations. Any thorough discussion of accountability and transparency of regulatory regimes needs to acknowledge the numerous dimensions of any regulatory regime which require to be held to account and be transparent in order to remain within a subset of desired outcomes.

Linking a regulatory regime perspective with its five accountability and transparency dimensions to the discussion of legitimate policy instruments provides the basis for more broad discussion of transparency and accountability as well as for analytical and empirical investigation. In particular, the focus on administrative doctrines, with their different conceptions as to the appropriate locus of authority and different understandings of information costs occurring to individual users, points to the normative basis of many discussions on accountability and transparency. This chapter has neither aimed to advance a particular normative viewpoint nor sought to develop a close link between 'how to' regulatory discussions and wider discussions on normative understandings of democracy. Instead, it has sought to suggest a more responsive or contingency-based view; that is, it has sought to advance a view that accountability and transparency should be designed in a way that is responsive to the specific circumstances of particular policy domains. Furthermore, it attempted to highlight potential tradeoffs that are inherent in particular choices of instruments that are supposed to advance accountability and transparency.

Talking about accountability and transparency is far from a mere obsession with institutional furniture arrangements or degrees of delegation between 'principals' and 'agents'. Accountability and transparency are not just a 'good thing' of which we should just have 'more'. The way in which such instruments are designed into a regulatory regime fundamentally affects the way in which power is allocated and negotiated in any regulatory regime and leads to potential intended and unintended consequences that are associated with particular and potentially substantial costs and benefits.

NOTES

1. Much of the following builds on most fruitful cooperation with Lindsay Stirton, inspiration by Teresa Elósegui and comments on an earlier version by Colin Scott, Kai Wegrich, Jacint Jordana, David Levi-Faur, Ian Bartle, Andrea Goldstein, Ulrika Mörth and Anthony Ogus. I thank the Policy Institute at Trinity College Dublin and the Political Science, Administration and Organization Department at the University of Potsdam for space to complete the drafting of this chapter. I nevertheless remain solely accountable for this output. Whether I have been transparent is for the reader to decide.
2. Baldwin et al. suggest that an attempt by the imaginary Ada Smith to establish a pin-making plant encounters six regulatory regimes based on at least six different legal regimes from the point of establishing the company to the eventual marketing of products (Baldwin et al., 1998, 1).
3. This discussion is biased towards holding the 'hardwired' bargain under control; it does not discuss the ways in which a 'hardwired' regime needs to be accountable in terms of responsiveness.
4. The analysis is informed by cultural theory. However, it does not deal with fatalism or 'contrived randomness' as a mode of control. A fatalist would rely on 'told you so' reporting and unannounced and unpredictable instruments.
5. Let alone the accountability of so-called 'total institutions', such as prisons, which, by nature, lack day-to-day transparency in their operating procedures.

6. This discussion ignores the potential difficulties in coming to the appropriate assessment of 'desirable' and 'undesirable' side-effects (and of decision-making processes to come to an assessment).
7. Arguably, the key argument would be that participation in the production of the regulated activities would reduce the need for control.
8. Such a view has been stressed, for example, by Jeremy Bentham, and often made in debatesas to whether to allow for presidential or board-type regulatory bodies.

REFERENCES

Ayres, I. and J. Braithwaite (1992), *Responsive Regulation*, New York: Oxford University Press.
Baldwin, R. and M. Cave (1999), *Understanding Regulation*, Oxford: Oxford University Press.
Baldwin, R., C. Scott and C. Hood (1998), 'Introduction', in R. Baldwin, C. Scott and C. Hood (eds), *Reader on Regulation*, Oxford: Oxford University Press, pp. 1–55.
Berry, W.D. (1979), 'Utility Regulation in the States: The Policy Effects of Professionalism and Salience to the Consumer', *American Journal of Political Science*, **23** (2), 263–77.
Bovens, M. (1998), *The Quest for Responsibility*, Cambridge: Cambridge University Press.
Bozeman, B. (2002), 'Public Value Failure: When Efficient Markets May Not Do', *Public Administration Review*, **62** (2), 145–61.
Breyer, S. (1993), *Breaking through Vicious Circles*, Cambridge, MA: Harvard University Press.
Epstein, D. and S. O'Halloran (1999), *Delegating Powers*, Cambridge: Cambridge University Press.
Falconer, P. and K. Ross (1999), 'Citizen's Charters and Public Service Provision: Lessons from the UK Experience', *International Review of Administrative Sciences*, **65** (3), 339–51.
Graham, C. (1997), *Is there a Crisis in Regulatory Accountability?*, Centre for the Study of Regulated Industries.
Hancher, L. and M. Moran (1989), 'Conclusions: Organising Regulatory Space', in L. Hancher and M. Moran (eds), *Capitalism, Culture and Economic Regulation*, Oxford: Clarendon Press, pp. 271–98.
Haque, S. (2001), 'The Diminishing Publicness of Public Service under the Current Mode of Governance', *Public Administration Review*, **6** (1), 65–82.
Hood, C. (1983), *Tools of Government*, London: Macmillan.
Hood, C. (1986), *Administrative Analysis*, London: Harvester Wheatsheaf.
Hood, C. (1997), 'Which Contract State? Four Perspectives on Over-Outsourcing for Public Services', *Australian Journal of Public Administration*, **56** (3), 120–31.
Hood, C. (1998), *The Art of the State*, Oxford: Oxford University Press.
Hood, C. and M. Jackson (1991), *Administrative Argument*, Aldershot: Dartmouth.
Hood, C., H. Rothstein and R. Baldwin (2001), *The Government of Risk*, Oxford: Oxford University Press.
Horn, M. (1995), *The Political Economy of Public Administration*, Cambridge: Cambridge University Press.
Huber, J.D. and C.R. Shipan (2000), 'The Costs of Control: Legislators, Agencies, and Transaction Costs', *Legislative Studies Quarterly*, **25** (1), 25–52.

Levine, M.E. and J.L. Forrence (1990), 'Regulatory Capture, Public Interest and the Public Agenda: Towards a Synthesis', *Journal of Law, Economics, and Organisation*, **6** (special issue), 167–98.

Lodge, M. (2001), 'From Varieties of the Welfare State to Convergence of the Regulatory State? The "Europeanisation" of Regulatory Transparency', *Queen's Papers on Europeanisation*, 10/2001, Belfast. (http://www.qub.ac.uk/ies/onlinepapers/poe10-01.pdf)

Lodge, M. (2002), 'Varieties of Europeanisation and the National Regulatory State', *Public Policy and Administration*, **17** (2), 43–67.

Lodge, M. and C. Hood (2002), 'Pavlovian Policy Responses to Media Feeding Frenzies? Dangerous Dogs Regulation in Comparative Perspective', *Journal of Contingencies and Crisis Management*, **10** (1), 1–13.

Lodge, M. and L. Stirton (2001), 'Regulating in the Interest of the Citizen: Towards a Single Model of Regulatory Transparency?', *Social and Economic Studies*, **50** (2), 103–37.

Loughlin, M. and C. Scott (1997), 'The Regulatory State', in P. Dunleavy, A. Gamble, I. Holliday and G. Peele (eds), *Developments in British Politics 5*, Basingstoke: Macmillan, pp. 205–18.

Macey, J.R. (1992), 'Organizational Design and Political Control of Administrative Agencies', *Journal of Law, Economics and Organisation*, **8** (1), 93–110.

Majone, G. (1997), 'From the Positive to the Regulatory State – Causes and Consequences from Changes in the Modes of Governance', *Journal of Public Policy*, **17** (2), 139–67.

Majone, G. (1999), 'The Regulatory State and its Legitimacy Problems', *West European Politics*, **22** (1), 1–24.

Makkai, T. and J. Braithwaite (1995), 'In and Out of the Revolving Door: Making Sense of Regulatory Capture', *Journal of Public Policy*, **12** (1), 61–78.

McCubbins M., R.G. Noll and B. Weingast (1987), 'Administrative Procedures as Instruments of Political Control', *Journal of Law, Economics and Organization*, **3** (2), 243–77.

Moran, M. (2001), 'Property, Business Power and the Constitution', *Public Administration*, **79** (2), 277–96.

Moran, M. (2002), 'Review Article: Understanding the Regulatory State', *British Journal of Political Science*, **32** (2), 391–413.

Romsek, B. (2000), 'Dynamics of Public Sector Accountability in an Era of Reform', *International Review of Administrative Sciences*, **66** (1), 21–44.

Scott, C. (2000), 'Accountability in the Regulatory State', *Journal of Law and Society*, **27** (1), 38–60.

Scott, C. (2001), 'Analysing Regulatory Space: Fragmented Resources and Institutional Design', *Public Law*, Summer, 329–352.

Stewart, J. (1992), 'The Rebuilding of Public Accountability', in J. Stewart, N. Lewis and D. Longley (eds), *Accountability to the Public*, London: European Policy Forum.

Stigler, G. (1971), 'The Theory of Economic Regulation', *Bell Journal of Economic and Management Science*, **2** (1), 3–21.

Stirton, L. and M. Lodge (2001), 'Transparency Mechanisms: Building Publicness into Public Services', *Journal of Law and Society*, 28 (4), 471–89.

7. Regulation in the age of governance: the rise of the post-regulatory state

Colin Scott[*]

1. INTRODUCTION

This chapter forms part of a larger project examining governance 'beyond the regulatory state'. Governance has been defined in a variety of ways in both official and secondary literatures. In this chapter the 'age of governance' is conceived in terms of recognizing the dispersal of capacities and resources relevant to the exercise of power among a wide range of state, non-state and supranational actors. It is claimed that '[t]he essence of governance is its focus on governing mechanisms which do not rest on recourse to the authority and sanctions of government' (Stoker, 1998, 17). An analysis in which governing is no longer seen as the exclusive prerogative of the nation-state presents a challenge to the literature, which argues that the last years of the twentieth century witnessed 'the rise of the regulatory state' (Majone, 1994).

In this chapter three core assumptions of the regulatory state movement are scrutinized using theoretical and empirical literatures which challenge one or more of these central ideas: regulation is instrumental in character; the state is necessarily central to regulatory governance; state law is a central instrument of regulatory governance. Each of these assumptions has a descriptive and a normative dimension, both of which are assessed in the critique. The objective of the analysis is not to dispense wholly with the assumptions but rather to act as a corrective to an influential literature which, because of its neglect of the non-instrumental dimension of regulation, non-state regulation and regulation which deploys non-state law, is incomplete in its mapping of regulatory governance arrangements.

This chapter focuses on one aspect of the critique concerning the centrality of state law to regulation. It argues for shifting the focus of analysis from state law to the wider range of norms and mechanisms through which control is asserted or achieved, however indirectly. The exercise is complementary to policy moves towards 'alternatives to state regulation' (Better Regulation Task Force, 2000). The approach constitutes something of a mirror-image to those who are arguing that the centrality of the state is too little rather than too much assumed (Weiss, 1998). The question at the heart of this chapter is to what extent can we or should we think of regulatory governance functioning in a manner not dependent on state law or in which state law is not central (cf. Black, 2001a).

The chapter maps current thinking on the nature of the 'regulatory state' and then sets out, in critical fashion, a range of theoretical approaches which challenge thinking about regulation which is oriented to the capacities of the state. Underlying this 'post-regulatory' thinking are concerns that the assertion of control by state regulatory bodies is, in many cases, implausible. Set against this, many instances of well-ordered economic and social relations are observable in environments where there is little state activity.

This chapter invites the reader not to wholly discard conventional conceptions of the state role in regulation. Indeed, other chapters in this volume deploy related arguments about variety in regulatory norms to enrich rather than challenge the idea of the regulatory state (Knill and Lenschow, Chapter 10). The alternative offered here is to think about governance in a different way so as to admit a wider range of norms, institutions and processes as constituting a way of thinking labelled 'the post-regulatory state'.

2.   REGULATION AND CONTROL

Regulation scholars have not, generally, agreed on what the target of their research should be. Economic theories of regulation have tended to follow economic thinking generally in positing a sharp distinction between markets and regulation (Daintith, 1997, 8–9). On this analysis the state provides basic rules of contract and property rights which are essential to the transactional basis of a capitalist economy and regulation is deployed where the market is judged to fail, for example because of natural monopoly, information problems or externalities (Baldwin and Cave, 1999, ch. 2). Hayek (1982, vol. 1, 52) characterized markets as a form of 'spontaneous order', amenable to improvement through fine tuning of the general rules of law, but in which specific interventions or commands would destroy the balance of the market ordering. Regulators could never know enough about how the market operated to intervene effectively. Political science has tended largely to follow the economic analysis in its characterization of the sharp distinction between regulation and markets (Mitnick, 1980, Wilson, 1980). Sociological analysis, oriented towards the analysis of power in its diverse forms, has tended to reject this sharp distinction. Shearing (1993), for example, argues that regulation is a central factor in shaping conduct generally and is *constitutive* of markets. I suggest that a defining characteristic of 'post-regulatory state' thinking generally is a blunting of the sharp distinction between states and markets and between the public and the private. Julia Black (2001a) has described this process of rethinking regulation as one of 'de-centring'.

Underlying the scepticism about the regulatory state, the various analyses have in common an attempt to grapple with the problem of control. At the highest level of abstraction any system of control consists of (1) some kind of standard, goal, or set of values against which perceptions of what is happening within the environment to be controlled are compared, through (2) some mechanism of monitoring or feedback which in turn triggers (3) some form of action which attempts to align the controlled variables, as they are perceived by the monitoring component with the goal component (Hood et al., 2001, 23–7). For classical regulation the goal component is represented typically by some legal rule or standard, the feedback component by monitoring by a regulatory agency, government department or self-regulatory organization and the realignment component by the application of sanctions for breach of standards.

These component functions of control are often split between different organizations. The United States is rather exceptional in the extent to which all three components are often delegated to regulatory agencies. Within most OECD countries regulatory rule-making is assigned to legislative bodies, monitoring is split between government departments, specialist agencies and non-state bodies, with formal capacity to apply sanctions reserved to the courts at the initiation of the monitoring organizations or some third party (Francis, 1993). Accordingly it may be helpful to think about regulation in terms of regimes with diffuse parts (Eisner, 2000, ch. 1). Socio-legal research has shown that the operation of such classical regulatory regimes frequently diverges from the hierarchical model suggested here because, for example, of incomplete monitoring, a lack of common understanding of the interpretation of regulatory rules (Reichman, 1992), and enforcement practices which are patchy and/or oriented towards negotiating consensual solutions to problems with regulatees rather than routinely applying formal sanctions (Grabosky and Braithwaite, 1986). The whole architecture of regulation built upon the rule of law is undermined by the elaboration of the numerous ways in which regulatory law is liable to be fuzzy (Cohn, 2001).

The post-regulatory state takes these observations and works with them to identify greater variety in control processes which invoke other bases of control than hierarchy and state law – notably the norms and practices of society or communities; the tendency towards rivalry or competition in organizational settings; and the capacity of design (for example of buildings or software) for controlling behaviour. In each case hierarchical structures or state law may have a partial role in the control system, but not a monopoly. Related to this is a shift in our understanding of who controls and who is controlled within regimes.

3. THE REGULATORY STATE

The concept of the 'regulatory state' was developed to distinguish a distinctive and emergent form of governance from the practices and institutions of the welfare state (Sunstein, 1990b; Majone, 1994; Pildes and Sunstein, 1995; Loughlin and Scott, 1997; Braithwaite, 2000; Moran, 2001a, 2001b, 2002). The welfare state deploys the instruments of public ownership, direct state provision of benefits and services, integration of policy-making and operational functions. By contrast the regulatory state governance form involves a complex set of changes in public management involving the separation of operational from regulatory activities in some policy areas (sometimes linked to privatization), a trend towards separating purchasers and providers of public services (through policies of contracting out and market-testing) and towards separation of operational from policy tasks within government departments and the creation of executive agencies. Each of these policies shifts the emphasis of control, to a greater or lesser degree, from traditional bureaucratic mechanisms towards instruments of regulation. Government departments (or nominated agencies or self-regulatory bodies) now regulate the provision of services (setting down standards, monitoring for compliance and enforcing) through the instruments of statutory regulation and contract and their near relations self- and co-regulation and quasi-contract. Linked to these changes, greater emphasis is placed on formal rules and monitoring by free-standing agencies. Regulatory state developments not only reform the manner in which public power over economy and society is exercised, but also draw into the process areas of social and economic life in which controls were characterized predominantly as self-regulatory in character (Moran, 2001b, 22–3).

Even as the process of displacement of the welfare state instruments was beginning, a number of distinctive literatures were emerging which were sceptical either of the descriptive utility or normative desirability of the concept of regulation. In a comprehensive review of the literature on the regulatory state, Moran offers a number of possible conclusions as to the validity and utility of the regulatory state concept. Most optimistically, the regulatory state literature may identify a central aspect of the 'new governing paradigm' of governance. It may just be a useful fiction, good for enabling increasingly specialized scholars to communicate with one another. Alternatively, regulatory states may exist, but with a 'character contingent on national setting' (Moran, 2002, 412).

Moran's own review is very much oriented to the US and UK experience, within which quite distinctive patterns in the emergence of regulatory governance can be identified. In the United States the rise of the regulatory state is linked to a cultural preference for private economic activity, and a concomitant requirement for the state to steer that activity to secure social and economic objectives. A key growth period in the American regulatory state was associated with the New Deal and then with the enhancement of social rights in the 1960s (Sunstein, 1990a). By the 1990s American public policy was seeking to move beyond the regulatory state through processes of 'reinvention' (Pildes and Sunstein, 1995). Conversely the UK regulatory state has arisen out of a *withdrawal* of the state from key economic activities in the 1980s and 1990s, a by-product of the centralizing manner in which the policy was carried out.

In other European states more limited trends towards regulatory governance can be ascribed to attempts by the European Union institutions to complete the single European market, requiring not only the liberalization of utilities sectors once dominated by national monopolists, but also that the states create independent regulatory capacities to promote competition, for example by ending cross-subsidies and promoting non-discrimination by dominant incumbents (Henry et al., 2000) The EU policy institutions place considerable emphasis on law and hierarchical control as cornerstones of reform processes (Wilks, 1996). This characteristic makes it difficult to envision EU policy readily moving towards post-regulatory governance structures which make greater use of non-legal control mechanisms and non-state institutions. However, there is growing evidence of the EU institutions using new governance approaches which give greater discretion to regulatees and member states as to how objectives are met, and which create lower levels of obligation, for example because they have non-binding soft law at their core (Knill and Lenschow, Chapter 10 in this volume). Such new approaches to governance reflect, in part, a recognition of the problems of steering member states and their citizens through coercive regulatory instruments, from the perspective of both legitimacy and effectiveness. The difficulties of regulatory governance in the EU are reflected in global governance more generally in debates as to the extent to which distinctive or autonomous supranational regulatory or legal orders can be created (Held, 2002). For some, autonomous global governance institutions represent a threat to democratic state governments, while for others such supranational regulatory initiatives are only likely to be effective when anchored to the capacities of sovereign states (Weiss, 1998). A third perspective suggests that supranational linkages of non-state regulatory actors are likely to be powerful within structures of global governance (Ronit, 2001).

If we look elsewhere in the OECD we find different patterns again. Governance of economic activities in postwar Japan, for example, has been dominated by monolithic state ministries engendering close and informal relationships with key businesses (Kagan, 2000, 225–6). Limited evidence of more formal and juridical enforcement styles only qualifies this picture slightly (Kagan, 2000, 229–31). We might respond to these observations either by suggesting that the regulatory state literature has little to say about the Japanese case, or suggest that international pressures will create 'pressures for more transparent and hence more legalistic modes of regulation' (ibid., 241). In other words, if the regulatory state concept fails to capture the characteristics of the current regime, then it will, almost inevitably, have relevance to the future. This hypothesis is questioned in a path-breaking study of 'cooperative capitalism' in Japan which suggests that as the power of the ministries both to protect and regulate industry is diminished, the vacuum is being filled by trade associations exercising self-regulatory functions, and extensive cooperation by firms within particular industries, a development supported by competition laws which are lenient in respect of restrictive agreements (Schaede, 2000, 7). Schaede (ibid., 3) further suggests that this form of development is more typical of Asian and continental European countries than the regulatory governance style which has emerged in the 'Anglo-American' countries.

Grabosky (1994) has offered the most sustained criticism of the regulatory state concept, rejecting, in particular, its focus on state activities and exclusion of non-state governance institutions. Grabosky (1995), whose focus is on Australia, the United States and the United Kingdom, points to well-established and growing trends to enlist non-state actors in regulatory governance (See also Anleu et al., 2000; Gunningham and Grabosky, 1998; Kraakman, 1986; Scott, 2002). There is also an important role for spontaneous market order (for example purchasing decisions and contractual terms of large firms) in such areas as environmental protection and equality (Grabosky, 1994; Richardson, forthcoming). Thinking in terms of the regulatory state is neither descriptively accurate nor normatively desirable. Whereas the central target of Grabosky's analysis is the assumption that the key actors in regulatory governance are state actors, the main basis of this chapter is the assumption that the key instruments and relationships are based on state law and hierarchy.

4.   THEORIES OF THE POST-REGULATORY STATE

The diverse theoretical perspectives which touch on the question set out in the introduction offer a number of different critiques which can be expressed with the following statements: (1) the capacity of law to exert control is limited; (2) control based on law is marginal to contemporary processes of ordering; and (3) state law is only likely to be effective when linked to other ordering processes. The first of these statements forms a core part of the descriptive analysis of the legal theory of autopoiesis (LTA), and the second is a central descriptive claim of the Foucauldian literature on governmentality. The LTA and the theory of responsive regulation each offer a version of the normative claim of the third statement. This section of the chapter offers a detailed critique of these different theoretical positions and the following section looks at how these theories might conceive of a post-regulatory state.

4.1 Legal Theory of Autopoiesis

For the legal theory of autopoiesis (LTA) the problem of control is a problem of communication. Autopoiesis is a term developed initially in biological sciences, derived from Greek words meaning self-producing, and refers to the idea that law reproduces itself according to its own norms. The problem which the theory addresses is centrally concerned with the difficulties that politics, economy, society and law have in communicating with each other and thus exercising control. Can legislatures create new legal rules and simply expect that they will be translated into laws which are effective in the legal system and which produce the desired changes in behaviour by economic and social actors? The central hypothesis of LTA is that such an expectation would, generally, be far-fetched. LTA provides an explanatory theory for the problems of regulatory control with some ideas as to how such problems might be addressed.

Developing a systems theory perspective associated with the work of Niklas Luhmann LTA perceives the world as consisting of differentiated and autonomous social subsystems (Anleu, 2000, 44).[1] These subsystems – the political, the legal, the social and the economic are the subsystems central to regulation – are said to be cognitively open but normatively and operatively closed. Thus a subsystem is open to 'facts, situations and events of its environment' (Luhmann, 1992, 145). This means that no subsystem is immune from the stimulation of its external environment, but such stimulation occurs as disturbance or perturbation. Stimuli are processed according to the normative structure of the subsystem and not the normative structure of the external environment. In the case of the legal system the distinctive character of its differentiation is its adoption of a binary code – in which actions are classified as legal or illegal, lawful or unlawful – to which its operations are oriented (Luhmann, 1992, 145–6).

To take a simple regulatory example, within the political subsystem there may be legislation created which assigns criminal penalties to breaches of rules set down in a regulatory statute. The legislation is the instrument of communication between political and legal subsystems. The legal subsystem, operationalized through a court, receives the legislation on its own terms, processing it according to the wider normative principles of criminal law. The instrumental objectives of the political subsystem in prohibiting the targeted conduct are of no interest within the legal subsystem. The legal norms emphasize principles protective of defendants such as a requirement that intent is proven, that guilt is proved beyond reasonable doubt, and so on. The stringent application of these principles often cuts across the instrumental objectives of a regulatory regime (Scott, 1995).

It may be the case that differentiated subsystems are well aligned with each other in particular domains. It is said, for example, that in many legal systems contract law and market principles of exchange within the economy have a reasonable fit with each other (Teubner, 1993, 92). Similarly the organizational forms used for business organizations' and corporations' law statutes are often quite well aligned. For LTA these alignments represent 'structural coupling' between systems. Such linkages are perceived as being a product of 'co-evolution' (Hutter, 1992).

The leading exponent of LTA, Gunther Teubner, describes his hypothesis as to the effects of the inherent problems of communications between subsystems in terms of a 'regulatory trilemma'. At its simplest the trilemma describes the three types of problem that can arise in the relationship between law and other subsystems: law may be irrelevant to the other subsystem and of no effect ('mutual indifference'); through creeping legalism law may damage the other system which is to be regulated by inhibiting its capacity for self-reproduction; the self-reproductive capacity of the legal subsystem may be damaged through an 'oversocialisation of law' (Teubner [1987] (1998), 406–14); Anleu, 2000, 47).

The aspect of the analysis which has received most attention is creeping legalism or juridification damaging other subsystems (Santos, 2002, 55–61). This is as much a problem for the welfare state as for the regulatory state (Anleu, 2000, 51). If we take the example of a regulatory regime over a utilities sector, decisions might largely be taken through negotiation over the needs of the sector consistent with a view as to what the regulatory policy requires. Law is present, but on the boundaries of regulatory interaction. Changes within the regulated sector, for example liberalization and an influx of new firms, might shatter the regulatory consensus and cause law to be drawn into the resolution of disputes more frequently. This is not simply about litigation, but also an increasing presence for lawyers in drafting documents and negotiating over regulatory decision-making. To the extent that lawyers operate within the meaning structures of the legal system they will seek to import legal norms about how things are done. This is perhaps most true in court settings, where judges are likely to resolve questions through appeal to the general norms of administrative or contract law rather than values more directly related to the instrumental objectives of the regulatory regime (Scott, 1998). For Teubner this poses the risk that private law will be further fragmented as it is asked to provide solutions to problems outside its normative experience or it will be hybridized and combined with other normative structures as it seeks to respond (Teubner, 1998).

Applying LTA to empirical questions provides a distinctive insight into problems of regulatory control. It displaces a linear governance pattern in which policy is translated into legislation, then regulatory action and regulatory effects with an image of 'a multitude of autonomous but interfering fields of action in each of which, in an acausal and simultaneous manner, recursive processes of differences take place' (Paterson and Teubner, 1998, 457). The challenge, in these terms, is to find ways to reduce or minimize the differences between the different fields of action through securing 'structural coupling' (ibid., 457). Such effects arise in quite unpredictable ways. This may be investigated empirically by drawing complex cognitive maps to demonstrate the self-regulatory processes of the various fields of action and to show their points of communication or non-communication (ibid., figs 5 and 6).

LTA envisions a post-regulatory state in which the legal subsystem relates to other subsystems not through highly specified, or materialized, regulatory law, but rather through working with the grain of the understanding of ordering within other subsystems. Put another way, the successful implementation of regulatory law is dependent on achieving some measure of 'structural coupling' (Teubner [1987] (1998), 415; cf. Clune, 1991/2). For Teubner the interesting ways to address the problem do not follow the economic theorists down a deregulatory route emphasizing the control functions of markets, but rather towards more sophisticated, abstract and indirect forms of regulatory intervention, which he describes as 'control of self-regulation' (see also Black, 1996), but which is also captured in the concepts 'collibration' (Dunsire, 1996), 'reflexive law', 'meta-governance' (Jessop, 1998, 2003), and 'meta-regulation' (Morgan, 1999; Parker, 2002). This approach recognizes the 'inner logic' of social systems and sets law the challenge of seeking to steer those social systems. A key aspect of this approach is re-casting the function of law from direct control to proceduralization (Black, 2000, 2001b). Such a shift in regulatory law would not end processes of juridification, but 'would help steer the process into more socially compatible channels' (Teubner [1987] (1998), 428). This modest conception of law's capabilities has led to a concern with targeting the internal management systems of regulated entities in order to secure compliance with regulatory goals (Gunningham and Grabosky, 1998; Parker, 2002).

Thinking about the problem of the relationship between mechanisms of global governance and regulatory law, Teubner (1997) himself has invoked ideas of legal pluralism as a complement to LTA. It is, claims Teubner, civil society rather than international governance organizations which is generating effective global regulatory rules (cf. Braithwaite and Drahos, 2000), effective in the sense that they are structurally coupled to the economic subsystem to which they apply. The key example he cites is the *lex mercatoria*, the ancient system of legal rules governing economic transactions, but he refers also to the regimes established within multinational enterprises to govern their global affairs. We could think also of international rules governing such matters as sustainability of forests and the protection of the environment from chemical pollution (Gunninham and Grabosky, 1998, ch. 4; Gunningham and Sinclair, 1999; Meidinger 2002).

The legal theory of autopoiesis highlights important limitations to the use of law as a regulatory instrument, encouraging us to think about the normative structures within other subsystems which might provide the key to control in respect of particular sets of values. The theory suggests a modest role of law in steering or proceduralizing those activities over which control is sought, thus seeking control indirectly. It is implausible to think of direct hierarchical control, and thus we must think of ways of intervening which work with the recursive practices of subsystems, seeking, for example, the alignment of regulatory norms set by legislators, legal norms generated as a response by the legal subsystem, and the activities over which control is sought. The capacity of the analysis to offer causal explanations and to predict the outcomes of particular interventions makes it extremely difficult to sell as a policy tool (Paterson and Teubner, 1998, 454–5).

4.2 Governmentality

The governmentality literature, originating with Foucault's well-known lecture, emphasizes the disparate practices and technologies which control and govern in contemporary states. The central problem addressed by the theory is the observation that much of the governance or control seen in modern societies is not focused on law and the state. Such an analysis leads to a conception of regulation which is pluralistic or decentred in character. A central characteristic of the governmentality literature is the approach to power, and the deployment of power for the purposes of governing. Foucault saw the art of government as representing a continuum between the power we have to govern ourselves, families and environment, and the sovereign power of the state (Foucault, 1991, 91–2). Thus conventional approaches to governmental power, which emphasize its legitimacy and basis in consent (Hindess, 1996, 105ff.), are displaced by greater emphasis on 'local or capillary power' (Hunt, 1993, 272). This is not to say that Foucault claimed to have developed any general theory of power. Indeed it has been suggested that Foucault's approach to power has more to offer legal scholarship in terms of methodology for understanding power than as providing a theory of power (Simon, 1994, 954).

However, it would be wrong to think of governmentality scholarship as conceiving of a shift towards a post-regulatory phase of governance. The diffusion of power and the emergence of new practices and technologies of control which are not dependent upon the sovereign state was in full swing in the eighteenth century. The governmentality scholarship invites us to reconceive the nature of regulatory governance rather than highlighting recent change. A number of Foucault-influenced legal scholars attribute the turn in legal scholarship away from a traditional conception of power oriented around legal sovereignty and consent towards a more diffuse and fragmented conception largely to the work of Foucault (Murphy, 1997, 204). I think it might equally well be attributed to pluralisms of the kind found in both legal scholarship and political science. Certainly the political science version of pluralism has been very influential in regulatory legal scholarship.

By the same token attention to private government in legal scholarship long pre-dates Foucault. The American critical legal studies movement looked to the work of Robert Hale, a law and economics scholar working in the first half of the twentieth century, to support arguments which undermine the juridical public/private distinction (Duxbury, 1990, 434). For Hale it was the possession of *economic* power which grounded the capacity of non-state actors to govern or coerce. Such private government calls for regulation of the inequalities which result. Foucault's analysis moves beyond these economic arguments by identifying other sources of power, central among these being professional expertise – whether in psychiatry, medicine or actuarial science (Rose, 1994). We can also detect the rise of professional power in constructing and practising within regulatory fields (Dezalay, 1996).

Law had a somewhat marginal place in Foucault's explication of governmentality. Government was not by law, but rather the use of law was one among a 'range of multiform tactics' for governing (Foucault, 1991, 95). Some with governmental power will have greater capacity to deploy law and others less. For Foucault, mercantalism, as a tactic of government, was defeated because it was excessively dependent on sovereign power of the law. Mercantilism was premised upon a thin theory of government wedded to sovereignty (Foucault, 1991, 98). The ascendancy of 'governmentality' in the eighteenth century was a product of the recognition of the wide range of tactics for governing and, necessarily, a more limited role for law. Hunt describes Foucault's views on modernity in terms that as the sovereignty of the monarch is displaced so is law, as the expression of sovereign will, expelled (Hunt, 1993, 272). The idea that sovereign law has been displaced by disciplinary power is premised on the two being incompatible, the operation of one excluding the operation of the other (Santos, 2002, 6).

This idea of the explulsion of law is premised on a definition of law as sovereign law which is contestable. Legal pluralism scholarship offers the most vigorous challenge to such a monolithic concept of law, with its emphasis on the plurality of forms and sources of law (Hunt, 1993, 307, 320ff.). There is plenty of justiciable law which, though by definition it is ultimately backed by state authority, is nevertheless made locally either through the rather traditional form of delegation of statutory power (Murphy, 1997, 203) (for example to local authorities and corporations) or through contract. Beyond that which is justiciable there are local rules and standards made within families, communities and organizations constituting self-government and government of others.

A key move made by pluralistic regulation scholars is to emphasize that law is just one form of effective norm. Norms are effective because they form part of a wider scheme of regulation which has monitoring and behaviour-modifying mechanisms. These may or may not be part of the legal system. This is not a new insight – it was a core aspect of the 'sociological jurisprudence' movement of the early twentieth century and is a basic tenet of both sociological and psychological understandings of ordering. The novelty lies in applying this conception of ordering through legal and non-legal norms to regulatory fields. In her study of educational reforms Anne Barron has emphasized the key role of law in the reform process. It is not that statutory reform has 'itself generated change within schools', rather law has tended to act on the 'discourses and practices' already found within the school system, 'triggering their elaboration or refinement; modifying them in ways that imbues them with a certain institutional force and stability' (Barron, 1996, 196).

The governmentality literature offers a modest conception of the role of law in the ordering of society. Highlighting the diffuse technologies and practices through which control occurs, it displaces the state from the centre of our thinking about ordering. Recent work by Alan Hunt, for example, places 'self-governance' at the centre of a study of moral regulation, with a rather tangential relationship to the legal regulation of the state (Hunt, 1999). Mariana Valverde's (1998) study of alcoholism examines the wide variety of state regulatory measures which form a rather peripheral part of the governance of alcohol consumption.

The governmentality literature is less strong, perhaps less interested, in suggesting how this reconception of ordering might be deployed in future regulatory policy. More generally it is difficult to discern any normative agenda. It is a literature which is at its most effective in reformulating our understanding through the analysis of the micro-detail of particular social and institutional practices. The reluctance to develop general knowledge which might ground a normative approach to governance issues has generated con-siderable debate within the governmentality literature as to the responsibilities of scholars to develop critique (O'Malley et al., 1997; Stenson, 1998).

4.3   Responsive Regulation

The theory of responsive regulation is centrally concerned with designing regulatory institutions and processes which stimulate and respond to the regulatory capacities which already exist within regulated firms, attempting to keep regulatory intervention to the minimum level necessary to secure the desired outcomes, while retaining the capacity to intervene more (in terms of more stringent enforcement or the introduction of a more interventionist regime).

On the basis of the governmentality analysis, regulation, if not always law, is a key constitutive element of contemporary societies (cf. Hunt, 1993, ch. 13; Shearing, 1993). The emphasis on regulation, particularly within the theory of responsive regulation, highlights a residual role for law at the apex of pyramids of both regulatory enforcement and regulatory technique. Thus the enforcement pyramid envisages that most regulatory interaction will be in the nature of education and advice ('persuasion') to regulatees. Where compliance is not forthcoming, regulators will escalate their enforcement activity, with warning letters and then civil or criminal penalties. The most stringent sanctions (for example licence revocation) will be at the apex of the pyramid (Ayres and Braithwaite, 1992, 35). Regulators and regulatees have incentives to operate largely at the base of the pyramid with relatively informal interaction. The technique pyramid has governments encouraging businesses to self-regulate at the base of the pyramid. Where self-regulation is not forthcoming or effective, governments may become involved with enforced self-regulation, under which firms are required to set down rules for themselves and report them to a regulatory agency for monitoring and enforcement. Where enforced self-regulation is not deemed effective, governments need to be able to escalate to command regulation, first with discretionary punishment and then with non-discretionary punishment (Ayres and Braithwaite, 1992, 39).

One might say that responsive regulation brings the idea of law back into governance, irrespective of whether law is actually invoked or actually perceived as a reason for cooperating with regulators or making self-regulation work. Central aspects of the theory are the development of pyramidal approaches to enforcement and the application of regulatory technique. The enforcement pyramid, reasoned inductively from empirical analyses, has regulators using low-level sanctions such as advice and warnings at the base of the pyramid and only escalating to more drastic remedies in the event that regulatees are unresponsive at the lower level. Higher-level sanctions might include application of fines, prosecutions and revocation of licences. Within the theory a regulator with the credible capacity to escalate to high-level sanctions should be able to operate mainly at the lower levels of the pyramid – 'speaking softly while carrying a big stick'. The technique pyramid has governments encouraging businesses to self-regulate at the base of the pyramid with the potential for escalating to more intrusive techniques should self-regulation prove ineffective (Ayres and Braithwaite, 1992).

Key aspects of the responsive regulation theory are vulnerable to claims that few countries exhibit a sufficiently unified or strong state capacity for regulatory power to be capable of sustained manipulation to secure desired regulatory outcomes. Contemporary regulatory law is rarely within the control of a single regulatory unit with capacity to deploy law coherently for instrumental purposes. Within the Westminster democracies legislatures are jealous of their power to make rules and to establish and reform regimes. Legislatures are additionally reluctant to delegate to agencies powers to apply formal legal sanctions (a prejudice commonly reinforced by the protections afforded in human rights legislation). Additionally key powers are held by non-state actors deriving from information, wealth and organizational capacities (Daintith, 1997; Hood, 1984; Scott, 2001). Powerful businesses may dominate the interpretation and application of regulatory legislation. Interest groups' rhetorical stances may render problematic the legitimacy of formal rules when they are applied.

In the Japanese case the criticism is that the responsive regulation model 'builds on the assumption of a strong regulatory state, with existing precedents and a large legal machinery – a condition that does not exist in Japan' (Schaede, 2000, 271). Self-regulation in Japan is typically more independent of the state than would be true in many other OECD countries. If, under these conditions, self-regulation is effective notwithstanding the absence of credible capacities by the state to escalate regulatory technique, it appears to challenge the general validity of the responsive regulation theory in this respect. Deakin and Cook (1999), referring to the German case, suggest the effectiveness of commercial norms in regulating business transactions is linked to their fit with principles of high-level commercial law, rather than to presence of state regulatory capacities.

The consequences of interdependencies within Westminster-style regulatory regimes are that it is difficult to imagine circumstances when enforcement agencies can coherently deploy law to pursue instrumental objectives in securing compliance. Put more starkly, enforcement pyramids are likely to be broken, incomplete or outside the control of instrumentally oriented agencies (Haines, 1997). In one empirical study it was suggested that occupational health and safety inspectors who appeared to be using a pyramidal strategy are in fact frequently using a split approach in which routine inspection activities occur in the base segments of the pyramid whereas reports of workplace injuries are met with responses almost exclusively in the upper, punitive half of the pyramid (Gunningham and Johnson, 1999, 122). This represents a more general pattern of regulatory responses to resource limitations within which it is more usually a matter of selecting the appropriate arrow from the quiver rather than running through the pyramidal approach with each regulatee. Accordingly there are 'different points of entry' to the enforcement pyramid, determined by reference to the characteristics of the regulatee and risk or nature of any infraction (Gunningham and Johnson, 1999, 124–5).

With pyramids of regulatory technique, legislators and/or regulators are liable to find it difficult to show credible commitment to the escalating of techniques. This is because instrumental enforcement is liable to be diluted by political considerations. The scope for such political considerations will vary according to the structure of dependencies within the regime. These limits to the application of the theory of responsive regulation cannot be corrected better by educating agencies, business, government and interest groups in what the model requires. They are, to a lesser or greater extent, structural features of contemporary societies and their governance structures, and represent a vindication of Foucault's dispersed power governmentality model. This objection has been addressed by reconceiving the enforcement pyramid in three dimensions, with government and agencies on one face, regulated businesses on the second face and third parties (whether NGOs or other businesses) on the third face (Gunningham and Grabosky, 1998, 398). This elaboration of the enforcement pyramid has the merit of modelling empirical evidence in a manner truer to the multi-party environments which typically characterize regulatory regimes. It demonstrates that control may be exercised even where state bodies are unable or unwilling to use their powers. So, for example, the capacity of an NGO to 'name and shame' or to take direct action against a business may constitute the peak sanctions in an enforcement pyramid. It envisages not only different parties, but also different instruments of control (Gunningham and Grabosky, 1998, 399–400). This pluralist reconception of the pyramidal approach makes clear the limitations for instrumental or integrated regulatory action. The potential for multiple and overlapping control possibilities which might operate indirectly is reminiscent of the approach within autopoietic theory which seeks to rebalance checks already within the systems – referred to as 'collibration' (Dunsire, 1996).

It is not clear how compatible even a modified theory of responsive regulation is with theories of legal pluralism. The difficulty centres on the privileging of state law conceived of as substantive norms and procedures of enforcement. Responsive regulation may be reworked to focus on the legitimacy of the procedures by which regulatory norms are generated or of the institutions within which they are implemented (Vincent-Jones, 2002b). In this formulation the theory takes us away from the inductively reasoned scholarship of Ayres and Braithwaite to the normative concerns of Nonet and Selznick (1978).

For some, the responsive regulation model has been insufficiently ambitious. Parker (1999, 71) suggests that it could 'provide a normative foundation for solving general problems of doing justice in democratic societies'. The enforcement pyramid should be deployed not only by regulators but by 'mothers, lovers, bosses, creditors, unions, and generals struggling for justice in child-rearing, relationships, employee management, finance, industrial relations, international trade, and warfare'. In one of the key elaborations of the responsive regulation theory Parker (1999, 76) offers a pyramidal model in which indigenous ordering is at the base with informal justice in the middle segment and formal legal justice at the apex. This innovation marries legal pluralism with responsive regulation, recognizing the capacities for control or ordering without state law. Where legal pluralists might question Parker's model is in her retention of the Braithwaitian assumption that effectiveness of indigenous ordering at the base of the pyramid is dependent upon the credible capacity of escalation to more formal law at the apex of the pyramid.

The responsive regulation theory offers us an inductively reasoned model for regulating both more effectively and with greater consent. It seeks to 'transcend' the deregulation debate by showing the continuing relevance and possibility of regulatory activity in a period of profound scepticism. It has the great merit that when shown the various pyramids, many regulators and policy-makers immediately seem to understand them descriptively and offer examples. But the retention of a strong and unified state within the model is a significant weakness, since it renders the theory problematic in situations characterized by either fragmented or weak states. In the context of this chapter the weakness feeds through into assumptions about how law may work within regulatory regimes.

5.   CHARACTERIZING THE POST-REGULATORY STATE

A critical analysis of the three theoretical perspectives discussed in the previous section provides the basis for questioning the capacity and desirability of depending on state law and hierarchical forms of control within the regulatory state, and provides the basis for conceiving of a post-regulatory state. The main focus of the preliminary analysis is alternative conceptions of control – alternatives to state law and alternatives to hierarchical control. We see variety in the components of control systems – the form which goals or standards take, the mechanisms for feedback or monitoring, and the mechanisms for realigning where deviation from the standards is detected, and variety in who is controlling and who is controlled.

5.1 Variety in Norms

We can think of the core norms of the regulatory state as primary and secondary legislation, the only forms of rule-making in which the state uses its monopoly of legal force over economic and social actors. Even here there is a plurality of state actors with formal rule-making capacity (including agencies, subnational governments, supranational institutions, as with the EU) such that rules may be multiple and overlapping, with meaning assigned to regimes through processes of interpretation which are contingent upon a variety of non-legal factors (Scott, 2001). A condition of 'internal legal pluralism' arises where there coexist 'different logics of regulation carried out by different state institutions with very little communication between them' (Santos, 2002, 95). Such conditions may be facilitated by the tendency of state actors to deploy a wide range of alternative forms of norm. Thus instruments of 'soft law' (more accurately portrayed in French as *normes douces*) such as guidance, circulars and letters of comfort are widely deployed with the intention of shaping the behaviour of those to whom they are directed, but without the necessity of using formal law (Lex Fori, 2000, 53). Soft law instruments enable departments and agencies to avoid the more elaborate procedural requirements of formal law and/or to address issues outside their formal mandates. State organizations may also use terms set down in contracts as instruments of control, either in the context of normal procurement processes (Daintith, 1979), or in the context of creating statutory regimes based on contractual or near-contractual governance (Vincent-Jones, 2002a). Contractual rules are, for the most part, set by the parties but underpinned by state laws relating to their enforcement and the filling in of gaps. Socio-legal research has found that in particular sets of business relationships strict contractual rules play a limited role in governing the conduct of the parties (Macaulay, 1963). It is difficult to develop a more general hypothesis as to the importance of state law for underpinning contractual relations.

Contractual rules are also extensively used as regulatory instruments by non-state actors. Such rules take both collectivized and individuated forms. Collectivized contractual rules are typically used to establish and make binding self-regulatory regimes. While it may be correct to think of signing up to membership of a self-regulatory regime (in the absence of irresistible market or governmental pressures) as voluntary, within common law countries at least, a member is then bound by the rules and procedures set down. Self-regulatory bodies are frequently much more complete regulators, in the sense that they combine rule-making, monitoring and sanctioning powers within a single organization, something which is rare for state regulatory agencies (Scott, 2002). Norms are also set down in individuated contractual agreements, enabling large companies to exert controls over the conduct of both their customers and their suppliers, not only through setting down rules, but also through introducing processes of monitoring, audit or certification for compliance.

A further form of non-state rule-making, not linked to contract, is found in processes of standard-setting or normalization. Private standards institutes in the industrialized states date from the early part of the twentieth century and have developed into extensive bureaucracies receiving state support both through funding and through the incorporation of standards into legal regulatory requirements. More recently general and specialized standardization bodies have emerged at the supranational level, notably in the European Union. Such private standards are also rendered effective through their incorporation into contracts.

The post-regulatory analysis of the plural legal norms emphasizes the development of principles and practices for regulating rule-making. A well-developed example of such meta-regulation is found in the principles for control over the imposition of regulatory burdens developed in the United States, the United Kingdom and many other OECD countries (Froud et al., 1998; Pildes and Sunstein, 1995). These regimes have in common procedural requirements that rule-makers carry out regulatory impact assessments on new regulatory rules. Such regimes typically apply to primary and secondary legal rules. The Australian federal government applies its regulation review regime additionally to soft-law instruments made by public authorities (Productivity Commission, 2001). The Australian National Competition Policy involves the federal Office of Regulation Review assessing the progress made by state and territory governments in reducing regulatory measures which reduce competition, and includes the capacity for the federal Treasurer to apply financial sanctions (Morgan, 1999). The UK government has extended the regulatory reform regime by administrative measures to encompass regulatory burdens imposed on the public sector, pursuing reviews of the burdens applying to public hospitals, schools, local government and universities.

State use of contracts as regulatory instruments over the public sector is also subject to quite developed regimes in many OECD countries. It was common practice in the UK for public authorities to use procurement processes to pursue unrelated policy objectives such as minimum wage and anti-discrimination policies through imposing contractual conditions. This practice was substantially ended by the application by domestic rules on compulsory competitive tendering and EU procurement rules which preclude taking such considerations into account when entering into contracts. The Australian Commonwealth government continues to pursue industrial policy, pay equity and environmental policies through its procurement rules, a preference which has precluded its accession to the WTO Agreement on Government Procurement (Department of Finance and Administration, n.d., 2002).

The theoretical literature linked to the legal theory of autopoiesis (LTA) further envisages the proceduralization of self-regulatory regimes (Black, 1996, 2000, 2001b). Such meta-regulatory rule-making might involve the setting of minimum requirements for particular types of standards set by individual firms or organizations, as with attempts to set minimum terms for manufacturers' guarantees.[2] More typical of such regimes is that they set minimum standards for collective codes of conduct developed through trade associations. The UK Office of Fair Trading (OFT) has used statutory powers to approve consumer codes under the Fair Trading Act 1973 to set down minimum standards that codes should comply with, including the provision of effective consumer redress regimes (Scott and Black, 2000, ch. 2). The UK Enterprise Act 2002 has reformed the regime, now requiring the OFT to issue minimum standards and to grant a common approval mark to schemes which are approved. The 'reinventing regulation' initiative in the US has spawned a number of attempts to use Braithwaite's 'enforced self-regulation' model, under which firms are either required or incentivized to write their own rules. The Environmental Protection Agency, for example, encouraged businesses to develop their own regimes in return for less burdensome regulation (Freeman, 1997), though the leading scheme, Project XL, appears to have failed because of 'delays in approval, ongoing demands for information' and bureaucratic resistance (Eisner, 2002, 25). This kind of initiative does, in any case, fall short of the kind of proceduralized law suggested by LTA.

A wide variety of norms is deployed in regulatory governance. In this section we have noted that formal legal rules may be developed by state and non-state bodies in a form other than primary and secondary legislation, and in particular through contract. We have also noted that instruments of soft law, which are not legally binding, are of considerable importance to state bodies, both government departments and agencies. Such soft-law norms typically derive at least some of their force from their location within a matrix of hierarchical state power. For example, an agency may prefer to operate through guidance which is effective because all parties know that legal rules are likely to be forthcoming if the guidance is not followed. Alternatively there may be a willingness to follow guidance as part of a more general pattern of cooperation. Other norms entail the deployment, or at least existence, of non-hierarchical mechanisms of control, as with social norms, standards relating to price and quality set through competition. These are discussed in the next section.

5.2 Variety in Control Mechanisms

If a central characteristic of the regulatory state is an emphasis on hierarchy as an instrument of control, then a key feature of the post-regulatory state is a shift towards other bases for control. This is a key theme of the governance literature. This change may be one of thinking rather than underlying mechanisms, since it has long been clear that the period of organized capitalism is characterized by a mixture of state, market and community within social control processes (Offe, 2000; Santos, 2002: 44–51). The shift in thinking is well exemplified in the work of Lawrence Lessig, with his division of control mechanisms into four basic types – law; social norms; markets; architecture. Lessig (1999) observes that contemporary developments in information technology give a particular prominence to the architecture of software as an instrument of control. Among the most celebrated aspects of Foucault's analysis of changes in disciplinary power was his revival of Bentham's panopticon model of prison design and claim that this architecturally oriented form of governance over prisoners was emblematic of a shift towards government through surveillance (Foucault, 1977, 195–228). A wide range of studies emphasize different forms of spatial control (Newman, 1972; Shearing and Stenning, 1985; Katyal, 2002; Merry, 2001). In its more basic forms control or regulation by architecture could not be less responsive. There is no enforcement pyramid with a concrete parking bollard, no exceptions to the application of the complete exclusion of parking, even if we can imagine any number of emergencies which a parking regulator (and an even greater number of drivers) might think justified an exceptional approach. Lawrence Lessig's (1999) well-known metaphor 'code is law' captures his assertion that the controls which are built into computer software (whether at the instigation of firms or government) offer an architectural alternative to the deployment of legal rules. Code can be deployed to inhibit international arbitrage by consumers of DVDs (digital versatile disks) or to prevent access to particular websites by unsupervised children, to provide two examples, each without the potential or actual application of legal sanction.

The search for greater variety in bases of control is consistent with the 'law of requisite variety', developed in cybernetics to capture the idea that in order to exert effective control, the controller must have at least as much variety in its control mechanisms as the system to be controlled (Beer, 1966). We have elsewhere adopted the central four-part division of the bases of control, though making significant revisions to the terminology and characterization of the four bases. We label these hierarchy, community, competition and design (Murray and Scott, 2002). Perhaps most importantly, we attach greater significance to the various hybrid forms of control which can be derived from the four basic types. The theory of responsive regulation is very much organized around the development of hybrid forms which deploy hierarchy and community as their basis, notably in the well-known model of 'enforced self-regulation' (defined as the activities of individual firms without and with direct monitoring and approval in setting and applying standards to themselves). Indeed, we could say that LTA, responsive regulation and governmentality are each peculiarly interested in one or more forms of self-regulation as a key basis for contemporary governance. Responsive regulation also draws on a hierarchy/competition hybrid in the model of partial industry regulation.

5.3 Variety in Controllers

Within the regulatory state literature state regulatory bodies are accorded a special place. In contrast, no special legitimacy or value is placed on attributing control functions to state bodies – government departments, agencies and courts – within post-regulatory state thinking. Standard-setting is observed at supranational level through a wide range of general and specific governance institutions. Trade associations operate both nationally and internationally to set standards, for example in respect of environmental protection. Businesses and NGOs frequently have both the interest and the capacity to monitor the activities of both government and businesses for compliance with norms of their or others' making. Thus banks, insurers, accreditation bodies and credit-rating agencies can all be thought of as contributing at least some components of control systems over risk-related behaviour and compliance with more general standards (Anleu et al., 2000; Heimer, 2002; Richardson, forthcoming). It is quite common for airlines and other carriers to be given incentives to effectively monitor for compliance with immigration rules and refuse passage to those in breach. Trade unions and NGOs may be formally empowered as enforcers of regulatory rules, for example in respect of occupational health and safety, animal welfare and consumer protection. NGOs may alternatively seek such powers through the use of media, litigation and other strategies to modify the behaviour of those seen in breach of implicit or explicit standards. When we use competition as the basis for control we may be empowering individuals to control through the aggregation of their market or other competitive behaviour.

5.4 Variety in Controllees

The regulatory state literature has traditionally viewed businesses as the key regulatees. The post-regulatory state perspective takes a wider view, recognizing that the behaviour of a wider range of actors is relevant to the outcomes of ordering social and economic life. Thus we may study controls over government itself, both in its regulatory activities noted above, and its more general capacities (Hood et al., 1999). We may also think of individuals as targets of control, using variety in control mechanisms to secure outcomes which might have been sought otherwise through regulating businesses.

Furthermore, we may be selective about whom we control. Partial industry regulation may be applied either where only a segment of a particular sector poses policy problems (as with dominant incumbents in the utilities or broadcasting sectors) or because we observe that the relationship between partial control and unregulated behaviour produces superior outcomes to either no or complete regulation (Ayres and Braithwaite, 1992). Many regulatory bodies now use risk analysis to determine whom they regulate and how intensively. Thus low-risk activities or organizations may fall substantially outside the regime, while riskier businesses are subjected to its full rigour.

6.   CONCLUSION

The term 'post-regulatory state' in the title of this chapter is not used in the sense of the body politic denoted in the phrases welfare state and regulatory state. Rather, the post-regulatory state is a state of mind which seeks to test the assumptions that states are the main loci of control over social and economic life or that they ought to have such a position and role. In the age of governance regulatory control is perceived as diffused through society with less emphasis on the sovereign state. This preliminary investigation of the legal dimension to the post-regulatory state is a long way from asserting the unimportance of law to contemporary regulation. At a descriptive level the analysis offers a wider array of norm types and control mechanisms relevant to understanding regulatory governance than is common in functionalist analyses of the regulatory state. Normatively the analysis is suggestive of alternative functions for law to asserting command. In particular it emphasizes the role of law in structuring or proceduralizing both state and non-state activities which are premised upon alternative instruments and/or institutions of control. But there are both theoretical and empirical challenges to be addressed.

One empirical problem with the analysis is that it fails adequately to reflect the impetus within governments to resort to 'command-and-control' regulation. Disasters and scandals of one kind or another routinely call forth responses which emphasize more prescriptive rules, more powerful regulatory authorities and related features. We need only think of the responses to BSE (bovine spongiform encephalopathy) in Europe and the Enron collapse in the United States, each with global reverberations. Unrelated to this is a concern identifiable within governments in the US, UK, Australia and elsewhere with asserting control over public sector bodies which has tended to generate more formal and externalized regulatory controls, dependent to a greater degree than hitherto on law. Set against this there are examples where the official response to disasters characterized as regulatory failure have been to *reduce* the intensity of external regulatory oversight and place more emphasis on the internal capacities of regulatees, as with occupational health and safety regulation in the UK oil industry following the Piper Alpha disaster (Paterson and Teubner, 1998, 474) and where controls over government bodies is asserted not through command and control but through trying to stimulate self-regulation and competition (Hood et al., 2000). But these examples of post-regulatory thinking appear to be more the exception than the rule.

The whole concept of the 'post-regulatory' may also be problematic, first because it might be taken to imply progression towards superior, as opposed to different, ways of thinking about governance, and second, because it raises the difficulty of addressing those jurisdictions where evidence for the emergence of a regulatory state is limited. Pre-regulatory states, such as those of North Asia, arguably demonstrate more of the kind of post-regulatory approach than would be true of the UK and the US, for example in the emphasis on informal steering of self-regulatory mechanisms. If we think of official policies towards developing countries, the agenda of the international financial institutions for the governance of developing countries is oriented around building up rather than displacing state capacity (World Bank, 1997). Thus, under the influence of international organizations, many states are looking to construct the institutions which will make state governance more effective, rather than to dismantle them (Levy and Spiller, 1996). We may therefore prefer to think of points on a continuum between regulatory and non-regulatory states within which some countries move towards the regulatory end and, to the extent to which they exhibit post-regulatory (or pre-regulatory) approaches, this represents a shift towards the non-regulatory end.

A theoretical objection to this chapter is to recognize that processes of control not focused on state law are important, but claim that such processes do not come within the rubric of regulation which is defined to refer only to that subset characterized by the deployment of state law by state agencies in instrumental fashion. This objection is at the heart of the project begun with this chapter. My response is to say that the 'enlarging the regulatory envelope' effects of my analysis are only a by-product and that the main reason for looking beyond the regulatory state is to secure a better understanding of the core state governance functions and the relationship between them and other ordering processes. Put another way, we enrich our understanding of regulation when we have better tools to understand the pervasiveness of non-state law and non-hierarchical control processes and their effects on regulatory processes as they are more conventionally conceived. Such an approach enables us to refocus the analysis in three ways.

First, there is the suggestion of a role for law in regulatory settings which is less concerned with setting down rules and powers. A common theme in contemporary governmentality and responsive regulation scholarship is an emphasis on what Foucault called 'conduct of conduct' (Rose, 2000) but which has similarities to what Christine Parker, building on her responsive regulation work, refers to as 'meta-regulation' (Parker, 2002, 297). It is no coincidence that a similar emphasis on the steering of internal control mechanisms is also found in the legal scholarship influenced by LTA. Is this hybrid form, with its emphasis on legal underpinning for indirect control over internal normative systems, capable of generating a new consensus on the role of law in regulation? This approach is defined by its retention of a central place for hierarchy as a steering mechanism. A post-regulatory state might look beyond hybrid forms which loosen command-based legal control, but, as with responsive regulation, retain it in at least some residual form such that ends are ultimately set and determined by the sovereign state.

Second, the chapter is suggestive of providing greater recognition to other types of legal and non-legal norms in processes of control. Where such norm structures exist or can be stimulated they may be preferable (because they may be more effective or more efficient) to regulatory law. Third, and linking the first two points, we might ask to what extent the hierarchical control dimension to regulation may be displaced by control processes built on community, competition and design, either singly or in hybrid combination. This shift has variously been described as a move away from hierarchies towards heterarchies (Black, 2001a, 145) or networks (Salamon, 2001, 1628). A governmentality approach recognizes, indeed emphasizes, situations where control arises from exercise of power not underpinned by sovereign law, though there is a hint of the role of sovereign law in underpinning hybrid governance arrangements in the governmentality literature too (Stenson, 1998, 337). Examples here include the electrical manufacturers who program DVD players only to read North American-coded DVDs and the communities which exercise control through defining what is thinkable or do-able. Some processes which lack state law underpinning may even deliver what are perceived as public interest objectives, such as development of software for controlling Internet access (a contested case) and the granting of consumer remedies in excess of legal rights.

The key here may be to identify the conditions under which the incentives for acting within competitive or community control structures are sufficiently (if not totally) aligned with conceptions of public interest, such that the state law underpinning is unnecessary. This would be a broad-brush exercise, rather than a micro-policy analysis, and arguably accords with what governments already do in determining the boundaries of regulatory intervention. I am broadly sympathetic to the view that markets are unable to function without some (however distant) underpinning of state law (Shearing, 1993). That argument needs further investigation in the case of community-based and design-based control which appear more radical when proffered distinctly from any hierarchical or sovereign law underpinning. Viewed in this way, the post-regulatory state may provide a way of thinking about regulatory governance which is complementary to the regulatory state literature, generating both new insights and new challenges.

NOTES

* The research and writing of this chapter were carried out while the author was on secondment as Senior Fellow in Public Law, Law Program and Regulatory Institutions Network, Research School of Social Sciences, Australian National University. The chapter was originally presented at the Politics of Regulation Workshop, Universitat Pompeu Fabra, Barcelona, November 2002. The author is grateful to John Braithwaite, Imelda Maher, Michael Moran, Anthony Ogus and Peter Vincent-Jones for comments on an earlier draft.

1. Approaches to control premised upon systems theory can also be found in the public administration literature, notably in the work of Dunsire (1996) and Hood (1984). See also Kickert (1993); and t'Veld (1991).
2. For example in Directive 1999/44/EC on Consumer Guarantees OJ L 171/12, 7.7.1999, Article 6.

REFERENCES

Anleu, Sharon L. Roach (2000), *Law and Social Change*, London: Sage.

Anleu, Sharyn L. Roach, Lorraine Green Mazerolle and Lois Presser (2000), 'Third-Party Policing and Insurance: The Case of Market-Based Crime Prevention', *Law and Policy*, **22**, 67–87.

Ayres, Ian and John Braithwaite (1992), *Responsive Regulation: Transcending the Deregulation Debate*, Oxford: Oxford University Press.

Baldwin, Robert and Martin Cave (1999), *Understanding Regulation*, Oxford: Oxford University Press.

Barron, Anne (1996), 'The Governance of Schooling: Genealogies of Control and Empowerment in the Reform of Public Education', *Studies in Law, Politics and Society*, **15**, 167–204.

Beer, Stafford (1966), *Decision and Control: The Meaning of Operational Research and Management Cybernetics*, London: Wiley.

Better Regulation Task Force (2000), 'Alternatives to State Regulation', London: Cabinet Office.

Black, Julia (1996), 'Constitutionalising Self-Regulation', *Modern Law Review*, **59**, 24–56.

Black, Julia (2000), 'Proceduralizing Regulation: Part I', *Oxford Journal of Legal Studies*, **20**, 597–614.

Black, Julia (2001a), 'Decentring Regulation: The Role of Regulation and Self-Regulation in a "Post-Regulatory" World', *Current Legal Problems* [2001], 103–46.

Black, Julia (2001b), 'Proceduralizing Regulation: Part II', *Oxford Journal of Legal Studies*, **21**, 33–58.

Braithwaite, John (2000), 'The New Regulatory State and the Transformation of Criminology', *British Journal of Criminology*, **40**, 222–38.

Braithwaite, John and Peter Drahos (2000), *Global Business Regulation*, Cambridge: Cambridge University Press.

Clune, William H. (1991/2), 'Implementation as Autopoietic Interaction of Auto-poietic Organizations', *European Yearbook in the Sociology of Law* (1991–2), 485–513.

Cohn, Margit (2001), 'Fuzzy Legality in Regulation: The Legislative Mandate Revisited', *Law and Policy*, **23**, 469–97.

Daintith, Terence (1979), 'Regulation by Contract: The New Prerogative', *Current Legal Problems*, 42–64.

Daintith, Terence (1997), 'Regulation' (Chapter 10 of the *International Encyclopaedia of Comparative Law*), Tübingen: Mohr Siebeck.

Deakin, Simon and Jacqueline Cook (1999), 'Regulation and the Boundaries of the Law', in ESRC Centre for Business Research (ed.), *Literature Survey on Factual, Empirical and Legal Issues,* papers prepared for the DIT Company Law Review, London: Department of Trade and Industry, http://www.dti.gov.uk/cld/may2000/esrc9.pdf.

Department of Finance and Administration (n.d.), 'World Trade Organisation Agreement on Government Procurement – Review of Membership Implications', Canberra: DOFA.

Department of Finance and Administration (2002), 'Commonwealth Procurement Guidelines', Canberra: DOFA.

Dezalay, Yves (1996), 'Between the State, Law and the Market: The Social and Professional Stakes in the Construction and Definition of a Regulatory Arena', in William W. Bratton, Joseph McCahery, Sol Picciotto and Colin Scott (eds), *International Regulatory Competition and Coordination*, Oxford: Oxford University Press, pp. 59–87.

Dunsire, Andrew (1996), 'Tipping the Balance: Autopoiesis and Governance', *Administration & Society*, **28**, 299–334.

Duxbury, Neil (1990), 'Robert Hale and the Economy of Legal Force', *Modern Law Review*, **53**, 421–44.

Eisner, Marc Allen (2000), *Regulatory Politics in Transition*, 2nd edn, Baltimore: Johns Hopkins University Press.

Eisner, Marc Allen (2002), 'Protecting the Environment at the Margin: The Role of Economic Analysis in Regulatory Design and Decision Making', paper presented to Law's Experts Conference, ANU, Canberra.

Foucault, Michel (1977), *Discipline and Punish: The Birth of the Prison*, Harmondsworth: Penguin.

Foucault, Michel (1991), 'Governmentality', in Graham Burchell, Colin Gordon and Peter Miller (eds), *The Foucault Effect: Studies in Governmentality*, Hemel Hempstead: Wheatsheaf, pp. 87–104.

Francis, John (1993), *The Politics of Regulation*, Oxford: Blackwell.

Freeman, Jody (1997), 'Collaborative Governance in the Administrative State', *UCLA Law Review*, **45**, 1–98.

Froud, Julie, Rebecca Boden and Anthony Ogus (1998), *Controlling the Regulators*, London: Macmillan.

Grabosky, Peter (1994), 'Beyond the Regulatory State', *Australian and New Zealand Journal of Criminology*, **27**, 192–7.

Grabosky, Peter N. (1995), 'Using Non-Governmental Resources to Foster Regulatory Compliance', *Governance*, **8**, 527–50.

Grabosky, Peter and John Braithwaite (1986), *Of Manners Gentle: Enforcement*

Strategies of Australian Business Regulatory Agencies, Melbourne: Oxford University Press.

Gunningham, Neil and Peter Grabosky (1998), *Smart Regulation: Designing Environmental Policy*, Oxford: Oxford University Press.

Gunningham, Neil and Richard Johnson (1999), *Regulating Workplace Safety: Systems and Sanctions*, Oxford: Oxford University Press.

Gunningham, Neil and Darren Sinclair (1999), 'Regulatory Pluralism: Designing Policy Mixes for Environmental Protection', *Law and Policy*, **21**, 49–76.

Haines, Fiona (1997), *Corporate Regulation: Beyond 'Punish or Persuade'*, Oxford: Oxford University Press.

Hayek, F.A. (1982), *Law, Legislation and Liberty: A New Statement of the Liberal Principles of Justice and Political Economy*, London: Routledge.

Heimer, Carol (2002), 'Insuring More, Ensuring Less: The Costs and Benefits of Private Regulation Through Insurance', in Tom Baker and Jonathan Simon (eds), *Embracing Risk: The Changing Culture of Insurance and Responsibility*, Chicago: Chicago University Press, pp. 116–45.

Held, David (2002), 'Law of States, Law of Peoples', *Legal Theory*, **8**, 1–44.

Henry, Claude, Michel Matheu and Alain Jeunemaître (eds) (2000), *Regulation of Network Utilities,* Oxford: Oxford University Press.

Hindess, Barry (1996), *Discourses of Power: From Hobbes to Foucault*, Oxford: Blackwell.

Hood, Christopher (1984), *The Tools of Government*, London: Macmillan.

Hood, Christopher, Oliver James and Colin Scott (2000), 'Regulation inside Government: Has it Increased, is it Increasing, Should it be Diminished?', *Public Administration*, **78**, 283–304.

Hood, Christopher, Henry Rothstein and Robert Baldwin (2001), *The Government of Risk*, Oxford: Oxford University Press.

Hood, Christopher, Colin Scott, Oliver James, George Jones and Tony Travers (1999), *Regulation Inside Government: Waste-Watchers, Quality Police, and Sleaze-Busters*, Oxford: Oxford University Press.

Hunt, Alan (1993), *Explorations in Law and Society: Towards a Constitutive Theory of Law*, London: Routledge.

Hunt, Alan (1999), *Governing Morals: A Social History of Moral Regulation*, Cambridge: Cambridge University Press.

Hutter, Michael (1992), 'How the Economy Talks the Law into Co-Evolution: An Exercise in Autpoietic Social Theory', *European Yearbook in the Sociology of Law* (1991–92), 263–93.

Jessop, Bob (1998), 'The Rise of Governance and the Risks of Failure: The Case of Economic Development', *International Social Science Journal*, **155**, 29–45.

Jessop, Bob (2003), 'Governance and Metagovernance: On Reflexivity, Requisite Variety and Requisite Irony', in H. Bang (ed.), *Governance, Governmentality and Democracy*, Lancaster: Department of Sociology, Lancaster University, http://www.comp.lancs.ac.uk/sociology/soc108rj.htm

Kagan, Robert A. (2000), 'Introduction: Comparing National Styles of Regulation in Japan and the United States', *Law and Policy*, **22**, 225–44.

Katyal, Neal Kumar (2002), 'Architecture as Crime Control', *Yale Law Journal*, **111**, 1039–139.

Kickert, Walter J.M. (1993), 'Autopoiesis and the Science of (Public) Administration: Essence, Sense and Nonsense', *Organization Studies*, **14**, 273–88.

Kraakman, Reinier H. (1986), 'Gatekeepers: The Anatomy of a Third Party Enforcement Strategy', *Journal of Law, Economics and Organization*, **2**, 53–104.

Lessig, Lawrence (1999), *Code: and Other Laws of Cyberspace*, New York: Basic Books.

Levy, Brian and Pablo Spiller (eds) (1996), *Regulation, Institutions and Commitment*, Cambridge, Cambridge University Press.

Lex Fori (2000), 'La Meilleure Pratique dans les Recours à des Norms Juridiques "Douces" et son Application sux Consommateurs au Seine de l'Union Europenne', Brussels: European Commission.

Loughlin, Martin and Colin Scott (1997), 'The Regulatory State', in Patrick Dunleavy, Ian Holliday, Andrew Gamble and Gillian Peele (eds), *Developments in British Politics 5*, Basingstoke: Macmillan, pp. 5–219.

Luhmann, Niklas (1992), 'The Coding of the Legal System', *European Yearbook in the Sociology of Law* (1991–92), 145–85.

Macaulay, Stuart (1963), 'Non-Contractual Relations in Business: A Preliminary Study', *American Sociological Review*, **28**, 55–83.

Majone, Giandomenico (1994), 'The Rise of the Regulatory State in Europe', *West European Politics*, **17**, 77–101.

Meidinger, Errol (2002), 'Forest Certification as a Global Civil Society Regulatory Institution', in Errol Meidinger, Chris Elliot and Gerhard Oesten (eds), *Social and Political Dimensions of Forest Certification*, Freiburg: Institut für Forstökonomie, pp. 265–89.

Merry, Sally Engle (2001), 'Spatial Governmentality and the New Urban Social Order: Controlling Gender Violence Through Law', *American Anthropologist*, **103**, 16–29.

Mitnick, Barry M. (1980), *The Political Economy of Regulation: Creating, Designing and Removing Regulatory Forms*, New York: Columbia University Press.

Moran, Michael (2001a), 'Not Steering but Drowning: Policy Catastrophes and the Regulatory State', *Political Quarterly*, **72**, 414–27.

Moran, Michael (2001b), 'The Rise of the Regulatory State in Britain', *Parliamentary Affairs*, **54**, 19–34.

Moran, Michael (2002), 'Review Article: Understanding the Regulatory State', *British Journal of Political Science*, **32**, 391–413.

Morgan, Bronwen (1999), 'Regulating the Regulators: Meta-Regulation as a Strategy for Reinventing Government in Australia', *Public Management*, **1**, 49–65.

Murphy, Tim (1997), *The Oldest Social Science? Configurations of Law and Modernity*, Oxford: Oxford University Press.

Murray, Andrew and Colin Scott (2002), 'Controlling the New Media: Hybrid Responses to New Forms of Power', *Modern Law Review*, **65**, 491–516.

Newman, Oscar (1972), *Defensible Space: Crime Prevention Through Urban Design*, New York: Macmillan.

Nonet, Philippe and Philip Selznick (1978), *Law and Society in Transition: Towards Responsive Law*, New York: Harper and Row.

Offe, Claus (2000), 'Civil Society and Social Order: Demarcating and Combining Market, State and Community', *Revue Européenne de Sociologie*, **XLI**, 71–93.

O'Malley, Pat, Lorna Weir and Clifford Shearing (1997), 'Governmentality, Criticism, Politics', *Economy and Society*, **26**, 501–17.

Parker, Christine (1999), *Just Lawyers*, Oxford: Oxford University Press.

Parker, Christine (2002), *The Open Corporation: Self-Regulation and Democracy*, Melbourne: Cambridge University Press.

Paterson, John and Gunther Teubner (1998), 'Changing Maps: Empirical Legal Autopoiesis', *Social and Legal Studies*, **7**, 451–86.

Pildes, Richard H. and Cass R. Sunstein (1995), 'Reinventing the Regulatory State', *University of Chicago Law Review*, **62**, 1–129.

Productivity Commission (2001), 'Regulation and Its Review', Canberra: AusInfo.

Reichman, Nancy (1992), 'Moving Backstage: Uncovering the Role of Compliance Practices in Shaping Regulatory Policy', in Kip Schlegel and David Weisburd (eds), *White-Collar Crime Reconsidered*, Boston: Northeastern University Press, pp. 245–67.

Richardson, Ben (forthcoming), 'Diffusing Environmental Regulation through the Financial Services Sector: Reforms in the EU and other Jurisdictions', *Maastricht Journal of European and Comparative Law*, **10**.

Ronit, Karsten (2001), 'Institutions of Private Authority in Global Governance: Linking Territorial Forms of Self-Regulation', *Administration & Society*, **33**, 555–78.

Rose, Nikolas (1994), 'Expertise and the Government of Conduct', *Studies in Law, Politics and Society*, **14**, 359–97.

Rose, Nikolas (2000), 'Government and Control', *British Journal of Criminology*, **40**, 321–39.

Salamon, Lester M. (2001), 'The New Governance and the Tools of Public Action: An Introduction', *Fordham Urban Law Journal*, **28**, 1611–74.

Santos, Boaventura de Sousa (2002), *Towards a New Legal Common Sense*, London: Butterworths.

Schaede, Ulrike (2000), *Cooperative Capitalism: Self-Regulation, Trade Associations and the Antimonopoly Law in Japan*, Oxford: Oxford University Press.

Scott, Colin (1995), 'Criminalising the Trader to Protect the Consumer', in Ian Loveland (ed.), *Frontiers of Criminal Law*, London: Sweet & Maxwell, pp. 149–72.

Scott, Colin (1998), 'The Juridification of Regulatory Relations in the UK Utilities Sectors', in Julia Black, Peter Muchlinski and Paul Walker (eds), *Commercial Regulation and Judicial Review*, Oxford: Hart, pp. 19–61.

Scott, Colin (2001), 'Analysing Regulatory Space: Fragmented Resources and Institutional Design', *Public Law*, 329–53.

Scott, Colin (2002), 'Private Regulation of the Public Sector: A Neglected Facet of Contemporary Governance', *Journal of Law and Society*, **29**, 56–76.

Scott, Colin and Julia Black (2000), *Cranston's Consumers and the Law*, London, Butterworths.

Shearing, Clifford (1993), 'A Constitutive Conception of Regulation', in John Braithwaite and Peter Grabosky (eds), *Business Regulation in Australia's Future*, Canberra: Australian Institute of Criminology, pp. 67–79.

Shearing, Clifford D. and Philip C. Stenning (1985), 'From the Panopticon to Disney World: The Development of the Discipline', in Anthony N. Doob and Edward L. Greenspan (eds), *Perspectives in Criminal Law*, Toronto: Canada Law Book Inc, pp. 330–50.

Simon, Jonathan (1994), 'Between Power and Knowledge: Habermas, Foucault, and the Future of Legal Studies', *Law and Society Review*, **28**, 947–61.

Stenson, K. (1998), 'Beyond Histories of the Present', *Economy and Society*, **27**, 333–52.

Stoker, Gerry (1998), 'Governance as Theory: Five Propositions', *International Social Science Journal*, **155**, 17–27.

Sunstein, Cass (1990a), *After the Rights Revolution*, Cambridge, MA: Harvard University Press.

Sunstein, Cass R. (1990b), 'Paradoxes of the Regulatory State', *University of Chicago Law Review*, **57**, 407–41.

Teubner, Gunther (1993), *Law as an Autopoietic System*, Oxford: Blackwell.

Teubner, Gunther (1997), '"Global Bukowina": Legal Pluralism in the World Society', in Gunther Teubner (ed.), *Global Law without a State*, Aldershot: Dartmouth, pp. 3–30.

Teubner, Gunther (1998), 'After Privatization: The Many Autonomies of Private Law', *Current Legal Problems*, **51**, 393–424.

Teubner, Gunther [1987] (1998), 'Juridification: Concepts, Aspects, Limits, Solutions', in Robert Baldwin, Colin Scott and Christopher Hood (eds), *Socio-Legal Reader on Regulation*, Oxford: Oxford University Press.

t'Veld, Roeland J., Catrien J.A.M. Termeer, Linze Schaap and Mark J.W. van Twist (eds) (1991), *Autopoiesis and Configuration Theory: New Approaches to Societal Steering*, Dordrecht: Martinus Nijhoff.

Valverde, Mariana (1998), *Diseases of the Will: Alcohol and Dilemmas of Freedom*, Cambridge: Cambridge University Press.

Vincent-Jones, Peter (2002a), 'Regulating Government by Contract: Towards a Public Law Framework?', *Modern Law Review*, **65**, 611–28.

Vincent-Jones, Peter (2002b), 'Values and Purpose in Government: Central–Local Relations in Regulatory Perspective', *Journal of Law and Society*, **29**, 27–55.

Weiss, Linda (1998), *The Myth of the Powerless State*, Cambridge: Polity Press.

Wilks, Stephen (1996), 'Regulatory Compliance and Capitalist Diversity in Europe', *Journal of European Public Policy*, **3**, 536–9.

Wilson, James Q. (1980), *The Politics of Regulation*, New York: Basic Books.

World Bank (1997), *World Development Report 1997*, Oxford: Oxford University Press and World Bank.

PART II

Comparative perspectives on the
politics of regulation

8. Comparative research designs in the study of regulation: how to increase the number of cases without compromising the strengths of case-oriented analysis

David Levi-Faur[*]

Regulatory reforms have gained immense global popularity and are widely pervasive across regions, countries and sectors. Very few countries have kept aloof from this sweeping trend. Still, amidst the wave of reforms some puzzling variations in their advance are discernible. For one, variations are clearly visible in the timing of the reforms. It might be possible to identify pioneering countries (for example Britain), fence-sitters (for example Germany), and laggards (for example France). Similarly, it is possible to distinguish countries that moved towards reforms after severe economic crises and with the active encouragement of international institutions such as the World Bank and the IMF (for example a number of Latin American countries). At the same time, some countries took a pro-active approach and autonomously reformed their regimes in the hope of strengthening their competitiveness in global markets (for example New Zealand, The Netherlands). Finally, some countries adopted rapid reforms across many sectors (for example Bolivia) while others were more picky and opted for reform only in a small number of sectors (for example Japan). At the sectoral level, some sectors are prone to reforms (for example air transport), others much less so (for example water). Some regions of the world boast widespread regulatory reforms (for example Europe) while in others they are barely noticeable (for example the Arab world). Whereas some reforms have often been subject to international agreements (for example trade), others have been left to national discretion (for example occupational health and safety).

The general advance of regulatory reforms, and consequently the new capitalist order itself, is beset by temporal, spatial, sectoral, national and international-level variations. These variations present yet a further layer of complication for social scientists who are already plagued by complex methodological and theoretical problems. Still, these variations are not merely a burden but are actually a blessing for comparativists, for two main reasons. First, while we generally seek regularities in human and social behaviour, variations are the most powerful engines of causal analysis. Without variations we cannot establish associations between variables, and without associations the causes, processes and outcomes of the reforms remain obscure. Second, variations are often the subject of research. Why is water, for example, less prone to regulatory reforms than air travel? Or why do regulatory reforms in the social sphere (social regulations) lag so markedly behind reforms in the economic sphere (economic regulation)? The aims of this chapter are to explore the role of variations and similarities in comparative research and to suggest a technique of compound designs that could maximize their explanatory power.

The context of this discussion is the search for research designs in the study of comparative politics that will enable researchers to deal systematically with political analysis in a shrinking world, where political action is conducted in various arenas simultaneously. At the same time, our discussion should be interpreted as part of the search for new techniques for finding a new balance between 'depth and breadth' in social science methodology (Ragin, 2000, 22). This is conducted through a careful process of increasing the number of observations while staying in the framework of case-oriented research (Ragin, 1987, 1994, 2000; King et al., 1994). Accordingly, the first part of this chapter identifies four popular approaches to case selection in comparative analysis: the national patterns approach (NPA), the policy sector approach (PSA), the international regime approach (IRA) and the temporal patterns approach (TPA).[1] The distinction between these approaches is based on theoretical preference in regard to the cases that need to be compared and the variations that they will display (see Table 8.1). The national patterns approach (NPA), which predicts that national variations will be the major determinants of reforms, advocates comparison of nations (for example Vogel, 1986; Waarden, 1995). The policy sector approach (PSA) predicts that sector-level variables will be the major determinant of reforms and advocates comparisons of sectors (for example Atkinson and Coleman, 1989; Hollingsworth et al., 1994). The international regime approach (IRA) suggests that the major determinants of the spread and depth of regulatory reforms are variations in the strength and scope of international regimes and it therefore focuses on the comparative analysis of regimes. Finally, the temporal patterns approach (TPA) suggests that the major variations in the reforms are shaped by past events, that is, by the particular situation of countries, sectors and international regimes at a particular time (for example the breakdown date of the old order) (for example Collier and Collier, 1991; Pierson, 1994, 2002).

Table 8.1   Four common approaches to comparative analysis

Approach	Cases to be compared	Predictions as to variations	Predictions as to similarities
National patterns approach (NPA)	Nations	Across nations	Across sectors, time and international regimes
Policy sector approach (PSA)	Sectors	Across sectors	Across nations, time and international regimes
International regime approach (IRA)	International regimes	Across international regimes	Across sectors, time, and nations
Temporal patterns approach (TPA)	Politics before and after major event	Across time	Across sectors, nations, and international regimes

The second part of this chapter focuses on the particular comparative design in Steven K. Vogel's *Freer Market, More Rules* (1996). This is a most remarkable study in its effort to employ some combinations of these approaches and thus selectively and systematically to increase the number of cases. Vogel's study is especially suitable to illustrate a technique for increasing the number of cases while retaining the benefits of case-oriented research (most notably, in-depth knowledge of one's cases). Most research in the study of regulation is confined to case studies (most often one country–one sector) or to statistical–quantitative analyses. The important terrain of medium-*N* research (more than two and less than circa 100 cases) is *terra incognita* for many.[2] This is an unfortunate state of affairs as medium-*N* designs might serve as shared space where quantitative and qualitative researchers can debate theory and evidence much more freely than in their own (often) exclusive domains. It is also the terrain where consensus can emerge about the value of generalizations on the one hand and about the importance of in-depth knowledge of one's case on the other. Medium-*N* research designs strive to preserve most of the valuable assets of the case-oriented approach while maximizing the explanatory power of the relevant theory through a careful selection of additional cases.

While there might be various useful strategies for increasing one's cases within the terrain of medium-*N* design, we suggest here a particular technique that we label 'compound research design'.[3] It is based on systematic combinations of any two out of the four common comparative approaches employed in the study of regulation (and public policy in general) in a way that at least doubles the original number of cases. Indeed, it is often possible to identify some combinations of some of the four research approaches isolated here. Yet only rarely are combinations of cases selected meticulously. A more formal and structured process of case-selection in comparative research designs may well support the goal of increasing the number of cases in one's research while maintaining most of the advantages of case-oriented analysis.

1. FOUR APPROACHES TO THE STUDY OF REGULATION IN A GLOBAL WORLD

As already presented (see Table 8.1), there are at least four popular approaches to case selection in comparative research designs. Let us explore each of them.

The National Patterns Approach

The national patterns approach (NPA) suggests that national-level characteristics exert a major impact on policy, politics, economics and society. Cross-national comparative designs are expected therefore to show significant diversity across the countries studied and to explain major variations in the policy process and outcomes, and the factors that shape them. The NPA has strong roots in the discipline of politics, as some of its major works employ a cross-national design. Alexis de Tocqueville's *Democracy in America* (1945 [1835, 1840]), Barrington Moore's study of *The Social Origins of Dictatorship and Democracy* (1966), and Theda Skocpol's *States and Social Revolutions* (1979) are some of these remarkable studies that explicitly draw on the comparative method and specifically on cross-national analysis. When applied to the study of regulation, the NPA suggests that political processes and outcomes are shaped by a country's unique national and historically determined characteristics embedded in specific state traditions.

The pioneering work of Andrew Shonfield (1965) on the different approaches and capacities of the British and French states to economic planning is one of the main departure points for students of comparative public policy and comparative political economy when they embark on the study of 'varieties of capitalism'. Typical for this research approach is the suggestion that policy making is determined at a specific national centre and predominantly by national institutions. These institutions are products of historical circumstances and cultural characteristics that create specific 'national institutional Gestalts' (Waarden, 1992, 158; see also Castles, 1993).

Some of the critical cross-national variations especially emphasized by cross-national comparativists include the national form of intermediation between state and society (pluralism versus étatism versus corporatism); preferences for action (active versus reactive policies); the policies' extent of integration (comprehensive versus fragmented); flexibility of rule formulation and application (legalism versus pragmatism); state–clientele relations (adversarialism versus consensualism versus paternalism); and network social relations (formal versus informal) (Waarden, 1995).

How do we know that a certain comparative research is grounded in the NPA? Since scholars do not always explicitly state their basic assumptions and their general methodological approach, it may be useful to identify two archetypes of studies in the NPA tradition. First, and most probably the most common in this tradition, are studies that compare two or more countries and ask why they differ in certain aspects of their policy or regulatory regimes. Here state-level characteristics are usually expected to offer a solution to the puzzling differences. Not uncommon would be to ascribe the resolute move to privatization and liberalization in the USA and Britain to the common liberal heritage; the hesitant move of Germany to the semi-sovereign characteristics of the German state; and the reluctant move in this direction by the French to the étatist tradition of the French polity and economy. Second, and rather less common, is the 'paradoxical design'. Here the comparison is based on two or more countries which by their characteristics would supposedly have adopted different policies but in practice converged. The question then is why have both étatist France and liberal America kept large segments of their water supply under private ownership? While this puzzle may be explained by variables and explanatory mechanisms not necessarily grounded in the national level, the basic premises of the research questions are built on the assumption that nations usually differ. While in the first research design national variations are the explanatory variables, in the second the absence of national variations is itself the subject of the research question.

The Policy Sector Approach

The policy sector approach emphasizes the autonomous political characteristics of distinct policy sectors, hence the multiplicity of political patterns in any single country. The major point might be summarized in two major propositions: '[First] that the style of policy making and the nature of political conflicts in a country will vary significantly from sector to sector. ... [And second] that policy making in a particular sector will exhibit strong similarities, whatever its national context' (Freeman, 1986, 486). These claims clearly challenge the notion of 'national patterns' that suggest significant similarities in the modes of political process across different sectors in any given country. In the field of comparative public policy it is the policy networks and meso-corporatism literature that best represent the policy sector approach. They call for a disaggregated view of the state, of the network of policy-making, and of the national level of policy-making (Atkinson and Coleman, 1989). The implications for policy analysis were clearly stated:

> Capitalism can no longer be studied as a whole, but must be broken down into its parts ... Both to capture the diversity of capitalism and to render it manageable, *it seems useful to focus on the sector as the key unit for comparative analysis* ... A number of changes in technology, market structure, and public policy seem to have converged to make this meso-level ... increasingly salient. (Hollingsworth et al., 1994, 8–9).[4]

Let us indicate some problems involved in a decision to identify a study as following or not following the PSA. James Q. Wilson's edited volume *The Politics of Regulation* (1980) assembles nine studies of regulatory agencies and regulatory politics in the United States that served as the basis for Wilson's introduction and conclusion. This 'collaborative' research design, where different sectors are examined and implicitly compared, and where the national level (United States) is constant (that is, under control), has some affinities with the PSA but cannot be considered an ideal representative of the approach. The reason is simple: the PSA design expects variations across sectors, and to identify variations one has to move from the implicit comparisons evident in Wilson's conclusions to an explicit and systematic study of variations in the 'politics of regulation' across sectors. In other words, an ideal research design from the PSA standpoint will allow explicit comparison across the sectors under research. A notable example of a study that does exactly that is Harris and Milkis's *The Politics of Regulatory Change: A Tale of Two Agencies* (1996), which compares the dynamics of administrative politics in the Federal Trade Commission and the Environmental Protection Agency.

The International Regime Approach

The international regime approach suggests that the major determinant of the extent and depth of regulatory reforms is variations in the strength and scope of international regimes. Regimes at the international level are considered to have their own autonomous characteristics and to differ in a number of important aspects (Krasner, 1983; Hasenclever et al., 1997). While much of the discussion around international regimes is directed to verification and negation of some meta-theories of international relations such as neo-realism, neo-liberalism and constructivism, in the last decade growing attention has been paid to the nuances of similarities and variations across regimes. This recognition is followed by a more widespread use of comparative research designs in the study of international relations and international political economy. A pioneering book in this tradition is Keohane and Nye's *Power and Interdependence* 1977 [1989]), which compares international regimes for oceans and money.

The growing recognition of the importance of comparative methodology in the fields of international relations (IR) and international political economy (IPE) is at least partly the result of the challenges of globalization, internationalization and Europeanization, which have narrowed the gap between the national and the international. As these forces and processes are hardly reversible, comparative methodologies may be expected to continue to grow in importance in the fields of IPE/IR. Increasing interdependence of the national (hence the sectoral) and the international requires us to reconsider the boundaries of cases and levels, and to analyse simultaneous deeds on various levels of political action (Tsebelis, 1990). It is also expected to be a major force beyond the reach of compound research design in the study of politics and policy.

John Braithwaite and Peter Drahos's *Global Business Regulation* (2000) may serve as an example of a comprehensive and penetrating study of international regimes in various spheres of political and economic action. The study covers 13 international regimes, from trade to financial regulation and from labour standards to marine transport. The empirical basis for the 13 studies is a comprehensive study of secondary material and 500 interviews conducted by the two scholars. The studies are followed by a comparative analysis across the 13 cases that focuses on three issues: actors, mechanisms and principles. Across each of the cases the study identifies key actors (for example organization of states, states, international business organizations, corporations and epistemic communities), governing principles (for example lowest-cost location, best practice, deregulation, strategic trade, rule compliance and most-favoured nation), and mechanisms of globalization (for example military coercion, economic coercion, systems of reward, capacity-building and reciprocal adjustment). Another notable example is Zacher and Sutton's (1996) comparative study of international regimes for transport (shipping and air travel) and communications (telecoms and post).

The Temporal Patterns Approach

The temporal patterns approach suggests that systematic diachronic comparisons of sectors, nations, or international regimes may reveal some of the most important features and determinants of the spread of regulatory reforms. Certain 'remarkable' events, such as the rise to power of a new leader, the appearance of new technology, the spread of some ideas beyond the critical threshold, wars and revolutions, serve as turning points and mark a boundary between the 'old' and the 'new' orders. The researcher then undertakes a comparative analysis of similarities and variations in the old and the new orders. Examples of such studies are Peter Gourevitch's (1986) comparative study of the economic depressions of 1873 and 1929 and the Colliers' study of critical junctures in the interaction of the Latin American labour movement with the state (1991). Some systematic modelling of the effect of time and sequencing in political analysis is evident in Pierson's work (1994, 2000, 2003).

The temporal patterns approach has a close affinity with historical approaches of research as both kinds are highly sensitive to time and context. Yet unlike traditional historical research, temporal patterns conceptualize the different eras as 'cases', and subject these cases to the regular tests of 'case selection' (for an excellent discussion of various issues related to temporal comparisons see Bartolini, 1993). The basic premises of the approach are widely used in comparative research, and not many readers will object to the idea that certain patterns of politics are time-dependent and that these patterns should therefore be compared systematically. More controversial, perhaps, would be a stronger claim that regulatory politics critically depends on the temporal dimensions of the case rather than on within-time (or synchronic) variations across nations, sectors, or international regimes. As will be demonstrated below, this stronger claim can be systematically examined in a compound research design, but for the moment let us keep the tension between different approaches to comparative research on hold, and explore some examples of the TPA.

There are two archetypes of TPA studies. First, and probably the most common in this tradition, are studies that compare two eras, one before and one after a major event, and ask why they differ on one point or another. Many accounts of the development of the regulatory state in the United States stand firmly on this approach. An example is Eisner's *Regulatory Politics in Transition* (2000, 2nd edn), which focuses on the temporal development of regulatory regimes in the United States in a comparable manner: the market regime (with the rise of big business), the associational regime (expansion of economic regulation in the progressive and the New Deal era), the societal regime (the rise of social regulation in the 1960s and early 1970s), and the efficiency regime (the deregulation era since the second half of the 1970s).

A second type of study in this approach is the 'paradoxical design'. Here the comparison is based on two or more 'eras' and the expectation that they will be characterized by different patterns of regulatory politics. The researcher's quandary arises from 'paradoxical findings' that point to similar outcomes across the eras despite the opposite predications of the TPA. While this puzzle may be explained by variables and explanatory mechanisms that are not necessarily grounded in the level of the international regimes, the basic premises of the research question arise from the assumption that 'temporal cases' should exhibit variations. An example is Stigler and Friedland's 'What Can Regulators Regulate? The Case of Electricity' (1962). Their paper treats the establishment of regulatory authorities for electricity as a turning point in the history of regulation, and suggests that if 'regulation matters', then the 'era of regulation' will be characterized by lower electricity tariffs. The puzzling evidence that they do not substantially differ was used to criticize public interest theories of regulation and to substantiate private interest theories.

Why Distinguish between these Approaches?

So what are the benefits of these distinctions? I can think of three. First, the distinctions clarify and formalize prevailing notions and practices of comparative analysis. Second, they assert the importance of variations in the selection of cases for comparison in order to avoid the problem of selection on the dependent variable. Third, they help us to increase the number of cases without compromising the strength of the case-oriented approach. This critical advantage is demonstrated in the next section.

2.   THE ROAD TO MEDIUM-*N* DESIGNS: VOGEL'S STUDY OF REGULATORY REFORMS

Steven Vogel's *Freer Markets, More Rules: Regulatory Reform in Advanced Industrial Countries* is widely considered as one of the best studies of the subject. One of the major strengths of the book is its comparative research design that makes use of a stepwise increase in the number of cases and meticulously combines some major comparative approaches. This part of the chapter discusses four important issues in Vogel's research design: (a) his stepwise increase in the number of cases, while staying firmly in the framework of case-oriented research; (b) his conception of what is a case; (c) his case-selection; (d) his technique for combining various comparative approaches. The range of issues that this discussion raises is critical for the further advance of medium-*N* research designs.

From Few to Many: Stepwise Increase of the Number of Cases

Figure 8.1 summarizes Vogel's stepwise technique of non-random selection of cases. The figure distinguishes six different steps in the aggregation of empirical evidence. The first is a comparison of the two primary countries studied (Britain and Japan) with emphasis on the variations in their ideological orientation and institutional constellations prior to the reform.[5] The second step introduces two additional sets of comparisons. In the first set the old and the new telecom regimes in Britain are compared, and in the second the same comparison is made in regard to Japan. The third step repeats this comparison but in respect of the financial sector in each of the countries. In the fourth step

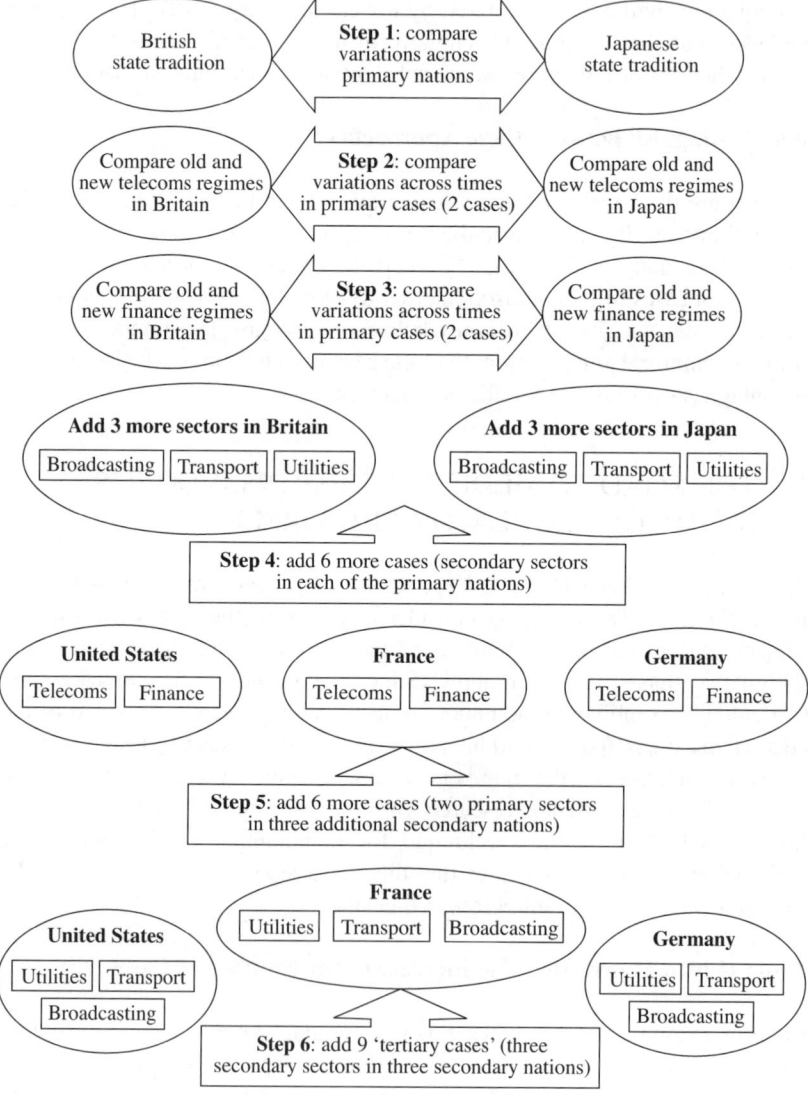

Figure 8.1   Vogel's stepwise research design

Vogel adds three more sectors (broadcasting, transport and utilities) in Britain and Japan. In the fifth step he adds three countries (France, the USA and Germany) and in each he examines the two primary sectors (finance and telecoms). In the sixth step he adds the three secondary sectors (broadcasting, transport and utilities) for the three secondary countries.

The gradual increase in the number of cases is remarkable, not least because Vogel employs different types of cases: more nations and sectors, as well as old and new sectoral regimes. The increase in the number of cases is not mechanistic and random, as in quantitative research. The selection is made with care and variations are sought on different dimensions (sectoral, national and temporal). This selection process, which maximizes the type of variations against which Vogel's arguments are framed, increases the validity of the conclusions. Vogel seems well aware that in non-random comparative research strategies not all cases are methodologically or theoretically equal, and that the variety of cases is often more important than their sheer number. At the same time Vogel includes cases that are not studied in depth (broadcasting, transport and utilities; Germany, the USA and France). As it is impossible to cover so many cases in depth, he opts for a rather limited coverage of these cases rather than dropping them. His choice opens the door to the medium-*N* terrain of political enquiry.

Types of Cases in Vogel's Research Designs

A puzzling aspect in Vogel's design, however, is his conception of a 'case'. According to Vogel's own count, the number of cases in his study is 25. With some adding up and multiplying it becomes clear that a case for Vogel is only a sector, and the 25 reflect the fact that he studies five sectors in five different countries (see Table 8.2). This is a puzzling calculation because the countries and the temporal regimes are not considered cases even though he explicitly compares British and Japanese political economy before the reforms and the old and new regimes for telecommunications and finance. An even larger number of cases might be identified if we distinguish five types of cases in Vogel's study. These cases vary in (a) the extent to which they involve in-depth inquiry, (b) their dimensions and (c) their inferential role in the study.

The first type of cases includes four 'primary cases': British telecoms, British finance, Japanese telecoms and Japanese finance. These cases are 'primary' in the sense that they are studied 'in depth' and serve as the pillars of Vogel's theoretical construction. The second type of cases in the study includes 12 'secondary cases'.[6] These add three more sectors (broadcasting, transport and utilities) first in Britain and then in Japan. A comparison of the four primary cases reveals that the secondary cases are studied in less depth and are reviewed more briefly. The third type of cases includes nine 'tertiary

Table 8.2   What is a case?

Type of case	The cases	Number of cases	Cumulative number of cases	Counted by Vogel
Primary cases	4 primary sectors	4	4	Yes
Secondary cases	3 secondary sectors in each of the primary nations plus 2 primary sectors in each of the 3 secondary nations	12	16	Yes
Tertiary cases	3 secondary sectors in each of the 3 secondary nations	9	25	Yes
Composite cases	5 countries after the reforms	5	30	No
Temporal sectoral cases	The old regimes in each of the 5 countries and 5 sectors	25	55	No
Temporal composite cases	5 countries before the reforms	5	60	No

cases', which are not specifically addressed in his study but none the less are integrated into his analysis in the final chapter (Vogel, 1996, 259). These cases cover the reforms in the three secondary sectors (broadcasting, transport and utilities) in the three secondary nations (the USA, France and Germany).

Yet cases are not discovered but are defined by the researcher (for an extensive discussion of this issue, see Ragin and Becker, 1992). It is the researcher who decides when one regime ends and another starts, which activities and actors are included in a sector and which are not, and similarly what is the particular 'regulatory orientation' or 'policy characteristics' of a country. Three additional types of cases may be pointed out that are missing from Vogel's 'official count' but are nevertheless very substantial to his analysis. The first of these is the 'composite case', namely cases that take their value (or character) from cases at a lower level. Specifically they include five nations that draw their 'national style of regulation' from the direction and extent of regulatory reforms in each of the five sectors studied. Two of these five composite cases – Japan and Britain – are primary cases while the other three are 'tertiary cases' (composed largely but not exclusively of secondary sectors in secondary countries). The second type of 'missing' case is the temporal sectoral case. Here the old and the new regimes in each sector might be conceptualized as different cases and thereafter compared diachronically. Thus, we can add five old sectoral regimes for each of the five countries to our counting. Third, we can add the temporal compound cases that include the countries before the reforms. When one adds to the 25 cases counted by Vogel the five compound cases, the 25 temporal sectoral cases, and finally the five temporal compound cases, the grand total is 60 cases.

One possible objection to my count of cases would focus on the count of the old regimes (sectoral and national) as cases. Vogel is after all interested in regulatory reforms that happened during the 1980s and not in the old regimes that were dominated by Keynesian policies. My answer to this objection is simple. The old regimes represent cases of no reforms and as such supply variations in the dependent variable. In many respects they are the answer to the problem of selection bias that plagues much case-oriented research (Geddes, 1990).[7] Another objection might question the argument that there is any value in counting the countries (and not only the sectors) as cases to be compared. Vogel, after all, made the most of the country-level comparison even without counting countries as cases. Here I would suggest that it might be beneficial to turn implicit comparisons into explicit comparisons and thus to make comparative research less of an art and more a technique that can be taught for graduate students, analysed easily by reviewers, and formalized as a professional standard. Counting the countries as cases is the first step in this direction.

From Simple to Compound Research Designs

Vogel's research design is exceptional also in the combination of different comparative strategies that give him powerful leverage later, when he examines the process of reforms. Specifically, he employs the temporal patterns approach (comparing old with new regimes), the national patterns approach (most explicitly in comparing Japan and Britain), and the policy sector approach (most explicitly in comparing telecommunications and finance). Yet despite his achievements in this task, his case-selection is open to criticism for three major reasons. First, it does not always follow the rule of 'choose the least favourable cases for your argument'.[8] Second, he does not explicitly define the variations across his sectoral cases (telecoms and finance). Finally, he does not explicitly present and discuss the full range of outcomes that arise from his decision to include different types of cases in his analysis. Let us consider his case selection with regard first to the primary nations and then to the primary sectors.

Vogel's choice of primary nations is justified on the following grounds:

> The United Kingdom and Japan began their regulatory reforms programs at the same time and under the similar circumstances, and extended their programs to a similar range of sectors. They were similarly influenced by the U.S. deregulation movement and faced common international market pressures. Thus they provide a good comparative fit: any differences in reform outcomes are likely to reflect differences in domestic politics. The British and Japanese governments adopted a similar rhetoric of 'liberalization' and 'deregulation', yet produced strikingly different reforms. This divergence cannot be explained by a market or interest groups model, but only through an examination of the ideas and institutions that shaped the two countries' reform strategies. (Vogel, 1996, 43)

Is this justification for case-selection convincing? Only partly. A more convincing argument for the effect of domestic politics and national institutions would have come from a study of countries that are as similar as possible (MSSD) on the relevant control variables.[9] Everything that Vogel advocates in this paragraph might have been argued more convincingly on some other pairs of countries. One example is a possible comparison of the UK and the USA. Evidence of divergent responses in these countries would have been more puzzling than the divergence between Japan, whose political economy is characterized by an étatist tradition, and the UK, which has a strong liberal tradition.[10] Vogel's case of diverging outcomes between the UK and Japan is more favourable for his argument about states' diverging responses to common pressures than is a case of varied outcomes between the UK and the USA.

Vogel's selection of sectors and application of the PSA is problematic. Let us examine the justification for his case-selection at the sectoral level:

> Even in the most dynamic and the most global of industries – telecommunications and financial services – I find that governments are hardly overwhelmed by international market pressures. (Vogel, 1996, 2)

It is clear from this sentence that Vogel is not looking for variations across these sectors, but instead uses them as two 'critical cases' in order to assess the arguments about the retreat of the state. The observation that telecoms and financial services are among the most global and most dynamic sectors is widely accepted, so each of the sectors makes a good case. Yet one may question the logic of choosing sectors that vary so little. Few would doubt the benefits of adding cases when one's aim is to generalize. Yet if one's goal is to show that ideas and institutions are important determinants of the reforms, it might be best to choose one case where markets and technologies are very important and one case where markets and technological changes are radically less important. We may suggest a comparison of financial services (very dynamic and global) and transport (much less dynamic and global). A study that shows that even in the most critical cases (financial services) governments are hardly overwhelmed by international market pressures, and that even in the most static cases (transport) governments are reforming their regulatory regimes (and therefore acting on their own preferences), will be more forceful in its conclusion than a simple repetition of the same conclusion in two similar cases. Moreover, since there are not enough variations in his primary sectoral cases, Vogel does not allow for the possibility that variations in governance structures are more important across sectors than across nations. Given that Vogel's approach is entrenched in the tradition of the NPA, it seems that the research design – in so far as we are concerned with the choice of sectors – is pretty favourable to his argument.

But how can one know in advance that one's cases include the desired variations and similarities? What might seem obvious after doing the research (namely the lack of obvious and salient sectoral variations between telecoms and finance as regards regulatory reforms) was not that obvious beforehand. One way to go about this is to conduct a pilot study before committing oneself to certain cases. While this might be a costly solution, the benefits might be great enough to justify them.

The Range of Outcomes in Vogel's Research Design

Using different types of cases (or comparative approaches) in one's research design changes the range of possible political outcomes. While a 'simple research design' can summarize along one dimension (yes, no, degrees of yes), a 'compound research design' is characterized by outcomes that vary along two or more dimensions. Take for example Vogel's four major cases (two nations and two sectors). The four possible outcomes are similarities across nations and sectors, variations across sectors and nations, variations across nations but not sectors, and variations across sectors but not nations.

Let us start with the one outcome that Vogel discusses extensively, namely variations across nations but not across sectors. This is Vogel's major finding. In discussing it he reasserts not only the argument about the state-led process of reforms but also the one about the relevance of comparative studies of nations as the major professional enterprise. Somewhat less attention is given to the possibility of variations across sectors and of similarities across nations. This is a clearly one possible outcome of the research but Vogel seems not really interested in cross-sectoral variations as his choice for comparison of most-similar cases. While he clearly shows that there are variations between telecoms, finance and broadcasting (with extensive regulatory change) and transport and utilities (where regulatory change is much less evident) he does not explicitly discuss them (see Vogel, 1996, p. 259, fig. 3). A third possible outcome is of similarities across nations and sectors. Vogel is aware that important similarities exist across nations and sectors in the 25 cases that he analyses, but this outcome is not a significant part of his research agenda. Instead he assumes that marketplace changes, macroeconomic trends, and export of the American 'deregulation' are responsible for this common trend of change. Finally, there is the possible outcome of variations across both sectors and nations, which is overlooked – at least when one seeks a systematic discussion of this specific outcome of the reforms.

In sum, Vogel offers an innovative research design that increases the number of cases without turning into a quantitative–econometric analysis. At the same time, however, his case-selection has some weaknesses, and he does not cover the wider range of possible outcomes that naturally arise when one moves from simple to compound research designs. In what follows we move to the major aim of this chapter and suggest a technique of combining two or more of the different research approaches that may help to overcome these problems.

3. FORMALIZING COMPOUND RESEARCH DESIGNS IN THE MEDIUM-*N* TERRAIN

Problems of case-selection are inherent in all research based on non-random selection of cases. One of the most notable warnings as to problems of selection bias in case-oriented research refers to selection on the dependent variable, already mentioned. Yet there are other types of selection bias that often go unnoticed, and these might prove crucial in any research design. One is the problem of selecting on particular variations. This problem occurs when there is arbitrary selection of one type of variation while others are ignored. For example, such a bias might occur if variations in the advance of regulatory reforms are studied on the level of the European Union without regard to sector-level variations. What explains variations across the food and occupational safety regimes in the European Union? The power of EU-level interest groups, or the food-safety scandals in one of the larger states?[11]

A second problem is that of selection bias owing to focusing on either variations or similarities. If variations and similarities are both an important dimension of the reforms, an analysis that focuses (or is constructed) on only one of them might be biased. Our technique might be at least partly handy here. Let us demonstrate the advantages of the technique in an example of a research design that combines the national patterns approach and the policy sector approach. The technique might be useful in studies that combine each of the two common comparative approaches (that is, also IRA and NPA, IRA and PSA, TPA and NPA, TPA and PSA, and TPA and IRA).

Our starting point is the differences between the predictions of the NPA and the PSA as to the extent of similarities and variations across nations and sectors. When contrasted in one research design, the NPA predicts cross-national variations and cross-sectoral similarities, while the PSA predicts cross-national similarities and cross-sectoral variations. The four possible outcomes when these predictions are considered are portrayed in Table 8.3.

Table 8.3   Possible patterns of variations and similarities of outcomes in a compound research design that combines comparisons of nations and sectors

	Cross-sectoral similarities	Cross-sectoral variations
Cross-national similarities	Evidence does *not* support either of the two approaches. Move to another level of analysis	Evidence supports the policy sector approach (PSA)
Cross-national variations	Evidence supports the national patterns approach (NPA)	Evidence supports both approaches simultaneously. Explore the conditions where one is more acceptable than the other

First, one can expect cross-national similarities and cross-sectoral variations. Such an outcome will confirm the PSA and thus will guide the researcher to look for sectoral-level factors that shape the regulatory reforms. Second, one can expect cross-sectoral similarities and cross-national variations to prevail. Such an outcome will confirm the NPA and thus will guide the researcher to look for nation-level factors. Third, one can expect similarities across both sectors and nations. Such an outcome implies that there are extra-national and extra-sectoral forces, probably global, which affect the governance regimes of all sectors and nations. The solution here is to move to the global level of analysis and to apply research tools that are more in tune with international relations than with comparative politics and comparative public policy. Finally, one can expect both cross-sectoral and cross-national variations. Such an outcome requires the researcher to explain *when* and *why* one of the approaches is more useful than the other.

It might be useful to illustrate these various potential outcomes with two concrete examples of hypothetical research designs (see application in Levi-Faur, 2003). Let us start with a research design with four cases: the privatization of water and electricity facilities in Germany and France. This design of two countries and two sectors is compound in that it derives its power from both the NPA and the PSA (see Table 8.4). From the NPA standpoint there are two cases to be compared: Germany and France. From the PSA standpoint the two cases to be compared are water and electricity. The NPA predicts considerable variations in attitudes to privatization across the two countries but minimal variations across the sectors. Specifically, the NPA expects France or Germany to adopt or reject privatization across *both* sectors. The PSA by contrast suggests that privatization is subject to sector-level politics, so it predicts that privatization will vary across the sectors and will vary less or not at all across nations. Specifically, one may expect, according to the PSA, that water ownership will keep its private (or public) characteristics in *both* countries. Yet there are other possibilities. First, one is likely to find privatization in both countries and in both sectors (see the top left cell in Table 8.4). Second, one is likely to find privatization in the two sectors in one of the countries but only in one sector in the other country (see the bottom right cell in Table 8.4).

A second illustration of the use of the technique demonstrates how one can increase the number of cases from four to about forty. In the example we include ten liberal countries and ten étatist countries in the same two sectors, water and electricity. The number of cases in this example is 40 (20 countries

Table 8.4   Possible patterns of variations and similarities of outcomes in a compound research design: comparing water and electricity privatization in France and Germany

	Cross-sectoral similarities	Cross-sectoral variations
Cross-national similarities	Privatization in both water and electricity and in both Germany and France	Privatization only in water (or electricity) in both Germany and France
Cross-national variations	Privatization in both water and electricity in Germany (or France) but not in France (Germany)	Privatization in both water and electricity in Germany (or France) but only in water (electricity) in France (Germany)

times two sectors). Table 8.5 presents fictional outcomes of the propensity to privatization in each of the countries and each of the sectors. As is evident from the table, evidence of a large number of privatizations (83 per cent of the 40 possible cases) supports the possibility of similarities across nations and sectors. Yet clear evidence exists for each of the other options. Cross-sectoral variations are evident from the greater propensity of water to privatization than electricity. Cross-national variations are evident from the greater propensity of liberal countries to privatize than étatist countries. Finally, evidence is present of variations across both sectors and nations. These variations are revealed in the tendency of liberal countries to privatize electricity more than water.

Table 8.5   Possible patterns of variations and similarities of outcomes in a compound research design: comparing water and electricity privatization in 10 liberal and 10 étatist countries

	Cross-sectoral similarities	Cross-sectoral variations
Cross-national similarities	Privatization in 33 out of 40 possible cases	Water is more prone to privatization (18 cases of water privatization but only 15 of electricity)
Cross-national variations	Liberal countries privatized in 18 out of 20 cases while étatist countries privatized in 13 out of 20 possible cases	Liberal countries tend to privatize electricity more than water. Étatist countries privatized water more than electricity

In the world of small-*N* research (and deterministic outcomes) exemplified in Table 8.4 it is highly possible that one of the four potential outcomes will win clear empirical support. But in the world of medium-*N* research, shown in Table 8.5 (as well as in large-*N* research), it is highly likely that all four of these approaches will get some support. This requires the researcher to examine his or her explanations against various outcomes. Clearly, some costs are involved as the challenges to any explanatory framework are bigger, but there are some benefits. First, simple and swift arguments that dismiss one or more mechanism of political change might be more difficult to propose. At the same time it may solve at least partly the two problems of case-selection discussed above: selecting on particular variations and selecting on variations rather than similarities (and vice versa).

4.   CONCLUSIONS: REGULATORY ANALYSIS IN THE MEDIUM-N's TERRAIN

Let us recall the subject of the book. One of our main assertions was that the politics of regulation in the age of governance is a matter for multi-level analysis. Multi-level political action requires multi-level analysis, and our compound research design and call for more systematic case-selection are meant to tackle old and new political problems in a new political reality. Comparative analysis is needed more than ever, yet disregard for methodological issues seems to be too frequent in comparative research (De Meur and Berg-Schlosser, 1994, 193–4). One indication of this situation is the repeated references to methodological studies from the early 1970s in current comparative research.[12] This stagnation is partly due to the fact that the methodological training in the political sciences and sociology is primarily oriented to statistical training. Yet statistical training, important as it is, is not the only methodology, and arguably not the major methodology in political studies, and there is an urgent need for methodological training in comparative strategies. A significant foundation for progress in this regard was laid by the work of Charles Ragin (1987, 1994, 2000) and the Compass research network.[13] No less important are the efforts to promote multi-method research designs (for example Bennett, 2002; Lieberman, 2002).

In the spirit of these efforts to promote the use of comparative strategies in political research, this chapter distinguished four major approaches to comparative research. It then offered a technique of comparisons that allows the researcher to increase the number of his or her cases without compromising the benefits of case-oriented research. Using Steven Vogel's technique of a stepwise research design, we showed how this could be done effectively. In addition, the chapter set forth a technique of a compound research design that allows systematic examination of all possible outcomes when two or more of the four comparative approaches are employed in one's research design. It is now up to scholars and students of regulatory reforms to decide to what extent these methodological suggestions might be useful in their own research.

NOTES

* I am grateful to Martin Minogue, who 'commissioned' this paper for the International Workshop of the Centre on Regulation and Competition, 4–6 September 2002, University of Manchester. Comments from Benoît Rihoux, Jacint Jordana, Martin Minogue, Raphael Schapiro and Steven Vogel on an earlier draft were very helpful. All the usual disclaimers apply.
  1.   For an alternative typology of comparative strategies, one which is oriented towards the formalization of inferential methods, see Mahoney (2000).
  2.   It might be useful to clarify that this terrain is titled a small-N terrain by some researchers

(for example the Compass group). Yet I think that it would be counter-productive to our goal to emphasize the similarities to the case-study approach. In fact, I interpret the work of Ragin et al. as a challenge to the case-study approach as much as it is to the quantitative–statistical approach.

3. Alternative labels that were considered are 'complex', 'multi-faceted', 'multi-dimensional', and 'multi-level' research designs.

4. The policy sector approach is on the rise in the study of governance issues. According to Vivien Schmidt, it is likely that at 'some point soon, ... sectors across Europe [will be] the most appropriate focus' (Schmidt, 2002, 307). Yet while the PSA has given birth to some excellent research, not one study has made a critical impact on the discipline of politics akin to the seminal works that are associated with the NPA.

5. See the summary on p. 45 of his book.

6. Vogel's term is 'mini-cases': see p. 256.

7. In her formulation, selection bias occurs when only positive cases of whatever political phenomenon (for example revolutions, revolts, policy change) are selected without regard to variations in the occurrence. Selection of cases, King et al. (1994) remind us, 'should allow for the possibility of at least some variation on the dependent variable' (ibid., 129).

8. As the scientific status of a theory or an argument is closely connected to the stringency of its tests, one's conclusions will be more convincing if the evidence holds in the least likely circumstance.

9. Selection according to the most similar system design (MSSD) takes cases that are as similar as possible, on the assumption that the more similar the cases being compared, the more possible it should be to control the effects of different variables. The most different system design (MDSD) compares cases that are as different as possible in order to show the robustness of a relationship between dependent and independent variables. For a somewhat confusing exposition of this critical distinction see Przeworksi and Teune, (1970).

10. The UK and the USA are generally perceived to belong to the same 'family of nations' and thus to have similar approaches. Yet has been shown admirably by David Vogel (1986) the commonalities between these countries are accompanied by significant variations in policy styles.

11. This point is a major assertion of the multi-level analysis approach to the study of European politics; unfortunately these assertions were not followed by the developments of systematic techniques for the study of multi-level politics.

12. These studies most often include references to Lijphart's oft-cited papers (1971, 1975) and more rarely to Przeworski and Teune (1970).

13. Compass stands for Comparative Methods for the Advancements of Systematic Cross-case Analysis and Small-*N* Studies. It brings together scholars and practitioners who share a common interest in theoretical, methodological and practical advances by a systematic comparative case approach to research that stresses the use of a configurational logic, the existence of multiple causality, and the importance of a careful construction of research populations. See http://www.compasss.org/

REFERENCES

Atkinson, M.M. and D.W. Coleman (1989), 'Strong States and Weak States: Sectorial Policy Networks in Advanced Capitalist Economies', *British Journal of Political Science*, **19**, 47–67.

Bartolini, Stefano (1993), 'On Time and Comparative Research', *Journal of Theoretical Politics*, **5** (2), 131–67.

Bennett, Andrew (2002), 'Where the Model Frequently Meets the Road: Combining Statistical, Formal and Case Study Methods', unpublished manuscript.

Braithwaite, John and Peter Drahos (2000), *Global Business Regulation*, Cambridge: Cambridge University Press.

Castles, Francis G. (ed.) (1993), *Families of Nations: Patterns of Public Policy in Western Democracies*, Aldershot: Dartmouth.

Collier, Ruth Berins and David Collier (1991), *Shaping the Political Arena*, Princeton: Princeton University Press.

De Meur, Gisèle and Dirk Berg-Schlosser (1994), 'Comparing Political Systems: Establishing Similarities and Dissimilarities', *European Journal of Political Research*, **26** (2), 193–219.

Eisner, Marc Allen (2000), *Regulatory Politics in Transition*, 2nd edn, Baltimore and London: Johns Hopkins University Press.

Freeman, G. (1986), 'National Styles and Policy Sectors: Explaining Structured Variation', *Journal of Public Policy*, **5**, 467–96.

Geddes, Barbara (1990), 'How the Cases You Choose Affect the Answers You Get: Selection Bias in Comparative Politics', *Political Analysis*, **2**, 131–50.

Gourevitch, Peter (1986), *Politics in Hard Times: Comparative Responses to International Economic Crises*, Ithaca: Cornell University Press.

Harris, A. Richard and M. Sidney Milkis (1996), *The Politics of Regulatory Change: A Tale of Two Agencies*, New York and Oxford: Oxford University Press.

Hasenclever, Andreas, Peter Mayer and Volker Rittberger (1997), *Theories of International Regimes*, Cambridge: Cambridge University Press.

Hollingsworth, J.R., P.C. Schmitter and W. Streeck (1994), 'Capitalism, Sectors, Institutions and Performance', in R. Hollingsworth et al. (eds), *Governing Capitalist Economies*, New York and Oxford: Oxford University Press, pp. 3–16.

Keohane, Robert O. and Joseph Nye (1977 [1989]), *Power and Interdependence*, Boston: Little Brown.

King, Gary, Robert O. Keohane and Sidney Verba (1994), *Designing Social Inquiry: Scientific Inference in Qualitative Research*, Princeton: Princeton University Press.

Krasner, Stephen D. (1983), *International Regimes*, Ithaca: Cornell University Press.

Levi-Faur, David (2003), 'The Politics of Liberalisation: Privatisation and Regulation-for-Competition in Europe's and Latin America's Telecoms and Electricity Industries', *European Journal of Political Research*, **42** (5), pp. 705–40.

Lieberman, S. Evan (2002), 'Seeing Both the Forest and the Trees: Nested Analysis in Cross-National Research', prepared for delivery at the Annual Meeting of the American Political Science Association, 29 August–1 September 2002.

Lijphart A. (1971), 'Comparative Politics and the Comparative Method', *American Political Science Review*, **65** (3), pp. 682–93.

Lijphart, A. (1975), 'The Comparable-Cases Strategy in Comparative Research', *Comparative Political Studies*, **8**, 169–81.

Mahoney, James (2000), 'Strategies of Causal Inference in Small-*N* Analysis', *Sociological Methods & Research*, **28** (4), 387–424.

Moore, Barrington (1966), *The Social Origins of Dictatorship and Democracy: Lord and Peasant in the Making of the Modern World*, Boston: Beacon Press.

Pierson, Paul (1994), *Dismantling the Welfare State? Reagan, Thatcher, and the Politics of Retrenchment*, Cambridge: Cambridge University Press.

Pierson, Paul (2000), 'Not Just What, but When: Timing and Sequence in Political Processes', *Studies in American Political Development*, **14** (1), 73–93.

Pierson, Paul (2003), 'Big, Slow-Moving, and … Invisible: Macro-Social Processes in the Study of Comparative Politics', in Jim Mahoney and Dietrich Rueschemeyer (eds), *Comparative Historical Analysis in the Social Science*, Cambridge: Cambridge University Press, pp. 177–207.

Przeworski, A. and H. Teune (1970), *The Logic of Comparative Social Inquiry*, New York: Wiley-Interscience.

Ragin, C.C. (1987), *The Comparative Method: Moving beyond Qualitative and Quantitative Strategies*, Berkeley: University of California Press.

Ragin, C.C. (1994), *Constructing Social Research: The Unity and Diversity of Method*, Thousand Oaks, CA: Pine Forge Press.

Ragin, C.C. (2000), *Fuzzy-Set Social Science*, Chicago: Chicago University Press.

Ragin, C.C. and S.H. Becker (eds) (1992), *What Is a Case? Exploring the Foundations of Social Inquiry*, Cambridge: Cambridge University Press.

Schmidt, A. Vivien (2003), *The Future of European Capitalism*, Oxford: Oxford University Press.

Shonfield, Andrew (1965), *Modern Capitalism: The Changing Balance of Public and Private Power*, Oxford: Oxford University Press.

Skocpol, Theda (1979), *States and Social Revolutions: A Comparative Analysis of France, Russia, and China*, Cambridge, Cambridge University Press.

Stigler, George and Claire Friedland (1962), 'What Can Regulators Regulate?: The Case of Electricity', *Journal of Law and Economics*, reprinted in George Stigler, *The Citizen and the State*, Chicago: The University of Chicago Press, 1975, pp. 61–77.

Tocqueville, Alexis de (1945 [1835, 1840]), *Democracy in America*, 2 vols, New York: Vintage Books.

Tsebelis, G. (1990), *Nested Games: Rational Choice in Comparative Politics*, Berkeley, CA: University of California Press.

Vogel, David (1986), *National Styles of Regulation: Environmental Policy in Great Britain and the United States*, Ithaca and London: Cornell University Press.

Vogel, K. Steven (1996), *Freer Markets, More Rules: Regulatory Reform in Advanced Industrial Countries*, Ithaca and London: Cornell University Press.

Waarden, Frans van (1992), 'The Historical Institutionalization of Typical National Patterns in Policy Networks between State and Industry: A Comparison of the USA and the Netherlands', *European Journal of Political Research*, **21**, 131–62.

Waarden, Frans van (1995), 'Persistence of National Policy Styles: A Study of Their Institutional Foundations', in Brigitte Unger and Frans van Waarden (eds), *Convergence or Diversity? Internationalization and Economic Policy Response*, Aldershot: Avebury, pp. 333–72.

Wilson, James Q. (ed.) (1980), *The Politics of Regulation*, New York: Basic Books.

Zacher, W. Mark and A. Brent Sutton (1996), *Governing Global Networks: International Regimes for Transportation and Communications*, 2nd edn, Cambridge: Cambridge University Press.

9. The political foundations of the European regulatory state

Nicolas Jabko

The recent renewal of scholarly interest in regulation as a particular mode of economic governance can be understood as the academic acknowledgement of a real-world phenomenon. In the last 20 years, the role of government in economic development has been the subject of intense debates in advanced industrialized economies. These debates were perhaps most vivid in Western Europe, where the post-World War II consensus on the existence of a strong public sector alongside the private sector was profoundly shaken. And in many respects, the new market-oriented reform agenda of the European Union clearly expressed the alteration of this consensus. During the 1980s and the 1990s, it is no exaggeration to say that the political economy of the European Union underwent a quiet revolution. The member states of the EU first agreed to complete an 'internal market' by the year 1992, then rushed toward this objective by way of extensive liberalization and regulatory reforms at the EU level. And the march toward economic and monetary union (EMU) involved a number of important reforms on top of this already crowded policy agenda – the creation of the euro, the European Central Bank, and new mechanisms of policy-making and regulation at the EU level. As a result of all these reforms, the European Union increasingly appeared as the archetype of a 'regulatory state'.

Yet beyond the most obvious and observable characteristics of the rise of the regulatory state at the EU level, the factors that caused the EU's quiet revolution and in fact the very nature of the reforms at stake require an interpretation. Many scholarly accounts of EU events relate them to a variety of trends that contributed to the 'globalization' of national markets. Without doubt, the 1980s and 1990s witnessed an increase in international economic competition and an acceleration of technological change in certain key economic sectors. And the process of regulatory reform, especially the worldwide multiplication of independent agencies and regulatory authorities, went hand in hand with this evolution. Thus, what happened in the EU can easily appear as the local artifact of evolving functional requirements of a modern economy, alias globalization.

This chapter challenges this conventional view of European regulatory reforms as a local artifact of globalization. As it happened, EU reforms came after a long period of 'Euro-sclerosis' and policy fragmentation from the mid-1960s through the mid-1980s, which was universally interpreted as a consequence of economic globalization. If globalization can be a cause of both policy convergence and divergence, then its causal status with respect to regulatory reforms in Europe becomes more debatable. The shift away from *dirigiste* policies and toward a more market-based model of public oversight of the economy – which is central to Giandomenico Majone's definition of the 'regulatory state' – is certainly a global phenomenon with a strong economic rationale, but the European manifestations of this phenomenon are not the result of global economic trends.

Based on a comparative analysis of new regulatory mechanisms recently set up in the European Union, this chapter argues that the emergence of new goals and new regulators is the result of political manoeuvring, rather than evolving functional requirements. In sectors characterized by intense market competition and technological innovation, national regulators constantly have to adapt in order to defend their turf. Therefore, would-be regulatory entrepreneurs are generally out-manoeuvred, and new regulatory agencies not frequently created. By contrast, regulatory innovation often occurs in policy sectors where technological evolution is so slow that significant increases in economic efficiency cannot come from incremental regulatory intervention. Under such conditions, the very inertia of this situation creates manoeuvring room for new regulatory–political initiatives. Regulatory innovation occurs because actors exploit contingencies, not because the evolution of the market requires it. In other words, the regulatory state is a product of politics, rather than economic modernization.

The argument proceeds in two steps. Section 1 serves to critique a conventional view of recent European integration as a process of economic modernization on a global scale. It highlights the problematic nature of the link between European regulatory reforms and market globalization. Section 2 offers a political interpretation of European regulatory reforms in the 1980s and 1990s. It stresses the importance of the historical and strategic context of reform, in contrast to the globalization view of regulatory reform.

1. THE PROBLEMATIC LINK BETWEEN EUROPEAN INTEGRATION AND GLOBALIZATION

The regulatory reforms that were adopted at the European level in the 1980s and 1990s can appear as a local artifact of broad global economic trends toward market reforms. In the recent literature on the EU, there are basically two versions of this European-integration-as-globalization argument. In a first version of the argument, the EU is an agent of economic modernization at the service of its member states. Due to economic evolution, the configuration of domestic interests changes, which in turn involves an economically motivated 'choice for Europe'. According to Andrew Moravcsik, 'European integration resulted from a series of rational choices made by national leaders who consistently pursued economic interests ... that evolved slowly in response to structural incentives in the global economy' (Moravcsik, 1998, 3; see also Frieden, 1991, *passim*). Firms involved in international trade benefit from market globalization and therefore lobby in favour of more openness and stability in the institutional insertion of national economies within global markets. In turn, the aggregation of such preferences at the level of national governments explains the single market and monetary union initiatives of the 1980s and 1990s in Europe.

Another version of the globalization argument focuses on the emergence of the EU as a 'regulatory state'. According to Giandomenico Majone, 'regulation has a single normative justification: improving the efficiency of the economy by correcting specific forms of market failures such as monopoly, imperfect information, and negative externalities' (Majone, 1994, 79; see also Majone, 1996, 1998). EU bodies are able to acquire some autonomy as they are able to expand their turf not so much on the traditional *dirigiste* domains of European governmental activities, but in the new sphere of economic regulation. The EU is successful because it is a modest, economically liberal state, well suited to the tasks of modern economic governance and the pursuit of efficiency. Its legitimacy rests on legal and economic expertise, and is buttressed by its independence from elected governments. This non-interventionist, non-political model of economic governance has its roots in the United States and then spreads around the world by virtue of its superior economic rationale. For example, the 1980s and 1990s upgrade of EU competition policy mirrors postwar trends in US antitrust policies. Both policies are driven by legal and economic principles aimed at making the market work better, rather than providing an active substitute for market governance.

Thus, depending on which version of the modernization argument we accept, the EU appears either as an international regime or as an opportunistic actor that rode a global wave of market-oriented regulatory reforms – which bore familiar labels such as 'deregulation', 'liberalization', 'privatization' or, more generically, 'market reforms'. On the surface, these interpretations appear to make a lot of sense. The models of economic governance that prospered after World War II in Europe – which generally involved what Shonfield called a 'balance of public and private power' (Shonfield, 1969) – seemed to have exhausted their usefulness in the early 1970s. On a macroeconomic level, capital mobility was undermining the capacity of governments to conduct domestically centred Keynesian policies of demand management. And, if we consider issues of microeconomic governance, technological change and the acceleration of business cycles and market uncertainty meant that old-style industrial policies were ineffective, as they produced 'white elephants' and 'lame ducks' more often than industrial champions.

The question, however, is to what extent the globalization perspective writ large really *explains* what happens at the EU level, and whether it says much about the causes of regulatory reform. On a theoretical level, leading scholars of regulation have repeatedly questioned the legitimacy of an approach that asserts the superiority of non-majoritarian decision-making for the pursuit of economic efficiency, and thus largely leaves politics out of the story of regulatory reform. As Michael Moran recently said about the literature sparked by Giandomenico Majone, 'regulation as an activity is itself highly problematic. ... How strange, then, that the identification of the regulatory state in Europe has been accompanied by the claim that it is actually a solution to other pathologies of command in political and economic life' (Moran, 2002, 399; see also Lowi, 1984). If we consider the nature of regulatory reform at the EU level, the evidence points to a dual set of changes in the overall orientation of regulation and in the actors in charge of performing regulatory tasks. On the one hand, there was a shift in the orientation of economic governance, away from interventionist policies and toward a more market-based model of governance – a phenomenon that can be defined as marketization. This shift was best symbolized by the rush to create a single market. There is a sense in which efficiency and competitiveness overshadowed other goals – like social equality or national security – on the policy agenda.

On the other hand, recent market-oriented reforms were accompanied by a real build-up of power at the EU level, not just a reform of the state. The shift from national toward EU governance – alias 'Europeanization' – meant that the EU moved into the business of economic governance. Economic and monetary union is perhaps the best symbol of this movement, as it involved an empowerment of the EU as a separate institutional sphere, so far mostly at the level of the European Central Bank. While the first phenomenon – that is, marketization – could be interpreted as a result of globalization, there is no a priori reason why this should happen at the EU level. Back in the 1970s, most observers actually predicted an increasing *fragmentation* of European interests and policies in an age of increasing global interdependence (Cooper, 1972; Haas, 1975). If anything, global interdependence in the 1970s seemed to carry the seeds of a renationalization of economic policy-making and reforms. European responses to the 1970s oil shocks and the global recession highlighted the differences between national models of political economy in a more visible way than ever since the end of World War II (Katzenstein, 1978).

As soon as we probe into the process and motivations of the dual phenomenon of marketization cum Europeanization, the causal power of market globalization considered as a requirement of economic modernity is no longer so clear. First, the process went beyond a pure logic of cost–benefit analysis. Once economic governance models began to change, Europeanization gained momentum in a way that cannot be easily understood from an economic perspective. The nature as well as the role of the state underwent profound change. For example, in the field of monetary regulation, some scholars have spoken of a 'de-territorialization of money' (Cohen, 1998; McNamara, 2002). As a result of monetary union, national states no longer have exclusive jurisdiction over the management of their own currencies. This represents an important leap that is not adequately captured in terms of international regime creation, or in terms of a reform of state action. Market globalization alone was arguably more likely to provoke a retrenchment of monetary regulation to the national level, rather than a full-fledged Europeanization (Jabko, 1999).

Second, the motivations behind EU-level reforms do not conform very well to a story of globalization. As it happened, regulatory reform went much further than what could be reasonably inferred from the intentions of its initiators. We need to remember that, at the time, the Single Act was received with reserve or even scepticism by long-time observers of European politics. European governments wanted more European unity for very different reasons in the mid-1980s. They did not see globalization as a hard constraint requiring a combination of marketization and Europeanization, but simply as an economic context in which to pursue a variety of political goals. To take only three salient examples, British free-market conservatives like Thatcher saw Europe merely as an outlet for their policy agenda and the interests of their constituencies, while French socialists like Mitterrand sought to reassert state power and the left's agenda at the European level, and Kohl pursued Germany's longstanding postwar foreign policy of supporting European integration in a rather open-ended manner. Given the diverse motivations behind regulatory reform at the EU level, it is amazing to see that anything was achieved.

2.   THE POLITICS OF REGULATORY REFORM

Upon closer examination, the phenomenon of marketization cum Europeanization undercuts the globalization story because it presents a number of anomalies. According to the globalization hypothesis, we should observe the most profound changes in issue areas and sectors where market forces are the most prevalent and where the momentum of change is least resistible. We should also observe that Europeanization and marketization move in lockstep, since Europeanization is considered mostly as an artifact of market globalization. Yet we observe, in fact, that marketization and especially Europeanization has extended into areas where market forces did not threaten to overwhelm publicly defined goals, and into areas where public prerogatives remain paramount. A good example of this dynamic is the provision of collective, alias 'public', services like telecommunications, transportation, or energy. In cases such as telecommunications, one could reasonably argue that the irruption of market pressures was an inescapable reality, once the need for technological progress was recognized. This was much less the case, however, in slow-moving sectors like the energy sector, where the EU has become a key factor of sectoral evolution.

Furthermore, we observe that the depth of marketization is inversely related to the phenomenon of Europeanization. The European Union becomes an imposing presence not so much in order to facilitate economies of scale and gains from trade, but above all in order to channel or even prevent the free operation of market forces when the result of market dynamics is deemed counterproductive. When the two goals are compatible, this contradiction between marketization and Europeanization does not arise. Up to a certain point, the build-up of regulatory capacity and the marketization process can perfectly go hand in hand. But when policy-makers are forced to choose between restraints on the operation of market forces and net loss of control, they generally attempt to retain control and to use the EU as an instrument for that purpose. In other words, when there is a conflict of objectives, the political logic of control tends to supersede the pure economic logic of market pressures. A good example of this is the European Commission's often aggressive enforcement of competition policy. Market forces generally ensure competition between economic actors, but they also give them strong incentives to pursue economies of scale. And there are cases where these two market dynamics are in conflict, since the race for economic gigantism can ultimately lead to a decrease in the level of effective market competition. An aggressive competition policy means, in practice, that the welfare costs that are associated with market-induced dominant positions are considered higher than the benefits that stem from economies of scale, which in turn justifies a bias in favour of maintaining the level playing-field. This cannot be considered as a direct result of market globalization, since in many respects the market is not left to operate freely (for a full development of this theme, see Vogel, 1996). Thus the establishment of a certain level and kind of political control over the modalities of globalization appears to be a key dimension of Europeanization.

How can we make sense of these anomalies? In order to understand the emergence of the regulatory state, it is useful to consider what occurred at the EU level as a broad change in the institutional regime that governed the European economy. Let us examine this process of regime change. Some of its aspects are particularly intriguing even in the context of globalization, and therefore deserve special attention. In varying proportions, many reforms at stake exhibit, across a variety of policy areas, at least one and usually several of the four following characteristics:

1. The *rapid pace* of regime change must be explained. Substantial market reforms took place very rapidly in the 1980s and 1990s, perhaps most dramatically in the area of financial integration. While market pressures had become very pressing and certainly pushed the financial sector in the direction of change, the sudden acceleration of reforms is none the less surprising because one would generally expect institutional equilibria to exhibit a substantial degree of inertia. Changes in financial regimes are generally difficult to carry out because financial establishments are nationally entrenched and prone to wage political resistance against reforms.

2. The *wide scope* of EU regime change is intriguing. The European market reform movement spread to areas where market forces for change were not extremely pressing. For example, energy is a relatively slow-moving sector, where economic pressures are attenuated by the importance of sunk costs and the relatively slow pace of technological progress. Yet EU countries engaged in a process of liberalizing the energy supply industry, to an extent that goes well beyond the level that could be justified by economic pressures only. Again, this is surprising because incumbent public utilities, often in a monopolistic position, were important political actors and able to wage a political fight against reform.

3. The *divergent focus* of EU-level reforms deserves to be explained. Regime change at the EU level did not only centre on the agenda of market integration, but also reached into areas that are highly tangential to – if not contradictory with – that agenda. For example, the EU budget was multiplied by four, mostly to cover an increase in the so-called EC Structural Funds. Through two successive reforms in 1988 and 1993, the member states agreed to set up a redistributive budgetary mechanism between EU regions. While the budget surely remained modest even after this increase, the occurrence of reform in this area is puzzling none the less, not only because the wealthiest and biggest member states stood to lose from EU-wide interregional transfers, but also because it seemed to counteract the competitive market-based allocation of resources across European regions.

4. The *high political profile* of EU reforms requires some explanation. Some reforms undertaken at the EU level are extremely political and dynamic, in the sense that the stakes involved are high, the ultimate distribution of costs and benefits largely elusive, and the long-term consequences potentially enormous. This is most clearly the case for the process of economic and monetary union, culminating with the creation of a single currency, the euro, managed by an independent European Central Bank. In this case, the surprise stems from the fact that a core group of EU member states actively prepared for and carried through what was in many respects a leap of faith, both economically and politically.

Thus different dimensions of the European Union's development can be systematically compared as combinatorial variants of these different characteristic. Table 9.1 illustrates a range of observed variation on the dependent variable. In each case, the process of regime change exhibits a particular combination, in various proportions, of the above characteristics of which at least one stands out as particularly important.

This short chapter obviously cannot do justice to the analytic underpinnings and empirical details of each case. But it should already be clear that, for explanatory purposes, the most important characteristics are precisely those that are the most counter-intuitive. These characteristics appear in bold in Table 9.1. For example, institutional inertia makes fast-paced EU-level reforms in the financial sector puzzling, all other things being equal. By comparison, the relatively limited scope of financial liberalization, its centrality to the market-building project as outlined in the '1992' agenda, and the moderate political profile of financial liberalization given the prior

Table 9.1 Characteristics of regime change

Select cases of regime change	Speed	Scope	Focus	Salience
Single financial area	**High**	Moderate	Central	Moderate
Internal energy market	Low	**Expanded**	Peripheral	Moderate
Structural funds reforms	Moderate	**Expanded**	**Extremely tangential**	Moderate
Economic and monetary union	Low	**Dramatically expanded**	**Peripheral/ tangential**	**High**

technological and political momentum fuelling it, deserve fewer explanations. The more we investigate the counter-intuitive characteristics, the more we will learn about the process of recent European integration, and the better we will be able to characterize its outcomes.

To see the scope of marketization and Europeanization, let us first consider the regulated provision of public services in relatively slow-moving sectors, like energy. Of course, the pace of change in these sectors has been relatively slow in relation to other sectors, for example telecommunications. The single market for energy only came about in the late 1990s and remains in infancy to this day, since many segments of the market are not effectively open to market competition. But if we consider the fact that these sectors were arenas that were not subject to overwhelming market forces in the first place, then the steps that have been achieved on the way toward a more liberal regulatory regime are remarkable (Eising and Jabko, 2001). If we now consider the provision and regulation of money encapsulated in Europe's economic and monetary union (EMU), we see that there has been a dramatic change in the regulatory regime and a full Europeanization of policy and regulation. The European Central Bank is now fully in charge of defining monetary policy at the EU level. It does so within a completely Europeanized policy-making framework. This does not mean, however, that public prerogatives have ceased to matter and that the setting of monetary policy has been transferred to the market. Quite to the contrary, the ECB's monetary policy now serves for euro-zone countries as a shield against market turbulences and currency tensions. Since all these countries share a single currency, it is no longer possible for market forces to directly discipline the policies of any single country by imposing on it the burden of a falling exchange rate. In this sense, Europeanization has gone much further than marketization.

The example of EMU is also interesting because it illustrates the inverse relationship between deep marketization and Europeanization. One of the benefits of EMU is to domesticate market forces and to blunt their power of nuisance for the member states of the euro zone. This may appear as a paradox, since the first phase and indeed one of the cornerstones of the EMU process was the full liberalization of capital movements within the EU (effective on 1 July 1990). In fact, while marketization went hand in hand with Europeanization up to a certain point, this correlation ceased to operate as soon as the exchange rates between currencies were irreversibly fixed on 1 January 1999. This example of an antagonistic relationship between Europeanization and marketization is not an isolated one. In areas where market forces were considered as fully legitimate and beneficial, marketization was a given, but Europeanization *per se* was often not a central characteristic of regulatory change. To the extent that there was some Europeanization, its relative importance pales in comparison with the marketization process. For example, the countries of the EU all experienced a more or less sudden shift from administrative or semi-public allocation schemes to market mechanisms for the provision of corporate capital in the 1980s and 1990s. A series of national reforms were passed in this area in the mid-1980s, and a number of EU directives followed these domestic financial reforms in the late 1980s and the 1990s. Yet the EU reforms were mostly aimed at achieving a satisfactory degree of coordination and 'mutual recognition' – a 'single financial area' – between otherwise different regulatory regimes for banking, investment services, insurance, and so on. Whatever convergence occurred between national financial regulations came about because of bottom-up market competition between firms and the political pressures that these firms brought onto national regulators, rather than from a top-down process of policy Europeanization.

In order to understand the paradox of a Europeanization process that occurs to the greatest extent in areas where it was least to be expected from a globalization perspective, it is helpful to think of the single market and EMU as an example of *market-building*. As Karl Polanyi showed in his classic study of nineteenth-century industrialization, markets are political creations (Polanyi, 1944). This applies to the EU's single market as well. When governments tried to create a Europe-wide market, they soon realized that it required a huge build-up of political power to establish and maintain that market at the EU level. Except in areas where market competition was already intense at the national level, there were very few actors eagerly waiting in the wings to capture the gains from trade on a wider scale. In many important areas there was no significant market competition before the single market. Monopolies were the name of the game, especially in the provision of collective services such as telecommunications, energy, or transportation. Another typical situation was one in which national markets remained strictly segmented and specialized in the provision of very heterogeneous or idiosyncratic goods and services, such as national currencies, regional economic infrastructures, pensions, medical care, education, and so on.

In hindsight, it is possible to see that these slow-moving sectors where change was not a foregone conclusion have actually undergone a rather dramatic evolution. Regulatory innovation and important Europeanization have occurred most often in policy sectors where technological evolution is slow and where market forces did not dictate sectoral evolution. In such sectors, the significant increases in economic efficiency that could be expected from widening the scale of markets, from national to EU-wide markets, could not come just from incremental regulatory reform. The paradox is that the very inertia of the situation created manoeuvring room for new regulatory–political initiatives. The global rush to 'market reforms' in the 1980s and 1990s gave legitimacy to various calls for 'new regulatory approaches' or 'new governance' oriented toward the market. Actors who had a generic interest in moving away from the *status quo* jumped on the bandwagon of market reform (for a suggestive analysis of this type of 'herding' behaviour, see Levi-Faur, 2002). This applied not only to politicians who were ideologically committed to the market, but also to important elite constituencies within both the private and the public sector. The well-publicized failures of direct public intervention – the 'lame ducks' of public sector industry – and the context of fiscal consolidation or retrenchment in most EU member states – which became especially acute given the convergence criteria and the growing burden of social protection – contributed to a much greater political acceptance of market liberalization. In the end, the regulatory state at the EU level was built in this historically favourable context for marketization. Once its principle was adopted, the creation of a genuine internal market at the European level justified a particularly strong exercise of political power, both in the process of legislating about it and in the kinds of regulatory arrangements that were made in order to establish and enforce market competition.

This stands in sharp contrast with the relatively low level of Europeanization in fast-changing sectors where the market had already become a fact of life before the single market and EMU. Since regulatory reform was already under way at the national level under the control of domestic actors, the intervention of EU actors was merely seen as unnecessary meddling on the part of the European Commission. Thus, beyond the establishment of a minimum 'level playing-field', European governments were reluctant to go in the direction of Europeanizing financial regulations. Since marketization was already in effect at the domestic level, the functional and political need for building power at the EU level was much less acute than in cases where marketization had to be forced against the will of well-entrenched domestic actors. In such cases, market forces and rapid technological progress usually prevailed even before the single market initiative, and national regulators constantly strove to adapt in order to defend their turf. The single market only created incentives to beef up coordination capacities so as to facilitate joint adaptation. Turf expansion by would-be regulators in the European Commission was severely bounded by the lack of political space for newcomers and new forms of regulation. For example, in the regulation of finance, only a loose level of coordination was established at the EU level, since competitive markets already existed on a national level and the problem was just to ensure adequate market access for suppliers and buyers of financial services from other EU member states. Thus, in areas that were technologically driven and highly exposed to international competition, the creation of a single market was important but not particularly problematic. Regulatory entrepreneurs were out-manoeuvred, and new regulatory agencies not frequently created. The Commission today has a very limited role in financial regulation, since most EU regulation happens at the committee level between national regulators who simply coordinate more than they used to in order to ensure a level playing-field. In such sectors, the name of the game was and remains the 'mutual recognition' of national regulations, combined with a procedure to establish 'minimum essential requirements' usually performed by way of regulatory coordination.

As a consequence, European integration went the furthest not in the sectors where the market was a fact of life, but precisely in those sectors where it was necessary to build and exert power in order to obtain otherwise unlikely market-oriented reforms. For example, when the member states decided to liberalize their energy markets in 1996 (electricity) and 1998 (gas), the supporters of liberalization understood that the EU alone would be able to bring about a series of regulatory reforms that would have been very difficult to sell at a domestic level only. While there obviously remained some room in these sectors to enhance efficiency – as is almost always the case – there was no built-in mechanism such as market competition to ensure the relentless pursuit of greater productivity and lower costs. In most cases, only certain segments of the elite were in favour of market-oriented liberalization at the outset. Yet EU officials, especially within the Commission, responded to this demand for liberalization by supplying a framework that enabled an otherwise unlikely series of reforms. In this process, they were able to build power in the area of liberalization and regulatory reform, both because the supporters of reform within the member states were willing to extend a political payment in exchange for the Commission's services as facilitators of reform, and because they saw this power build-up as a guarantee that market-oriented reforms would actually be implemented across the European Union. In the case of electricity, the EU directive not only required a certain level of liberalization, but also provided for 'reciprocity' in market access among member states. This meant that the member states could only gain access to their neighbours' markets if they agreed to liberalize theirs. In practice, the member states relied on the Commission to monitor their partners' progress in implementing the directive, since it was difficult for any given government to unilaterally justify reciprocity-based restrictions in the general context of liberalization. The Commission could also use its powers in the area of competition policy, especially merger regulation, as leverage to enforce liberalization on reluctant member states. Very concretely, this meant that member states whose firms wanted to engage in mergers and acquisitions in newly liberalized sectors across the EU first had to prove that they were taking steps to liberalize their own domestic markets. The Commission thus became a powerful arbiter and watchdog of liberalization, precisely because it was acting in sectors where this particular brand of regulatory reform was bound to be the most controversial.

In summary, the main analytic differences between a globalization-as-driver perspective and a politics-as-driver perspective to explain the emergence of the regulatory state can be shown as in Table 9.2.

To make the case for politics rather than economics in the birth of the regulatory state does not at all amount to a belief in the unlimited power of

Table 9.2   Emergence of the regulatory state explained by different perspectives

	Globalization-as-driver perspective	Politics-as-driver perspective
Main causal mechanism	Market forces translated as political interests	Political strategies that utilize market ideas
Main actors	Established political actors acting as interest group representatives and in response to an economic context	Political entrepreneurs acting opportunistically and in response to an ideational context
Enabling condition	Economic evolution shifts the distribution of political resources and empowers new groups	Broad revival of market ideas creates opportunities for actors to advocate Europeanization in highly insulated sectors
Confirming evidence	Europeanization dictated by economic imperatives (e.g. the objective economic interests of social groups or nations)	Europeanization shaped by political considerations (e.g. the build-up of political power and/or the active promotion of values)
Anomaly/ disconfirming evidence	Europeanization in market-insulated sectors and/or minimal Europeanization in market-exposed sectors	Marketization overriding the expected build-up of political power and/or the promotion of political values
Interpretation of the rise of the regulatory state	Modernization process driven by economic forces on a global scale	Political development with local specificities in a favourable global ideational context

political entrepreneurs to shape outcomes. Quite the contrary; the emergence of the regulatory state must be understood as a historical event which, as such, could be reversed or reoriented in the foreseeable future. Since it cuts across so many economic sectors and policy areas, the trajectory of EU competition policy provides a good illustration of the depth and the same time the limits of this power-building dynamic. European policy-makers had realized in the late 1980s that the single market could not prosper without a competition policy to prevent the development of giant Euro-monopolies. Thus the Merger Control Regulation was passed in 1989 and the EU significantly increased its activities in the area of competition policy. Yet this was only the beginning of a considerable build-up of Commission powers in this area, which was rarely foreseen in the member states. Competition policy was a good base for building up the regulatory state, since it placed the Commission in the position of imposing a new orientation in economic governance across the European Union. Perhaps most significantly, the European Commission's antitrust policy increasingly moved on the politically sensitive terrain of 'state aids' to industry (Smith, 1998). Given the European governments' tendencies to assist industrial firms through various forms of financial aid, this evolution is equivalent to a new deal in business–government relations. It also affects the capacity of member states to conduct their own regional development policy, since any outlay of capital in the form of tax incentives comes under the scrutiny of competition policy beneath the heading of state aid. The EU *de facto* increasingly defines the trends of regional development policy – the type of action that is permissible or not – through the active combination of its competition policy and its cohesion policy. Incidentally, this dual role of the EU in these two very different policy areas can be understood as a source of practical coherence rather than of doctrinal incoherence – something that is completely impossible to understand if the 'regulatory state' is seen as a pure efficiency-oriented regime and as fundamentally incompatible with redistribution (for example Majone, 1998). As a regulatory state with a role in structural policy especially at the regional level, the EU is uniquely positioned to define both the terms of a level playing-field and the criteria under which state aids can be extended without creating unwarranted trade distortions. The powers of the Commission are in a sense more extensive in the area of antitrust than those of the US government, since Commission decisions are immediately applicable and can only be challenged in court after the fact. The power of EU bodies is felt even beyond the borders of the EU single market, with the recent vetoing of a merger between two US corporate giants, General Electric and Honeywell – a merger that had been previously approved by US antitrust authorities.

At the same time, it is not clear whether this build-up of power at the EU level will continue indefinitely. Critics argue that the European Commission is now the 'judge, jury, and executioner' of a policy that has a profound impact on the day-to-day conduct of business in the EU. In cases such as the prohibited merger of GE and Honeywell, the Commission has been criticized for abusing its powers under competition policy and there are certain indications that a political backlash may be under way. In the recent past, EU member governments have increasingly challenged competition policy decisions in court, both because they substantively disagreed with these decisions and because they saw them as abuses of power on the part of the European Commission. In certain cases, the European Court of Justice and the European Court of First Instance have ruled against two high-profile Commission prohibitions of mergers (namely, the Airtours and the Legrand–Schneider cases).[1] At the same time, other recent judicial rulings have reinforced the hand of the Commission, especially on the issue of 'golden shares' – a system that gave national governments in some European countries certain prerogatives in defining the shareholding structures of big domestic firms. On the whole, what can be said for now is that the EU has really acquired some power, and is less shy about flexing this new muscle. This does not only apply to the European Commission, but also to other EU-level institutions, which should be considered as part of the EU 'regulatory state'. This trend tends to disprove globalization stories, which rest on the assumption that economic and regulatory reforms are relatively easy and politically neutral to undertake. The quiet revolution of marketization cum Europeanization incurred major effects on the actors. The example of EU competition policy has transformed the European Commission into a major force shaping the global regulatory agenda. This is a political development that cannot be understood simply as the outcome of a globalization story. We are witnessing not a simple battle between the supporters and the enemies of economic modernity, but more importantly a political struggle for power in the new governance structure of the European economy. While the relaunching of Europe in the 1980s and 1990s happened in a global economic context, it also meant a change in the institutional framework that defined Europe's mode of insertion into the global economy.

3.   CONCLUSION – SEEING THE REGULATORY STATE AS A STATE

While advanced industrial societies are constantly engaged in a process of economic modernization, the purely functional/economic dimension of the rise of a European regulatory state glosses over the politics of this process. Regulatory innovation and market reforms at the EU level have gone far beyond the functional requirements of modernization. As a result, Europe's political economy is a very different world now than it was 20 years ago. It makes sense to speak of a quiet revolution in European political economy over this period. The process of market-oriented regulatory reform in Europe in the last two decades has entailed a fundamental change in the nature of political power and the conception of the role of the state. But it has *not* meant the emergence of an a-political regulatory state solely devoted to the pursuit of efficiency and completely divorced from a more traditional conception of the state that would stress the pursuit of political power, societal values and distributional goals. Starting from a position of complete marginality, the European Union as a sphere of decision-making, and especially EU actors such as the European Commission and the European Central Bank, were considerably empowered – both *vis-à-vis* EU member states and on a global level. While public officials in the member states are still concerned about national sovereignty and their capacity to influence outcomes, the new centrality of EU institutions changes the very nature of sovereignty and the parameters of public action in Europe. And while the emergence of 'the regulatory state' is indeed a very remarkable phenomenon, there are good reasons to doubt that the regulatory state is synonymous with a depoliticized pursuit of aggregate welfare, completely detached from the realm of power, values and distributive stakes. In other words, it is important to see the regulatory state for what it is, that is, a form of coercive state power instead of a non-political and arguably utopian form of state power.

Such a political reading of the European Union's regulatory state also has important consequences. If the rise of the regulatory state is understood as a phenomenon of power rather than just a straightforward pursuit of economic efficiency, then certain questions arise more vividly. On a practical level, the empowerment of the European Union raises the open-ended question of what purpose and societal vision this new power is supposed to serve. If the European Union is not primarily about the pursuit of efficiency, then what should it be about? After the completion of the single market and EMU and on the eve of a major enlargement of the European Union, a discussion of the political origins of the EU as a regulatory state can thus serve as a rejoinder to the timely debate about the *'finalités'* of the European Union. From a theoretical perspective, the main lesson is that we need to bring *politics* back into our understanding of the logic of regulation and regulatory change. This parallels the efforts of comparative historical scholars to 'bring the state back in' (Evans et al., 1985), but with an EU twist to the story – since a number of state officials from different member states with different purposes interact in a process of regulatory reforms in which they are not the only and (arguably) not even the most pivotal actors. The rise of the regulatory state is certainly a worldwide phenomenon, but it is not a seamless process and certainly not an a-political process. Thus it cannot be understood on a theoretical level without reference to the particular forms of local and international politics that contribute to its emergence and persistence. It is toward this kind of mid-range theorizing combined with a historical perspective and awareness that scholars of regulatory politics should pay more systematic attention.

NOTE

1. In 2002, the Court ruled in favour of Britain and France, which had challenged the Commission's decision to prohibit these two high-profile industrial mergers. The two reversals of Commission decisions in the area of EU merger policy were unprecedented and therefore received a great deal of publicity.

REFERENCES

Cohen, Benjamin J. (1998), *The Geography of Money*, Ithaca: Cornell University Press.

Cooper, Richard N. (1972), 'Economic Interdependence and Foreign Policy in the Seventies', *World Politics*, **24** (2).

Eising, Rainer and Nicolas Jabko (2001), 'Moving Targets: Institutional Embeddedness and Domestic Politics in the Liberalization of EU Electricity Markets', *Comparative Political Studies*, **34** (7).

Evans, Peter B., Dietrich Rueschemeyer and Theda Skocpol (1985), *Bringing the State Back In*, Cambridge: Cambridge University Press.

Frieden, Jeffry (1991), 'Invested Interests: The Politics of National Economic Policy in a World of Global Finance', *International Organization*, **45**, 425–51.

Haas, Ernst B. (1975), *The Obsolescence of Regional Integration Theory*, Berkeley: Institute of International Studies.

Jabko, Nicolas (1999), 'In the Name of the Market: How the European Commission Paved the Way for Monetary Union', *Journal of European Public Policy*, **6** (3), 475–95.

Katzenstein, Peter J. (ed.) (1978), *Between Power and Plenty: Foreign Economic Policies of Advanced Industrial States*, Madison: University of Wisconsin Press.

Levi-Faur, David (2002), 'Herding towards a New Convention: On herds, shepherds, and lost sheep in the liberalization of the telecommunications and electricity industries', paper delivered at the Workshop on Theories of Regulation, Nuffield College, Oxford, 25–26 May 2002.

Lowi, Theodore (1985), 'The State in Politics: The Relations Between Policy and Administration', in Roger Noll (ed.), *Regulatory Policy and the Social Sciences*, Berkeley and Los Angeles: University of California Press, pp. 67–105.

Majone, Giandomenico (1994), 'The Rise of the Regulatory State in Europe', *West European Politics*, **17** (3), 77–101.

Majone, Giandomenico (1996), *Regulating Europe*, London: Routledge.

Majone, Giandomenico (1998), 'State, Market, and Regulatory Competition in the EU', in Andrew Moravcsik (ed.), *Centralization or Fragmentation*, New York: Council on Foreign Relations, pp. 94–123.

McNamara, Kathleen R. (2002), 'Making Money', manuscript, Princeton University.

Moran, Michael (2002), 'Understanding the Regulatory State', *British Journal of Political Science*, **32** (2), 391–413.

Moravcsik, Andrew (1998), *The Choice for Europe: Social Purpose and State Power from Messina to Maastricht*, Ithaca: Cornell University Press.

Polanyi, Karl (1957), *The Great Transformation: The Political and Economic Origins of Our Time*, Boston: Beacon Press, [1944].

Shonfield, Andrew (1969), *Modern Capitalism: The Changing Balance of Public and Private Power*, London: Oxford University Press.

Smith, Mitchell P. (1998), 'Autonomy by the Rules: The European Commission and the Development of State Aid Policy', *Journal of Common Market Studies*, **36** (1), 55–78.

Vogel, Steven K. (1996), *Freer Markets, More Rules: Regulatory Reform in Advanced Industrialized Countries*, Ithaca: Cornell University Press.

10. Modes of regulation in the governance of the European Union: towards a comprehensive evaluation

Christoph Knill and Andrea Lenschow

1. INTRODUCTION[1]

Forms of governance are in transition on an international scale. Neither the juxtaposition of the market and state regulation nor that of public versus private actors in governing society match well with the multiple faces of modern governance. The classical regulatory state, which has emerged as an alternative to the welfare state – both however with the intent to complement or correct market mechanisms – is gradually changing its distinctive face of top-down authoritative control of market and society and is joining with other steering mechanisms.[2] The process of regulating is being decentralized, allowing access to and spreading responsibilities across economic and societal actors; the regulations themselves are taking on various forms ranging from substantive rules to incentives and procedural requirements; chains of control are blurring and mechanisms of control softening with the emphasis shifting towards more responsiveness and self-responsibility.

While this trend is a general one, the European Union (EU), which has been characterized as a regulatory state *par excellence* (Majone, 1994, 85–92), represents a particularly good example to investigate and evaluate it. As part of a larger governance debate in Europe, triggered by the declining competitiveness of the European economy globally and concerns with regard to the protection of citizens in an increasingly uncertain environment (characterized by rapid technological change as well as open borders, and the fading capacities of national states to cope with these challenges), the EU is experimenting with a variety of different regulatory approaches. Historically, the EU regulators were caught between functional needs and political pressures and, hence, the EU regulatory apparatus developed *ad hoc* and in patchwork style. Nevertheless, we can observe the emergence of less authoritative, less interventionist, more participatory regulatory forms.

The political system of the EU reveals several characteristics that are particularly favourable for engaging in this development. Of particular importance in this respect is its nature as a multi-level system. The complex intermeshing of powers and competencies of public and private actors at varying institutional levels poses enormous challenges with respect to the accommodation of diverse interests in order to ensure the system's overall legitimacy, both in terms of input (democratic standards) and output criteria (decision-making, implementation, problem-solving). As a consequence, we observe a complex picture of coexisting and overlapping patterns of regulation both within and across different policy sectors.

Based on this observation, this chapter has two objectives. First, it is our aim to structure the complex picture of different modes of EU regulation. To arrive at a differentiated picture of the EU regulatory state, we develop a typology of different modes of European regulation ranging from classical legal instruments to softer forms of steering the economy and society (akin to Scott's concept of the (post-)regulatory state; Chapter 7 in this volume). In a second step, we are looking at the regulatory transition from a normative angle. Although the choice of regulatory instruments will always be the result of political processes shaped by interests, power as well as institutional constellations, the functionality of regulatory instruments in terms of policy outcome and societal impact is likely to enter the debate. This is true especially in the EU, which continues to suffer from unstable support in the population as well as in parts of the political elite. Hence we analyse the various modes of regulation employed in EU policy-making on the basis of several evaluation criteria, offering a critical commentary on regulatory modes and trends.

2. EUROPEAN GOVERNANCE: A TYPOLOGY OF REGULATORY MODES

In order to classify the varying patterns of regulation characterizing European governance, we proceed in two steps. First, we look at different *forms of intervention* which emerge from the specific allocation of competencies within the multi-level system. In a second step, we attempt to develop this typology further by analysing the process set in motion through these forms of intervention, that is, the *steering mechanisms* by which the intended policy objectives shall be achieved.

2.1 Forms of Intervention

Considering that we are dealing with the EU, we need to pay particular attention to the multi-level structure framing regulatory processes. This institutional context forces us to consider the distribution of responsibilities across regulatory centres (such as the EU, national executives or non-state actors). We therefore focus on two dimensions of regulatory intervention: the level of obligation and the level of discretion. EU regulatory policy may differ in terms of its obligatory nature imposed on its addressees; hence the level of legal authority associated with EU intervention. In addition, EU regulatory policy may differ with respect to the distribution of tasks across the tiers of governance and the level of discretion they grant to decentralized actors in the implementation process. While both dimensions may apply to regulatory approaches in general, they are particularly central in the evolution of the EU regulatory state.

Table 10.1 summarizes the mix of regulatory patterns that currently coexists in the EU. Combining the two dimensions of regulation – obligation and discretion – we arrive at four modes of intervention. In the table we identify those classes of regulatory instruments that are representative for each mode.[3]

The 'substantive and procedural regulatory standards' fit the image of the EU regulatory state – and true enough, these regulatory instruments remain the dominant form of intervention in the European single market and other spheres of social life (cf. Héritier, 2002; Holzinger et al., 2003). Regulatory standards usually entail obligatory and detailed rules, allowing the EU Commission – at least in theory – to control the level of compliance on the national and regional level (Baldwin and Cave, 1999, 160). Concentrating on both standard-setting and legal control at the supranational level, this is the most hierarchical (top-down) mode of regulation.

The so-called 'new instruments' are a mixed bag of regulatory tools.[5] What

Table 10.1   Modes of regulation in the EU

	High level of obligation imposed by the regulator on implementing actor/ authority	Low level of obligation imposed by the regulator on implementing actor/ authority
High level of discretion for implementing actor/authority	New instruments: economic, communicative, framework regulation	Open method of coordination[4] (OMC)
Low level of discretion for implementing actor/authority	Regulatory standards: substantive, procedural	Self-regulation in the shadow of the state

they have in common is a more indirect approach towards achieving behavioural change. While the level of obligation for the national administration is high, the addressees of these policy instruments have broad leeway to comply within a relatively open regulatory space (framework regulation) or to react to new procedural or incentive structures (economic and communicative instruments).

Framework regulations leave it to decentralized levels of governance to add regulatory substance fitting local conditions into the European framework defining obligatory general guidelines and goals (Baldwin and Cave, 1999, 161). Economic and communicative instruments have been designed to target the problem perception and incentive structures of economic and social actors. Instead of hierarchy, these regulations emphasize participation, self-initiative and voluntarism. Procedural requirements are meant to contribute to achieving substantive objectives (cf. Knill and Lenschow, 2000).

The instruments listed in the second row of the table shift regulatory responsibility away from the EU level to private actors or national authorities. The 'self-regulatory model' is based on private actors devising concrete regulatory standards – in the shadow of the state. Typically, an industrial association (as opposed to government or firm) sets rules and standards (codes of practice) for the conduct of the associated firms (Gunningham and Rees, 1997, 365). The level of control shifts from EU to the industry level, although the failure to self-regulate may trigger the return to the regulatory standards approach.

In the EU, private self-regulation can be observed in two basic forms. First, self-regulation is based on voluntary agreements between the Commission and sectoral associations. In these agreements (which officially are declared as Commission recommendations), industry commits itself to the implementation of certain requirements. A second pattern can be observed in the field of social policy. Based on the Social Protocol of the Maastricht Treaty, the Commission is not only legally required to consult the European peak associations of industry and trade unions before developing social policy proposals. The member states have also accepted that negotiations between these associations can serve as a substitute for traditional European regulatory processes (Falkner, 2000). The final agreement of the corporatist partners, however, takes the traditional form of an EU directive.

While all types discussed so far have to do with rules to be followed, the 'OMC' (open method of coordination) follows a mere process model. While certain policy benchmarks are set for the Union, national responses are formulated independently and without the threat of formal sanctions. The EU merely provides a context and enabling structures for cooperation and learning among national policy-makers. The regulatory impact of this approach rests on dissemination of best practice and the provision of incentives (peer review) rather than legal obligation and control. Hence the level of obligation to a regulatory centre is low and a wide range of policy strategies to achieve general EU targets could be chosen.

2.2 Dominant Mechanisms of Steering

Each regulatory type implies a different mechanism of policy adaptation on the national level and hence, also a different model of governance in the European multi-level system. We can distinguish three general mechanisms through which regulators might seek to affect the behaviour of the regulated: (a) they may be coerced to comply with the regulation, (b) they may be 'tempted' to change their behaviour due to incentive effects of the regulation and (c) they may learn, that is, redefine their interests on the basis of new knowledge gathered due to the regulatory context and subsequently adapt their behaviour. As most regulatory instruments are characterized by various mechanisms, we developed a ranking. In Table 10.2 we distinguish between

Table 10.2   Steering mechanisms and modes of regulation

	Regulatory standards	New instruments	Self-regulation	OMC
Coercion	++ Legally binding standards	+ Framework and procedural rules	+ Shadow of hierarchy	+ Reporting and monitoring
Incentive structures	0	++ Changes of procedural and/or material opportunities	++ Private actors influence regulatory standards	+ Peer pressure
Learning	0	0	+ Communication in private networks	++ Best-practice models
Overall steering model	Hierarchy model: of power coercion	Public delegation model: subsidiarity	Private delegation model	Radical subsidiarity model: public learning approach

three levels of relevance (++ dominant mechanism; + relevant mechanism; 0 irrelevant mechanism). In assessing the relative importance of steering mechanisms, the analytical focus is on the underlying intentions of the regulators rather than the actual performance or 'objective' relevance of these mechanisms.

We argue that different modes of regulations entail different models of governance. The early European regulatory state relied primarily on the hierarchy model with its implied powers of coercion. This model makes no attempt to influence the addressees' awareness of the problem structure by tackling either strategic or cognitive foundations of individual behaviour.

The new modes depart from the hierarchical model to different degrees. The least radical departure leads to the application of new instruments. This public delegation model relies on an authoritative framework, but places particular emphasis on creating incentive structures at the EU level and leaving discretionary space for public administration on lower levels of governance to add the relevant administrative procedures. The widespread inability or unwillingness of lower-level administrative agents to implement detailed EU regulation has been one reason for experimenting with such softer instruments.

A more far-reaching departure from the hierarchical model of regulation is the delegation model based on private self-regulation (Black, 1996; Ogus, 1995). The EU calls especially on economic actors to form a private network in order to solve particular problems collectively. The private network is responsible for setting regulatory standards and for ensuring compliance. The dominant mechanism leading to behavioural change relies on the provision of incentives as the self-regulatory approach induces economic actors to comply with rules formulated 'in their name' and in view of their needs and capacities. Nevertheless, it is important to note that this model generally exists with a 'fall-back regulatory option', that is, in conjunction and in the shadow of the hierarchical state. Moreover, learning effects among the members of the private network constitute a supplementary steering mechanism.

Finally, the most fundamental departure from the hierarchy model is the OMC. Here, hierarchy does not even feature as a fall-back option. Regulatory responsibility is entirely located at the national level (where the hierarchical model may still apply, however), hence the notion of radical subsidiarity (cf. Hodson and Maher, 2001). The EU assumes a completely new governance function in facilitating coordination and mutual learning among national policy elites. There is no formal attempt to control outcomes, although the method is dependent on the prior agreement on general principles and goals in the policy area in question (de la Porte and Pochet, 2002; Scott and Trubek, 2002). Moreover, hierarchical elements in terms of reporting requirements and the reliance on incentive structures (peer pressure) are complementary steering mechanisms that stimulate learning and diffusion processes.

3.   'GOOD GOVERNANCE'? EVALUATING THE DIFFERENT MODES OF REGULATION

To decide whether a certain mode of regulation reflects 'good governance' or not, we need to be clear about the benchmarks of such an evaluation (cf. Baldwin, 1995; Baldwin and Cave, 1999, 76). When considering the current political and scientific discussion on 'good governance' in the EU, it becomes obvious that these criteria are debatable. The main conflict deals with the question whether either input or output legitimacy of European regulation should serve as primary evaluation criteria (Scharpf, 1999).

Traditionally, output factors constitute the major focus of legitimizing EU regulatory policy. Particular attention is paid to three factors: (1) the extent to which the EU has the capacity of taking political decisions in a certain area; (2) the extent to which these decisions are actually implemented and complied with at the national level; and (3) the degree to which the policies in question achieve their intended objectives (problem-solving capacity). The concern with these factors can be traced to the nature of the EU political system, where high consensus requirements in the decision-making process and lacking powers of hierarchical intervention during the implementation stage constitute far-reaching problems for efficient and effective governance.

The intensive concern with decision-making and implementation diverted attention from questions of input legitimacy. While this narrow evaluative base did fit the technocratic image of the EU as an institution established to deal with problem-solving deficiencies of the nation-state, it is inadequate once we consider the EU as a new policy and fairly 'grown-up' system of governance. With the waning acceptance of EU policy-making among the European citizens in recent years, the democratic quality of the EU has finally been taken up in the academic debate on EU governance (cf. Abromeit, 1998; Zürn, 1996).

The recognition of this multiple legitimization challenge among EU policy-makers is visible not only in the publication of the White Paper on Governance, but also in the general regulatory practice as described above. But general analysis of the merits of different regulatory modes with respect to the various normative criteria has not been performed so far. In the following, we will therefore attempt such an evaluation.[6] Of course, we acknowledge that the actual politics of regulatory choice is only partially normatively driven and rather the result of multiple interests interacting in a complex institutional setting. Nevertheless, the present existential debates within the EU open windows of opportunity for normative evaluation to influence future policy-making.

There are certain limits to such evaluations: We will not weigh the relative significance of the individual performance indicators because in our view such weighing depends on the particular policy context as well as individual (or cultural) preferences. Hence we do not claim to develop a final rank order of regulatory approaches in this chapter; rather, we try to develop a general template for assessing the potential of EU policy in light of particular circumstances. Only knowledge of the circumstances will enable the regulator to make choices with respect to potential tradeoffs between two performance criteria. Notwithstanding these problems of evaluation, we think that much can be said for trying to assess regulatory performance. We will get an idea to what extent (and at what costs) the shift from the hierarchical mode of regulation towards alternative forms of EU intervention may actually result in an overall improvement of regulatory performance. Furthermore, we will gain some insights into the question to what extent a certain regulatory approach can be significantly improved on one of the four criteria without substantive loss on another. In other words, we are able to compare the relative strengths and weaknesses of different regulatory approaches with respect to their input and output legitimacy.

3.1 Decision-making Capacity

A necessary, albeit not sufficient, condition for effective regulation is the capability of governments to take a regulatory decision (or to enact a legislative mandate). This capacity can hardly be taken for granted, but varies across different political systems, depending on the specific institutional rules characterizing the decision-making process. With respect to the EU, Scharpf (1999) in particular emphasized far-reaching structural deficits in this regard, given the high consensus requirements in the Council. Although this view is not uncontested in the literature (cf. Benz, 1998; Héritier et al., 1996), there seems to be a general agreement that decision-making at the European level is a demanding process that, in many instances, requires the use of 'subterfuges' (Héritier, 1999) in order to escape from deadlock.

This general statement needs to be differentiated, however. Scharpf (1997) developed an important distinction between product and process standards (see also Holzinger, 2001). Moreover, as will be argued in the following, the decision-making capacity of the EU multi-level system also varies with the underlying mode of regulation.

More precisely, there exists a close linkage between this capacity and respective levels of discretion and obligation implied by different modes of regulation. Quite obviously decision-making capacity decreases if the level of regulatory discretion goes down. The challenges to reach a consensus in the Council rise the more EU policies are based on very detailed regulatory arrangements, significantly constraining the options of national governments and authorities or private actors for adjusting to EU requirements. At the same time, the task to achieve an agreement between heterogeneous national interests increases with the extent to which regulatory requirements impose legally binding obligations on the decision-makers.

Consequently, the ability to reach decisions can be expected to be lowest if the EU adopts the model of hierarchical intervention by regulatory standards. As outlined above, this approach typically implies the prescription of rather detailed and legally binding requirements which have to be implemented and enforced by the member states. At first glance, this finding is in sharp contrast with the very high number of regulatory standards which still constitute the dominant form of European regulation. This feature of the EU regulatory regime, however, is basically the result of the member states' general consensus towards the establishment of a common market which is based on harmonized national rules and standards. But this 'permissive consensus' in favour of harmonization varies across policy areas and problem types. With respect to market-making regulations and product standards the adoption of regulatory standards is more likely than in fields of market-shaping regulations defining requirements for national production and process standards (Scharpf, 1997). Against this backdrop, it is hardly surprising that the Commission has increasingly experimented with other modes of regulation in order to overcome potential deadlocks in decision-making (Knill and Héritier, 1996).

In sharp contrast with the regulatory standards approach, decision-making is relatively unproblematic in the OMC case. Agreement on benchmarks and guidelines between the member states is facilitated by the fact that they enjoy broad leeway in achieving these rather general and non-obligatory objectives. The relatively frictionless decision-making might explain why this mode of regulation is of particular importance in areas where the hierarchical approach of regulatory standards turned out to be highly ineffective such as social or home affairs policy (Working Group, 2001). The extent to which such discretionary format is suitable for decision-making 'beyond the *status quo*' still remains to be seen, however.[7]

The performance of the remaining modes of regulation (new instruments and private self-regulation) can be located in between the extreme poles defined by regulatory standards and OMC. In the case of new instruments, a mixed account emerges from the fact that they generally define broad, but nevertheless legally binding, requirements. While considerable discretion for domestic compliance places them close to the OMC, their obligatory nature underlines their proximity to regulatory intervention. In the end, the decision-making dynamics depend on the specific mixture of hierarchical and non-hierarchical elements in the Commission proposal, which might vary from case to case. Thus, in the case of economic and communicative instruments it can often be observed that substantive discretion (in terms of goal attainment) coincides with highly detailed procedural rules, limiting the member states' actual implementation choices. Such rules apply typically to consultation requirements, reporting obligations and transparency concerns (Knill and Lenschow, 2000; Scott and Trubek, 2002). In the case of framework regulation, by contrast, non-hierarchical elements seem to play a more important role. Although framework directives may be combined with more detailed daughter directives, which tend to resemble the classical approach of hierarchical intervention, they exemplify flexible and differentiated forms of regulation in so far as they do not assume uniform national responses (Baldwin and Cave, 1999, 161).

Evaluating decision-making of private self-regulation, we arrive at a similarly ambiguous judgement, albeit for different reasons. On the one hand, self-regulatory arrangements are based on voluntary agreements in the private sector which should generally facilitate the establishment of such regimes. On the other hand, the low level of discretion characterizing this approach might reduce industry's preparedness to engage in self-regulation because the detailed prescriptions may impact unevenly on the relative competitiveness of industrial actors. It has been argued that these problems of decision-making disappear as soon as self-regulatory regimes are placed in 'the shadow of hierarchy' (that is, the threat of hierarchical intervention in case of non-agreement), because industry generally prefers self-regulation over top-down regulatory standards. For reasons outlined above, the EU's decision-making capacity in the case of regulatory standards is itself rather low; hence the effect of the legislative threat can hardly be taken for granted when it comes to the establishment of self-regulatory arrangements.

In sum, the analysis indicates that the capacity to decide regulatory norms in the EU multi-level system varies considerably across different modes of regulation. More specifically, decision-making capacity linked to the OMC clearly exceeds that of regulatory standards, while the performance of new instruments and private self-regulation lies somewhere in between these poles.

3.2 Implementation Effectiveness

Effective regulation not only depends on legislative decisions, but also on the extent to which these decisions are actually implemented and complied with. Generally, member states or private actors have to take the necessary steps in order to fulfil the objectives spelled out in European legislation or industrial agreements in both formal and practical terms (cf. Knill and Lenschow, 2000). To what extent do the four regulatory modes under investigation differ with respect to these aspects? At first glance, it seems to be rather difficult to identify significant differences. This can be traced to two factors.[8]

First, there are problems of equal relevance for all four approaches (cf.

Baldwin and Cave, 1999, 56). For instance, the practice of 'creative compliance', that is, the practice of avoiding the intention of a law without breaking the terms of the law, constitutes a common problem for all modes of regulation (cf. Cohn, 2002; McBarnet and Whelan, 1991). Second, effective implementation is likely to correlate with the 'goodness of fit' with national practices and the constellation of interests. Although there may be some policies which are more likely to find broad support for European regulation than others (cf. product regulation) and might be associated with higher compliance rates, generalization is less applicable to different regulatory instruments taken in isolation (Knill and Lenschow, 2000).[9] Third, not all regulatory characteristics in our classification have clear implications for implementation performance. This holds true in particular for regulatory discretion. On the one hand, there are numerous studies emphasizing the advantages of high discretion in terms of effective implementation, as it offers more leeway to adjust regulatory requirements to the social and political conditions at the national or subnational level (Lipsky, 1980; Berman, 1980). Other studies, by contrast, emphasize that highly specified rules provide a more promising basis for effective enforcement, since they define clear objectives and requirements for both implementers and addressees (Krämer, 1992; Lübbe-Wolff, 1996). Considering this tradeoff between broad and detailed legal requirements, the level of discretion constitutes no useful indicator for explaining variances in the implementation performance of the different regulatory approaches.

We focus therefore on those dimensions where the impact on implementation is less ambiguous, namely the level of obligation and the underlying steering mechanisms. Concerning the first, it is generally argued that highly obligatory rules have a higher potential for effective implementation, as the force of law can be used to impose the fixed standards or objectives (Baldwin and Cave, 1999, 35). In the absence of legally binding requirements, by contrast, this 'push-factor' is lacking and compliance rests solely on the 'goodwill' of the implementers. Hence, from this perspective the obligatory approaches (regulatory standards and new instruments) achieve a higher ranking than non-obligatory approaches (private self-regulation and OMC).

However, the level of obligation is not the only factor affecting the implementation of regulatory approaches. Of similar importance are 'pull factors', that are aspects which influence the willingness of implementing bodies and policy addressees to comply with European requirements. In this context, the underlying steering mechanisms by which regulatory objectives shall be achieved are of crucial importance. Thus we follow the argument that steering mechanisms that are responsive to the motivations and interests of implementers and the regulated actors contribute to effective implementation of the regulation in question effectively. Analysing the different modes of regulation from this perspective, we find that such responsive mechanisms are particularly relevant with respect to OMC and, although a little less, to new instruments. In the latter case, responsiveness emerges from the fact that new instruments explicitly seek to change incentive structures of the involved actors in order to stimulate and modify the domestic policy context in favour of effective compliance. Typical examples are economic incentives or participation and information rights. Incentives are also the steering logic behind the peer review of national policy developments in the context of the OMC. Moreover, the OMC promotes processes of coordination and mutual learning across national policy-makers.

Regulatory standards do not explicitly attempt to alter strategic opportunities or stimulate mutual learning processes among implementers and the addressees of regulation. Their primary steering mechanism is coercion; behavioural adjustment is to be achieved by hierarchical means of command and control.

At first sight, private self-regulation seems to rely positively on pull factors as the incentive to escape top-down regulations induces private regulators to formulate and comply with own rules. This incentive depends on the presence of a coercive threat, however. If the shadow of the hierarchy is perceived as weak, industry may respond to the opposite incentive to cheat. Private actors might implement regulatory rules in a rather light-handed way as the threat of enforcement or later top-down intervention in case of self-regulatory failure is low (Baldwin and Cave, 1999, 58).

Summing up this discussion on implementation performance, new instruments emerge as the most promising approach. They combine a high degree of obligation with an explicit orientation to alter domestic incentive structures in favour of effective compliance; they rely on both sticks and carrots. In the case of private self-regulation, by contrast, the effectiveness of the carrot depends on the stick component, which in the EU is not well developed, suggesting a high likelihood of implementation deficits. Regulatory standards and the OMC reveal mixed patterns, indicating a medium ranking. While the obligatory nature might positively affect the implementation of regulatory standards, their non-responsiveness towards the domestic context constitutes a major source of implementation failures. Exactly the opposite constellation can be found with respect to the OMC. Here, the emphasis on mutual learning and coordination might have very positive effects, while the voluntariness implies that there is little external push driving and guiding domestic activities.

3.3 Problem-solving Capacity

Even if we assume that regulatory policy is implemented effectively, this does not guarantee that it actually achieves its objectives; effective decision-making and implementation are not sufficient to ensure effective problem-solving. For one, it is a common phenomenon that – due to high scientific uncertainty and complexity – regulators have no full understanding of the causal mechanisms behind a given problem. Furthermore, regulators might well know how an effective regulatory approach should be designed, but lack the power and resources to carry their views through the decision-making process. In both scenarios, the regulatory design may be inappropriate for coping with the problems at hand. In view of this constellation, two questions are addressed in this section. First, we ask which factors might influence the quality of regulatory design. Second, we analyse the extent to which these factors are present or absent in the different modes of European regulation.

With regard to the general aspects which affect the quality of regulatory design, four factors are of particular importance. First, high adjustment flexibility allows for swift redesign of regulations in the light of technological innovations, new scientific evidence or experience with former approaches. Second, it makes a crucial difference for effective goal attainment whether regulators design their rules in view of the interests of the public at large or in the interests of the regulated group/industry (problem of capture) (Mitnick, 1980). Third, the problem-solving capacity can be expected to increase with the extent to which the regulatory design is responsive to different national and subnational problem constellations. Fourth, it is an essential requirement for effective regulation that regulators have clear indicators in order to develop sound predictions on potential regulatory outcomes (Baldwin and Cave, 1999, 43).

Table 10.3 shows that the different regulatory approaches under investigation reveal considerable differences with respect to these factors. They can be traced mainly to their distinctive characteristics in terms of obligation, discretion and dominant steering mechanisms.

Opportunities for flexible adjustment are closely linked to the level of obligation. Adjustment is particularly difficult when regulation is based on legally binding directives (regulatory standards and new instruments). The complex procedures characterizing EU policy-making and the need to accommodate a high diversity of interests turn the development of European legislation generally into a lengthy and cumbersome process. Since most changes of existing legislation require a new legislative decision, flexible responses in light of new regulatory, scientific or technological developments are difficult.[10] Flexible adjustment is much easier in cases where EU regulation is based on less demanding procedures. This applies in particular to the voluntary approaches of private self-regulation and the OMC (cf. Abbott and Snidal, 2000).

The extent to which regulatory decisions suffer from capture problems is

Table 10.3   Regulatory modes and problem-solving capacity

	Regulatory standards	New instruments	Self-regulation	OMC
Adjustment flexibility	Low	Low	High	High
Danger of capture	High	Low, but depending on national transposition	High	Low, but depending on national transposition
Context-responsiveness	Low	High	Low	High
Predictability of outcomes	High	Low	High	Low

affected by the level of discretion inherent in the different approaches. Generally, capture is more likely in cases of highly detailed regulation. In such constellations, regulators require a large amount of information in order to carry out their task. As the regulated industry itself is the best source of such information, this gives industry a degree of leverage over regulatory arrangements which, in the extreme case, might lead to capture. From this it follows that capture problems might be of particular relevance for the regulatory standards approach. The risk that regulatory rules primarily serve the interests of the industry also applies to private self-regulation where similar information asymmetries between the self-regulatory bodies and public enforcers exist.[11] The potential for capture at the European level is lower if regulation is based on the definition of broad objectives and hence requires no detailed technical information on the side of the EU regulator. This constellation characterizes new instruments and the OMC. However, a low potential for capture at the European level does not exclude selective access of certain private interests during the implementation stage. Thus the danger of capture is crucially dependent on domestic arrangements, which vary from country to country.

The level of discretion is also of relevance when accounting for the context-responsiveness of different regulatory approaches. Leeway for implementers in adjusting to regulatory requirements in the light of distinctive problem constellations at the national, regional or local levels enhances the chances for effective problem-solving. The realization of this potential, however, requires steering mechanisms which ensure that discretion is used in line with the overall objectives of the regulation, and hence rely on the modification and stimulation of the policy context in favour of effective compliance. Meeting both requirements (high discretion, responsive steering mechanisms) is the aim of new instruments and the OMC. In practice, however, there seems to be room for further improving the soft sanctioning implied in peer review as well as the effectiveness of other learning tools (cf. Hodson and Maher, 2003; Chalmers and Lodge, 2003).

At the same time, these features of new instruments and the OMC imply certain disadvantages with respect to the predictability of regulatory outcomes. Thus it is rather difficult to estimate if and to what extent changes in domestic incentive structures might actually result in desired behavioural changes and political results (cf. Knill and Lenschow, 2000). The same problem applies to the stimulation of mutual learning and coordination across national policy-makers. Considering these uncertainties and the broad leeway in terms of substantive objectives, both highly discretionary regulatory approaches achieve a poor ranking on predictability. The opposite holds for regulatory standards and private self-regulation, where clear substantive objectives provide a sounder basis for predicting results.[12]

3.4   Democratic Legitimacy

Ever since the rather unexpected opposition to the Maastricht Treaty, frequent reference has been made to a democratic deficit built into the EU polity. The transformation of the regulatory modes we are analysing in this chapter partly reflects a response to this perceived lack in 'input legitimacy'. Non-traditional regulatory instruments aim at gaining public acceptance through better communication with the addressees, higher responsiveness to national or regional problems and the invitation of public control. We see a trend toward decentralizing regulatory responsibilities to national and regional authorities and therefore a certain re-empowerment of national legislatures. Before turning to the democratic performance of the different regulatory modes in more detail, however, we need to shed some light on the interplay of democratic norms and structures in the EU. Generally, we can distinguish between three democratic models aiming to aggregate the public will in accordance with full and equal representation of the people. Depending on the existence of deep cleavages in society (tending to a polarization of opinions in the public) and the presence and depth of general solidarity in the political entity (affecting the willingness to accept a potential minority status), we have seen the evolution of two types of representative democracies – majoritarian and consensual – which are distinct in their relative protection of functional and territorial minorities (cf. Lijphart, 1984). Furthermore, territorial scope and functional differentiation of the modern state and the rising demands on elected officials have contributed to the emergence of the associational format (cf. Cohen and Rogers, 1995) where interest associations assume political functions and, due to their proximity to the public ear, contribute to enhance the sovereignty of the people.[13]

In the EU, we see a combination of all three models: policy-making based on the majoritarian model is dominant in the European Parliament (EP) representing the European public at large. It is directly elected by all citizens of the member states and operates on the basis of majority voting. However, the standard of equal representation has been altered in favour of minority protection by giving the electorate from small member states additional weight. The Council of Ministers derives its democratic legitimacy indirectly from national elections and is dominated by consensual norms. Traditionally, these have been rooted in the requirement of unanimity voting in politically salient questions and the need for rather strong majorities otherwise; in addition, small states are protected by the present arrangement of weighted votes. Increasingly, however, we see Council negotiations also influenced by majoritarian patterns that have been strengthened in all Treaty amendments since the mid-1980s. Finally, associational arrangements have entered into EU policy-making practices (Eising, 2001; Schmalz-Bruns, 1997).[14] At the stage of policy formulation in particular the Commission relies heavily on the input of various interest groups (Eising and Kohler-Koch, 1994, Greenwood and Aspinwall, 1998). More crucially, certain decision-making responsibilities have been conferred on interest associations. For instance, private organizations lead some processes of technical harmonization and norm-setting in the fields of social and environmental policy (Eichener and Voelzkow, 1994), corporatist structures have been introduced in the regulation of industrial relations (Falkner, 2000) and we see experiments with industrial self-regulation.

This mix of procedures and the interplay between the two representative institutions (Council, EP) and interest associations fails to fully match any conventional democratic quality standard. From the perspective of the majoritarian model, the criterion of equality is violated and the EP does not carry enough weight in decision-making; advocates of the consensus model will emphasize the non-existence of a European public glued together by a shared identity and trans-national solidarity and hence consider any majoritarian processes premature. Both schools are likely to be critical with respect to patterns of democratic control in the EU, pointing to limitations in parliamentary oversight, judicial review and direct scrutiny (cf. Baldwin and Cave, 1999, 152–3). Associational democracy is usually perceived as a complementary model to the conventional structures of democratic representation, shifting some responsibility from the state to the people while maintaining a framework for equal representation and control. Considering the potential distance of EU institutions from the people, associational structures have been perceived as a chance to involve the public more directly in policy-making, to close conflictual gaps in society and create a European public sphere; the ability to ensure equality and democratic control at the same time is viewed more critically.

On the basis of this brief discussion we can formulate three assumptions that will guide the following more detailed review of the democratic quality of the different regulatory modes in EU policy-making:

A1.   Due to the deep national cleavages characterizing the EU polity, the absence of a self-perceived 'European demos' and in the light of future enlargements, we consider the consensus model of democracy more adequate than the majoritarian model (cf. Kielmansegg, 1996).

A2.   The democratic legitimacy of associational decision-making processes depends on representative structures and practices internally and its embeddedness in conventional structures of representative democracy (cf. Cohen and Rogers, 1995, 69–71).

A3.   We assume the democratic legitimacy of national structures to be generally superior to that of the EU multi-level governance system.

Turning now to the evaluation of the four regulatory modes, we consider three sub-criteria: public mandate, due process and accountability. They capture the nature of the demos' input across all phases of policy-making – from policy formulation to implementation and evaluation – and hence, offer a full view of the democratic process.

Public mandate
The four modes of regulatory policy claim legitimacy on the basis of different procedures to establish the public mandate: notwithstanding the associative input indicated above, regulatory standards and new instruments are primarily based on a mix of majoritarian and consensual forms of representative authorisation. OMC relies at the decision-making stage merely on the consensus model, with some input from stakeholder representatives. Self-regulation, in turn, is based on the associational model.

Considering the societal structure of the EU, we consider the unanimous democratic mandate for OMC guidelines and benchmarks least problematic (cf. A1), although we need to acknowledge that the national representatives in the Council act at considerable distance from public discourses and, despite consultation arrangements with the EP and 'stakeholders', are vulnerable to developing an executive bias. The mandate for regulatory standards and new instruments is based on mixed patterns. The required majority in the Council under the qualified majority rule is high and Council decision-making remains influenced by consensual and reciprocity norms. Nevertheless, we witness a gradual shift towards majoritarian decision-making procedures which may be premature from a democratic angle. The critical issue in the case of self-regulation consists in the decision to delegate regulatory power to private actors. A democratic mandate for such a decision needs to be derived from conventional practices of representative democracy (A2). In this respect the self-regulatory practices in the EU tend to be only indirectly legitimized as most of them are initiated by the European Commission and, hence, the result of an administrative decision.[15] An exception is the Social Dialogue, which is based on a Treaty provision and framed by representative regulatory policy-making at the EU level in the sense that the proposal of the social partners needs to be agreed by Council and Parliament before being adopted as an EU directive. Here associative practices complement and potentially strengthen EU decision-making procedures by bridging distant EU institutions and society (cf. Falkner et al., 2002).

Considering the multi-level structure of EU regulatory policy-making, those forms of regulatory interventions that build on the democratic structures in the member states possess a clear(er) public mandate. Hence, the two subsidiarity models have a structural advantage *vis-à-vis* regulatory standards and self-regulation (cf. A3). OMC relies on national governments or legislatures to formulate and decide all concrete policy measures aiming to achieve the benchmarks set at the EU level. New instruments seek national democratic mandates merely for the specification and sometimes elaboration of EU law. Nevertheless, framework legislation in particular leaves real scope for national decision-making and exploits the democratic potential of subsidiarity.[16]

To sum up, the consensual style of decision-making at the EU level combined with the most discretionary practice places OMC at 'first place', followed by discretionary new instruments. Notably, OMC acknowledges the absence of a European demos while at the same time aims to build a European public sphere, though notably at the expense of European parliamentary input. Self-regulatory practices, bypassing any representative organ at the EU level, rank below even the regulatory standards relying on these organs. However, there may be variants that are backed legally and embedded in EU law. These pass as a legitimated form of associative democracy while at the same time closing the gap between the EU and society.

Due process

Due process relates to the decision-making and the implementation phase and claims public support on the basis of equal and wide participatory rights granted to and substantive equality provided for those affected by regulatory decisions. Both dimensions are especially challenging in the transnational and multi-level EU system.

The issue of participatory rights refers to the scope of participation in the formulation of regulatory policy by those affected or involved in the implementation. Here, we are confronted with two opposing images of regulatory policy-making in the EU: while some emphasize the extraordinary openness of the Commission, inviting input from all parts of society, others perceive the Commission as a gatekeeper and deplore the level of executive and bureaucratic discretion leading to potential biases in the public input and even to forms of clientelism. Lack of transparency is a main criticism put forward against the rise of committee-driven policy-making. While equal access of all interests remains an empirical question, lack of transparency generally hinders effective insurance of due process inside comitology.[17]

The delegation of regulatory responsibilities to private actors or to the member state level adds new dimensions to due process. Again, we will assume that all democratic standards are met at the national level. Furthermore, we even observe that the EU puts a lot of effort into designing and prescribing due process procedures for implementation and subsequent regulation in the member states. New instruments such as procedural rights to information or public hearings aim to enhance public involvement on the ground. OMC resembles new instruments in encouraging 'enlightened' policy-making at the EU and national level through new participatory structures.

In contrast to all forms of public regulation, it is the very point of self-regulation to closely involve those affected by the regulation; but in practice this has come at the risk of turning 'due process' on its head. The proverbial characteristic of self-regulation is its industrial bias constraining the input of the general public, the consumers, the residents and so on. This bias is related to the desire to form a coherent group, sharing similar problems and pressures, in order to arrive at a solution before the dog – in the form of the EU regulator – bites. Of course, the European Court of Justice (ECJ) operates as a watchdog and self-regulatory systems can be structured inclusively from the start (recall A3).

With respect to the second dimension of due process, substantive equality, the much-praised regulatory discretion may turn out to be a problem. Discretion makes room for unequal treatment of the regulated, inconsistencies within or between policies and distortions of the market due to different local regulatory patterns. From this perspective, EU public or private standard-setting is superior to the two subsidiarity models, although the capacity of the EU regulators to ensure that self-regulatory networks guarantee the application of the private norms is limited. The insistence on substantive equality is not uncontroversial, however, as it may go hand in hand with a great insensitivity to the circumstances experienced by those affected by regulatory decisions. Uniform regulation does not take account of different administrative structures, established technologies or problem saliencies. Hence we need to distinguish between regulatory content that requires uniform application in the EU due to the presence of trans-boundary effects or market distortions and regulatory content that can be achieved flexibly. The combination of regulatory uniformity and discretion is the main philosophy of new instruments. The recognition of national diversity also explains the high discretionary practice of OMC. However, while OMC aims to facilitate learning and public involvement, hoping for national improvements and – in the longer run – more consistent regulatory structures in the EU in areas where EU regulation is absent, it does not establish any firm regulatory framework guaranteeing activity at the national or regional level.

To sum up the discussion on due process, on two dimensions we saw ambiguous effects. While regulatory discretion is likely to impact positively on the level of access and participation, discretion does not contribute to substantive equality. The relative importance of this latter criterion varies with the regulatory intent, however. Second, the choice of steering mechanisms also affects due process. The coercive model contributes to substantive equality, while treating the openness of procedures and involvement of stakeholders as secondary; the learning model emphasizes openness of the process more than equal outcomes. In this ambiguous picture new instruments stand out as performing quite well on all counts.

Accountability

Regulators may claim democratic legitimacy even in cases where the public has not been involved in the rule-making process if the people have the possibility to exercise public control over the regulatory authority. Once again, we need to take into consideration the multi-level structure of the European Union. Focusing on Brussels, Baldwin and Cave (1999, 152–3) arrive at generally sceptical conclusions, pointing to the constrained controlling powers of the EP and the weak control most national parliaments have over their governments acting in the European arena. Also, they observe that the ECJ's resources are limited; review tends to be sporadic and dependent on the existence of a party with the knowledge and financing to bring about action. Furthermore, the ECJ looks to the legality, not merits or substance, of regulatory rules or actions. This perspective applies to the classical form of regulatory intervention, namely EU regulatory standards.

Both parliamentary and direct public control are enhanced by decentralizing regulatory tasks to regional or national public authorities (cf. A3) through the use of discretionary new instruments. The fact that in practice this may come at the expense of some confusion over the relevant locus of responsibility does not negate their potential to facilitate a higher level of control in a multi-level system. In the case of OMC this benefit of subsidiarity is taken even further as national parliamentary and electoral control mechanisms apply to the bulk of actual regulatory activity. Furthermore, OMC attempts to compensate for intransparent structures at the EU level with soft methods of accountability like peer review and reporting requirements, combined with a high level of publicity, aiming to ensure that member state governments meet the agreed benchmarks. The process of benchmarking at the EU level, establishing the framework for national policy-making, requires closer analysis, however. On the one hand, this process seems to escape the – even though deficient – traditional forms of control in Brussels, making bad things worse. The EP is largely excluded from the process and judicial review is secondary due to the weak legal context.[18] On the other hand, the consensual structure (cf. A1) and participation of stakeholders links the benchmarking process to national parliaments and associative representatives of the general public, creating alternative ways towards public control.

Self-regulation is clearly most problematic in terms of public control. Besides the remote sanctioning powers of public authorities, self-regulatory systems risk being captured by groups that are not representative of the general public – or even those affected by the regulation – and isolated from public oversight. In principle self-regulatory systems could be accountable, however; statutory prescriptions, ministerial or parliamentary guidelines, reporting and publication requirements, and so on, would subject self-regulators to public control and scrutiny (cf. A2). The implicit threat of legislative intervention in case of self-regulatory failure may have a similar effect.

Table 10.4 summarizes the preceding discussion. While a summarizing score is impossible given the complexity of the issue, we observe generally good performance in the two subsidiarity models, due to their reliance on national democratic structures and a partial opening of decision-making procedures to the wider public, paving the ground for an emerging European public sphere.

4. CONCLUSION

Although methodological problems make it impossible to establish an overall performance ranking of the different modes of European regulation, the comparatively favourable evaluation of new instruments and OMC is somewhat surprising. The question that immediately emerges is 'Why are regulatory standards still the dominating mode of intervention in EU policy-making?' Several factors should be emphasized.

First, regulatory standards represent the traditional mode of EU policy-

Table 10.4   Democratic legitimacy of four regulatory modes

	Regulatory standards	New instruments	Self-regulation	OMC
Democratic mandate	*EU level:* deficient	*EU level:* deficient *National level:* good	*EU level:* mostly poor *SR-level:* typically biased	*EU level:* acceptable *National level:* good
Due process	*Participation:* at the discretion of the EU executive	*Participation:* at EU level as RS; emphasized at national level	*Participation:* great reliance on 'those affected', but danger of bias	*Participation:* stakeholder participation at both levels of governance
	Substantive equality: yes – disregarding local circumstances	*Substantive equality:* partial– combined with responsiveness to local conditions	*Substantive equality:* yes – assuming authority of self-regulatory network *vis-à-vis* its members	*Substantive equality:* weak – indirect encouragement of local adjustments
Accountability	*Control:* deficient at EU level	*Control:* deficiency at EU level is partly corrected at national level	*Control:* weak in practice, but possible in theory	*Control:* ambiguous at EU level; traditional + soft mechanisms applied to national activity

making and institutional inertia prevents most organizations from engaging in quick and radical reforms. Second, our choice of evaluation criteria has been selective. Although we have focused on the most common factors, we can hardly claim that our selection is encompassing. This is crucial, in particular, in the case of OMC, which has a number of limitations potentially reducing its regulatory utility: (a) both its regulatory claim (to merely establish guidelines and benchmarks) and the consensual decision-making process may result in an undemanding framework for national policy-making. It is no surprise that OMC is applied primarily in policy areas where national governments hesitate to give up competence. Hence there may be a tradeoff between democratic decision-making and reliable steering capacity; (b) effective implementation is made dependent on internal learning processes and therefore cannot be expected immediately; (c) OMC relies on an experimental process of problem-solving, hence is not designed to ensure precisely defined results; (d) OMC accepts the unequal treatment of regulatory addressees in the member states, it is not suitable for creating a level playing-field.

Third, the choice of regulatory approaches is rarely the result of a careful normative evaluation on the part of the policy-makers, but it reflects underlying interest constellations and strategic interactions shaping the decision-making processes at the European and national level. From this perspective, and as indicated, both new instruments and OMC constitute rather unsuitable approaches if harmonization is the main interest of the regulators. Such an aim is best served through hierarchical regulatory standards. The same holds true if the decision-makers share a preference for predictable and reliable regulatory arrangements. The regulatory framework of OMC and new instruments is likely to be too flexible, whereas hierarchical norms give clearly defined directions. As the dominance of classical approaches suggests, these considerations have obviously been of crucial importance in EU governance and its emphasis on market creation.

However, this does not imply an inevitable dominance of the regulatory standards approach. Both new instruments and OMC could be preferable options if the maintenance of national diversity is desirable or unchangeable. This is equally the case in constellations where risk and insecurity characterize the regulatory context, with the effect that no clear and generally applicable regulatory solution is in supply.

In sum, any final evaluation of a regulatory format depends on the weighing of the individual criteria, which in turn needs to be based on the character of the policy problem to be solved. While regional diversity, and hence a discretionary policy design, may be perfectly acceptable in some areas, the economic context (competition, mobility and so on), the presence of external and in particular transnational effects, the expressed pursuit of shared values or the commonly perceived problem salience may call for uniform standards or procedures in all member states. It was the intent of this chapter to develop a template that would facilitate any such contextualized evaluation. We have provided criteria and an overview of structural advantages and disadvantages; the weighing of the criteria needs to be done on a case-by-case basis. In addition, further analysis needs to be done with respect to the combination of regulatory modes. For instance, is there a certain mix of steering mechanisms that is most capable in problem solving? This chapter has provided the necessary elements for such future investigations.

NOTES

1. For constructive comments on earlier versions of this chapter we are particularly grateful to the editors of this volume, Helge Joergens, Rainer Eising as well as the participants of the regulation and governance workshops in Oxford, Barcelona and Jena.
2. Compare Moran (2002) for an excellent review as well as Scott, Chapter 7 in this volume.
3. It is important to emphasize in this context that this typology, based on the two dimensions of regulatory discretion and obligation, does not deny that the approaches grouped together in one box reveal important differences with respect to other criteria, such as underlying steering mechanisms or policy addressees. Moreover, in referring to 'new instruments' we do not imply that this term only encompasses regulatory approaches that have been developed very recently. Rather we use the term to classify a distinctive form of regulation to be found at the European level.
4. The OMC is not exclusively a regulatory policy; it was first applied in the area of macro-economic steering in the EU (Hodson and Maher, 2003; Chalmers and Lodge, 2003). Since then most OMC experiments have been started in social policy, setting and coordinating distributive and regulatory benchmarks. Here, the OMC is part of a regulatory reform process creating a framework – at least in theory – for learning in a context-responsive and inclusive format. It shares features with Ayres and Braithwaite's (1992) 'responsive regulation' although the emphasis lies on allowing for flexibility in national and local adaptation and only secondarily on responsiveness to the interest of stakeholders.
5. Also self-regulation and OMC are new forms of governance but distinct from the so-called new instruments in their more radical departure from traditional law-based patterns of intervention.
6. To be sure, judging the extent to which a certain mode of regulation is legitimate in terms of input and output criteria is not to offer an assessment of the actual support that a regulator enjoys. It is rather an assessment of the legitimacy that a regulator *deserves*. What matters is the collective justificatory power of the arguments that can be made with respect to the four criteria in question (cf. Baldwin and Cave, 1999, 82).
7. For a sceptical assessment see Chalmers and Lodge (2003).
8. While implementation effectiveness might be affected by a broad range of factors, we restrict our analytical focus here to one aspect which is of crucial relevance for domestic compliance with EU policies, namely the adjustment of formal and informal institutions to the requirements spelled out in European legislation (cf. Knill and Lenschow, 2000).
9. It is true of course that not all modes of regulation discussed in this chapter are equally applied to all policy and issue areas. In this chapter we are not focusing on implementation performance that is related to the level of agreement with respect to the issue at hand although we realize that this might also impact on the average performance of certain instruments chosen to produce certain types of public goods.
10. In some contexts, the comitology procedure provides for an alternative to lengthy legislative negotiations and allows for faster adjustment to typically technological or scientific developments.
11. The problem of capture will generally be much more pronounced in cases where public interests (such as environmental or consumer organization) are excluded from the decision-making process.
12. Of course, even the predictability of outcomes of clear regulatory standards is limited in many problem areas that are characterized by high levels of scientific uncertainty and, hence, risk.
13. This, of course, depends on the internal organizational characteristics of interest associations as well as the degree to which associative constellations succeed in representing the plurality of public opinion.

14. Furthermore, the mode of *direct democracy* exists in the EU – however, only with regard to constitutional questions and not in the process of regulatory policy-making. Hence we can ignore this democratic form in our discussion.
15. The Commission receives its mandate from democratically legitimated institutions – Council and Parliament – which delegate certain tasks to it, and from the provisions of the EU Treaty.
16. In the regulatory practice of the EU, framework legislation tends to be coupled with the drafting of more detailed daughter directives, however, leaving the regulatory responsibility with policy-makers in Brussels.
17. It must be noted that committees do not exist outside legal oversight (cf. Comitology Decision 87/373/EEC) and therefore may also contribute to the rationalization of regulatory processes and the creation of mutually agreeable and cooperative solutions (cf. Joerges, 2002).
18. Some, but not all, forms of national policy coordination have been introduced directly to the Treaties, though in very generic terms. Besides, OMC benchmarks or guidelines are not legally binding (Working Group, 2001).

REFERENCES

Abbott, K.W. and D. Snidal (2000), 'Hard and Soft Law in International Governance', *International Organization*, **54** (3), 421–56.

Abromeit, H. (1998), 'Ein Vorschlag zur Demokratisierung des europäischen Entscheidungssystems', in B. Kohler-Koch (ed.), *Regieren in entgrenzten Räumen*, PVS Sonderheft 29, Opladen: Westdeutscher Verlag, pp. 80–90.

Ayres, I. and J. Braithwaite (1992), *Responsive Regulation. Transcending the Deregulatory Debate*, Oxford: Oxford University Press.

Baldwin, R. and M. Cave (1999), *Understanding Regulation: Theory, Strategy, and Practice*, Oxford: Oxford University Press.

Baldwin, R. (1995), *Rules and Government*, Oxford: Oxford University Press.

Benz, A. (1998), 'Politikverflechtung und Politikverflechtungsfalle. Koordination und Strukturdynamik im europäischen Mehrebenensystem', in B. Kohler-Koch (ed.), *Regieren in entgrenzten Räumen*, PVS Sonderheft 29, Opladen: Westdeutscher Verlag, pp. 558–89.

Berman, Paul (1980), 'Thinking About Programmed and Adaptive Implementation: Matching Strategies to Situations', in H. Ingram and D. Mann (eds), *Why Policies Succeed or Fail*, London: Sage, pp. 205–27.

Black, J.M. (1996), 'Constitutionalising Self-Regulation', *Modern Law Review*, **59**, 24–55.

Chalmers, D. and M. Lodge (2003), 'The Open Method of Co-ordination and the European Welfare State', paper prepared for the EUSA 8th Biennial Conference, Nashville, 27–29 March.

Cohen, J. and J. Rogers (1995), 'Secondary Associations and Democratic Governance', in J. Cohen and J. Rogers (eds), *Associations and Democracy*, London: Verso, pp. 236–67.

Cohn, M. (2002), 'Fuzzy Legality in Regulation: The Legislative Mandate Revisited', *Law and Policy*, **23**, 469–97.

De la Porte, C. and P. Pochet (eds) (2002), *Building Social Europe through the Open Method of Co-ordination*, Brussels: P.I.E.–Peter Lang.

Eichener, V. and H. Voelzkow (1994), *Europäische Integration und verbandliche Interessenvermittlung*, Marburg: Metropolis Verlag.

Eising, R. (2001), 'Assoziative Demokratie in der europäischen Union?', in A. Zimmer and B. Wessels (eds), *Verbände und Demokratie in Deutschland*, Opladen: Leske + Budrich, pp. 293–329.

Eising, R. and B. Kohler-Koch (1994), 'Inflation und Zerfaserung: Trends der Interessenvermittlung in der Europäischen Gemeinschaft', in W. Streeck (ed.), *Staat und Verbände*, PVS Sonderheft 25, Opladen: Westdeutscher Verlag, pp. 175–206.

Falkner, G. (2000), 'Problemlösungsfähigkeit im europäischen Mehrebenensystem: Die soziale Dimension', in E. Grande and M. Jachtenfuchs (eds), *Wie problemlösungsfähig ist die EU? Regieren im europäischen Mehrebenensystem*, Baden-Baden: Nomos, pp. 283–311.†

Falkner, G., M. Hartlapp, S. Leiber and O. Treib (2002), 'Democracy, Social Dialogue and Citizenship in the European Multi-level System,' paper presented at the 1st Pan-European Conference on European Union Politics, 'The Politics of European Integration: Academic Acquis and Future Challenges', Bordeaux, 26–28 September.

Gunningham, N. and J. Rees (1997), 'Industry Self-Regulation: An Institutionalist Perspective', *Law and Policy*, **19** (4), 363–414.

Greenwood, J. and M. Aspinwall (eds) (1998), *Collective Action in the European Union*, London: Routledge.

Héritier, A. (1999), *Policy-Making and Diversity in Europe: Escape from Deadlock*, Cambridge: Cambridge University Press.

Héritier, A. (2002), 'New Modes of Governance in Europe: Policy Making Without Legislating?', in A. Héritier (ed.), *The Provision of Common Goods: Governance across Multiple Arenas*, Boulder, CO: Rowman & Littlefield, pp. 185–206.

Héritier, A., C. Knill and S. Mingers (1996), *Ringing the Changes in Europe. Regulatory Competition and the Transformation of the State*, Berlin: de Gruyter.

Hodson, D. and I. Maher (2001), 'The Open Method as a New Mode of Governance', *Journal of Common Market Studies*, **39** (4), 719–46.

Hodson, D. and I. Maher (2003), 'Hard, Soft and Open Methods of Policy Coordination and the Reform of the Stability and Growth Pact', paper prepared for 'Building EU Economic Government: Revising the Rules?' organized by NYU in London and UACES, 25–26 April.

Holzinger, K. (2001), 'Aggregation Technology of Common Goods and its Strategic Consequences. Global Warming, Biodiversity and Siting Conflicts', *European Journal of Political Research*, **40**, 117–38.

Holzinger, K., C. Knill and A. Schäfer (2003), 'Steuerungswandel in der europäischen Umweltpolitik?', in K. Holzinger, C. Knill and D. Lehmkuhl (eds), *Politische Steuerung im Wandel: Der Einfluss von Ideen und Problemstrukturen*, Opladen: Leske + Budrich, pp. 103–32.

Joerges, C. (2002), 'Deliberative Supranationalism – Two Defences', *European Law Journal*, **8** (1), 133–51.

Kielmansegg, P. Graf (1996), 'Integration und Demokratie', in M. Jachtenfuchs and B. Kohler-Koch (eds), *Europäische Integration*, Opladen: Leske + Budrich, pp. 47–72.

Knill, C. and A. Héritier (1996), 'Neue Instrumente in der europäischen Umweltpolitik: Strategien für eine effektivere Implementation', in G. Lübbe-Wolff (ed.), *Der Vollzug des europäischen Umweltrechts*, Berlin: Erich Schmidt Verlag, pp. 209–34.

Knill, C. and A. Lenschow (eds) (2000), *Implementing EU Environmental Policy: New Directions and Old Problems*, Manchester: Manchester University Press.

Krämer, L. (1992), *Focus on European Environmental Law*, London: Sweet & Maxwell.

Lijphart, A. (1984), *Democracies. Patterns of Majoritarian and Consensus Government in Twenty-one Countries*, New Haven: Yale University Press.

Lipsky, M. (1980), *Street-Level Bureaucracy*, New York: Russell Sage.

Lübbe-Wolff, G. (1996), 'Stand und Instrumente der Implementation des Umweltrechts in Deutschland', in G. Lübbe-Wolff (ed.), *Der Vollzug des europäischen Umweltrechts*, Berlin: Erich Schmidt Verlag, pp. 77–106.

Majone, G. (1994), 'The Rise of the Regulatory State in Europe', *West European Politics*, **17** (3), 77–101.

McBarnet, D. and C. Whelan (1991), 'The Elusive Spirit of the Law: Formalism and the Struggle of Legal Control', *Modern Law Review*, **54**, 848–73.

Mitnick, B. (1980), *The Political Economy of Regulation*, New York: Columbia University Press.

Moran, M. (2002), 'Review Article: Understanding the Regulatory State', *British Journal of Political Science*, **32**, 391–413.

Ogus, A. (1995), 'Rethinking Self-Regulation', *Oxford Journal of Legal Studies*, **15** (97), 87–108.

Scharpf, F. (1997), *Games Real Actors Play: Actor-Centered Institutionalism in Policy Analysis*, Boulder: Westview Press.

Scharpf, F. (1999), *Governing in Europe: Effective and Democratic?*, Oxford: Oxford University Press.

Schmalz-Bruns, R. (1997), 'Bürgergesellschaftliche Politik – ein Modell der Demokratisierung der europäischen Union?', in K.-D. Wolf (ed.), *Projekt Europa im Übergang*, Baden-Baden: Nomos, pp. 63-90.

Scott, J. and D.M. Trubek (2002), 'Mind the Gap: Law and New Approaches to Governance in the European Union', *European Law Journal*, **8** (1), 1–18.

Working Group (2001), European Commission: *Involving Experts in the Process of National Policy Convergence*, report by Working Group 4a, June, http://europa.eu.int/com/governance/areas/group8/report_en.pdf.

Zürn, M. (1996), 'Über den Staat und die Demokratie im europäischen Mehrebenensystem', *Politische Vierteljahresschrift*, **37**, 27–55.

11. Divergent convergence: structures and functions of national regulatory authorities in the telecommunications sector

Marc Tenbücken and Volker Schneider[1]

1. INTRODUCTION

Starting with developments in the USA at the end of the 1970s, the wave of liberalization and privatization spread globally to the telecommunications sector of almost all nations one by one. The pressures evoked by the phenomenon of globalization forced different states to carry out extensive institutional reforms to position themselves favourably to face growing international competition (Berger and Dore, 1996; Hall, 1992; Strange, 1996). At the beginning of the twenty-first century formerly closed markets are now opened for private contractors, state monopolies have been dismantled, and public telecommunications companies have been partially or completely privatized.

However, parallel to liberalization and privatization developments, we detect a global trend towards 'reregulation' (Vogel, 1996).[2] In the course of the paradigmatic change from the positive to the regulative state, most countries have established national regulatory authorities (NRAs). These are equipped with their own regulatory responsibilities, resources and, in organizational terms, are detached from ministries and thus not subject to the direct influence of politicians or government officials (Doern and Wilks, 1996; Gilardi, 2002; Levy and Spiller, 1996; Majone, 1997; Thatcher, 2002a, 2002b, among others). The main task of the NRAs is to control the market power of the former state monopolists and provide for fair competition in the liberalized infrastructural sectors. Thus far, in over 100 countries NRAs have taken responsibility for the regulation of the telecommunications sector (cf. Levi-Faur, 2003, 23). This entails, for example, various tasks concerning interconnection disputes, unbundling of the local loop or licence allocation and control in mobile- and fixed-voice telephony.

The central question in this chapter is whether the regulatory reform process led to the adoption of a relatively unitary NRA model, for example the British blueprint Oftel (Office of Telecommunications) as the first NRA to be established in the course of liberalization, or whether the countries reacted differently to this paradigm change in institutional terms. Did the diffusion of telecommunications reform make countries adopt similar organizational structures and delegate equivalent regulatory competencies[3] to their NRAs? Some organizational as well as functional configurations give greater political independence to the NRA than others. Thus the decision to reform the provision of telecommunications services, which was a relatively common reaction by all OECD countries to the demands of globalization, does not allow causal inferences on the material independence of the authority. According to Grande and Risse (2000, 244), in most cases 'there is an interaction effect between convergence brought on by globalization pressures, and path dependency created by traditional national structures'. Analysing the liberalization process in telecommunications, we are interested in finding out if national deviations in the adoption of the new regulatory model did in fact result and what they look like in more detail. In addition, we will be able to construct an index of independence from the individual results obtained in the detailed NRA comparison.

The next section briefly summarizes the liberalization developments in the telecommunications sector and the proliferation of the new regulatory paradigm. Afterwards, we shall present the analytical framework and introduce facet theory, a methodology that helps to compare complex institutional configurations. In doing so, the fourth section presents the organizational structures and regulatory competencies of the NRAs and compares them applying partial order scalogram analysis (POSA), an instrument to illustrate institutional configurations on the basis of facet theory. We discuss differences and similarities and corroborate the hypothesis that the diffusion of regulatory reform in telecommunications led to nation-specific institutional configurations and, thus, to divergent convergence in the global reform process. The conclusion summarizes the most significant results of the chapter and outlines interesting points for further research.

2.   LIBERALIZATION, PRIVATIZATION AND THE EMERGENCE OF NATIONAL REGULATORY AUTHORITIES

Over the past 20 years, we have been able to observe vivid reform activities of governments in the telecommunications sector around the globe (cf. Schneider, 2001a). Together with aviation and electricity, telecommunications belongs to those infrastructure sectors that experienced the most significant transformation processes from monopoly to competition. However, telecommunications is the only sector in which, next to liberalization and privatization measures, almost all reform-oriented nations have established NRAs to guide the process of market opening. Hence this sector offers the broadest analytical basis for testing the hypothesis that policy convergence can bring about institutional divergence at the same time. The organizational structures and regulatory functions of the NRAs are thus in the focus of the subsequent analysis.

Regulatory Authorities as an Institutional Prerequisite for Market Opening

The literature on regulation often assumes that a functional change in the role of the state from the 'positive' or interventionist state to the 'regulatory' state has occurred on the basis of the developments since the early 1980s (Majone, 1997; Seidman and Gilmour, 1986). The central dilemma of the transition from a monopoly situation to that of stable and functioning competition in telecommunications entails guaranteeing new network administrators and service providers fair access to the market and controlling the dominant position of the former Public Telecommunications Operator (PTO) on the market (Grande, 1994). Hence the need to ensure competitive markets for new entrants and for consumers alike was the major reason behind the creation of new regulatory bodies and the implementation of new regulatory rules such as licensing, numbering, interconnection, universal service, and rights of way.

In the European Union, harmonization among the member states had been facilitated by the Commission, which developed a 'common regulatory framework' (CRF) for the telecommunications sector.[4] Among others, this CRF considers the role of NRAs in national telecommunications regulation. The establishment of NRAs that are as independent as possible from the influence of state actors and private interest groups and watch over the new sector-specific regulation imperatives is thus the most visible institutional result of the regulatory reforms in the telecommunications sector to date (Thatcher, 2002b).

NRAs function primarily as a referee to secure the politically and economically desired competition among entrepreneurs. In doing so, they deal with issues of loop-unbundling, interconnection disputes or licensing of fixed and mobile networks. NRAs further face a growing number of consumer complaints. Oftel, the British regulatory authority, for instance, has to deal with around 80000 complaints every year. In order to be able to handle the challenges that emerge from consumer interests and functioning markets in a globalizing economy, NRAs have to possess a specific regulatory profile. In addition, the convergence of telephony, broadcasting and Internet-based services demands new responses from governments as regards the cooperation or merger of NRAs which are responsible for those sectors which so far could be regulated separately.

Both the liberalization and privatization developments as well as the establishment of the NRAs followed the pattern of a 'bandwagon' effect, where more and more states joined the privatization strategy over time. Figure 11.1 clearly demonstrates that an extensive liberalization and privatization development did not set in until the beginning of the 1990s, and was most extensive between 1995 and 1998.[5] By 2002 all OECD states had begun to liberalize their market for fixed-voice telephony. With the exception of Luxembourg, all countries had at least partially privatized their PTO and, with the exception of Japan and New Zealand, established an NRA. In Japan,

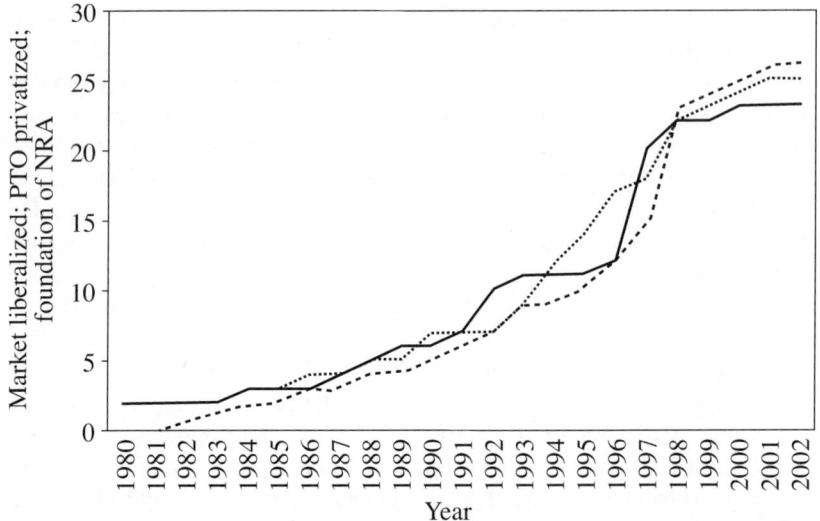

----- Market liberalized ········· Privatization of PTO ——— Foundation of NRA

Notes: Market liberalized: year in which the telecommunications sector was opened for competition; privatization of PTO: year in which the first shares of the PTO were sold to the public; foundation of NRA: year in which the NRA was *de facto* established.

This figure shows the development of regulatory reform in the telecommunications sector for 26 OECD countries. The curve demonstrates that liberalization, privatization and NRA establishment activity occurred almost in parallel and was highest in the mid- and late 1990s. The NRA curve lies left to the liberalization curve, thus indicating that the establishment of NRAs was the institutional prerequisite for market opening. Today, all but two countries have established an NRA to regulate the national telecommunications sector.

*Figure 11.1   The reform process in telecommunications in the OECD
             countries since 1980*

the Ministry of Public Management, Home Affairs, Posts and Telecommunications is still responsible for regulation, and in New Zealand, the Commerce Commission enforces and controls regulatory provisions but does not constitute an NRA according to our definition. Contrary to assessments of the political science literature at the end of the 1980s and the beginning of the 1990s (cf. Grande and Schneider, 1991; Morgan and Webber, 1986; Rubsamen, 1989), we observe quite a pronounced convergence pattern for the politics of liberalization and regulation in the telecommunications sector. This does not mean, though, that there is no variation in detail, as we will see later in the comparison of the NRAs.

The steps of liberalization, privatization and foundation of an NRA have essentially run remarkably parallel. It is striking, though, that in all countries except for Great Britain, Sweden, The Netherlands and the Federal Republic of Germany, NRAs were created before market liberalization began. This means that the institutional set-up was implemented before the opening of the telecommunications monopoly. After a period of low-level activity between 1993 and 1996, many new NRAs were established in the years 1997 and 1998. [6] One might also observe that the market in numerous countries was not opened until the PTO had been (partially) privatized. Between 1993 and 1997 in particular there was more extensive and continuous privatization than liberalization activity. The USA and Canada, however, are special cases since the telecommunications sector had always been entirely or partially privately organized in both countries. The private monopoly in the USA lasted until the divestiture of AT&T in 1982. Concerning regulation, in both countries, NRAs were founded very early: the FCC (Federal Communications Commission) in 1934 and the Canadian CRTC (Canadian Radio–television and Telecommunications Commission) in 1976.

One view held in the literature is that formal and informal networking leads to the recognition of mutual problems and best practice solutions. David Coen for instance argues that '[w]ith the creation of agencies throughout the member states [of the EU] it is possible to envisage that we will see increasing convergence of regulatory solutions' (Coen, 2002, 142). While it is claimed that path dependency leads to divergence in features at the micro level of NRAs, such as administrative structures or decision-making procedures, authors identify increasing similarities in the institutional design and in the acceptance of guiding principles at the *macro level* (Böllhoff, 2002; Eyre and Sitter, 1999).

We challenge this view. The global development towards the NRA-model cannot blur the fact that divergence does not only occur at the micro level but also at the macro level. Consituting elements of NRAs such as the organizational structure and competencies delegated to them differ strongly between national regulatory systems. While most countries have indeed opted for the regulator model in the process of reregulation, a closer analysis of NRAs reveals significant differences in institutional design. Such differences can also be observed in the timing and scope of the liberalization and privatization processes of OECD countries (Schneider et al., 2003).[7] As we shall see, the organizational structure and the competencies endowed to the NRA in particular tend to greatly vary.

3. NATIONAL REGULATORY AUTHORITIES IN AN INSTITUTIONAL TOPOLOGY

As we have just shown, regulatory reform in telecommunications exhibits the pattern of a relatively convergent process among Western industrial nations. Almost all countries liberalized and privatized their telecommunication systems and created organizationally separate NRAs. A closer look, however, reveals that most of these authorities show quite particular organizational and functional profiles. Comparing the NRAs can help us to identify if the reform process created convergent organizational structures at the level of regulation or if countries reacted rather differently to the challenge of national regulatory design.

In a methodological perspective, our goal is thus (1) to develop a general yardstick by which institutional convergence of organizations such as NRAs can be measured, and (2) to apply this method to a systematic comparison of the NRAs of OECD countries. If we conceive institutional convergence as process by which the similarity between different institutional structures is increasing, we can refer to measurement strategies used in network analysis (Scott, 2000; Wasserman and Faust, 1997). This methodological domain provides for a number of options in which the similarity (or dissimilarity) between two or more relational structures (for example a communication network) is measured by some indices of similarity (or dissimilarity). For instance, if we represent the various communications relations one actor has with other actors in a matrix, then the rows of this matrix represent the communication profiles of the various actors. A range of similarity indices (for example correlation coefficient, number of matches, and so on) then enables us to quantify the degree of similarity between different communication profiles. A computation of similarity indices between all the communications profiles then leads to a new symmetrical matrix in which the various cells express the degrees of similarity between the different communication profiles. Then, in a second step, multidimensional scaling can be used to visualize the similarity of these relational profiles in a kind of 'social map' (Young and Hamer, 1987). This method is implemented in most of the advanced statistical computer programs.

The statistical procedure finally computes a configuration of points that can be represented in a scattergram, where the profile similarity between the various pairs of actors is expressed in terms of geometric distances between these actors. For instance, actors in a network that have almost identical communication relations to all other actors are depicted very close to each other, whereas actors with very different communication profiles are depicted rather far away from each other. This rule is applied to all possible pairs of actors. The difficulty of this analytical procedure is to find a configuration in which all the geometrical distances between the different points (representing actors) correspond – more or less – to the structural similarity between actors.

This basic idea can also be applied to the comparative analysis of organizational structures. In such a perspective an institutional configuration such as an NRA is conceived as a specific combination of institutional elements. The presence or absence of different institutional traits may be conceived as a distinct institutional profile (Schneider, 2001b). Thus the degree of profile similarity (dissimilarity) between different NRAs (institutional profiles, functional profiles, and so on) may be used as a measure of institutional convergence (divergence). Accordingly, the similarity of institutions may be visualized by the above-mentioned method of multidimensional scaling in which the geometric distance between all pairs of NRAs express their relative institutional similarity.

In this respect, however, we have to cope with yet another problem. As we deal with institutional qualities, we are in most cases only able to establish nominal or ordinal classifications. The use of statistical analytical techniques such as metrical multidimensional scaling is therefore problematic and sometimes its application is severely restricted. A possible solution, however, is to have recourse to more advanced ordinal scaling techniques which have been developed during the last 15 or 20 years. One of these classification and measurement techniques is known in the profession as 'facet theory'.

In the following we will use this measurement approach to depict the various organizational and functional combinations that make up an NRA in its relative geometrical positioning. Applying this method, we are able to make our multidimensional classification procedure more explicit in the comparison of institutional configurations, while partial order scalogram analysis (POSA) as a specific form of multidimensional scaling allows us to visualize the profiles of the regulatory authorities in two-dimensional scattergrams. Since facet theory and POSA have only recently gained attention in political and organizational research (Lang and Grote, 2004; Schneider, 2001b), we will first briefly elaborate on the methodological and theoretical aspects of this form of analysis and presentation.

Facet Theory and Partial Orders

In the past, facet theory has primarily been used by psychologists in areas of research such as intelligence tests, attitudes and values of individuals, organizational psychology and environmental studies (Guttman and Greenbaum, 1998, 13). As a powerful method of structural analysis, facet theory has yet to gain attention in political science. For this reason, we will briefly outline the core elements of this analytical approach before applying it to the comparison of NRAs.

The basic idea behind facet theory is that every analytical object can be decomposed into a certain number of distinct dimensions (facets), where each facet can be decomposed into ordered values. A combination of different facets is called a 'structuple', each of the facet elements being a 'struct'. For example, the analytical object 'person' could be decomposed into personal characteristics (facets) such as age, height, physical strength or intelligence. We would then attribute different elements, such as small (1), medium (2) and large (3), to each of the four facets. If data are metric, as in the case of 'height', for example, these data have to be categorized. Hence the analytical object which has a medium age (2), is very tall (3), possesses medium physical strength (2) and only little intelligence (1) would end up with the structuple $\{2321\}$. This structuple is only one realization of 81 (3^4) possible combinations. Where all structuples of a whole are comparable with each other, we are dealing with a linear or complete order. The comparability of two structuples has been established once at least one struct of a structuple possesses a higher value than the corresponding struct of another structuple and no other struct holds a lower value.[8] It is then possible to compare these structuples along a perfectly one-dimensional scale, the 'Guttman scale'.

However, in complex social science phenomena, it is difficult to compare all structuples of a data set, for example the structuples $\{1312\}$ and $\{1222\}$ – so that it is necessary to present the structuples in a two- or multidimensional space. The lacking comparability of all existing structuples is thus the main difference between a linear order (Gutmann scale) and a 'partial order' (Borg and Shye, 1995, 107). The geometrical presentation of this kind of data is possible with various techniques of multidimensional scaling. For the visual presentation of multivariate distributions where actors – in our case NRAs – can be assigned different profiles, 'multidimensional structuple analysis' (MSA) may be used. MSA maps out structuples by points in a multidimensional space which in turn can be partitioned into different regions with every facet serving as the basis of the structuple, in which only points with the same struct lie. However, for doing so the data must demonstrate a particular structure (Borg and Shye, 1995, 96). For MSA there is neither an a priori requirement for the distributive structure of the variables in the data set, nor for the interrelation between them. In addition, metric data can be categorized (Guttman and Greenbaum, 1998, 25).

For our comparison of NRAs, we apply a particular form of MSA known as 'partial order scalogram analysis', POSA (Levy, 1998, 5). POSA distinguishes itself from MSA in that each variable can be ordered in the same direction, that is, if 1<2<3<4 ... <*n* holds for the elements of all facets. In order to determine the smallest possible dimensionality to depict this partial order while strictly maintaining the order, we use 'POSA with base coordinates' (POSAC). Very similar to conventional multidimensional scaling, POSAC orders all existing structuples and depicts these as points in a two-dimensional space using geometric distances on the basis of profile similarities (Guttman and Greenbaum, 1998, 27). A further step in POSAC then consists in the identification of 'facet regions' delineated by dividing lines separating clusters of configurations in the two-dimensional diagram. The boundary specification of respective facet regions may also be realized by other structural methods such as cluster analysis.

Data Set and Analytical Methodology

The NRAs in the OECD countries differ considerably in terms of their organizational traits and regulatory competencies. While some do come very close to the ideal type of an independent NRA, others demonstrate characteristics that imply a persistently above-average dependency on state principals. With the help of POSAC we are able to offer a comparison of the organizational and functional profiles of the NRA in a fitness landscape and thus spatially illustrate their degree of independence. In doing so, we consider the fitness landscape to be a two-dimensional space in which the profile with the lowest degree of independence is located in the lower left corner while the profile with the highest degree of independence is nested in the upper right corner. The geometric distances between the points refer to the similarity of the organizational structure and the competencies of the NRA. Regulatory authorities with a similar organizational structure and comparable regulatory functions are thus closer to each other than those having clearly different structures or competencies.

In contrast to additive indices (cf. Gilardi, 2002), multidimensional scaling on the basis of partial orders allows us to depict institutional configurations visually. The advantage is that we can distinguish between objects which have different values on different facets and thus show different institutional configurations. With a pure additive index, this differentiation cannot be done. Moreover, it can simply be problematic to add certain institutional characteristics together, a little bit like apples and pears. Consider, for instance, the case of two NRAs in which one NRA shows exactly the opposite values on half of the organizational or functional characteristics and the other shows the opposite values on the other half of the characteristics (that is, the structuples {111333} and {333111}). Using an additive index, we would receive exactly the same independence score for both NRAs without being able to recognize that the institutional configurations are as divergent as they could possibly be in this case.

For the POSAC, data were collected on the organizational structure and the regulatory competencies of the regulatory authorities in 26 OECD countries.[9] These data were transformed along a coding scheme for the POSAC (see Appendix A and B). For the comparison of the organizational profiles a variable representing a high degree of independence is coded with '3', a moderate degree of independence with '2' and a low degree with '1'. For the sake of comparison of the functional profiles we code such cases in which the NRA has the sole or partial regulatory responsibility with '2' and cases where other regulatory institutions fulfil this task (for example ministry, cartel office) are coded with '1'.

As a result of this transformation, we get the corresponding structuples for the organizational (Appendix A) and the functional (Appendix B) profiles of the NRAs. However, in the following analysis, we do not consider the facets regulatory institutions {RI} and independence from political power {IP} because of a lack of variance between the 23 NRAs on these two facets. To make the coding procedure more transparent, let us consider the example of Danish NITA (National IT and Telecom Agency). According to the coding for the organizational profile, we obtain the structuple {311213113}.[10] Table 11.1 shows how this transformation is being made.

For all other countries, the procedure was analogous. Data were then further reduced using the computer program 'SYSTAT'. The POSAC function in SYSTAT calculates the relative position of each structuple in the two-dimensional space so that the partial orders on each of the former nine (organizational profile) and 11 (functional profile) dimensions are preserved as well as possible.

4.   'INDEPENDENT' REGULATORY AUTHORITIES – RHETORIC OR REALITY?

Having presented the convergent development of the liberalization and regulation politics in the telecommunications sector and the analytical method, we now compare and contrast the NRAs in detail and examine the degree of their independence from political actors and the state administration.

We believe that it is necessary to distinguish between formal, material and *de facto* independence. Formal independence refers to the nominal or

Table 11.1 Coding example – the Danish NRA

Facet	Abbr.	Data value	Coding value
Country number	CR	3	–
Country name	CN	DK	–
Regulatory institutions	RI	SR, C	1
Staff per inhabitant (mill.)	ST	Large	3
Independence from political power	IP	Yes	3
Reports to	RT	Ministry	1
Autonomy of decision-making	AD	Yes	1
Overturning of decisions	OD	Telecom. complaints board and telecom. consumer board	2
Approval of budget	AB	Ministry	1
Form of financing	FF	Fees and appropriation	3
Collegial body	CB	No	1
Appointment of head	AH	Ministry	1
Term of office	TO	Indefinite	3

Notes:
Facets {Rl} and {IP} omitted.
The corresponding coding scheme is shown in Appendix A.

rhetorical claims of politicians or state officials as regards the status of independence of the regulatory authority. For instance, political rhetoric could be an instrument to enhance credibility in liberalization programmes initiated by governments under globalization or budgetary pressures. By contrast, material independence describes the status of an NRA according to the legal acts establishing the authority. Thus it considers all officially delegated powers of the NRA on the basis of either laws by the Parliament or decrees and ordinances of the executive. Finally, *de facto* independence describes the status of an NRA as it manifests itself in daily regulatory praxis. It refers to the observable relationship between the NRA and other regulatory institutions, such as Parliament, ministries and competition authorities.

Hence an NRA can be materially independent in terms of political statues and administratively delegated powers, but still be only semi- or partially independent from the legislative or the executive when it comes to concrete regulatory decisions. Measuring and comparing *de facto* independence among all 26 OECD countries would, however, require a very complex and voluminous research design. That is why we limit our analysis here to the dimension of material independence.

We want to demonstrate that, despite formal proclamations of governments that the national regulatory body for the telecommunications sector is independent from any political influence, NRAs are in fact often only partially or semi-independent. The assumption that there is a gap between formal and material independence could, among other things, be based on the fact that governments want to enhance their credibility in order to attract foreign direct investment (cf. Majone, 1997). Formal delegation to NRAs might further the credibility of liberalization steps and privatization measures of the PTO, without having to disturb the established power distribution between those institutions which have been responsible for regulation in the past.

In the following section, we compare the organizational structures of the NRAs (Table 11A.2, Appendix A) and their regulatory competencies (Table 11A.4, Appendix B). Finally, we combine these two dimensions in order to create an index of material independence (Table 11A.5, Appendix C).

Organizational Structure of the NRAs

Analysis of the organizational profiles is based on a total of nine variables which measure the essential organizational characteristics of an NRA with respect to its internal and external environment. These variables indicate control relations between the political-administrative system and the NRA, such as the procedures foreseen for the appointment of the NRA's head and the approval of the budget, or the authorities' official reporting responsibilities. They further measure the organizational characteristics of the NRA's head, such as size or term of office and control for the decision authority and autonomy of the NRA. Finally, a third set of variables considers the organizational size with respect to staff per one million inhabitants or aspects of the financing structure.

As already exemplified in Table 11.1, for the organizational profile of 23 OECD countries[11] we considered nine facets and omitted two of them due to a lack of variance. The facets 'Collegial body', 'Appointment of head', 'Reports to', 'Autonomy of decision-making (licensing)', 'Approval of budget', 'Overturning of decisions', 'Form of finance', 'Term of office' and 'Staff' together form the structuple {CB, AH, RT, AD, AB, OD, FF, TO, ST}. Comparing all 23 profiles along a multidimensional scale, we end up with the topography illustrated in Figure 11.2. Data are listed in Appendix A.

The fitness landscape demonstrates a relatively large degree of variation, as a unitary organizational model in the OECD countries has evidently not yet emerged. As for their organization structure, the NRAs still vary considerably and have approached the ideal model of an independent sector regulator

POSAC profile plot

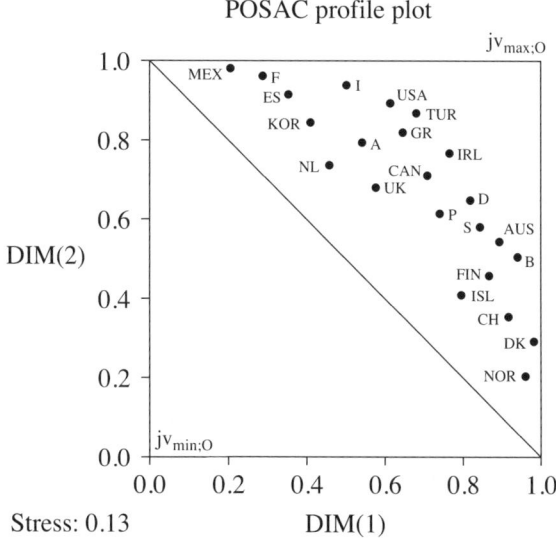

Stress: 0.13

Notes: The stress factor indicates the percentage of structuples not correctly represented in the POSAC. Due to a reduction of nine to just two dimensions, there is some error. In general, a stress factor of <0.20 is considered to be acceptable for the POSAC.

The figure shows the POSAC for the organizational profiles of the NRAs. In this case, POSAC orders the NRAs along nine dimensions according to each facet, reduces the data and depicts them in a two-dimensional space. NRAs that lie closer to the upper right corner ($jv_{max;O}$) show a high level of independence, whereas those closer to the lower left corner ($jv_{min;O}$) possess a low level of independence. Those NRAs having the same distance to the diagonal possess the same level of independence. DIM(1) and DIM(2) are the result of the data reduction calculated by the POSAC when *n* dimensions are reduced to only two in order to represent multiple dimensions in a Euclidean space. The stress factor indicates what percentage of the structuples are not correctly represented after this reduction. Hence DIM(1) and DIM(2) are artificial or constructed dimensions which do not exclusively represent one of the facets of the structuple. They are comparable to those factors in a factor analysis which load high for the variables. The Euclidean distance between each pair of NRAs represents the similarity of the NRAs on the basis of the initial partial ordering on nine dimensions. The figure shows great variation, thus indicating that many NRAs differ significantly in terms of organizational structure. No unitary NRA model has yet emerged. Many NRAs, however, possess a similar level of independence, which can be seen from the fact that several points are at an equal distance from the diagonal line.

Figure 11.2   Fitness landscape of organizational NRA profiles

(represented by $jv_{max;O}$ in the upper right corner) following highly diversified patterns. However, all countries possess a level of independence that is closer to the maximal value (complete material independence) than to zero (complete material dependence). This is recognizable by the fact that all NRAs are located to the right of the diagonal and thus closer to $jv_{max;O}$ (highest level of independence) than to $jv_{min;O}$ (lowest level of independence). In terms of their organization profile, Turkey, Ireland and the USA are the most independent of the 23 countries analysed. The least independent NRAs are those of the Netherlands, Norway and Mexico.

Significantly, the FCC, often considered as the 'mother of all national regulatory authorities', marks the highest independence score. Indeed, the USA was the first nation to have established an NRA for the telecommunications sector, namely in 1934. But this fact alone cannot explain the outcome of our analysis. In the literature, however, the FCC is frequently considered as a typical example of an 'independent regulatory authority' (cf. Oberlander, 2001). In addition, it is a common perception that the British regulatory authority Oftel, the first telecommunications NRA in Europe, was modelled after the US blueprint FCC.

The position of Turkey, however, strikes our attention. With a joint value[12] of 0.772, it demonstrates the greatest independence score in the comparison of organizational profiles. This is surprising, if we consider the fact that Turkey is a real latecomer in terms of liberalization and privatization and that it has a longstanding tradition of strong central government authority, especially as regards regulation. This contradiction could be explained by the fact that Turkey did indeed establish an NRA for telecommunications because of initial formal liberalization measures, but transferred only very few competencies to the authority in the course of the sluggish privatization of TürkTelekom.

A closer look at the data reveals that the distances between the single NRA positions and the ideal position in the profile plot ($jv_{max;O}$ with the structuple {3333 …}) do not vary very much. In other words, the levels of independence concerning the organizational profiles are pretty much the same for all NRAs. The levels only range from 0.581 for Norway, which has the lowest POSAC score, to 0.772 for Turkey. Considering the specification of POSAC, these scores constitute only minor variations. What does vary, though, and what can be seen instantaneously from the profile plot, are the specific organizational characteristics of each NRA.

To illustrate this point a little further, let us consider the cases of Denmark and France. Both countries show about the same level of independence according to our POSAC ($jv_{DK;O} = 0.634$; $jv_{F;O} = 0.623$). However, in some points, the two NRAs differ substantially. Whereas the Danish NRA shows high independence values for the organizational variables 'number of staff' (ST), 'term of office' (TO) and 'forms of finance' (FF), the French NRA possesses significantly higher values for 'autonomy of decision-making' (AD), 'approval of the regulator's head' (AH) and the 'composition of the regulator's head' (CB). Thus, although both NRAs have different values for specific organizational variables, in total this sums up to a comparable level of independence for the NRAs in both countries.

The asymmetry between NRAs showing a great deal of variation in their specific organizational set-up on the one side and a comparable level of independence on the other seems to further indicate that governments selectively grant their NRAs considerable autonomy on certain dimensions and not on others. It appears to be an individual national decision which organizational elements of the NRAs are being granted high and which low levels of independence. Two mechanisms might be at work here. First, the organizational divergence might be a result of the political will of the government which was in charge at the time the NRA was set up. Partisan politics might be one reason for the emergence of different levels of independence on certain organizational facets constituting a NRA. Whereas left parties might tend not to delegate too many powers to NRAs, centre-right governments might favour a rather clear separation between official state activities and sector regulation in order to reduce the powers of the state. Second, the regulatory traditions in the respective country might determine the distribution of power between the government, in most cases the ministry, and a newly created sector regulator (cf. Coen and Héritier, 2000).

Regulatory Competencies of the NRAs

A second macro-picture can be obtained by analysing the similarity of functional profiles of the NRAs. Each NRA has a spectrum of tasks and functions ranging from licensing (fixed-voice and mobile-voice telephony), licence oversight, merger approval, interconnection charges, dispute resolution, spectrum planning and allocation, numbering planning to price regulation. In order to convert regulatory functions into numbers, we have coded the involvement of the sector regulator alone or in cooperation with the ministry as '2', and the responsibilities of the ministry alone or of other institutions as '1'. Since two of the activities, dispute resolution and numbering allocation, are invariant among the 23 NRAs analysed, the POSAC restricts itself to the scaling of ten variables.

For the POSAC of the competence profiles the ten variables 'spectrum planning', 'spectrum allocation', 'issuing of mobile licences', 'numbering planning', 'numbering allocation', 'issuing of fixed licences', 'merger approval', 'oversight of licence requirements', 'regulatory body for pricing' and 'interconnection charges' were chosen from the data set. Hence the fitness landscape shown in Figure 11.3 coincides with the 23 profiles with the structuple {SP, SA, ML, NP, NA, FL, MA, OL, RB, IC}. Data are listed in Appendix B.

Here we detect an even greater variation than in the case of the organizational profiles. Both extreme positions in the lower left and the upper right corner are realized in the analysis. The USA and the Federal Republic of Germany are those countries that have granted their respective NRAs the most comprehensive regulatory competencies. They reach the (maximal) POSAC

POSAC functional profiles

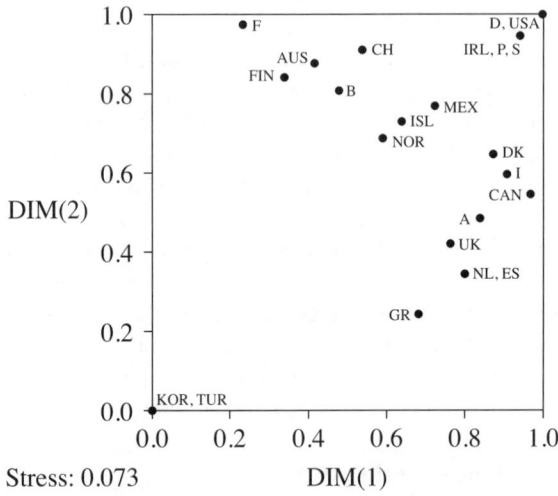

Stress: 0.073

Notes: The figure shows the POSAC for the functional profiles of the NRAs. In this case, POSAC orders the NRAs along ten dimensions according to each facet, reduces the data and depicts them in a two-dimensional space. The Euclidian distance between each pair of NRAs represents the similarity of the NRAs on the basis of the initial partial ordering on ten dimensions. The figure shows even greater variation than in Figure 11.2, thus indicating that NRAs differ even more significantly in terms of regulatory competencies. As a consequence, the NRAs show very different levels of independence. See Figure 11.2 for an explanation of how to read the figure and what the stress factor indicates.

Figure 11.3   Fitness landscape of functional NRA profiles

score of $jv_{max;F}$ = 1000, illustrated by the position in the upper right of the profile plot. Again, the result is no surprise for the American FCC, which had been delegated more and more competencies over the years since its creation in 1934. German RegTP, on the other side, belongs to the relatively young NRAs which have just been created as a consequence of EU liberalization pressures. Other European countries such as Ireland, Portugal and Sweden have also delegated extensive competencies to their NRAs. Their NRAs possess exactly the same functional profiles. So far, only Finland and the United Kingdom have tackled the new challenges based on the convergence of classic telephony, broadcasting and Internet-based services, by merging formerly independent authorities to one new 'super-regulator'. These new bodies, however, do not belong to the most independent of the NRAs analysed.

In South Korea and Turkey, none of the analysed regulatory functions are executed by the NRA. In these countries, as in Japan and New Zealand, which were not part of the analysis, the ministry remains responsible for all matters of regulation. The result for Turkey is surprising, though, as its NRA showed a relatively high degree of independence in the analysis of the organizational structure. Where regulatory authorities in the telecommunications sector experienced an evolutionary process aimed at completely independent institutions in a material sense, these countries' NRAs would still be at the very beginning of the process.

Unlike for the organizational characteristics, the great variation among the NRAs is equivalent to highly different levels of independence as regards the functional profiles. Whereas some NRAs come close to the ideal position of Germany and the USA, others have relatively little say in the regulation of telecommunications. However, EU member countries all show at least a moderate level of regulatory competencies. The two countries that did not delegate any regulatory power to their NRAs are non-EU countries. In addition, South Korea and Turkey are perfect cases for which the distinction between formal and material independence can most clearly be exemplified. Both have created NRAs which possess rather high levels of independence as regards their organizational characteristics and the lowest scores as regards their functional profiles. This asymmetry most probably originates in the fact that the creation of an NRA was a rather symbolic move to comply with harmonization requirements at the OECD and WTO level and to enhance policy credibility in order to attract foreign direct investment (cf. Gilardi, 2002).

The Material Independence of the NRAs

By means of these partial results we are now able to produce an index of independence that takes the organizational structure and regulatory competencies of the NRA equally into account. For each country the arithmetic mean was calculated from the POSAC joint values for the organizational and the functional profile. Using these mean values, we are able to set up a rank order of the countries as regards the degree of material independence of their NRAs (see Appendix C).

A graphic representation of this index is offered by Figure 11.4. For each NRA, the joint values of the organizational and the functional profile were used to determine its position on the x and y axis of the diagram.

The most independent NRAs are again located to the upper right of the diagram. The most independent regulatory authority, closely followed by the RegTP of the Federal Republic of Germany and ComReg in Ireland. Of the ten most independent regulatory authorities, six of them belong to a country of the European Union. We can further see from Figure 11.4 that there exists a significant variance between the levels of material independence of the NRAs.

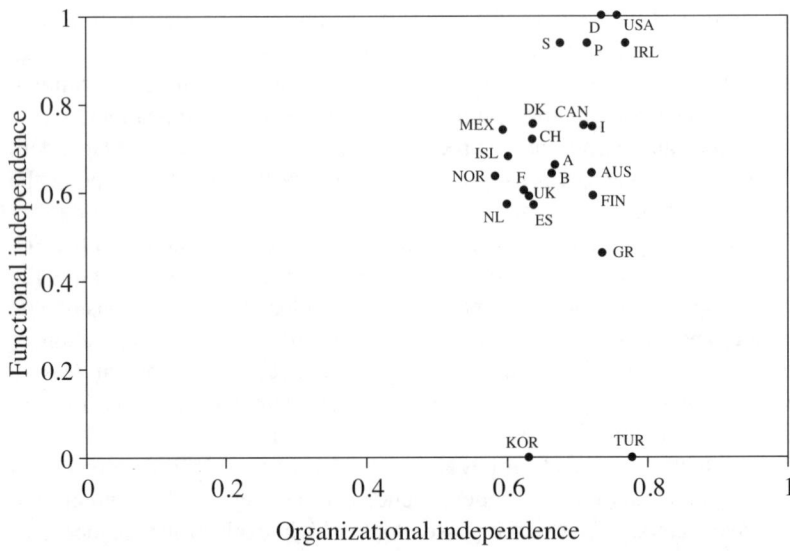

Notes: The figure represents graphically the level of material independence for the 23 NRAs on the basis of the two POSACs we conducted for the organizational and the functional profiles. The x axis shows the joint values for the POSAC of the organizational structure, and the y axis shows the joint values for the POSAC of the competencies. The high variation in this figure indicates that NRAs differ significantly in terms of material independence.

Figure 11.4   Material independence of NRAs in the telecommunications sector

The variance is much more explicit on the y axis, that is, the functional dimension of our analysis. On the organizational dimension, the NRAs do not vary too much. However, this is only true for the 'level of independence'. A closer look at the organizational structures reveals that there are explicit differences between the NRAs which equalize each other for the calculation of independence. This is nicely depicted in Figure 11.2 above.

Together with the results from the POSAC above, this confirms our hypothesis that despite a worldwide diffusion of NRAs, there are by no means in all cases equally independent regulatory authorities with comparable competencies. Hence the fact that almost all OECD countries have complemented the opening of the telecommunications market with the creation of formally independent NRAs left us with the question of how the institutional implementation was actually carried out in practice. The answer to that question is that, until now, no unitary model has emerged and penetrated all countries, nor has there been a mere emulation or spread of the American FCC model.

However, some European NRAs have been attributed structures and competencies that come close to those of the FCC, for example, RegTP in Germany or ComReg in Ireland. Those institutions often labelled by the literature as classic examples of independent NRAs, such as Oftel (from autumn 2003: Office of Communications, Ofcom) in Great Britain or Opta (Onafhankelijke Post en Telecommunicatie Autoriteit) in the Netherlands, demonstrate a surprisingly low degree of material independence. And in Spain and Austria as well, the ministry continues to hold significant regulatory responsibility at the costs of the influence and independence of CMT (Comisión del Mercado de las Telecomunicaciones) and TKK (Telekom-Control Kommission). In Italy and Sweden, on the other hand, AGCOM (Autorità per le Garanzie nelle Comunicazioni) and PTS (Post-och Telestyrelsen) today are authorized to decide autonomously on almost all questions of telecommunications regulation.

5. CONCLUSION

The global reform process in telecommunications has brought about a clear trend towards policy convergence. However, major national differences persist. In this chapter, we have established that despite the fact that the convergence process intensified with time, we observe a strong variation in the institutional implementation of the regulatory reforms of the telecommunications sector. Although the regulatory reform of the telecommunications sector was sparked by developments in the USA and had a great impact on all other states, they have not merely copied the American blueprint of a materially independent NRA with extensive regulatory competencies. In contrast to predictions by the literature (Coen, 2002; Eyre and Sitter, 1999), the spread of the new regulatory paradigm has not led to convergence in the institutional design and competencies of NRAs. While it seems clear that there are distinct national features at the micro-level (Böllhoff, 2002), even at the macro-level we cannot speak of pure convergence. Although almost all countries have established NRAs in telecommunications, the agencies differ strongly as regards some of their constituting elements which should be considered as important also for the macro-organizational level. The OECD countries essentially created NRAs with various organizational structures and often very different regulatory competencies delegated to them, leading to the observed phenomenon of divergent convergence.

The institutional diversity, in turn, has direct repercussions on the level of material independence of the individual NRAs. Whereas all countries claim to possess formally independent NRAs, we find a very visible gap between countries with a comparatively materially independent NRA, such as the USA, the Federal Republic of Germany, or Ireland, and those states whose institutions (ministries, cartel offices) still maintain far-reaching regulatory authorities in the telecommunications sector, such as Japan, New Zealand or South Korea.

One of the questions we are left with at the end of this discussion is: which factors are responsible for the significant degree of variation in the organizational structure and the regulatory competencies of the NRAs? Are national factors causing country-specific adaptation to the internationally present reform agenda (Haverland, 2001; Schmidt, 2002)? This would not be surprising given the large differences in the political and administrative systems and in the legal traditions between the OECD countries. The answer to this question, we believe, must be based on further detailed research on the global diffusion of regulatory reform processes.

NOTES

1. We would like to thank Nadja Schorowsky for her help with data collection and Michael Dobbins for his linguistic support. We further would like to thank Fabrizio Gilardi, Jacint Jordana and David Levi-Faur for helpful comments on earlier versions of this chapter. All errors are ours.
2. Deregulation must be distinguished from reregulation to the extent that the former refers to the reduction or elimination of government regulations while reregulation pertains to the reformulation of existing and the creation of new rules to facilitate the transformation from monopoly to competition (Vogel, 1996, 3).
3. We use the terms 'regulatory competencies' and 'regulatory functions' interchangeably in the context of the chapter.
4. The main document of this new European legal framework is the 'Directive on a common regulatory framework for electronic communication networks and services' from 7 March 2002 (European Parliament, 2002).
5. The main reason for the abundance of liberalization measures at the end of 1990s is EU Directive 96/19/EC, providing that all EU member states completely open their markets for fixed-net telephony starting 1 January 1998 and that the PTOs allow new providers free access to their network infrastructure (European Commission, 1996).
6. Note that the NRA curve has the form of a typical s-shaped diffusion curve.
7. Whereas by the end of 2002 six OECD countries (Denmark, Great Britain, Ireland, Mexico, New Zealand and Spain) had completely privatized their PTO, others have yet to undergo any steps towards privatization (for example Luxembourg) or the majority of the company is still controlled by the state (for example Belgium, France and Norway). The telecommunications firms in Canada and the USA had always been entirely in private hands.
8. For example, the structuple {2321} is larger than the structuple {2221}, if 1<2<3 holds for all structs; both structuples can thus be compared with each other.
9. The data set is based on information provided by the ITU and OECD as well as our own research. It can be accessed at http://www.uni-konstanz.de/FuF/Verwiss/Schneider/redimensionierung.htm.
10. Consider, however, that the facet order of the structuples *after* the POSAC is usually not identical with the order after the coding procedure. The reason for this is that POSAC rearranges the initial facet order of the structuple according to the best comparability of the structuples on the basis of ordinal scaling.
11. We consider only 23 out of 26 OECD countries since insufficient data for Luxembourg were available. Japan and New Zealand do not possess an NRA. In Japan, all regulatory functions are still fulfilled by the Ministry of Public Management, Home Affairs, Posts and

Telecommunications. And in New Zealand only one Commissioner in the Commerce Commission is exclusively responsible for telecommunications affairs.
12. The joint value is the arithmetic mean of the values for DIM(1) and DIM(2).

REFERENCES

Berger, Suzanne and Ronald Dore (eds) (1996), *National Diversity and Global Capitalism*, Ithaca: Cornell University Press.

Böllhoff, Dominik (2000), 'The new regulatory regime: the institutional design of telecommunications regulation at the national level', in Adrienne Héritier (ed.), *Common Goods, Reinventing European and International Governance*, Lanham, US: Rowman & Littlefield, pp. 235–61.

Borg, Ingwer and Samuel Shye (1995), *Facet Theory. Form and Content*, London: Sage.

Coen, David (2002), 'The politics of regulation in Europe', *Journal of European Public Policy*, **9** (1), 141–5.

Coen, David and Adrienne Héritier (2000), 'Business perspectives on German and British regulation: telecoms, energy and rail', *Business Strategy Review*, **11** (4), 29–37.

Doern, Bruce and Stephen Wilks (eds) (1996), *Comparative Competition Policy: National Institutions in a Global Market*, Oxford: Oxford University Press.

European Commission (1995), 'Directive on the application of open network provision to voice telephony', 95/62/EC, published in OJ L 321/6, 30.12.1995.

European Commission (1996), 'Directive regarding the implementation of full competition in telecommunications markets', 96/19/EC, published in OJ L 74/13, 22.03.1996.

European Parliament (2002), 'Directive on a common regulatory framework for electronic communication networks and services', 2002/21/EC, published in OJ L 108/33, 24.4.2002.

Eyre, Sebastian and Nick Sitter (1999), 'From PTT to NRA: towards a new regulatory regime?', in Kjell A. Eliasson and Marit Sjovaag (eds), *European Telecommunications Liberalization*, London: Routledge, pp. 55–73.

Gilardi, Fabrizio (2002), 'Policy credibility and delegation to independent regulatory agencies: a comparative empirical analysis', *Journal of European Public Policy*, **9** (6), 873–93.

Grande, Edgar (1994), 'The new role of the state in telecommunications', *West European Politics*, **17** (3), 138–57.

Grande, Edgar and Thomas Risse (2000), 'Bridging the gap. Konzeptionelle Anforderungen an die politikwissenschaftliche Analyse von Globalisierungsprozessen', *Zeitschrift für Internationale Beziehungen*, **7** (2), 235–66.

Grande, Edgar and Volker Schneider (1991), 'Reformstrategien und staatliche Handlungskapazitäten. Eine vergleichende Analyse institutionellen Wandels in der Telekommunikation in Westeuropa', *Politische Vierteljahresschrift*, **32** (3), 452–78.

Guttman, Ruth and Charles W. Greenbaum (1998), 'Facet theory: its development and current status', *European Psychologist*, **3** (1), 13–36.

Hall, Peter A. (1992), 'The movement from Keynesianism to monetarism: Institutional analysis and British economic policy in the 1970s', in Sven Steinmo, Kathleen Thelen and Frank Longstreth (eds), *Structuring politics. Historical institutionalism in comparative analysis*, Cambridge, UK: Cambridge University Press, pp. 90–113.

Haverland, Markus (2001), 'National adaptation to European integration: the importance of institutional veto points', *Journal of Public Policy*, **20** (1), 83–103.

ITU (2003), 'International Telecommunications Union Regulatory Reform Unit', available: http://www.itu.int/ITU-D/treg/index.html.

Lang, Achim and Jürgen R. Grote (2004), 'Facetten des Wandels – Anpassungsstrategien von Wirtschaftsverbänden an ihre Umwelt', in Beate Kohler-Koch and Roland Eising (eds), *Interessendurchsetzung im Mehrebenensystem*, Baden-Baden: Nomos (forthcoming).

Levi-Faur, David (2003), 'Herding towards a New Convention: On herds, shepherds, and lost sheep in the liberalization of the telecommunications and electricity industries', paper presented at the workshop 'The Internationalization of Regulatory Reform', Berkeley, 26/27 April 2003.

Levy, Brian J. and Pablo T. Spiller (eds) (1996), *Regulation, Institutions and Commitment: Comparative Studies of Telecommunications*, Cambridge, UK: Cambridge University Press.

Levy, Shlomit (1998), 'A typology of partial-order: the case of drug use in Israel', *Quality & Quantity*, **32**, 1–14.

Majone, Giandomenico (1997), 'From the positive to the regulatory state: causes and consequences of changes in the mode of governance', *Journal of Public Policy*, **17** (2), 139–67.

Morgan, Kevin and Douglas Webber (1986), 'Divergent paths: political strategies for telecommunications in Britain, France and West Germany', in Kenneth Dyson and Peter Humphreys (eds), *The Politics of the Communications Revolution in Western Europe*, London: Frank Cass, pp. 56–79.

Oberlander, Susan E. (2001), 'Indicators of Independence in Regulatory Commissions', paper presented at the Telecommunications Policy Research Conference, October.

OECD (2003), International Regulation Database Homepage, available: http://www.oecd.org/EN/document/0,,EN-document-2-nodirectorate-no-1-18275-2,00.html.

Rubsamen, Valerie (1989), 'Deregulation and the state in comparative perspective: the case of telecommunications', *Comparative Politics*, **22** (1), 105–20.

Schmidt, Susanne K. (2002), 'The impact of mutual recognition – inbuilt limits and domestic responses to the single market', *Journal of European Public Policy*, **9** (6), 935–53.

Schneider, Volker, Simon Fink and Marc Tenbücken (2003), 'Measuring and Explaining Institutional Reform: The Privatization of Infrastructures', paper presented at the ECPR Joint Session of Workshops, Edinburgh, 28 March to 2 April.

Schneider, Volker (2001a), 'Institutional reform in telecommunications: The European Union in transnational policy diffusion', in Maria Green-Cowles, Jim Caporaso and Thomas Risse (eds), *Transforming Europe. Europeanization and Domestic Change*, Ithaca: Cornell University Press, pp. 60–78.

Schneider, Volker (2001b), *Die Transformation der Telekommunikation. Vom Staatsmonopol zum globalen Markt (1800–2000)*, Frankfurt am Main: Campus.

Scott, John (2000), *Social Network Analysis: A Handbook*, London: Sage.

Seidman, Harold and Robert Gilmour (1986), *Politics, Position, and Power. From the Positive to the Regulatory State*, 4th edn, New York: Oxford University Press.

Strange, Susan (1996), *The Retreat of the State. The Diffusion of Power in the World Economy*, Cambridge, UK: Cambridge University Press.

Thatcher, Mark (2002a), 'Delegation to independent regulatory agencies: pressures, functions and contextual mediation', *West European Politics*, **25** (1), 125–47.

Thatcher, Mark (2002b), 'Regulation after delegation: independent regulatory agencies in Europe', *Journal of European Public Policy*, **9** (6), 954–72.

Vogel, Steven K. (1996), *Freer Markets, More Rules. Regulatory Reform in Advanced Industrial Countries*, Ithaca: Cornell University Press.

Wasserman, Stanley and Katherine Faust (1997), *Social Network Analysis: Methods and Applications*, Cambridge, UK: Cambridge University Press.

Young, Forrest W. and Robert M. Hamer (1987), *Multidimensional Scaling: History, Theory and Applications*, New York: Erlbaum.

APPENDIX A

Table 11A.1   Coding for organizational profiles

CR	CN	RI	ST	IP	RT	AD	OD	AB	FF	CB	AH	TO
1	AUS	2	3	3	1	3	3	2*	1	2	1	2
2	A	1	1	3	1	3	3	3	2	2	1	2
3	B	1	2	3	1	1	3	1	1	1	1	3
4	CAN	1	2	3	3	3	1	1	2	3	1	2
5	DK	1	3	3	1	1	2	1	3	1	1	3
6	FIN	1	3	3	1	3	3	3	1	1	1	3
7	F	1	1	3	2	3	3	2	1	3	3	3
8	D	1	3	3	2	3	3	2	2	1	1	2
9	GR	1	1	3	3	3	3	1	2	3	3	2
10	ISL	2	3	3	1	3	3	1	1	1	1	2
11	IRL	2	2	3	3	3	3	3	3	2	1	3
12	I	1	1	3	2	3	3	3	2	3	3	3
13	KOR	2	1	3	3	3	3	2	1	3	1	1
14	MEX	1	1	3	1	1	1	1	1	3	3	3
15	NL	1	1	3	1	3	3	1	2	2	1	2
16	NOR	1	3	3	1	3	1	2*	1	1	1	3
17	P	1	3	3	3	3	3	1	1	2	1	2
18	ES	1	1	3	3	3	3	2	1	3	1	3
19	S	2	2	3	1	3	3	2*	1	3	1	1
20	CH	1	3	3	1	3	3	1	2	1	1	3
21	TUR	2	1	3	3	3	3	3	2	3	1	2
22	UK	1	1	3	2	3	2	1	2	1	1	2
23	USA	1	1	3	3	3	3	2	2	3	3	2

Note: Insufficient data for Luxembourg available. No NRAs in Japan and New Zealand.

Table 11A.2   Coding scheme for organizational profiles

Country number	CR	Countries from 1 to 14
Country name	CN	Names of countries
Regulatory institutions	RI	SR+C+M = 1; SR+C or SR+M or C+M = 2; SR = 3
Staff per inhabitant (mill.)	ST	small = 1; medium = 2; large = 3
Independence from political power	IP	No = 1; Yes = 3
Reports to	RT	M = 1; G or P = 2; G+P or M+P or Other = 3
Autonomy of decision-making	AD	No = 1; Partial = 2; Yes = 3
Overturning of decisions	OD	Political dependent institutions = 1 Political independent institutions = 2 Courts = 3
Approval of budget	AB	M or G = 1; P = 2; SR = 3
Form of financing	FF	1 source = 1; 2 sources = 2; 3 sources or more = 3
Collegial body	CB	No = 1; small (<4) = 2; large (>=4) = 3
Appointment of head	AH	M or G = 1; P = 2; SR or P+G = 3
Term of office	TO	<4 = 1; >=4 = 2; >=6 = 3

Note: M = Ministry; G = Government; P = Parliament; SR = Sector regulator; C = Competition authority; * = value estimated.

APPENDIX B

Table 11A.3   Coding for functional profiles

CR	CN	FL	ML	OL	MA	IC	DR	SP	SA	NP	NA	RB	FP
1	AUS	2	2	1	1	1	1	2	2	2	2	1	2
2	A	2	2	2	1*	2	2	1	1	1	2	2	1
3	B	1	1	2	1	2	2	2	2	2	2	1	2
4	CAN	2	1	2	2	2	2	1	1	2	2	2	2
5	DK	2*	2	2	1	2	2	1	2	2	2	2	2
6	FIN	1	1	1	1	2	2	2	2	2	2	1	2*
7	F	1	1	2	2	2	2	1	2	2	2	1	1
8	D	2	2	2	2	2	2	2	2	2	2	2	1
9	GR	1	1	2	1	2	2	1	1	1	2	2	2
10	ISL	2	2	2	1*	1	2	2*	2	2	2	2*	1*
11	IRL	2	2	2	1	2	2	2*	2	2	2	2	2
12	I	2	2	2	1	2	2	2	1	2	2	2	2
13	KOR	1	1	1	1	1	2	1	1	1	1	1	1
14	MEX	1	1	2	1	2	2	2	2	2	2	2	2
15	NL	2	1	2	1	2	2	1	1	1	2	2	2
16	NOR	1	1	1	1	1	2	2	2	2	2	2	1
17	P	2	2	2	1	2	2	2	2	2	2	2	2
18	ES	2	1	2	1	2	2	1	1	1	2	2	2
19	S	2	2	2	1	2	2	2	2	2	2	2	1
20	CH	2	2	2	1	2	2	2	2	2	2	2	1
21	TUR	1	1	1	1*	1	1	1	1	1	1	1	1
22	UK	1	1	2	1	2	2	1	1	2	2	2	2
23	USA	2	2	2	2	2	2	2	2	2	2	2	2

Note: Insufficient data for Luxembourg available. No NRAs in Japan and New Zealand.

Table 11A.4   Coding scheme for functional profiles

Country number	CR	Countries from 1 to 14
Country name	CN	Names of countries
Fixed-voice licence	FL	M = 1; SR = 2
Mobile-voice licence	ML	M = 1; SR = 2
Oversight licence requirements	OL	M = 1; SR or SR+M = 2
Merger approval	MA	Other = 1; SR or SR+C = 2
Interconnection charges	IC	M = 1; SR or SR+M = 2
Dispute resolution	DR	SR = 2
Spectrum planning	SP	Other = 1; SR or SR+M = 2
Spectrum allocation	SA	Other = 1; SR or SR+M = 2
Numbering planning	NP	Other = 1; SR or SR+M = 2
Numbering allocation	NA	Other = 1; SR = 2
Regulatory body (pricing)	RB	Other = 1; SR or SR+C or SR+C+M = 2
Fixed price regulation	FP	Other = 1; Price cap = 2

Note: M = Ministry; G = Government; P = Parliament; SR = Sector regulator; C = Competition authority; * = value estimated.

APPENDIX C

Table 11A.5   Independence ranking

Country number	Country name	**Joint value independence** ($jv_{CN;Ind.}$)	Joint value organizational profiles ($jv_{cn;O}$)	Joint value functional profiles ($jv_{CN;F}$)
1	USA	**0.876**	0.751	1.000
2	Denmark	**0.866**	0.731	1.000
3	Ireland	**0.852**	0.764	0.939
4	Portugal	**0.824**	0.709	0.939
5	Sweden	**0.807**	0.674	0.939
6	Italy	**0.735**	0.718	0.751
7	Canada	**0.732**	0.707	0.756
8	Denmark	**0.696**	0.634	0.758
9	Australia	**0.681**	0.715	0.647
10	Switzerland	**0.679**	0.633	0.725
11	Mexico	**0.670**	0.592	0.747
12	Austria	**0.664**	0.665	0.663
13	Finland	**0.655**	0.718	0.592
14	Belgium	**0.653**	0.661	0.645
15	Iceland	**0.642**	0.599	0.685
16	France	**0.615**	0.623	0.606
17	Norway	**0.611**	0.581	0.640
18	United Kingdom	**0.611**	0.627	0.594
19	Spain	**0.604**	0.633	0.574
20	Greece	**0.598**	0.731	0.464
21	Netherlands	**0.585**	0.596	0.574
22	Turkey	**0.386**	0.772	0.000
23	South Korea	**0.313**	0.625	0.000

12. Law in the age of governance: regulation, networks and lawyers

Patrick Schmidt[*]

The 'Age of Governance' has meant challenges to the centrality of state power, decreased relevance of formal models of administrative hierarchy, and recognition of interdependence among private and public actors (Haas, 1992; Marks et al., 1996; Strange, 1996; Pierre and Peters, 2000; Black, 2001a; Scott, 2001, Chapter 7 in this volume). At the same time, commentators have expressed a heightened concern for the expansion of US-style, adversarial legalism, which has been taken to mean heightened formality, rule-based relations and judicial management of regulatory interactions (Kagan, 2001; Keleman, 2002). The apparent paradox in the simultaneous decline of state-centred control and the rise of an 'age of legalism' dissolves on closer inspection: whereas it once might have been presumed that the state holds all the legal instruments of regulatory control, we now recognize that private sector regulated entities have numerous legal options available, and with those options firms have the ability to engage regulators at the bargaining table. The interdependence, continuing relationships and strategic interactions of public–private regulatory encounters are all consistent with a situation in which the legal setting of administrative regulation gives bargaining chips to both public and private actors.

These two phenomena – more generally, the politics of public–private regulatory interaction and the legal realm in which regulatory policy-making finds its effect – are difficult to bring into a single conversation. Certainly, a notion of law, usually meaning the 'hard law' of formal decrees and binding rules, has always been the background for the traditional accounts of administration offered by lawyers and even many social scientists. But many and diverse strains of research, into which this chapter itself fits, begin from the proposition that 'law is more marginal … than lawyers might assume' (Scott, 2001, 334). The formal law relied upon by hierarchical models of administration commonly becomes a foil for the emergence of informal norms, private sector self-regulation and non-state influence on regulatory outcomes. Having cast aside the bogeyman of formal law, social scientists have been slow to probe too deeply into the logic of law or to integrate accounts of legal actors into their theories of regulation, due perhaps to the complexity of legal issues or the belief (not discouraged by the legal profession itself) that law is only a 'technical' translation of regulatory policy-making (cf. Hall et al., 2000). For their part, many legal scholars work largely within a discourse that presumes the centrality of law and only occasionally bring empirical research to bear on these questions. Prosaically, the insightful theoretical work which might sit at the Archimedean point of legal and social scientific perspectives on regulation, including that of Teubner (1993) and Black (2000, 2001b) may fail to reach audiences who have more applied ambitions.

This chapter argues for greater attention to the way 'the law' is studied in social science research on regulation, and it advances one account of how legal forces factor into regulatory politics. Specifically, drawing on the case of the United States Occupational Safety and Health Administration (OSHA), I argue that law helps to unify the micro-level behaviour of private interests with the more general theoretical concerns of policy networks by serving as a focal point for political behaviour and a general stable of resources and influences that are often described in studies of administrative politics. The relatively enduring patterns of behaviour described by networks are both enduring and patterned because some force, either active or inertia, links individual interests across discrete political encounters. The understanding of 'law' adopted by those individuals can serve as that unifying presence. The behaviour of public and private actors is not only conditioned by legal considerations but is directed at making 'law' out of interest preferences. As parties understand and act upon their incentives (in part structured by the legal order), their actions in turn shape the future content of the law. A form of reflexivity is present in networks, then, and this reflexivity is demonstrated by OSHA's regulatory policy-making.

As a 'command-and-control' regulator, scholars have often subjected OSHA to scrutiny and used it to illustrate wider issues of regulatory politics (Kelman, 1981; Bardach and Kagan, 1982; Noble, 1986; Mendlehoff, 1988; McGarity and Shapiro, 1993; Scholz and Gray, 1997). As a case study of US administrative politics, the attention is warranted. Established by Congress in 1970, OSHA was the product of an optimistic era when social regulation offered the prospect of reining in the excesses and broad social damages of capitalism (Eisner, 1993). Like environmental and consumer product regulation, its mandate was broad and its powers thoroughgoing. Its two major components, rule-making and enforcement, were separate statutory grants of authority to establish rules centrally and then conduct inspections and sanction violators in the field. OSHA often serves as a useful case for observing legal forces because it is among the most contentious areas of regulatory policy-making, in the country held out as the most legalized regulatory environment.

For that reason, however, OSHA must be justified as relevant to other national and policy settings. A case from US regulatory politics, especially a setting as profoundly rooted in legal conflict as OSHA, represents to some observers from outside the United States a visit to another world that will always be foreign. Yet the pinnacle of legalism that is OSHA should not trigger a false dichotomy between adversarial and cooperative modes of regulation. Rather, at one end of a dimension for the centrality of law, OSHA makes explicit what is latent in other systems where a realm of law (whether hard law or soft law, formal law or informal legal norms) interacts more fluidly with other forms of knowledge and processes. Thus, sharing with other countries concerns for procedure, accountability and values of administrative justice, the American case offers the researcher the opportunity to consider the more general linkages between varieties of law and political forces.

Second, unique as OSHA's context may be, concerns about the juridification and legalization of regulatory policy-making are apparent beyond US shores. None would assume, of course, that the path to be taken in any national or transnational context will follow the US model. Yet as Daniel Keleman (2002) argues, adversarialism is a contagious condition, with traces appearing in the EU, for instance, even if profound differences will remain. Economic and social change can produce demands for accountability or transparency, leading to more formal regulation, even in states with deep-seated impulses toward consensual processes (Milhaupt and Miller, 2000). Further, we must not generalize too quickly about the nature of national regulatory styles. In different policy settings and periods of time any country can exhibit bursts of adversarialism (Kagan, 2000, 229). US regulatory policy in the second half of the twentieth century is a case in point, in that the postwar framework for administrative regulation (set by the Administrative Procedures Act of 1946) called for quasi-legislative 'informal' rule-making as an antidote to adversarial, quasi-judicial proceedings. Even the style of OSHA's policy-making was not set by its authorizing statute, but rather was shaped evolutionarily by the behaviour of actors in the regulatory network. Thus it is relevant to take OSHA apart to observe more clearly the dynamics of law in regulatory politics, knowing that such features may be replicated elsewhere in part or in concept.

The first section that follows takes up the theoretical issues surrounding regulatory politics as networked systems and I consider the role law has played in these accounts. The next three sections offer a closer look at the OSHA policy network in order to consider the significance of law to interactions there. As suggested already, law figures prominently in policy-making through OSHA, and at the micro-level, what 'the law' is – or is perceived to mean – is crucial to how interest representatives (lawyers and non-lawyers alike) engage the agency and one another. In the concluding section, I consider how a more robust conception of law is needed in social science theorizing about regulation. Like Scott's examination of the post-regulatory state, my aim is not to reassert the importance of hierarchical ordering in regulation. At a different level, I argue, the drive for law and law-like order in regulatory processes makes law an important vehicle for understanding micro-level behaviours within more permanent patterns in the sphere of regulation.

THE ROLE OF LAW IN ADMINISTRATIVE NETWORKS

The rise of political science as a discipline in the twentieth century was accompanied and perhaps inspired by a realization that formal law (particularly constitutions) explains a mere portion of applied policy-making in political systems. Between the intentions of the law's creators – whether envisioned legislatively, judicially, or administratively – and the targets of the laws, its meaning changes. No longer monolithic, law is a tool that is created and used by individual actors in a larger process, or more structurally, it is a realm that engages and clashes with other discourses. From its creation by high court judges or low-level bureaucrats, as other social scientists have observed, those involved in the practice of law reinterpret, redefine, recreate and reconstitute the meaning of law in its particulars (McBarnet, 1984; Dezalay, 1994; Conley and O'Barr, 1998). Though the hangover of the traditional focus on the state's legal commands has been felt in the study of regulation, both European and American scholars of policy networks have advanced perspectives on regulation rooted more firmly in institutional dynamics and political behaviour.

The concept of networks has pervaded the study of regulation in the past 20 years as one of a variety of efforts to describe decentred regulation (Black, 2001a). As a catchword, the term resonates with the entangled relationships and labyrinthine processes that, like a sausage-maker, press interests into law. If nothing else, 'the term "network" merely denotes suggestively the fact that policy making involves a large number and wide variety of public and private actors from the different levels and functional areas of government and society' (Hanf, 1978, 12). The enormous variation of terms used to theorize what are, broadly speaking, functional equivalents – among them, 'issue networks' (Heclo, 1978), 'professional networks' (Ham, 1981), 'iron duets' (Yishai, 1992) and 'corporatist policy communities' (Falkner, 1998) – demonstrate the underlying appeal of the concepts that are found in multiple disciplines, including organizational sciences, policy studies, political science and sociology.

In all its variants when applied to regulatory policy-making, the most important implication of describing regulation as a network is that the administrative agency is not the director or producer of the play, but an actor on the same stage, and even then not necessarily the star of the show. An agency of the state, such as OSHA, receives delegated authority and power to exercise over individuals and organizations in the private sector, but it comes with explicit and implicit limits, some of which are in the hands of private actors.

Three consequences flow from and fill out the understanding of regulatory relationships as networks: interdependence, enduring relations and strategic action. Interdependence means, simply, that no single individual, group or organization 'gets its way' repeatedly without enlisting the explicit or tacit support of others. This stricture includes government organizations, which are no more 'central' to understanding public policy than are private interests. Public bodies struggle to balance effective governance with their need to retain legitimacy (de Bruijn and Ringeling, 1997), and so seek cooperation and political support from private actors, particularly to the extent that constituencies (such as regulated entities or the interested public) could otherwise threaten agency authority with appeals to legislatures, courts or other higher authority. Mutual need begets resource exchanges, making cooperation between parties a desirable if not common occurrence (for example Braithwaite, 1985; Shapiro and Rabinowitz, 1997). Interdependence both encourages and takes place against a backdrop of more-or-less enduring relationships between government bodies and private organizations. Relationships, in turn, set the stage for decision-making in networks, particularly in routine affairs. Narrow and complex issues before many regulatory agencies discourage occasional involvement in administrative processes by individuals and generalist interest groups, leaving a limited set of recurring participants. As individual and institutional relationships develop among these parties, they gain advantages of expertise and access, which in turn solidifies the collective advantage of those inside the circle. Finally, interdependence and continuing relations combine to produce a third significant feature of regulatory policy-making: the prominence of strategic interaction. Governments share with private parties the need to devise strategies for networked political environments (Kickert et al., 1997).

Individuals act within formal and informal rules, assess possible courses of action, and use results of those actions to inform future strategies. What is vital is the recognition that regulatory interactions are more than simple consequences of political ambitions, but are also a constitutive part of political structures. 'Winning' means achieving desirable outcomes but also setting the stage for the future. In repeated regulatory encounters, as interactions of a political game, each result affects in some way the calculations of parties who will meet again. Government strategies for 'winning' inspire careful design of political processes and attempt to influence numerous aspects of networks, including membership, terms of exchange, access or coordination (Van Waarden, 1992). In so doing, agencies set the context for strategic decisions made by private parties, whose own repeated participation fosters development and evolution of practices and informal rules (Klijn and Teisman, 1997). Significant evidence already points to the factors influencing how such rules and processes evolve, including the size of a regulatory policy area, disparities of resources between parties, goals of the parties, perceptions and beliefs, and cultural and ideological commitments (Keohane and Ostrom, 1995).

The foci and *raison d'être* of regulatory networks is the creation and articulation of law. Standard-setting by a public body or in concert with private power aims toward the creation of governing rules, and implementation involves negotiation premised on the need to articulate the rules in specific cases (Freeman, 2000). A deficiency of existing empirical research has been the failure to treat 'the law' as much more than a background variable when examining regulation as a political and social phenomenon. Of course, law is a background variable, and it can take on multiple layers of complexity in the struggle to ensure compliance and accountability by private actors (Parker, 2002). The basic steps of the regulatory process, such as setting an agenda, deciding the form and content of public participation, making substantive decisions about outcomes and negotiating policy outcomes, are typically framed as they are because parties attend to a formal statement of the process, whether granted by statute or, as in the United States, elaborated by courts. Administrative politics, especially in the United States, rarely occurs far from the influence of the law and legal concepts, and these guide all stages of the process. Vitally, however, one cannot underplay the degree to which the law is open to debate and creativity. The process of finding and exposing gaps in the law in rule-making involves a level of intentionality usually overlooked. In US administrative politics, the view that administrative policy-making is an act of law-making – governed in the fullest sense by statutes and judges – makes law the medium for interaction and a malleable set of abstractions where political choices are hammered out.

Taking legal interactions seriously, then, adds another dimension to the richness of regulatory politics. Another, related absence – even in the American literature on regulation, with only a few exceptions – is concern for the role of lawyers as intermediaries. Empirical research on regulatory politics and research on lawyers share a common interest in linking the behaviour of public and private actors to wider structures of power in seemingly hierarchical governmental systems. Similar themes are present with any group of actors, such as compliance professionals or corporate officials, since in the age of governance a key question is to understand how the values of the state permeate into those of private parties (Parker, 2002). Yet while other groups look outside the law for their inspiration – as, for example, technical experts might look to their socialization to environmentalism – lawyers sit substantively and symbolically closer to the public sphere. Interplay between the research traditions regarding lawyers and regulatory networks offers advantages for each. For the former, the conceptual framework described in this section may aid the effort to generalize about legal work in a context that lawyers themselves often claim lacks routine and evades generalization. There may be order within public–private interactions concerning regulations, and the interactions of lawyers, clients and government bureaucracies may be a fruitful starting point. In regulatory networks, like political and social networks more generally, there is the need for coordination, strategizing and intermediation (Boissevain, 1974; Knoke, 1990), and lawyers may represent the specialization of those functions in the US context. For the latter research tradition, accounts of lawyers and legal work force social scientists to confront how law and legal norms affect behaviour, and they introduce new variables which otherwise pass unaccounted for. Ultimately, notions of law and legal interpretation can become a focal point for attempts to bridge the gap between the micro-level interactions of interests with the middle-range attempts to understand how the administrative state 'works'.

Some scholars have probed these directions. Perhaps the most sustained body of such research to have considered the role of law concerns international and transnational networks (Riles, 2000; Applebaum et al., 2001; Slaughter, 2001). Transnational affairs are usually only cousins of regulatory policy-making that is the focus here, yet the presence of 'law' in these accounts is striking and ironic because in the transnational realm very often the raw 'stuff' of the law is absent. In the domestic regulatory context, too, we can find developing notions that can integrate levels of analysis, where law and politics reflexively inform each other (Hancher and Moran, 1989; Hall et al., 2000; Scott, Chapter 7 in this volume). I will look more closely at these suggestions below, but first, the next section examines a specific case of regulatory policy-making by OSHA in order to suggest the ways that the US system – though atypical in its specifics – illustrates some of these wider problems.

LAW IN ADMINISTRATIVE NETWORKS: A US CASE

On 6 February 1990, OSHA published a proposed rule reducing the 'permissible exposure limit' (PEL) for cadmium. In its unavoidable technicalities, the rule would reduce the amount of the chemical to which workers could be exposed from 100 micrograms of cadmium per cubic meter (μg/m^3) for cadmium fumes and 200 (μg/m^3) for cadmium dust, to a uniform 1 (μg/m^3) for all cadmium compounds. OSHA did not arrive at a proposal without some provoking by pro-regulation forces. Both the Health Research Group of Public Citizen (the public interest group founded by the famed consumer advocate, Ralph Nader) and the International Chemical Workers' Union (ICWU) had petitioned OSHA for new, tougher standards. Several studies supported the claim that OSHA's then-current standard, adopted in 1971, was insufficient to prevent harm to workers' health. When OSHA denied the petition and the claim that there was a 'grave danger' facing workers, the Health Research Group and ICWU filed suit in the DC Circuit Court of Appeals – by statute, challenges to rule-making automatically proceeding to the tier of appellate courts immediately below the Supreme Court – and shortly thereafter the court began to monitor OSHA's progress towards a revised cadmium standard.

Cadmium metal and compounds are used widely in diverse products such as pigments, plastics and batteries. Because of cadmium's diverse forms and uses, OSHA confronted a complex rule-making problem when attempting to defend a uniform PEL. Scientifically, do cadmium dusts and fumes present similar risks? Can both be feasibly controlled to the same level? Are all industries affected by the rule economically able to comply? To answer these, OSHA contracted a consulting firm to perform a feasibility study. As required by the rule-making process – one premised on open deliberations and reasoned defences of regulatory decisions – OSHA invited letters of comment and participations in policy-making hearings. Throughout these processes, one of the most significant concerns by industry groups and companies was the accuracy of the estimates of cost.

In the public phase of the rule-making process, a number of industry groups voiced concern on behalf of the secondary 'dry colour formulator' industry, which mixes cadmium with other chemicals in small batches to produce colours for use in plastics, ceramics and other products. While primary manufacturers of raw cadmium were easily identified and few in number, one comment letter asserted that the dry colour formulators consisted of 'hundreds of companies and thousands of employees who will be affected by these proposed regulations'.[1] Industry groups asserted that the end-use market for cadmium was mostly very small companies that would not survive as formulators passed compliance costs on to them.

At the hearings, manufacturers of cadmium described a portfolio of companies that had purchased cadmium, but they mentioned no company names. Because OSHA had no 'average' formulator to use as a case study of feasibility, the record remained unclear as to the composition of the formulator 'industry'. For purposes of OSHA's analysis, the consultant's study lumped the dry colour formulators with all other industries that mix chemicals. The study assumed that all workers in industries which mix chemicals had similar exposure to airborne cadmium. Based on the study of other workplaces, OSHA then claimed that cost-efficient procedures and controls could be used by dry colour formulators to comply with the PEL. Although recognizing the weakness of the assumption, a Labor Department official confided, OSHA 'fudged it' and went forward with the final rule (confidential interview). There was little choice. Responding to an appeal by the Health Research Group and the ICWU, the DC court of appeals had ordered that the rule be completed by 31 August 1992.

The Color Pigments Manufacturers' Association,[2] represented by a New Jersey law firm, filed suit in federal court and were joined by the Cadmium Council, another industry group. With the OSHA statute and past decisions as their guide, the litigants contested, first, whether 'substantial evidence' supported a regulation for cadmium pigments (separate from other cadmium compounds), and second, whether the rule was technologically and economically 'feasible' for the dry colour formulator industry. In addition, five companies and two trade associations from other industries each filed suit in a total of four federal judicial circuits on other issues. All suits were consolidated to one court, the Eleventh Circuit.[3] Importantly, these seven other suits reached settlements with OSHA in mid-1993.

In March 1994, a three-judge panel ruled in the last suit that OSHA had acted on a rational basis and with substantial evidence when it included cadmium pigments in the PEL. The Eleventh Circuit judges noted their doubt and found an equally rational alternative in the record, but deferred to the agency's conclusion. The panel was not so charitable on other issues, however, firmly criticizing the agency for 'its failure to study any particular dry color formulators whatsoever' when determining the technical and economic feasibility of the rule as applied to this industry.[4] Because OSHA's findings were based on 'faulty assumptions' and 'flawed methodology', the court reversed the rule as applied to the industry and remanded the matter to OSHA for a specific enquiry about dry colour formulators. To date, OSHA has not responded to this remand order. In 1999, agency officials conceded that '[w]hile this remand issue remains a concern to OSHA, our resources have been applied to other priority activities'.[5]

Though hardly a health regulation of widespread concern, the cadmium case illustrates the problems and pathologies of regulatory law and politics under US conditions. First, while critical attention invariably tends to court judgments, apart from the suit by the Color Pigment Manufacturers' Association, OSHA reached settlements with industry petitioners, allowing all parties to avoid the time, resources and uncertainties of judicial resolutions. Indeed, the risk of full-blown litigation in most of the suits had never been a significant concern for some OSHA officials, since some of the parties filing suit quickly approached the agency to discuss settlement, hoping to find results 'they could live with'. As has been demonstrated in litigation against the EPA (Environmental Protection Agency), lawsuits challenging agency rules are frequently invitations to continued bargaining rather than signs of a breakdown in normal working relationships (Coglianese, 1996). This finding contradicts a long line of research which has viewed litigation as a strategy of last resort for parties with continuing relationships (Macaulay, 1963; Galanter, 1974; Stewart, 1985). Though the cadmium industry was not a 'repeat player' as fully as more notable union and industry groups have become, it did have the advice of a handful of Washington lawyers who had sustained experience working within the regulatory framework. Lawyers have developed the advantages of repeat players in administrative politics, such as experience, informational advantages and the ability to exploit legal strategies as a form of 'politics by other means'.

Second, regulatory policy-makers are dependent on information, but judicial oversight held OSHA to standards beyond the agency's reach. OSHA was unaware of the potential significance of the dry colour formulators as an industry subsector when the rule was in the early stages of development. The subsector received only slight mention in a few comment letters, and agency insiders felt that the trade associations 'had not been particularly forthcoming' with information about the industry. Indeed, the industry's contention that 'thousands of workers' would be affected was virtually unsubstantiated. As if to remind us of a meaningful public–private divide, the court required the agency, but not the industry, to be 'transparent'. In the US case, courts imposed the standards, but the more general problem is that 'proceduralizing' regulation (Black 2000, 2001b) changes the balance of power in the network by giving private actors resource advantages over public actors. Whether legislatures or more diffuse mechanisms of regulatory accountability similarly affect network dynamics remains a question for future research.

A hallmark of legalism is a commitment to proceduralism. In this rule-making, as in others (Schmidt, 2002), the process determined the possibilities for the agency, and here the possibilities were sharply constrained, with suits by private parties being the proverbial rock and hard place. On the one hand, OSHA was forced by the union's suit to promulgate a revised standard, putting into motion a 'notice and comment' procedure that would fulfil the statutory mandate. On the other, industry interests forced OSHA to develop as far as possible particular angles and justifications for the proposed rule, and when the agency could not, took it to task for its failure. OSHA's choice of a lesser evil was to consign one portion of the rule to a regulatory black hole.

ORGANIZING NETWORK PRACTICES: LEGAL STRUCTURE AND REGULATORY BEHAVIOUR

As a case study, the cadmium rule-making might leave one with the impression that litigation, while significant in the life of individual private actors, does not test the boundaries of regulatory interactions: the agency, while challenged on some points, was able to settle most of the suits on narrow terms or, at worst, suffer an industry-specific gap in coverage. In this way, law is sometimes conceived of as a fixed boundary that either establishes a process for regulatory encounters or places substantive limits on the state (sometimes enforceable by courts). This section considers the extent to which legal structures influence administrative behaviour. Again the approach is to delve into the level of micro-level behaviour, here the product of extensive elite interviews with interest group representatives, private lawyers and OSHA officials. At this level of enquiry, legal structures generate patterns of behaviour that have shaped the evolution of the regulatory system.

Although new cases present opportunities for judicial discretion, and although some issues of OSHA law remain contested, there is a consensus that key decisions have left much of OSHA law 'settled'. Landmark decisions from the US Supreme Court settled important questions of constitutional law and statutory interpretation, including how to interpret the inherent vagueness of the OSH Act, such as the meaning of 'significant risk', 'feasibility', and the role of cost–benefit analysis. Within these frameworks, courts do not adjust standards based on their own understanding of the scientific and economic evidence, but rather must determine whether, based on the record, OSHA acted reasonably in its decision. Judicial oversight of rule-making still invests considerable discretion in each case. How might a judge assess whether an agency has presented 'substantial evidence', taken to mean what evidence a 'reasonable mind might accept as adequate'? With the dim light of the law as its guide, the cadmium court faced a question saturated with substance: was the dry colour formulator industry so different from other chemical mixers and large users of cadmium pigments that OSHA's modelling was inappropriate? A question such as this requires that courts assess whether OSHA disregarded important evidence, mishandled the evidence it relied on or lacked evidence to justify its assumption.

The logic of the law does more than guide courts. The possibility of litigation casts a shadow over the 'informal' administrative process. Any interest group in the network with sufficient means and awareness can anticipate the possibility of judicial review and participate in rule-making accordingly. Lawyers acting for interest groups, companies and unions – but even experienced, non-lawyer representatives of interest groups acting alone – react to the possibility of subsequent litigation by attempting to answer the courts' questions before they are asked. That is, knowing from the established legal framework the questions a court might ask on review, parties have every incentive to place evidence and arguments on the record that will answer those questions. In the words of one Washington lawyer, the goal is to 'patrol the record':

> [Y]our task is not only making your client's affirmative case, demonstrating what their interests are, but ... trying to build an evidentiary fence around the record so that it leaves the government with very few options. ... [T]he task is to patrol the record by challenging submissions by the government and by others which seem to be at odds with your clients' interests, trying not only in terms of developing pre- and post-hearing comments to respond, but at the hearing trying to engage people in examination for the purpose of trying to discredit what they are saying. (Confidential interview)

That is, elite participants view a reviewing court as a check on OSHA that can be triggered or suppressed through the strategic development of the administrative process. In addition to stating their preferred version of the regulatory standard, private parties want OSHA to be concerned about how a court may look at the rule-making record. Yet the likelihood of success on appeal may not be strong, so it is not as simple as trying to create a winning case for the court. The more modest goal is to produce legal risk for the agency, such that OSHA either takes a cautious approach in its rule or must consider settlement in post-rule-making litigation. Courts hold discretionary authority, albeit limited, and judges may be more favourably disposed to the claims of clients.

Patrolling the record is both a substantive and a procedural activity, lodged between a legislative and an adjudicatory process. The courts seek to 'ensure that the regulations resulted from a process of reasoned decisionmaking'.[6] Procedurally, for example, courts in the 1970s twice set aside portions of standards when the notice of proposed rule-making did not advise the public of all issues under consideration.[7] But as OSHA gained experience, such objections became less frequent, and so participants developed more sophisticated ways of casting OSHA's decision-making into doubt. The task becomes more complex when conflicting interest groups – in OSHA issues, typically industry against labour unions – attempt to undercut the others' position while also either attacking or defending OSHA's position. The strategic options are complex and situational.

The outcomes are no less varied. Reviewing courts tend either to uphold an agency's action or remand a portion of the rule to the agency for further explanation and justification, as happened in the cadmium rule-making. The agency may make minor but consequential changes to the rule or alter its interpretation in the field so as to finesse the issue. From industry's perspective, even with no change in the rule, litigation may simply gain enough time to prepare for the costs of compliance and to adjust operations. Perhaps most important, as legal concerns have become engrained within the network, agency decisions have confirmed that the anticipated responses of agencies can amplify the effect of external forces (McGarity, 1993; Gilboy, 1995). OSHA may attempt to defend a rule by answering industry criticisms in great detail, but it also may capitulate by shaping a rule to a party's interest, even when agency decision-makers are not persuaded as a matter of substance. The desire to avoid litigation generates the goal of establishing a credible threat to the agency, made possible by acquiring skill in both rule-making and litigation. As one interviewee, an attorney for industry groups, stated:

> Our approach is to focus on making sure that the information in the record is sufficient that you cannot legally make a decision which goes against us, and if you do, we're going to have a very easy time of it because it's going to be clear to that appellate judge under the terms of the statute. (Confidential interview)

This interviewee concluded somewhat boastfully: 'I think at this point we have built a reputation with the agency that they ignore our comments at their peril.' Reputation may have such an effect, though ultimate success depends on a multitude of factors outside the immediate control of the agency and private parties alike, including the political ideology and deference of appellate court judges and, of course, the economic and scientific facts supporting a regulation.

The threat that skilled, repeat participants in rule-making may have on the agency is amplified further by the government lawyers who typically join OSHA's specialist staff on rule-making teams and help translate the reasons for administrative decisions into the most legally defensible terms. Translation is not value-free, however. The lawyers' professional independence, made worse by their organizational independence from OSHA, gives them a particularly significant role in advising the government about the shape of new rules and testing the agency's conclusions against the rule-making record. Sometimes this role is performed without incident, but at other times the probing exposes deficiencies in the record that prevent the staff from doing what they regard as 'the right thing to do'. Compounded by lack of control over the solicitors in the Department of Labor, OSHA's collective frustration at its lawyers is not irrational. The Solicitor's Office has been described as a bottleneck on the standard-setting process (McGarity and Shapiro, 1993). When a suit has been filed, OSHA's lawyers assume even greater influence. The possibility of losing a standard in litigation creates a strong incentive to settle, but settlement means compromise, and OSHA staff members are known to allege that attorneys will accept significant revisions to a rule in order to avoid litigation. On the other hand, lawyers are better positioned to appreciate the risks of litigation. The shape of the legal order surrounding OSHA has meant, then, that policy-making proceeds on terms that are partly policy-driven and partly court-driven, and that latter element is infused within the agency's internal organization. Like the shared understandings of elite private actors in the rule-making process, public actors organize and evolve structures that support instrumental goals.

INTEREST REPRESENTATION IN REGULATORY POLITICS

The previous section emphasized how litigation has created practices that pulsate at the heart of OSHA's administrative process. The incentives set in formal law and propelled by US courts reverberate through the network, with public and private actors adding advantages of resources, reputation or creativity to advance their interests. In the OSHA network, the legal influences are the 'hard law' of a statute and case law, and so the emphasis has been on lawyers. But the identities of these individuals as lawyers are not essential to the story. Most of the lawsuits in the cadmium rule-making led to public–private negotiation and settlement, and settlement across the public–private divide represents the more universal clash of interests across a negotiating table. What is essential is that interest representatives are commonly missing from mezo-level accounts of the regulatory process. This gap leaves an opportunity cost: the opportunity to see how individuals with continuing involvement in a network are shaped by network forces yet also transform it through their individual actions. We can find in interest representatives, then, a link between the law – whether that be formal or, as Colin Scott suggests, more informal – and the clients and sometimes infrequent participants who collectively make up the supposed network. This section pauses briefly to consider more generally the place of interest representatives in accounts of regulatory politics.

Political networks are known to nourish multiple types of intermediaries, such as coordinators, gatekeepers and liaisons who fill the brokering function basic to all social and political communities (Knoke, 1990, 144–5). Among the most provocative research is that looking at intermediaries in networks, which has provided a window into the communities surrounding American trial courts, systems that typically involve a relatively narrow set of recurring participants within an ordered legal structure (Blumberg, 1967; Flemming et al., 1992). There, the highly patterned and formal interactions give rise to a need for efficient solutions among interdependent network participants. Administrative bureaucracies present a higher order of complexity. Regulatory agencies are rarely single court organizations, but rather composite systems with distinct tasks. In occupational safety and health, for example, both administrative rule-making and enforcement have complicated internal structures, substantive intricacies and interwoven power structures. Dozens and sometimes hundreds of interested parties participate in agency rule-making efforts and bargain in the shadow of the law. Companies must overcome a knowledge deficit about regulations and substantive expertise affects the fortunes of parties in litigation. Further, the 'court systems' for many agencies spread nationwide and embrace peculiar combinations of regular and infrequent litigants. The tangled web of pressures in regulatory settings ensures that intermediaries have roles to play. Those roles, as suggested by the case reported here, span a wide range (see Table 12.1).

Table 12.1   Roles of lawyers as interest representatives

Role	Description
Advocate	Traditional advocacy in formal settings, through either written or oral communication
Shepherd	Guide through administrative processes
Educator	Informs client of norms in regulatory interactions, promotes compliance, cooperation or resistance to norms
Diplomat	Go-between or representative in negotiations
Power-broker	Strategist, with ability to leverage client's resources and advantages within network

While private firms and agency decision-makers both call on lawyers to serve as advocates when disputes reach judicial fora, lawyers orient their clients to the process and shape expectations, become the face of interest groups, use accumulated reputation on behalf of clients who are not repeat players and transform disputes with learned negotiation skills. Patrolling the record exemplifies another role offered by repeat-playing intermediaries – the opportunity to broker administrative policy-making by leveraging strategic position. Knowledgeable of the legal setting for rule-making, attorneys amplify pressures and checks within the system that must be activated to be effective.

Scholars have made very few attempts to examine forms of interest representation in regulatory networks. In the most noteworthy exception in the US context, a multidisciplinary group analysed the structure of representation in Washington across multiple policy domains (Heinz et al., 1993). After tracing interactions of both lawyer and non-lawyer representatives, they concluded that US regulatory networks have 'hollow cores' without central brokers able to exchange information, form coalitions and direct the development of policy. Instead, they found, interest groups and representatives maintain relatively close relationships with others sharing their own interests and ideology. Further, lawyers appeared infrequently among the most 'notable' representatives in each policy area and concentrated in specialized settings requiring either particular credentials (such as appearing in court) or knowledge of substantive regulations and processes. This massive project countered many misconceptions about interest representation, for contrary to myth, attorneys were found to hold no monopoly over policy-making and are limited to episodic demands for specialized expertise.

In their enquiry, Heinz et al. were looking explicitly for a particular type of lawyer–lobbyist, one who shapes policy-making across multiple policy domains. Looking with more focus to specific regulatory subsectors, such as health and safety within labour law, all agree that lawyers can be found in large numbers in US regulation. But what might we say lawyers *do*? Heinz et al. invited such an enquiry when they commented that their approach left unexamined the 'qualitative significance' of lawyers' work in regulatory areas (Nelson and Heinz, 1988). As suggested by the cadmium case, particular network dynamics flow from the complex substantive issues, specific legal standards and evolving behaviour of interest representatives.

In this context, at levels below those where the attorneys have been described systematically, lay support for the notion that the production of law and law-like norms represents a key goal of interest representatives in regulatory networks. Given the absence of brokers at the core of regulatory networks, Heinz et al. characterize administration within policy domains as pervasively and unyieldingly uncertain. Individual organizations and representatives lack control over the direction of policy, perhaps inevitably, attempts to produce norms in networks stem from the competition of interests in repeated play. The interdependencies, continuing relationships and strategic manoeuvring at the heart of networks includes issues that arrive at the individual level of personalities and relationships, as well as the situation at hand. Further, environmental factors come into play.

We can understand administrative settings only by accounting for the remarkable array of influences on regulators, regulated entities and intermediaries. The roles that lawyers may play, the capacity of law to affect private sector behaviour, the relative control exercised on one another by public and private forces, and the types of strategies designed to execute the political warfare of regulation are shaped by a wide palate of conditions and uncertainties. Table 12.2 brings together a range of influences that affect the

Table 12.2   Partial typology of influences in OSHA regulatory network

	Individual	Situational	Environmental
Client	• Repeat player • Ideological commitments	• Facts of case or situation • Economic cost benefits	• Competitive pressures • Norms and social expectations in client's industry
Attorney	• Specialization • Socialization, e.g., legal education, government experience	• Reputation with government officials • Strength of relationships with government and client	• Economic pressures • Professional liability and ethical codes
Government	• Professional orientation • Organization of decision-making within agency • Capacity for discretion	• Political controls from legislative or executive branches • Level of judicial oversight	• Resource limitations • Institutional culture • Diffuse effect of political controls
Common	• Personality	• Prior law (statutory, formal and informal precedents)	• Shared cost of breakdown in relationships

balance of powers in individual interactions. The politics of regulation may be slave to the individual personalities at work, or any of a host of other individual factors. Situational factors produce many of the case-by-case variations, while environmental factors frame and constrain interactions. These factors come into play selectively. All parties possess resources and liabilities that establish strategic positions. But the case-by-case influences on behaviour give way with repeated interactions to more enduring elements – the reputations that individuals may seek to maintain, or the law that is created and revised interstitially. Thus lawyers make use of the law as background but also articulate possible resolutions of individual disputes that would set precedents, standards, informal or formal law.

REFLEXIVITY AND REPRESENTATION IN REGULATORY THEORY

From many readings of how regulation and regulatory networks work in the twenty-first century, it might be wondered whether the state has been made to disappear. By some accounts, we approach a near total absence of hierarchy. Yet looking at the closest level of behaviour, the level of the individual, this should not be taken to mean that law has disappeared. Within any system established by statute or some variety of formal law, constraints will be felt at some pressure point (Parker, 2002). OSHA's case remains highly formal, but more generally administrative systems involve an attempt to produce norms autonomously (Galligan, 2001). A widened definition of law, including soft law and informal norms, captures the way that micro-level regulatory interactions still find order through the continuing interactions and interdependences of the network. Like the reassembled shards of a shattered stained-glass window, it may be difficult to find order in it, but it may still impress. This place for law is constructive and constructed rather than simple background. As observed in the case of the cadmium rule-making, the law and legal interactions shape the development of practices and organizational habits. Building on that example, numerous other theoretical formulations might be brought together into this window into regulation: law structures and engenders attitudes; law embodies cultural and technological assumptions under girding decision-making; law creates perceptions by actors about who possesses legitimate authority, thus helping to structure informal relationships; and further, the absence of formal law in some contexts – particularly the global economic sphere – can create space for the emergence of other forms of negotiations.

These possibilities might be thought to be in tension. On the one hand, law is the example *par excellence* of parties creating norms and law through social interaction, whether that be formally through legal encounters or, less formally, through the law of commercial transactions and informal law. On the other hand, law is commonly used in studies of regulatory politics as the background 'stuff' that positions actors in power relationships at 'time one' and provides the tools with which parties then carry on recurring engagements. Reflexivity between these two conceptions may be the most natural result. In the vagueness left in legislative acts (here I speak particularly of common law systems), regulation moves interstitially to fill in the gaps, and the 'law' is the product of regulatory interactions. Even within specific policy sectors, what we know as 'law' changes as a result of continuing relationships – the transformation of OSHA rulemaking being a case in point. The goal of interactions very often can be the creation of law itself as parties attempt to embed existing relationships in a more permanent structure. Thus the concept of law can operate as an intermediary concept between the micro-level of interactions that appear chaotic in our 'post-regulatory' world, because the need and the drive for order produces a range of formal and informal devices that are constructed and operate as forms of law. A more vigorous conception of law as a mezo-level organizing principle helps to bring together the disorder of individual regulatory interactions with the continuing patterns observed in the network phenomenon.

This account of law finds indirect support in recent work by other contributors to this volume. Colin Scott and Christopher Hood's use of the regulatory space concept (Hall et al., 2000; Scott, 2001) brings together the politics of individuals, organizations and culture in the development of regulatory policy. 'Regulatory space' builds on and shares features in common with 'networks' as received from the political science tradition, particularly the interdependence and informal linkages among parties. While the notion of regulatory space has been criticized for not offering a sophisticated role for law in policy interactions and, in a related criticism, being of little guidance to legal practitioners (Daintith, 1989; Black, 1997; but cf. Hancher 1990), its reappearance in recent work pushes toward reflexivity among the transitory and the permanent, the micro-level chaos and the higher-level concepts of law, politics and culture. Thus, in work by Scott and Hood, professional cultures and turnover within the UK's telecommunications regulator help to explain patterns of decision-making within the agency and the institutional conflicts that arise in regulatory space. By exposing the roots and consequences of intragovernmental and public/private competition, the approach makes more accessible the feedback loops between individual behaviour and the legal/policy environment.

Developing more robust linkages between 'networks' and legal processes will be an extensive project. Some theoretical commentary has already suggested the broad brush of such melding in socio-legal and institutional analysis (Scott, 2001; Black, 2000, 2001b), although this vein of thought has so far received expression only at an abstract level of theory. Scholarship has increasingly recognized that legal institutions constrain individual decision-making, while the politics that individuals create help to shape the legal environment. Variations on the network concept or on images of the 'law' employed by social scientists may prove too shallow to be anything other than a conceptual label, but if brought together, there is an opportunity to give meaning to the individual interactions that surround the post-regulatory state. The US example of OSHA illustrates the influence of formal law on regulatory politics, but a wider lesson may be to recognize that regulatory networks have constructed order where hierarchy is no longer thought to operate.

NOTES

* I would like to thank the editors, Colin Scott, Simon Halliday and Bronwen Morgan for their comments on this chapter.
1. Exhibit 19-40, letter from the Dry Color Manufacturers' Association to the Docket Officer, dated 11 May 1990, Docket No. H-057a, OSHA Docket Office, Washington, DC.
2. Formerly known as the Dry Color Manufacturers' Association.
3. The petitioners in five of these suits were represented by the same Washington, DC law firm that represented the Cadmium Council.
4. *Color Pigments Manufacturers' Association, Inc.* v. *OSHA*, 16 F. 3d 1157 (1994).
5. Richard E. Fairfax (Director of Compliance Programs, OSHA), Standard Interpretations, 'The PEL for cadmium at dry color formulator operations', 15 October 1999, available at www.osha.gov.
6. *AFL-CIO* v. *Marshall*, 617 F. 2d 415 (1979) at 649.
7. *Synthetic Organic Chemical Manufacturers' Association* v. *OSHA*, 503 F. 2d 1155 (3rd Cir. 1974); *American Iron & Steel Institute* v. *OSHA* 577 F. 2d 825 (3rd Cir. 1978).

REFERENCES

Applebaum, Richard P., William L.F. Felstiner and Volkmar Gessner (eds) (2001), *Rules and Networks: The Legal Culture of Global Business Transactions*, Oxford and Portland, OR: Hart Publishing.

Bardach, Eugene and Robert A. Kagan (1982), *Going By The Book: The Problem of Regulatory Unreasonableness*, Philadelphia: Temple University Press.

Black, Julia (1997), 'New Institutionalism and Naturalism in Socio-Legal Analysis: Institutionalist Approaches to Regulatory Decision Making', *Law and Policy*, **19**, 51–93.

Black, Julia (2000), 'Proceduralizing Regulation: Part I', *Oxford Journal of Legal Studies*, **20**, 597–614.

Black, Julia (2001a), 'Decentring Regulation: Understanding the Role of Regulation and Self-Regulation in a "Post-Regulatory" World', *Current Legal Problems*, **54**, 103–46.

Black, Julia (2001b), 'Proceduralizing Regulation: Part II', *Oxford Journal of Legal Studies*, **21**, 33–58.

Blumberg, Abraham (1967), 'The Practice of Law as Confidence Game: Organizational Cooptation of a Profession', *Law and Society Review*, **1**, 15–39.

Boissevain, Jeremy (1974), *Friends of Friends: Networks, Manipulators and Coalitions*, Oxford: Basil Blackwell.

Braithwaite, John (1985), *To Punish or Persuade: Enforcement of Coal Mine Safety*, Albany: State University of New York Press.

Coglianese, Cary (1996), 'Litigating Within Relationships: Disputes and Disturbance in the Regulatory Process', *Law and Society Review*, **30**, 735–65.

Conley, John M. and William M. O'Barr (1998), *Just Words: Law, Language, and Power*, Chicago: University of Chicago Press.

Daintith, Terence C. (1989), 'A Regulatory Space Agency?', *Oxford Journal of Legal Studies*, **9**, 534–56.

de Bruijn, Johan A. and Arthur B. Ringeling (1997), 'Normative Notes: Perspectives on Networks', in Walter J.M. Kickert, Erik-Hans Klijn and Joop F.M. Koppenjan, *Managing Complex Networks: Strategies for the Public Sector*, London: Sage, pp. 152–64.

de Bruijn, Johan A. and Ernst F. ten Heuvelhof (1995), 'Policy Networks and Governance', in David L. Weimer (ed.), *Institutional Design*, Boston: Kluwer Academic Publishers, pp. 161–79.

Dezalay, Yves (1994), 'The Forum Should Fit the Fuss: The Economics and Politics of Negotiated Justice', in Maureen Cain and Christine B. Harrington (eds), *Lawyers in a Postmodern World: Translation and Transgression*, New York: New York University Press, pp. 155–82.

Eisner, Marc Allen (1993), *Regulatory Politics in Transition*, Baltimore: Johns Hopkins University Press.

Falkner, Gerda (1998), *EU Social Policy in the 1990s: Towards a Corporatist Policy Community*, London: Routledge.

Flemming, Roy B., Peter F. Nardulli and James Eisenstein (1992), *The Craft of Justice: Politics and Work in Criminal Court Communities*, Philadelphia: University of Pennsylvania Press.

Freeman, Jody (2000), 'The Private Role in Public Governance', *New York University Law Review*, **75**, 543–675.

Galanter, Marc (1974), 'Why the "Haves" Come Out Ahead: Speculations on the Limits of Legal Change', *Law and Society Review*, **9**, 95–154.

Galligan, Denis (2001), 'Authoritarianism in Government and Administration: The Promise of Administrative Justice', *Current Legal Problems*, **54**, 79–102.

Gilboy, Janet A. (1995), 'Regulatory and Administrative Agency Behavior: Accommodation, Amplification, and Assimilation', *Law and Policy*, **17**, 3–22.

Haas, Peter (1992), 'Introduction: Epistemic Communities and International Policy Coordination', *International Organization*, **46**, 1–35.

Hall, Clare, Colin Scott and Christopher Hood (2000), *Telecommunications Regulation: Culture, Chaos and Interdependence Inside the Regulatory Process*, London: Routledge.

Ham, Christopher (1981), *Policy-making in the National Health Service: A Case Study of the Leeds Regional Hospital Board*, London: Macmillan Press.

Hancher, Leigh (1990), *Regulating for Competition: Government, Law, and the Pharmaceutical Industry in the United Kingdom and France*, Oxford: Clarendon Press.

Hancher, Leigh and Michael Moran (eds) (1989), *Capitalism, Culture, and Regulation*, Oxford: Clarendon Press.

Hanf, Kenneth (1978), 'Introduction', in Hanf and Fritz W. Scharpf (eds), *Interorganizational Policy Making: Limits to Coordination and Central Control*, London: Sage, pp. 1–15.

Heclo, Hugh (1978), 'Issue Networks and the Executive Establishment', in Anthony King (ed.), *The New American Political System*, Washington DC: American Enterprise Institute, pp. 87–124.

Heinz, John P., Robert L. Nelson, Edward O. Laumann and Robert H. Salisbury (1993), *The Hollow Core: Private Interests in National Policy Making*, Cambridge, MA: Harvard University Press.

Kagan, Robert A. (2000), 'Introduction: Comparing National Styles of Regulation in Japan and the United States', *Law and Policy*, **22**, 225–44.

Keleman, Daniel (2002), 'Regulatory Styles: The Diffusion of Adversarial Legalism?', paper presented to the workshop on 'Theories of Regulation', Barcelona, Spain, 29–30 November.

Kelman, Steven (1981), *Regulating America, Regulating Sweden: A Comparative Study of Occupational Safety and Health Policy*, Cambridge, MA: MIT Press.

Keohane, Robert O. and Elinor Ostrom (eds) (1995), *Local Commons and Global Independence: Heterogeneity and Cooperation in Two Domains*, London: Sage.

Kickert, Walter J.M., Erik-Hans Klijn and Joop F.M. Koppenjan (eds) (1997), *Managing Complex Networks: Strategies for the Public Sector*, London: Sage.

Klijn, Erik-Hans (1996), 'Analyzing and Managing Policy Processes in Complex Networks: A Theoretical Examination of the Concept Policy Network and Its Problems', *Administration & Society*, **28**, 90–119.

Klijn, Erik-Hans and G.R. Teisman (1997), 'Strategies and Games in Networks', in Walter J.M. Kickert, Erik-Hans Klijn and Joop F.M. Koppenjan (eds), *Managing Complex Networks: Strategies for the Public Sector*, London: Sage, pp. 98–118.

Knoke, David (1990), *Political Networks: The Structural Perspective*, New York: Cambridge University Press.

Macaulay, Stewart (1963), 'Non-Contractual Relations in Business: A Preliminary Study', *American Sociological Review*, **28**, 55–69.

Marks, Gary, Fritz W. Scharpf, Philippe C. Schmitter and Wolfgang Streeck (1996), *Governance in the European Union*, London: Sage.

McBarnet, Doreen (1984), 'Law and Capital: The Role of Legal Form and Legal Actors', *International Journal of the Sociology of Law*, **12**, 231–8.

McGarity, Thomas O. (1993), 'Some Thoughts on "Deossifying" the Rulemaking Process', *Duke Law Journal*, **41**, 1385–462 .

McGarity, Thomas O. and Sidney A. Shapiro (1993), *Workers At Risk: The Failed Promise of the Occupational Safety and Health Administration*, Westport, CT: Praeger Press.

Mendlehoff, John M. (1988), *The Dilemma of Toxic Substance Regulation: How Overregulation Causes Underregulation at OSHA*, Cambridge, MA: MIT Press.

Milhaupt, Curtis J. and Geoffrey P. Miller (2000), 'Regulatory Failure and the Collapse of Japan's Home Mortgage Lending Industry: A Legal and Economic Analysis', *Law and Policy*, **22**, 245–90.

Nelson, Robert L. and John P. Heinz, with Edward O. Laumann and Robert H. Salisbury (1988), 'Lawyers and the Structure of Influence in Washington', *Law and Society Review*, **22**, 237–300.

Noble, Charles (1986), *Liberalism at Work: The Rise and Fall of OSHA*, Philadelphia: Temple University Press.

Parker, Christine (2002), *The Open Corporation: Effective Self-regulation and Democracy*, Cambridge, UK: Cambridge University Press.

Pierre, Jon and B. Guy Peters (2000), *Governance, Politics and the State*, Basingstoke, UK: Palgrave Macmillan.

Riles, Annelise (2000), *The Network Inside Out*, Ann Arbor: University of Michigan Press.

Schmidt, Patrick (2002), 'Pursuing Regulatory Relief: Strategic Participation and Litigation in U.S. OSHA Rulemaking', *Business and Politics*, **4**, 71–89.

Scholz, John T. and Wayne B. Gray (1997), 'Can Government Facilitate Cooperation? An Informational Model of OSHA Enforcement', *American Journal of Political Science*, **41**, 693–717.

Scott, Colin (2001), 'Analysing Regulatory Space: Fragmented Resources and Institutional Design', *Public Law*, Summer, 329–53.

Shapiro, Sidney A. and Randy S. Rabinowitz (1997), 'Punishment Versus Cooperation in Regulatory Enforcement', *Administrative Law Review*, **49**, 703–37.

Slaughter, Anne-Marie (2001), 'Globalization, Accountability, and the Future of Administrative Law: The Accountability of Government Networks', *Indiana Journal of Global Legal Studies*, **8**, 347–67.

Stewart, Richard B. (1985), 'The Discontents of Legalism: Interest Group Relations in Administrative Regulation', *Wisconsin Law Review*, 655–86.

Strange, Susan (1996), *The Retreat of the State: The Diffusion of Power in the World Economy*, Cambridge, UK: Cambridge University Press.

Teubner, Gunther (1993), *Law as an Autopoietic System*, Oxford: Blackwell.

Van Waarden, Frans (1992), 'Dimensions and Types of Policy Networks', *European Journal of Political Research*, **21**, 29–52.

Yishai, Yael (1992), 'From an Iron Triangle to an Iron Duet?: Health Policy Making in Israel', *European Journal of Political Research*, **21**, 91–108.

13. Regulatory designs, institutional constellations and the study of the regulatory state

Jacint Jordana and David Sancho[1]

Over recent decades, many countries have actively promoted significant regulatory reforms in the governance of their economies. Privatization and market liberalization, combined with public initiatives aimed at regulating markets, have taken on a greater prominence in policy-making and institutional developments. The rise of the regulatory state has involved the creation of new institutions across countries and sectors. One of the most visible manifestations of these innovations has been the emergence of a European policy arena which is characterized by an extensive use of regulation (Majone, 1996) and of a massive diffusion of the autonomous regulatory agency as a new institutional model for public management both in Europe (Gilardi, 2002) and internationally (Levi-Faur, 2002).

These administrative innovations have attracted the attention of many scholars, from various disciplines and areas of interest, who analyse the changing nature of state (for a review see Moran, 2002). They have tended to focus on issues such as the advantages of autonomous agencies, the actual 'independence' attained, the effectiveness of the decisions made by the agency, and issues of transparency and accountability.[2] Much less attention has been devoted to these agencies' effects on the decision-making processes relevant for policy outcomes. The new regulatory institutions are embedded in institutional settings that were created in previous periods and for different kinds of public action. As a result, the accumulation of different institutions with the capacity to intervene has apparently made more complicated decision-making in regulatory policy than in most traditional interventionist policies. This resulting institutional setting combines comprehensive and specialized public bodies charged with various public mandates, also with different and often contradictory goals. Thus, autonomous regulatory agencies represent only one segment of the entire institutional arena in which regulatory policy is made and implemented.

While most scholarly attention has been focused on the new regulatory institutions as a major factor in shaping regulatory outcomes, this chapter suggests that it is the whole institutional arena, not just the new agencies, which makes the difference in policy processes and policy outcomes. We aim to address this lacuna in the study of the effects of regulatory design by identifying some distinctions between different institutional configurations in the regulatory arena. In this we share some perspectives, such as those of advocacy coalition theory (Sabatier and Jenkins-Smith, 1994), that recognize the existence of fragmentation in policy domains, but usually do not also integrate institutional configurations into their models, or the literature on policy communities and policy networks, although it has paid little attention to the implications of institutional structures for the analysis of the actors involved in the polity (Klijn, 2001). On the contrary, we will focus our attention on institutions, rather than actors, considering that particular configurations could emerge in different policy areas. The concept of institutional constellations is developed here to characterize these configurations, in which we also intend to recognize certain cultural components. In addition, we put forward some observations about the effects of the new regulatory settings on political conflicts generated by regulatory issues. In North American research on the conflict between regulatory agencies and legislative and executive principals, a large number of sophisticated analyses have been conducted about the actual level of autonomy that agencies enjoy. Research has also focused on the effectiveness of control mechanisms established by the Congress (for a review, see Pollack, 2002). However, these analyses have been based on the presidential logic of American institutions, without a more general approach to the problems of political conflict embedded in diverse institutional settings.

Our analysis is limited to the role played by existing institutions in the public realm, for two reasons: first, because we are interested in the study of institutions within the regulatory state, and second, for the sake of simplicity, we concentrate on more basic developments. Indeed, regulatory policy-making implies multiple modes of regulation, in which private institutions often play a fundamental role (Knill and Lenschow, Chapter 10, this volume; Scott, Chapter 7, this volume); but we postpone to a future occasion extending our arguments to them. In what follows, we first develop the concept of the institutional constellation, and distinguish between three key dimensions: institutional diversity, distribution of responsibility and power structure. Second, we focus in more detail on each of these dimensions, discussing the ways in which the emergence of autonomous regulatory agencies has altered traditional institutional landscapes. Third, we introduce two additional issues aimed at fully characterizing institutional constellations: collective and individual decision-making procedures, and the political culture that is embedded in any institutional constellation. Finally, we suggest a set of hypotheses concerning the effects of concrete institutional constellations. These hypotheses allow a deeper discussion of some of the consequences of different configurations for policy-making and may facilitate a comparative analysis of regulatory designs across issues, sectors and nations.

INSTITUTIONAL CONSTELLATIONS: A FRAMEWORK FOR ANALYSIS

Despite the creation of similar regulatory institutions in many sectors and countries, the broader institutional contexts are varied. Very different adaptations have been made to embed these innovations into existing decision-making procedures and legal traditions. Moreover, similar institutional innovations can produce divergent effects because companies and consumers, as well as professionals, bureaucrats and politicians – the fundamental actors in regulatory game – do not react identically in every political context (and the institutional incentives that are available do not match all the cases). In studying the regulatory state and its diffusion throughout the world in recent decades, it is essential to understand existing variations in decision-making processes that lie behind the formal similarities of many institutional innovations. The notion of institutional constellation aims to capture this diversity, making it analytically operational.

What are institutional constellations? We conceive them as entire sets of formal institutions and interconnected rules that shape public decision-making in a given regulatory arena, including shared interpretative structures, affecting the patterns of interaction by decision-makers within the sector. Considering that institutions consist of 'cognitive, normative and regulative structures and activities that provide stability and meaning to social behaviour' (Scott, 1995, 33), we can place institutional constellations as the aggregate level that assembles different single institutions interacting because of decisions related to the same policy area. A close concept was developed by G.A. Krause (1996, 1088) when presented the regulatory game in the North American case as 'a dynamic system of institutions that are interrelated with one another', stating that influence over policy decisions can flow from any institution to the others, and to determine the nature of these relations have to be done inductively. However, in our view, institutional constellations are not only a set of interdependent institutions, but also constrain and influence institutional behaviour, creating rules, rewards and punishments, and establish codified patters of meaning and value systems that operate at the level of the policy environment (Zucker, 1987).

Although institutional constellations in the regulatory state diverge greatly, they have some attributes in common in so far they are all related to regulatory policies. Regulatory policies impose obligations directly on individuals or organizations and determine their most basic forms of intervention through specific rules, which have direct consequences (Lowi, 1985, 74). The tasks of designing rules, controlling their compliance, and observing their effects form the core of these policies, and are also the main sources of political conflict (being either rules formalized by law or any variety of soft regulations). Regulatory designs play a central role in completing these tasks, assigning roles to institutions and actors, and distributing the power to impose obligations. There are at least three good reasons why institutional constellations are worthy of study: they shape to a great extent the problems of governance and policy change in regulatory policies, they distil political conflict, and they connect sector policy-making to other sectors' problems and priorities.

When focusing on any regulatory area, it is necessary to understand the dimension of policy change. One reason why any given policy change is usually complex is that the major decisions taken by relevant actors are exposed to many influences, whether national or international. However, if we consider actors' decisions in the context of their institutional settings, which have an impact on their scope – as it is developed within the 'actor-centred institutionalism' approach (Scharpf, 1997) – we should be able to identify the institutions and institutional networks that shape behaviour in the regulatory arena. This will in turn permit a more accurate analysis of policy change, considering also that actors' strategies are influenced by institutional constellations.

Institutional constellations are also worth studying because they help us understand the political conflicts we find in regulatory policy. Political conflict in regulatory policy is rooted in policy processes, in which costs and benefits are distributed among a defined set of group or companies, as in, for example, conflicts between established companies and new entrants to the market (Wilson, 1980), or between consumers and business users. A customer-oriented policy conflict emerges in the user area because costs are widely distributed among the majority of domestic consumers, while business users, who have greater negotiating power, obtain better rates (Chang, 1997, 712).

The role of existing institutional constellations is precisely to mediate in these types of conflicts, configuring paths – based on norms and rules – to articulate political struggles and making possible public policy decisions. Institutions and decision rules configuring institutional constellations often aggregate interests in sophisticated ways, shaping and reshaping them. As a common core of the new institutionalism, we assume here that institutions not only aggregate individual interests but also combine them into collective decisions by many possible formulas, producing results that are substantially different from the mere sum of preferences. The institutional rules, either formal or informal, shape directly the transformation of individual preferences into collective according to specific purposes (Immergut, 1998). Here we consider that collective preferences are constrained first, at the level of any single institution within the constellation, when specific audiences are close to particular institutional units, and second, at the constellation level, when the multifaceted set of policy positions and fragmentary decisions representing political conflict within the regulatory state leads in some way to significant policy decisions.

The concept of institutional constellations also enables us to recognize the extent to which a policy sector is isolated from external policy decisions. By focusing on institutional constellations rather than particular regulatory institutions, we are strategically placed to observe the ties connecting the different institutions – whether area-specialized or horizontal – that contribute to regulatory policy. As a consequence, we might be able to estimate the possible influence on sector policy decisions of major political institutions that might pursue a range of objectives across many policy areas. The regulatory state – in its institutional dimension – could be thus understood as a collection of institutional constellations, displaying varying degrees of autonomous power, and differing across sectors and national traditions.

Institutional constellations can be observed in three dimensions: institutional diversity, distribution of responsibility, and power structure. Table 13.1 describes these dimensions, providing a short definition for each

Table 13.1   Institutional constellations: key dimensions and their variation

Key dimensions	Definition	Range of variation	Absence of inst. constellation
Institutional diversity	Number of institutions involved	Degree of fragmentation (low–high)	Institutional unity
Distribution of responsibility	Allocation of policy decisions to different institutions	Degree of dispersion (low–high)	Concentrated responsibilities
Power structure	Institutional capacity to control final policy decisions	Degree of centralization (low–high)	Hierarchical power

and identifying the observable variable for each dimension. The most descriptive dimension is institutional diversity, since it identifies types of institutions. The other two dimensions, based on identifying responsibilities and power, effectively represent different features of the units identified by the dimension of institutional diversity.

In the institutional diversity dimension, we observe the number and character of the public institutions involved in formulating regulatory decisions. Special attention is paid to:

a. ministries: responsible for public policy in regulated sectors, they usually concentrate on sector-specific policy planning and strategic issues; they disband highly bureaucratic structures and have the goal of setting up strategic management and policy control cores;
b. competition authorities: traditional institutions that aim to control markets (competitive behaviour, authorizing mergers, and so forth) and to protect citizens as consumers, they act horizontally for the whole economy;
c. regulatory agencies: new specialized public bodies that guide and implement policy regulations, often combining legislative, executive and judicial functions, they tend to be independent or semi-independent of the classical ministerial structure. They often take charge of the implementation of policy instruments in a highly autonomous way, whereas policy definition and policy change are usually the domain of other institutional actors, like parliaments, courts, ministries, or other public authorities;
d. parliaments: they specialize in drawing up complex laws to determine the mechanisms of market regulation and tend to set up specialized supervisory commissions;
e. courts of justice: they play a role in the new system protecting citizens and firms, whether directly or as a last resort; and
f. others: the presidency, ministries other than those directly responsible for policy or state-owned companies, where they exist.

The degree of institution fragmentation refers to the number of these institutions active in regulatory policy; it is higher as the number of institutions involved increases. The institutional structure of regulatory regimes can assume many arrangements, as has been detailed by Ogus (2003), identifying different cases from complete government control to self-regulation.[3] Institutional unity represents the very extreme case of only one institution taking on all the policy-making within the sector, either ministry or agency. Nowadays, however, this is a rare configuration, and what is really interesting to observe is the existing degree of institutional diversity within an institutional constellation and the role played by each institution within it.

The distribution of responsibilities refers to how responsibility for policy decisions is dispersed among the institutions involved in the constellation. This dimension differs from institutional diversity because responsibilities are not necessarily allocated uniformly across the institutional actors. Many scenarios are possible. For example, an institutional constellation is possible in which responsibilities are concentrated basically in a few core institutions; while at the same time one may observe a different constellation in which responsibilities are more evenly distributed among institutions. A typical policy context characterized by simultaneous actions performed by several institutions that have different responsibilities could also display a certain overlap of responsibilities. In many cases there is no clear-cut separation of responsibilities, as for example when a competition authority from the judicial system intervenes in regulatory disputes. This could reflect either an inefficient institutional design or an intended system of checks and balances. Also, overlap is reinforced by cognitive limitations which arise from the difficulty involved in clearly defining limits on policy-related responsibilities. This situation is typically found in cross-sectional public policies, such as environmental policy, where the overlap of competencies, undefined limits on responsibility, and, often, the conflicting objectives and priorities of the different implied regulators (for example ministries of environment, health, industry), make consistent governmental action difficult (Underdal and Hanf, 2000).

Finally, power structures differ across issues, sectors and nations. Responsibility and power form separate dimensions because policy responsibility does not extend to control over final decisions. This is a matter of capacity rather than action (courts or the presidency perform this role in many cases). Hierarchical power structures, which are traditionally assumed to be a general feature of public policy-making, were designed to concentrate authority within a 'principal' institution enjoying democratic legitimacy (such as the legislature). Within the context of new regulatory policies, as the specialist literature has highlighted, it is of the utmost importance to examine the issue of delegation: specifically, to address the question of how much autonomous authority has been delegated to the specialized regulatory agencies. In addition, competition authorities, as well as courts, could exhibit a significant degree of autonomous authority. These factors together pave the way for the emergence of less hierarchical power structures, in which different institutions have some degree of autonomy and the centralization of power is reduced. The degree to which power is centralized can vary; this undoubtedly has different implications for the policy-making process.

INTERNAL DIVERSITY OF INSTITUTIONAL CONSTELLATIONS

Mechanisms for rule-making, supervision and imposition of sanctions do not necessarily have to be set up in the same institution, and can even be fragmented and divided among different institutions. As has been observed, quite a large number of public institutions can be involved in regulatory policy, ranging from governmental departments to specific judicial or legislative bodies. Whereas US-based regulatory commissions normally concentrate most of the regulatory functions within the same organization, this it is not common in Europe and elsewhere, even with new regulatory bodies. In Europe, different governmental bodies together with legislators and the new regulatory agencies are often actively involved in the regulation of the same sector (Baldwin et al., 1998). Nowadays, regulatory decision-making is more complex as it involves the promotion of rules or the issue of licences, as well as active market-making policies which are integrated into the rules themselves as a more interventionist form of regulation (Chang, 1997). For all these reasons, we find that many countries display a highly significant degree of institutional fragmentation in regulatory policy-making and implementation, since many of the available instruments remain within various existing institutions. In addition, regulatory agencies are more open to new actors entering the sector as a result of the opening of markets, while governments tend to continue to associate to a greater extent with the larger established companies in the sector.

There is a more deeply rooted tradition of specialist regulatory bodies in the American public sector than in the European, with the possible exception of some British precedents (McLean, Chapter 3, this volume; Moran, 2001). The radical decision of the USA not to create public monopolies and to leave the provision of public services to the market strengthened incentives for the establishment of more sophisticated systems of control and supervision to protect consumer rights (these agencies mostly didn't defend 'free competition'). In general, regulatory powers were awarded to specialist commissions on the grounds that they could bring together experts to take decisions on very technical matters of which neither the ordinary courts nor Congress itself had enough knowledge (Eisner, 2000; McCraw, 1984). Later, as these commissions started to develop their own organizational structure, they became generically known as agencies as well, that is, public bodies with a relative degree of autonomy.

By contrast, in Europe and many other parts of the world specialized regulatory public bodies removed from traditional ministerial structures are a relatively recent development. In Great Britain, it was only from the 1970s onwards that they began to appear. The purpose of these bodies was to supervise very specific tasks or activities such as civil aviation, television, or race relations. In each case, they were created for very different reasons from the American ones: it was believed that the specificity of the subject required special attention, and it was deemed necessary to establish controls and formulate consistent and very specific policies. More recently, many regulatory agencies were created in Europe in the 1990s, although they are very different from their counterparts in the United States.[4] However, the rhetoric, symbols and design of regulations were quite similar on both sides of the Atlantic.

Arguments justifying the creation of similar independent authorities cite a great variety of reasons. In the case of the telecommunications sector in northern EU countries, where states retained a considerable share of the capital of the incumbent operators, the introduction of independent agencies was justified as a means of preventing a conflict of interest within the government (Schneider, 2001)[5]. It is surprising, however, that the obvious alternative option was not chosen: why not privatize the company? However, in southern EU countries, where companies were fully privatized, the argument took a different turn: independence was justified more by the desire to maintain professional autonomy than as a means of preventing a conflict of interests between politicians (Jordana, 2002). Beyond Europe, the diversity of reasons given to establish regulatory agencies is even greater. In the USA, with its especially high level of fragmentation, the meaning of 'independence' is even less clear. In the cases where it is applied, it is used to characterize those agencies that answer to Congress but not to the president, although the president does have some control over the agencies' activity. Latin America differs again. Here, independent agencies take the form of special units within the public sector, which have special remunerations and professional selection criteria. Independence is fundamentally understood as meaning independence from the political parties – not so much because of conflict over policy aims but rather as a means of protection against the 'spoils' system which exists in practically all the countries in the region (Geddes, 1994).

The spread of the regulatory agency model throughout the world raises the question whether the diversity of motives to delegate has some influence on institutional design. Thus we should examine the extent to which the rhetoric about regulation has been accompanied by wholly superficial adaptations of these organizational set-ups, that is, cases where the dominant administrative traditions have adopted new symbols and codes to ensure their own organizational survival (Hood, 1998). It might not be surprising if the diversity of motives then resulted in different ways of inserting these new institutions into the constellation as a whole, thereby constructing new roles and also assigning different roles to the other institutions. The involvement of such traditional institutions as ministries, presidencies, courts or competition authorities tends not to disappear completely, but their function could change in different ways, often as a by-product of path-dependent historical legacies. In any case, these developments can show us the degree of institutional fragmentation introduced in an institutional constellation, in so far as we can identify the resulting number of relevant units that actively intervene in the regulatory policy.

DISTRIBUTION OF RESPONSIBILITIES IN THE REGULATORY ARENA

Responsibility for decisions relevant for the upholding of the policy is often dispersed within institutional constellations. We can find distribution of responsibilities among several institutional units, at different levels of government or within the same level, and in different branches of government or in different units belonging to the same branch. In fact, we often observe patterns of competition and cooperation in these multiple dimensions (Geradin and McCahery, Chapter 5, this volume). The degree of dispersion of responsibilities can also produce some overlap among the responsibilities of different units in these dimensions, that might configure a challenge for regulatory designs.

A typical argument used to justify the creation of agencies can help us to think about the dispersion of responsibilities in regulatory policies. This argument defends the creation of agencies as a function of politicians' need to commit their power to public policy in order to avoid certain short-term temptations (election cycles, interdependence on other policy sectors, and so on). These temptations would condition their decisions and introduce elements of distrust and distortion into regulated markets. It is worth remembering that this argument emerged in the case of central banks, a classic and fully independent agency model. The main rationale behind government commitment was not so much the precise regulation of the actual bank sector but rather attainment of a single aim: the control of inflation through the use of monetary policy. This is a relatively clear and specific task, in which a possible conflict with government is clearly and almost structurally defined (Elgie, 1998; Lohmann, 1998).

The regulation of a productive sector with market imperfections (which justify public intervention) is, however, quite a different matter from controlling monetary policy. Here, the clash of interests with those of government is not clearly defined (it may be occasional and variable), while regulatory and control tasks are not easily characterized by a clear aim either. An example is the typical debate that exists about whether to promote competition as much as possible in the short term, or to keep it in check by stimulating investment in infrastructure. This has an ultimately political component, which cannot be resolved with purely technical criteria given the existing uncertainties behind both options. This could explain why most governments retain many policy responsibilities in ministries and other public bodies when they create specialized regulatory agencies, which then as a result generate some dispersion of responsibility for the policy.[6] Concentration of policy responsibility in a single public body, whether ministry or agency, does not seem to be a very common configuration nowadays. This being the case, it is impossible to avoid a certain degree of controversy with respect to public policy, given the fact that responsibility is distributed among different bodies – each with specific intervention instruments – that might maintain different platforms even though there can be only one outcome.

The formal and complete separation of tasks and responsibilities, however, seems to be much more complicated in practice than in theory. Ideally, we should distinguish between regulators (who enforce rules and supervise their compliance within the market), judges (who control the regulators), and the government (which uses its different ministries to formulate the policies). By observing the specific capabilities and instruments within a policy area, we can formally identify the distribution of responsibilities amongst one or more public organizations. It is necessary to note, none the less, that responsibilities can easily overlap when different institutions share them. It is a formal as well as an informal phenomenon that occurs when different bodies, often with different objectives, use instruments available to them to act on a single policy aim. This subject is closely related to the existence of loopholes in a legal norm. The legal norms cannot anticipate all the cases and controversies that can arise in any regulatory process. The reality of administrative and political interaction always produces scenarios in which decision-making responsibility is not clearly predicted in the norm. Differences amongst legal interpretations leave some room for conflict amongst institutions, each of them struggling to maintain and extend its margin of responsibility and discretion over political intervention (Majone, 1996). We find examples of this situation in traditional confrontations over policy between regulative agencies and ministries. This scenario reappears in conflicts between different specialized regulatory agencies, such as arose between sector regulators (telecommunications or electricity) and general regulators of market competition (antitrust agencies) over the basic criteria of regulatory policy.

Overlap is, then, understood to refer more to responsibilities regarding policy aims than to responsibilities regarding instruments, whose division and delegation are clearly defined in the majority of cases, and whose use can be protected by a 'discretion zone' in which decisions can be made autonomously.[7] Some decision-making procedures, however, can conduce also to formal overlap, particularly when co-decision rules or mutual control designs exist. Furthermore, as the regulation of markets with imperfections, such as those of public utilities, gives rise to a large number of difficulties, public intervention must be very active and constant, and make a fundamental contribution to defining the business structure of the market.

POWER STRUCTURES IN THE INSTITUTIONAL CONSTELLATION

The diffusion of the regulatory agency model has challenged the structure of power in many countries, often reducing centralization in the governance of many policy sectors. However, we need to examine in more detail the extent to which, within the scope of public institutions, traditional hierarchies of power have been transformed into less centralized power structures. Here, the presence of decision-making procedures – delegation mechanisms, veto players and time stabilizers – that work as devices to articulate the structure of power within the constellation come into play.

By observing the emergence of the regulatory agency model in the American case, we can see that the independence of commissions from the executive was a result more of the politico-institutional functioning of the American governmental system, with its divisions and separations, than of some ideal set-up. Given the presidential model that existed in the USA, Congress did not want to grant regulatory powers to the executive on a permanent basis. Quite the contrary: its purpose was to limit presidential action in some policy areas. As Majone points out (1996, 17), the conferring of powers during the 1930s to a number of notable commissions (Federal Communications Commission, Securities and Exchange Commission, Civil Aeronautics Board, among others), was the price that President Roosevelt had to pay for the Congress and the Supreme Court accepting his extensive economic public intervention programmes, although his real purpose was to integrate these regulatory functions into the different ministerial departments.

Because of the particularities of the Westminster model of government, the privatization of public services in Great Britain in the 1980s gave rise to a new variety of organizational set-ups that were aimed at regulating public services through the figure of the manager, avoiding direct control by public servants. These managers, appointed by the corresponding ministries, were given regulatory power and aided by an autonomous government body. Thus the British model demonstrates some continuity in terms of hierarchical governmental structures in the dissemination of new public bodies specializing in regulatory tasks (and cutting down bureaucratic hierarchical structures). None the less, the complexity of the new system inevitably led to a reduction in the ministries' responsibilities and made necessary the redefinition of more sophisticated systems of accountability (Moran, 2001, 31).

As we see, the regulatory agency model did not spring from premeditated efforts to improve regulatory governance, but rather is the outcome of political or bureaucratic conflict. The worldwide diffusion of the agency model, however, allowed these particularities to be confronted with a variety of political and institutional contexts. In this way, we need to analyse how the relationship between traditional political institutions and regulatory agencies is articulated. Particular attention can be paid to a number of mechanisms. First of all is the way in which legislation establishes a statute to grant authority over a certain sector to a particular regulatory agency. The specification and details of objectives and the political directions to be followed restrict the agency's margin of discretionary activity. Second, the state's power to appoint specific individuals to positions in a regulatory direction, as well as the power to dismiss them, is an important tool of control over the regulatory body. Two basic criteria have traditionally guided these selection processes in many sectors: political affiliation and technical training (Noll, 1983). A new, third, element which structures the capacity of interaction between regulatory bodies and regulatory agents is the availability of resources (Duch, 1991), which comprise personnel, expert knowledge, access to relevant information, and material and economic resources. The ability to generate technical information is vital in order to ensure the agency's autonomy in the process of policy-making. Fourth, outside control over the regulating institutions is an important delegating mechanism: choice of the system of external control becomes critical (Spiller, 1993). Control could be predominantly judicial, governmental, or parliamentary. There are also systems in which the body exercising control consists of those associations that are interested in a regulated sector. Considering these different components that define the separation or 'formal' independence of regulatory agencies from traditional ministerial hierarchical structures, F. Gilardi (2002) has developed a detailed index to measure the extent to which delegation to these specialized institutions has been implemented. He identifies five basic variables: agency head status, management board member status, relations with government and parliament, financial and organizational autonomy, and regulatory competencies.

However, classifying regulatory agencies solely by their special position in the government set-up can be insufficient. It is important to stress that a regulatory agency cannot be characterized as having less hierarchical control because it has more responsibilities. Rather, its power should be measured by other factors that are more associated with effective autonomy over decision-making (no reversibility, no anticipation of preferences, accountability mechanisms, and so on). For example, an agency which has a wide range of responsibilities but which repeatedly follows the orientations of the parliament or the politicians has little effective power. With this in mind, it is possible to establish some distinctions. First, if a regulatory agency has few delegated powers, it could produce symbolic benefits by creating a 'special' highly visible unit in the policy sector, capable of obstructing the ability of politicians to change their minds over a short period. A certain level of internal competition within the government can also mean better management, greater transparency within the government itself, or less danger of capture by business. On the other hand, if there is a high degree of delegation (as where the agency is answerable only to parliament) or full delegation (as where the agency is answerable to the judiciary), the power structure within the public system affected by the new institutional set-up becomes less centralized. Executive or legislative commitments result in the establishment of a cross-control system to monitor the policy process, which makes it more difficult for the system to fail, although it reduces the likelihood of policy change. In the end, the regulatory agency emerges as a new actor with veto power within the institutional constellation.

DECISION-MAKING AND POLITICAL CULTURE

We consider that actors in institutional settings are guided by certain cultural practices when pursuing their own objectives. These practices consist of shared patterns of interaction that can, for example, be observed in an actor's reactions to policy disputes. These practices are also revealed when actors adopt informal rules to deal with political conflict, rules that can vary among countries and sectors and range from routine manifestations to symbolic acts. Existing formal institutions and decision-making rules and procedures are not completely capable of dealing unaided with political conflicts in the regulatory arena. There must be some shared set of values or practices in order to meet actors' expectations when interpreting a given rule or deducing what margins for manoeuvre are enjoyed by a specific institution involved in policy-making. In regulatory decision-making, the main conflicts appear to focus on command over incentives and controls (Majone, 1997a). Thus, some practices or values on how to exercise command and control in institutional constellations have to be shared by actors in order to delineate which type of public intervention is legitimate and which is not.

We identified three different values related to actors' political practices that are especially relevant to the policy process in regulatory arenas: policy dominance, consensus formation and policy coherence. The first represents actors' common understanding about who has more influence on command and control over the policy area: is there a basic dominance by some public institutions (or a coalition of them), or is there an unstable dominance exercised by two competing institutions? Traditions and cultures of state intervention are crucial here in order to distinguish between practices that influence the effectiveness of regulatory designs and those that leave room for the possibility of self-regulation. Most public actors might aim at full command and control over a policy sector if sufficiently reasonable criteria exist to justify its intervention (imperfect markets, monopolistic threats, and so on), but a particular political culture may view public intervention in a way that limits the fulfilment of this purpose. In addition, public authorities' espousal of policy dominance also raises the question of which institutional logic should be more appropriate in exercising policy dominance – given well-known problems such 'bureaucratic drift' or 'agency capture' (Baldwin and Cave, 1999).

The second value that we identified is the formation of consensus among all the actors in order to exercise command and control over policy. Consensus formation can be understood as the establishment of informal joint-decision systems without unanimity rule among the players involved in a regulatory arena. When we find this inclusive value to be strong in an institutional constellation, it is being actively enforced with the aim of avoiding political conflicts by means of cooperative decision-making (the opposite is represented by a confrontational attitude: to win is also to diminish the others). However, establishing consensus and pacts among actors in regulatory policies is very complex due to the presence of net winners and losers throughout the different steps of the regulatory process. In addition, it is necessary to keep in mind the problem of consensus technology: it avoids conflict losses and has low transaction costs, but also incorporates the risk of being transformed into a joint-decision trap, producing exacerbated side payments (Scharpf, 1997, 144–5). These difficulties, added to the appearance of new entrants in the sector, will no doubt hinder a political culture based on consensus formation in a regulatory sector.

We also need to note that the level of consensus orientation for policy decisions is related to the character of the institutions. Some institutional designs promote consensus, while others aggravate institutional isolation and foment conflict-oriented behaviour. For example, Oftel's case of agreements with operators linked to licensing conditions clearly favoured consensus formation. Agreements had to be ratified in turn by both the Competition Commission and the Secretary of State for the Department of Trade and Industry, both of which had veto power. If Oftel and the operators had been unable to reach an agreement, the Competition Commission would have determined the new conditions for the licence. Oftel and the operators normally agreed on regulations, since an appeal to the Competition Commission was not a desirable option for either the companies or Oftel. For the companies, it was risky because the process might take longer and their financial standing might be damaged during that time. For Oftel an appeal to the Competition Commission implied a loss of credibility (Thatcher, 1998).

The last value is policy coherence, as a way to limit command-and-control flexibility in regulatory policy. When this value is well established in the political culture of the actors, they participate in the common practice of defending policy coherence as a non-disputable issue. However, linking policy change and policy consistency, as a shared value, encounters many problems because ordinary politics often challenges the stability of policy-related decisions, which can at times be influenced by multiple actors with different time perspectives. A related aspect of policy coherence refers to time-consistency when there is a process of policy change. Also, policy interdependence is a very common phenomenon today that often produces incoherent policy decisions because of the indirect effects of decisions made in other policy sectors that cannot be resisted. Thus, the robustness of the actors' cultural practices with respect to policy coherence could represent a counterweight to many external influences that can affect any sector's policy-making.

Decision-making procedures are key components with which to articulate political conflict in so far as they establish mechanisms to generate policy outputs in which different institutions usually take part. There are many decision rules affecting the policy process, and many significant questions for the command and control of regulative policy are often linked to specific formal procedures. We consider that many of these procedures are usually designed to interconnect the institutional units within the constellation with respect to major policy decisions. Rules indicate which actors and institutions have the right to take a decision and under which conditions, and also who can revise and perhaps revoke decisions already taken by other units. Also, rules and procedures usually give precise descriptions of how and when collective or joint decisions are to be taken, and who has to participate. Obviously, some relationship exists between the type of decision-making procedures prevailing in an institutional constellation and the political culture and the formal structures that are observable in the same constellation. This will be discussed later, when we set forth some consequences for policy-making given particular combinations. It must be pointed out that decision-making procedures work as instrumental devices making some of the values related to a political culture easier to satisfy, and that these are often adopted as a way of stabilizing particular cultural and political settings.

We find many classifications of decision-making rules and procedures in the literature. They could probably help us to better analyse institutional constellations by identifying concrete characteristics and estimating their effects. However, as we focus in this chapter particularly on the basic features of institutional constellations, it is not necessary to discuss them in detail. Thus, instead of adopting any classification, we limit ourselves here to identifying a few basic and significant procedures. First, we find the existence of delegation mechanisms, that is, rules that define how 'delegated' decisions are taken and how they are controlled and reversed. These mechanisms permit some institutions acting as principals to entrust other institutions, acting as agents, to take decisions, maintaining some form of control over them.[8] Second, we have the presence of veto players (Tsebelis, 2002). Veto players can be understood as the number of institutions present in the constellation which, under the constellation's decision rules, have autonomous power to block any policy decision. This power can either be limited to some specific range of decisions, or affect any important decision relating to regulatory policy. Third, we can recognize the existence of time-consistency stabilizers in regulatory policy-making. Time stabilizers are decision rules conceived to hinder or delay – but not impede – decisions that could produce policy changes over time.[9] For example, decision procedures such double approbation, formal incubation periods, or transparency mechanisms could act as time-stabilizers. They can be either designed as special decision-making procedures for essential aspects of policy, or directly embedded in the design of specialized institutions. This last mechanism can also be understood as a way to protect institutions with well-defined behaviour and policy aims from making rapid decisions that challenge their traditional tasks and goals.

POLITICAL CONFLICT AND INSTITUTIONAL CONSTELLATIONS

Political conflict is mediated by institutional constellations, and the different characteristics they might display conduce to different expressions and resolutions of existing conflicts. Formerly, we identified in institutional constellations some variations in institutional diversity, distribution of responsibilities and power structures: low institutional fragmentation versus high fragmentation, low dispersion of responsibilities versus high dispersion, and low centralization of power versus high centralization. Now we will connect these variables to different decision-making procedures that prevail in different institutional constellations, taking into account the number of veto players, the intensity of delegation, or the strength of time-stabilizers. We should observe these procedures as indicators of each dimension in institutional constellations (see Table 13.2). Thus, specific decision-making procedures appear as a consequence of the characteristics each formal structure displays: institutional diversity can be measured by observing the intensity of delegation (when an autonomous unit exists), the power structure

Table 13.2 Institutional constellations: combining characteristics

	Low institutional fragmentation	High institutional fragmentation
High centralization of power Low dispersion of responsibilities	Few veto players Limited delegation Weak time-stabilizers	Few veto players Extensive delegation Weak time-stabilizers
High centralization of power High dispersion of responsibilities	Few veto players Limited delegation Strong time-stabilizers	Few veto players Extensive delegation Strong time-stabilizers
Low centralization of power Low dispersion of responsibilities	Many veto players Limited delegation Weak time-stabilizers	Many veto players Extensive delegation Weak time-stabilizers
Low centralization of power High dispersion of responsibilities	Many veto players Limited delegation Strong time-stabilizers	Many veto players Extensive delegation Strong time-stabilizers

can be identified by counting the number of veto players, and the distribution of responsibilities can be identified by observing the strength of time-stabilizers (the more responsibilities, the more possibilities to obstruct a decision-making process). Together, we find different types of institutional constellations and identify combinations of decision-making procedures for each of them. For simplicity's sake, we present this framework using only two values for each category, but a more detailed scale might be elaborated, identifying more degrees of variation and increasing the framework's plausibility.

Political conflict in regulatory policy can be mediated by very different institutional constellations – as seen in Table 13.2 – which will be conducive to diverse forms of policy process. Some of these forms imply a concentration of policy decisions in the hands of single actors, almost without constraint; other forms include important constraints on decision-makers; and yet other forms are based on many actors capable of taking final decisions, either with or without constraints. A better approach, however, to the characterization of political conflicts might be to resurrect the issue of political culture in terms of the different values that make up the actors' political practices in regulatory arenas. There exists some correspondence between institutional attributes and type of political culture in regulatory policy; each frequently reinforces the other. Thus we now explore how different institutional characteristics affect the values of policy dominance, consensus formation and policy coherence. We consider that the pursuit of each of these values leads to a specific type of political conflict.

The value of policy dominance refers to a common understanding about the most influential actors in institutional constellations. Thus political conflict appears when some actors challenge the dominant situation. For example, tensions produced by bureaucratic drift tend to appear when the degree of institutional fragmentation is low and delegation mechanisms are limited. Bureaucrats could question the established policy dominance, configuring a situation that represents a conflict, with the aim of transferring control of the policy to politicians. However, under a classic hierarchical structure in which a single player has veto power, elected politicians have last-resort control. Within low degrees of power centralization, and with more veto players, the struggle for policy dominance will probably be more intense – as it will be also when low institutional fragmentation forces actors to share the same space. Problems derived from agency capture by private interests tend to appear when the degree of power centralization is low, although when this is combined with low fragmentation these problems could be more reduced. Also, when a high degree of centralization persists, policy dominance conflicts are limited to a certain extent because agency has no veto power. In the case of low centralization with extensive delegation, however, political conflict appears to be more complicated, and the policy dominance value could be very unstable. To summarize, a policy dominance value could present more intense problems and potential for conflict to the extent that institutional fragmentation and power decentralization increase.

Consensus formation among the players is another value that can be present in the political culture of institutional constellations. Here, political conflict could appear when joint-decision systems are formed. Two different problems exist for the emergence of consensus. First, when responsibilities for the regulatory policy are clearly dispersed, the absence of common aims could make it more difficult to find shared issues and take joint decisions on them. Second, when responsibilities are scarcely dispersed, the potential for conflict might become greater as several players can focus their attention on putting pressure on the central institutions. These problems can be exacerbated or reduced depending of the character of delegation. For example, policy agreements based on consensus are a highly complex matter, as there is the danger of side exploitation when actors enjoy extensive delegation and are able to use strong time-stabilizers. In contrast, with limited delegation and weak time-stabilizers, it is unlikely that any participating actors will be able to pursue a separate path, which could lead to consensus formation and permit the construction of more complex views of problems. This is also a situation in which politicians, to overcome weak time-stabilizers for example, might introduce wider aims which go beyond the perspectives of the regulatory agencies and which might lead to improved technical precision and information on areas of a more political nature. If delegation is limited, problems might appear when dispersed responsibilities provoke ambiguities within a low-fragmented institutional constellation (limited delegation permits autonomous survival to specialized units that maintain few strong time-stabilizers).

The third type of political conflict in regulatory arenas that we consider here is produced by the aim of policy coherence. We identify several situations that might challenge coherence, such as the decisions of politicians influenced by the electoral cycle or decisions of regulatory agencies produced by direct business interests. The character of time-stabilizers and the number of veto players that are associated with each situation could affect these problems. Policy coherence in a highly centralized institutional structure confronts the peril of political decision-making guided by electoral considerations. Time-stabilizers, as specifically designed commitments, act as an antidote to this temptation. However, it is necessary to bear in mind that weak time-stabilizers could be easily overwhelmed, and strong ones could also impede time-consistent policy change. Also, an increase in the number of veto players reduces the possibility of any type of policy change, whether time-consistent or not. A similar process could occur with the problem of agency capture, producing incoherent decisions. In that case, the problem might well appear when the power structure displays a less centralized character. In any case, strong time-stabilizers and many veto players could easily amplify policy stability, but this could then reduce the chances of any policy change.

CONCLUSIONS

The distinctions drawn above about institutional constellations could help us understand why similar institutional innovations may promote a variety of outcomes, and represent a clear indication that it is necessary to analyse the whole institutional picture when we try to explain the role of institutions in policy-making and policy outputs. For example, delegation to non-majoritarian institutions has much more complex interaction effects than accounts of delegation usually allow for. When certain models of regulatory designs are promoted for a specific country or sector, it is necessary to take in account that their institutions are embedded in a larger institutional constellation. It is this particular configuration and their characteristics that shape the regulatory policy process and regulatory outcomes.

Analysing the influence of single institutions on decision-making could introduce many biases, but, at the same time, considering the complete institutional landscape could be very costly, and it could also be difficult to compare, given its uniqueness. With the aim of reducing institutional complexity in comparative analysis, the concept of the institutional constellation could offer an intermediate way by identifying a few dimensions that capture the basic dynamics of the whole institutional set.

Obviously, further steps have to be taken in order to construct and refine indicators for empirical analysis, but we believe that achieving a simple and basic level of fruitful comparative analysis across sectors and nations could help to overcome some difficulties in the analysis of regulatory policy. Providing contrasting hypotheses about the role of institutions of regulatory policy, which can be generalized, might represent a way of improving our knowledge about governance in the regulatory state. In this sense, when combining the different components and dimensions that we identified within the institutional constellation concept, we were able to establish some tentative hypotheses that connect institutional combinations with the most frequent types of political conflict that researchers are confronted with when analysing regulatory policy-making.

NOTES

1. We would like to thank Sharon Gilad, Victor Lapuente, David Levi-Faur and Martin Lodge for very useful comments on earlier versions of this chapter.
2. Discussions about these institutional innovations have generated explanations such as the one that underlines the idea of policy commitment; governments, for the sake of their own credibility, consider it convenient to bind themselves to avoid policy changes in the future for a given policy issue (Majone, 1997b). Other explanations point to the demand for policy-relevant expertise or to the existence of conflicting preferences. See, for example, Thatcher and Sweet (2002).
3. See also Doern and Wilks (1998), who compare regulatory institutions in the United Kingdom, the United States and Canada.
4. The relationship between agencies and traditional institutional structures took different forms; the parliamentarian tradition of government in European countries induced stronger controls, or new processes of quite active consensus formation (Coen and Doyle, 1999).
5. This need was repeatedly met by the EU in the shape of different directives throughout the liberalization process from 1990 onwards. For a more detailed definition, see the Parliament and Council's Directive on interconnection 97/33, art. 9.
6. The telecommunications and electricity sectors in several European countries after market liberalization are clear examples of these situations, where a significant degree of variation is observable (for a comparison between Germany and United Kingdom, see Böllhoff, 2001; for other countries see also Coen and Doyle, 1999).
7. The characteristics of the discretion zone affect the behaviour of the different actors, who attempt to prevent the emergence of constant conflict between different institutions. As Thatcher and Sweet indicate, 'The smaller the zone of discretion, the greater the agent's

interest will be in monitoring and anticipating the principal's reactions to activities, to the extent of the fear, or wish to avoid, having decisions overturned' (2002, 6).

8. For a discussion of the limits of this control, see Majone (2001).
9. Although it does not represent a decision rule, the notion of 'audience costs' developed by S. Lohmann (2002) can be understood as an additional time-stabilizer. To the extent that audiences misunderstand – and probably punish – changes that are introduced without deliberation or sufficient time to allow them to be convinced of the need for them, they act in fact as time-stabilizers embedded in the institutional action framework.

REFERENCES

Baldwin, R. and M. Cave (1999), *Understanding Regulation. Theory, Strategy and Practice*, Oxford: Oxford University Press.

Baldwin, R., C. Scott and C. Hood (1998), 'Introduction', in R. Baldwin, C. Scott and C. Hood (eds), *A Reader on Regulation*, Oxford: Oxford University Press.

Böllhoff, D. (2001), 'New Regulatory Agencies in British-German Comparison – The Impact of Public Sector Reform Policies', ECPR 29th Joint Sessions of Workshops, Grenoble, 6-11 April.

Chang, Ha-Joon (1997), 'The Economics and Politics of Regulation', *Cambridge Journal of Economics*, **21**, 703–28.

Coen, D. and C. Doyle (1999), 'Designing Economic Regulatory Institutions for European Network Industries', mimeo, London Business School, October.

Doern, G.B. and S. Wilks (1998), *Changing regulatory institutions in Britain and North America*, Toronto: University of Toronto Press.

Duch, R. (1991), *Privatising the Economy: Telecommunication Policy in Comparative Perspective*, Manchester: Manchester University Press.

Eisner, M.A. (2000), *Regulatory Politics in Transition*, Baltimore: Johns Hopkins University Press.

Elgie, R. (1998), 'Democratic Accountability and Central Bank Independence: Historical and Contemporary, National and European Perspectives', *West European Politics*, **21** (3), 53–76.

Geddes, B. (1994), *Politician's Dilemma: Building State Capacity in Latin America*, Berkeley: University of California Press.

Gilardi, F. (2002), 'Policy Credibility and Delegation to Independent Regulatory Agencies: A Comparative Empirical Analysis', *Journal of European Public Policy*, **9** (6), 873–93.

Gilardi, F. and D. Braun (2001), 'Delegation aus der Sicht der Principal – Agent Theorie. Ein Literaturbereicht', *Politische Vierteljaheresschrift*, **43** (1), 147–61.

Hood, C. (1998), *The Art of the State. Culture, Rhetoric and Public Management*, Oxford: Oxford University Press.

Immergut, Ellen M. (1998), 'The Theoretical Core of the New Institutionalism', *Politics & Society*, **26** (1), 5–34.

Jordana, J. (2002), 'The persistence of telecommunications policies in national states: Portugal and Spain in the European arena', in J. Jordana (ed.), *Governing Telecommunications and the New Information Society in Europe*, Cheltenham, UK and Northampton, USA: Edward Elgar.

Klijn, Eirik-Hans (2001), 'Rules as Institutional Context for Decision Making in Networks', *Administration & Society*, **33** (2), 133–64

Krause, George A. (1996), 'The Institutional Dynamics of Policy Administration: Bureaucratic Influence over Securities Regulation', *American Journal of Political Science*, **40** (4), 1083–121

Levi-Faur, D. (2002), 'Herding Towards a New Convention: On Herds, Shepherds, and Lost Sheep in the Liberalization of Telecommunications and Electricity Industry', Nuffield College Working Paper in Politics, W6-2002, Oxford.

Lohmann, S. (1998), 'Federalism and Central Bank Independence: The Politics of German Monetary Policy, 1957–92', *World Politics*, **50** (3), 401–46.

Lohmann, S. (2002), 'Why do Institutions Matter? An Audience-Cost Theory of Institutional Commitment', *Governance*, **16** (1), 95–110.

Lowi, T. (1985), 'The state in politics. The relation between policy and administration', in R.G. Noll (ed.), *Regulatory Policy and the Social Sciences*, Berkeley: University of California Press, pp. 67–105.

Majone, G. (1996), *Regulating Europe*, London: Routledge.

Majone, G. (1997a), 'From the Positive to the Regulatory State. Causes and Consequences of Changes in the Mode of Governance', *Journal of Public Policy*, **17** (2), 139–67.

Majone, G. (1997b), 'Independent Agencies and the Delegation Problem: Theoretical and Normative Dimensions', in B. Steuenberg and F. van Vught (eds), *Political Institutions and Public Policy*, Dordrecht: Kluwer, pp. 139–56.

Majone, G. (2001), 'Two logics of delegation. Agency and Fiduciary Relations in EU Governance', *European Union Politics*, **2** (1), 103–22.

McCraw, T.K. (1984), *Prophets of Regulation*, Cambridge: Belknap Press.

Moran, M. (2001), 'The Rise of the Regulatory State in Britain', *Parliamentary Affairs*, **54**, 19–34.

Moran, M. (2002), 'Understanding the Regulatory State', *British Journal of Political Science*, **32** (2), 391–414.

Noll, R. (1983), 'The Political Foundations of Regulatory Policy', *Zeitschrift für die gesamte Staatswissenschaft*, **139**, 377–404.

Ogus, A. (2003), 'Comparing regulatory systems', in D. Parker and D. Saal (eds), *Privatisation Handbook*, Cheltenham, UK and Northampton, USA: Edward Elgar, pp. 514–36.

Pollack, M.A. (2002), 'Learning from the Americanists (Again): Theory and Method in the Study of Delegation', *West European Politics*, **25** (1), 200–219.

Sabatier, P.A. and H.C. Jenkins-Smith (1994), *Policy change and learning an advocacy coalition approach*, Boulder: Westview.

Scharpf, F.W. (1997), *Games Real Actors Play. Actor-centered Institutionalism in Policy Research*, Boulder: Westview.

Schneider, V. (2001), 'Institutional reform in telecommunications: The European Union in transnational policy diffusion', in M. Green-Cowles, J. Caporaso and T. Risse (eds), *Transforming Europe. Europeanization and Domestic Change*, Ithaca, NY: Cornell University Press, pp. 60–78.

Scott, W.R. (1995), *Institutions and Organizations*, Thousand Oaks, CA: Sage.

Spiller, P. (1993), *Institutions and Regulatory Commitment in Utilities Privatization*, Washington: Institute for Policy Reform.

Thatcher, M. (1998): 'Institutions, Regulation, and Change: New Regulatory Agencies in the British Privatised Utilities', *West European Politics*, **21** (1), 120–47.

Thatcher, M. (2002), 'Delegation to Independent Regulatory Agencies: Pressures, Functions and Contextual Mediation', *West European Politics*, **25** (1), 125–47.

Thatcher, M. and A. Sweet (2002), 'Theory and Practice of Delegation to Non-Majoritarian Institutions', *West European Politics*, **25** (1), 1–22.

Tsebelis, G. (2002), *Veto Players. How Political Institutions Work*, Princeton: Russell Sage Foundation.

Underdal, A. and K. Hanf (2000), *International environmental agreements and domestic politics. The case of acid rain*, Aldershot: Ashgate.

Vogel, D. (1986), *National Styles of Regulation. Environmental Policy in Great Britain and the United States*, Ithaca and London: Cornell University Press.

Wilson, J. (1980) (ed.), *The Politics of Regulation*, New York: Basic Books.

Zucker, L.G. (1987), 'Institutional Theories of Organization', *Annual Review of Sociology*, **13**, 443–64.

Index